BASQUE DIASPOR
Gloria Totoricagü
specializes in Basque migration and diaspora studies.
She earned her doctorate degree in Comparative Politics
from the London School of Economics and Political Science, and currently researches and teaches at the Center
for Basque Studies at the University of Nevada, Reno. She
has conducted unparalleled fieldwork and investigation
with Basques from communities in over twenty countries and regularly serves as a consultant for institutions
in the Basque Country. Her work has been awarded and
recognized internationally, including the *Vasca Mun-
dial*, Worldly Basque, award in 2003, and when selected
as the President of the Committee of Academic Experts
from the Eusko Ikaskuntza, or Basque Studies Society,
initiative for EuskoSare, a worldwide network for Basque
studies.

Dr. Totoricagüena collaborates in various research
projects with homeland institutions and with those of
the Basque diaspora. She is a permanent delegate to the
North American Basque Organizations, and has represented the United States in each of the World Congresses
of Basque Collectivities. Her numerous publications
include more than thirty articles and several books
including: *Identity, Culture, and Politics in the Basque
Diaspora*; *The Basques of New York: A Cosmopolitan
Experience*; *Diáspora Vasca Comparada: Etnicidad, Cultura y Política en las Colectividades Vascas del Exterior*;
and *The Basques of Boise: Dreamers and Doers*.

Gloria Totoricagüena

Basque Diaspora
Migration and Transnational Identity

Basque Textbooks Series

Center for Basque Studies
University of Nevada, Reno

This book was published with generous financial
support from the Basque Government.

Library of Congress Cataloging-in-Publication Data

Totoricaguena, Gloria P. (Gloria Pilar), 1961–
    Basque diaspora : migration and transnational
    identity / Gloria Totoricaguena.
        p. cm. – (Basque textbooks series)
    ISBN 1-877802-45-X (paperback)
    ISBN 1-877802-46-8 (hardcover)
    ISBN 1-877802-47-6 (compact disk)
    1. Basques—Foreign countries—History. 2. País
Vasco (Spain)--Emigration and immigration—History.
3. Basques—Ethnic identity. I. Title. II. Series.
    DP302.B48T68 2004
    909'.049992--dc22

                      2004027242

Published by the Center for Basque Studies
University of Nevada, Reno /322
Reno, Nevada 89557-0012.

Printed in the United States of America.

CONTENTS

The Basque diaspora
A brief introduction

THE NOTION *of a "diaspora," or dispersion, is
derived from the Greek word for "to spread," "to
disperse," "to sow," or "to scatter." An original and
salient factor of Basque Studies includes the immigrant
populations and their descendants spread and sown
throughout the world living in the Basque diaspora,
the maintenance of their ethnic identity, and their connections to their homeland. This course will compare
transnational identities maintained in populations of
the Basque diaspora in more than twenty countries. Lectures and readings will combine theories from sociology,
political science, history, and anthropology to investigate
the specifics of Basque migrations, cultural representations, diasporic politics, and ethnonationalism. The
course will analyze the Basque Autonomous Government's international relations with various Basque communities abroad and compare them with other similar
homeland–ethnic diaspora relations. This unique course
aims to explore Basque diaspora studies by comparing
ethnonationalism, transnationalism, and identity maintenance in the numerous host countries that have significant Basque immigrant populations. We will evaluate
the historical, political, and economic dimensions of
migration and the creation of ethnic institutions in the
host countries. Students will examine Basque cultural
construction and maintenance and the effects of gender,
generation, geography, and globalization on Basque
communities outside of Euskal Herria.*

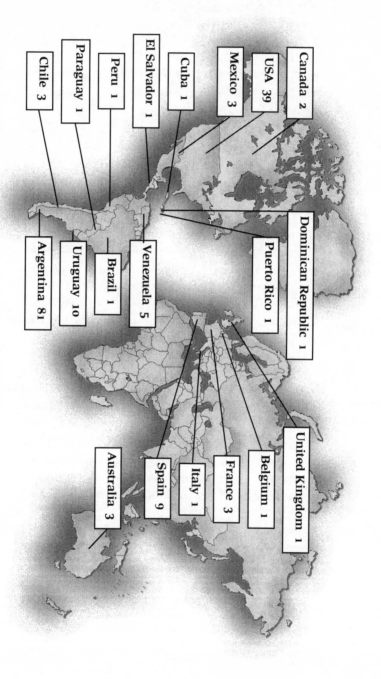

Basque Centers registered with the Government of the Basque Autonomous Community.

Chile 3
Paraguay 1
Peru 1
El Salvador 1
Cuba 1
Mexico 3
USA 39
Canada 2
Dominican Republic 1
Puerto Rico 1
Argentina 81
Uruguay 10
Brazil 1
Venezuela 5
United Kingdom 1
Belgium 1
France 3
Italy 1
Spain 9
Australia 3

BASQUES ON THE MOVE

Throughout the late Middle Ages, the Bay of Biscay's marine economy and commercial trade required Basques to travel and contact other cultures and societies, and Basque place-names dot the landscapes in

Basque Centers registered with the Government of the Basque Autonomous Community.

Argentina	81	Spain	9	USA	39
Australia	3	Madrid	3	Arizona	1
Melbourne	1	Barcelona	1	California	14
Sydney	1	Málaga	1	Florida	3
Belgium	1	Palma de		Idaho	5
Brazil	1	Mallorca	1	Nevada	7
Canada	2	Valladoid	1	New York	2
Chile	3	Valencia	1	Oregon	2
Santiago	2	Salou	1	Utah	1
Valpariso	1	United		Wyoming	2
Cuba	1	Kingdom	1	Washington	2
Dominican		Uruguay	10	Venezuela	4
Republic	1	Montevideo	3	Caracas	2
El Salvador	1	Carmelo	1	Valencia	1
France	3	Durazno	1	Puerto	
Paris	1	Minas	1	la Cruz	1
Burdeos	1	Rivera	1	Carabobo	1
Jurançon	1	Rosario	1		
Italy	1	Salto	1	Federations	
Mexico	3	Colonia	1	Argentina	
México DF	3			Spain	
Paraguay	1			United States	
Peru	1			Venezuela	
Puerto Rico	1			Uruguay	

coastal regions of Western Europe, Scandinavia, and Newfoundland. Basque whalers, merchants, and ship-builders, along with professional military men, were among these first emigrants. However, notable numbers of Basques did not begin to leave the Basque Country permanently until the colonial pursuits of the 1500s under the crown of Castile and later of Spain.

SPECIALISTS IN migration studies have argued that the political, economic, and social factors of human migration are varied and that these factors are specific to different epochs and different persons. We can, however, discriminate between factors that "push" emigrants out of their homelands and factors that "pull" them toward diasporic destinations elsewhere in the world, a distinction that we will employ throughout. In the case of Basque emigration, the most salient factors pushing Basques to emigrate included Spanish colonization of the Americas and the demand for clerics, military person-nel, and tradesmen; the restricted economic opportunity in the homeland; the physical position of Euskal Herria (the seven Basque provinces) between Spain and France and its use as a stage for Napoleonic military campaigns; the French Revolution (1789–1804); the First Carlist War (1833–39) and the Second Carlist War (1872–76); and the Spanish Civil War (1936–39) and the subsequent Franco dictatorship. The Spanish liberalization of emigration in 1853 also facilitated thousands of persons annually to depart for Latin America, as did the Basque primogeni-ture inheritance system and overpopulated rural areas. We will be investigating each of these variables and the ensuing effects on Basque emigration to various parts of the world.

New World economic and political opportunities, weighed against Old World uncertainties and upheavals, helped pull emigrants out of the Basque Country, to the

Americas and beyond. Basques pursued ethnically based trading networks to aid the expansion of their ambitions, and this was the foundation for a trade diaspora that was followed by economic, political, and sociocultural transnationalism. Until the beginning of the last century, commercial trade and military and religious conquests were the reasons for Basque emigration, an emigration that took place both inside a Basque transkingdom and transstate networks and inside the framework of the Spanish empire. Spanish and French conquests provided new options to Basques for overseas migration. Basque emigration to the Americas and the Philippines involved the transfer of the skilled and influential from an imperial country and its regions to its colonies, a colonial diaspora. This emigration was also often temporary, dominated by young males, and it was rare for an entire family to leave the Basque Country together.

THE INDEPENDENCE movements in Latin American territories and the Disaster, as it is known, of the 1898 Spanish-American War drew a line that divides the history of Basque emigration into two phases. In the first phase of large-scale emigration, at the beginning of the sixteenth century, the kingdom of Castile lacked sufficient population and economic resources to pursue colonialism on all fronts. Without military and commercial transportation, it could not possibly maintain its Old World holdings or develop its fledgling New World territories. Efforts to colonize would require reliable supplies of iron implements, and military campaigns would consume large amounts of weaponry. For Basques, who were experienced and skilled in producing such equipment in the homeland, the opening of the New World was an immediate stimulant to emigrate and provide this knowhow in the colonies, as well. William A. Douglass and Jon Bilbao (1975) have shown that Basque emigrants often

NOTITIA
VTRIVSQVE
VASCONIÆ,
TVM JBERICÆ,
TVM AQVITANICÆ,

QVA, PRÆTER SITVM REGIONIS ET ALIA
ſcitu digna, NAVARRÆ Regum Cæterarumque, in iis,
inſignium vetuſtate & dignitate familiarum ſtemmata
ex probatis Authoribus & vetuſtis monumentis
exhibentur.

Accedunt Catalogi Pontificum Vaſconiæ Aquitanicæ,
hactenus editis pleniores.

Authore ARNALDO OIHENARTO Mauleoſoleñ.

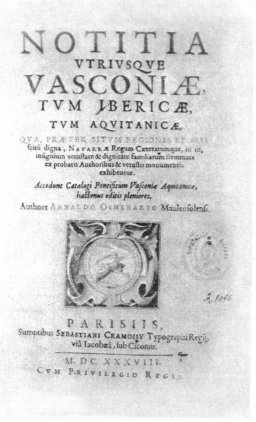

.ℜ. 1066

PARISIIS,
Sumptibus SEBASTIANI CRAMOISY Typographi Regij,
vià Iacobæâ, ſub Ciconiis.

M. DC. XXXVIII.

CVM PRIVILEGIO REGIS.

A Basque lawyer from Mauleon, Zuberoa, Arnaut
D'Oihenart y Echart published the first history of
the Basque Country, composed of three different
books, in 1638, with a second edition in 1658. Written
in Latin, the work includes family genealogies and
personal manuscripts and letters among the numerous
investigations. His anthropological definition of the
Basque Country led him to refute the contemporary
political divisions of Euskal Herria of his day.

acted as a self-aware ethnic group, maintaining ties to each other and to their homeland. This resulted in trade networks, collective action, mutual assistance programs, schools for Basque children, and associations and societies for the maintenance of Basque language, culture, and traditions, all examples of what we will categorize as diaspora activities.

THE SECOND phase was a part of a larger wave of emigration from Europe to former colonies in the New World, a transfer of people who were economically and/or politically oppressed and seeking relief. The population movements were massive. During this phase, the entire population growth in Iparralde for the last half of the nineteenth century was canceled by emigration (Jacob 1994, 46). This is a staggering fact.

Pulling these emigrants across the Atlantic were dreams of economic success, civil rights and political freedoms, and asylum. By the time that this second wave of Basque emigration began, however, the preferred earlier destinations—Mexico, Venezuela, and Peru—had been supplanted by Argentina and Uruguay in the south and later by the United States in the north. We will be examining each of these central elements of the Basque diaspora in depth, along with migrations to even more distant destinations, such as Australia.

In this second wave, as in the first, some searched for opportunities, while others fled difficulties, and the Basques were no exception. They were also no exception in that they again sought out earlier emigrants and used ethnic transnational networks in determining their destinations. As in the first phase of disaporic emigration, many Basques experienced the pull of family ties or other personal contacts from their villages. Those who departed without definite contacts in the New World to receive them knew from village folk stories that an established Basque group could be found in almost any of these New World trade regions. They knew about remittances to families in their areas and often witnessed the renovation or construction of new farmsteads and churches and improvements in agricultural equipment as results of those remittances. It was only natural to expect that their fellow Basques would be helpful in adapting to the new society and would help them find employment and housing.

At the onset of this phase, during and after the French Revolution, the northern Basque provinces were subjected to military occupation, and their ancient legal charters, their foral laws, were abolished. Basques were generally deprived of their lands and livestock, and while numerous Basques were interned in camps by revolutionary officials, there was also a forced deportation of more than three thousand Basques who were accused of treason with Spain. In 1793 in Baiona alone, more than sixty death penalties were pronounced for "complicity in illegal immigration or correspondence with priests in exile." Napoleon's rise to power and push to conquer the Iberian Peninsula resulted in several wars being fought in the Basque Country, with Basques themselves being recruited and conscripted by both sides. These were additional push factors that influenced the desire to escape the political oppression.

THE FIRST of the Carlist Wars in Spain commenced in 1833, with the rural Catholic and regionalist Basques (a majority of the Basque population) siding with the traditionalist challenger to the throne, Don Carlos, against the Liberals, supporters of the queen regent and her government. Meanwhile, Basques from the modernizing areas of Bilbao, Donostia–San Sebastián, and Vitoria-Gasteiz and those from the commercial and intellectual elite favored the Liberals. Financing the war resulted in taxation in most areas of the Basque Country and conscription by the Carlist forces. The defeat of the Carlists in 1839 left Basques with political and economic war debts and retributions, and six years of war had also disrupted the economy and agricultural output. An estimated eight thousand war exiles fled the Basque Country to Argentina, Uruguay, and Chile. A corn-crop failure and the famine of 1846–47 aggravated the already dire circumstances and gave impetus for many to abandon their economic, military, and political situations and seek relief in the Americas.

The French Revolution of 1848 once again found the Basques fighting on the losing side against revolutionary goals, and memories of repercussions from the earlier rebellions encouraged departures from the area. Between 1852 and 1855, there were 1,311 Basque military evaders—almost one-half of the French total. In Spain, the Second Carlist War (1872–76) saw a repeat of defeat and emigration to escape hardship. Maritime archives show that hundreds of military-aged men avoided or deserted their obligatory three-year military service, and others later fled the repercussions of the Liberals.

THE SPANISH Civil War (1936–39) also produced thousands of Basque political refugees. In all, across the globe, the final collapse of the Spanish Republic resulted in an estimated one hundred and fifty thousand exiled Basques. Those political exiles significantly influenced the diaspora communities' self-definitions and involvement in the maintenance of Basque identity by transporting the contemporary homeland nationalism of the day.

Although necessary as an escape from the political and economic pressures of the Basque region, emigration often created social problems, such as lack of youth, laborers, and especially eligible males for marriage. It significantly affected the roles and power of women in a society with fewer men, and single parenting is not a new phenomenon in the Basque Country, although traditional extended families provided many parents with aid, supervision of children, and affection.

It is important to note that emigration during any of these time periods was by no means an unusual option or a last resort to remedy hardship. There were enduring structural reasons in Basque culture that encouraged emigration. The rules of inheritance followed in rural Basque society constituted the single most important push factor in stimulating emigration out of Euskal Herria. Because of the small size of the farmsteads, or *baserris*, their limited productivity, and demographic pressures, they often could not support more than a single family at a time. By custom and foral law, primogeniture was the mode of inheritance, with the farmstead passing to a single heir, be it male or female, and often regardless of birth order. Consequently, as the other siblings in the family grew to maturity, they became candidates for emigration. De facto primogeniture pushed many Basques to emigrate.

IN ADDITION, during the nineteenth century, when political turmoil and war roiled the homeland, some hostland governments in the New World were actually recruiting Basques to fill the pressing needs of economic development in the newly minted states, enticing and pulling young Basques to leave their crowded *baserris* for the economic opportunities of South America. Uruguayan governments, beginning in 1832, had specifically requested Basque immigrants for the country's agriculture, and with the European Industrial Revolution there was a high demand for the products of the South American sheep industry, which was mainly controlled by Basques, and consequently there were high profits to

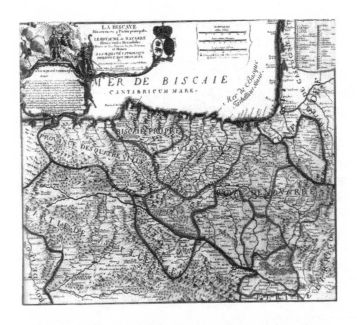

In 1704, Jean Baptiste Nolin prepared this map depicting
the contemporary political and geographical details of
the Basque Country. Nolin's family business in Paris
published and distributed continental and world atlases.
The map demonstrates an outsider's perception of the
Basque Country's political boundaries and political
alliances.

---

be made by them. By the 1840s, establishment of a sheep
industry has augmented the raising of cattle in the interior pampas regions, with Basque immigrants dominat-
ing sheep herding and cattle ranching in the so-called
"Southern Cone"—Chile, Argentina, Paraguay, and
Uruguay. The attractions of South America, formally and
informally conveyed, pulled many young Basques to the
New World.

By the time of the second phase of immigration, the typical emigrant thus was a single male between fifteen and twenty-five years old, sent for by relatives in the New World who needed agricultural laborers, or one going in search of relatives hoping they needed laborers. It was also a prime age for escaping mandatory military service. By the end of the nineteenth century, few women emigrated with their husbands, and occasionally single women would be sent to live and work with their kin in the Americas. More commonly, a husband would travel alone to find work and settle in the new community. After several years of saving money, he would either send for his wife and any children or would return to the homeland with the savings.

IMMIGRANT BACHELORS used Basque social networks to find mates in their new host society, and Basque endogamy rates were high in Argentina, Uruguay, and the United States. One survey showed that in the United States, of 119 Basque men who immigrated to Idaho between 1889 and 1939, 114 then married other Basques in the United States or by returning to the homeland for a bride (Edlefsen 1948, 65). Various Basque women in Euskal Herria married their fiancés in absentia in wedding ceremonies where a groom's brother, uncle, or cousin stood in for the new spouse. This way the woman was already technically married and more acceptable, according to Catholic Church leaders, for single travel to join her husband.

As we have seen, Basques frequently knew of fellow Basques escaping poverty and political and economic oppression, seeking employment and opportunity, and this knowledge exerted a more or less constant pull. The key to the decision to migrate in fact may well have been access to information. Jose C. Moya, for example, argues that immigrants from Spain to the Southern Cone tended to be from the coastal regions, close to international ports, and that their access to information, whatever the route to be taken, was essential to emigration (Moya 1998). The choice of destinations and the timing of departure depended on homeland circumstances, family and village ties, and employment opportunities, but ultimately on the information one had regarding other possibilities and the chances for success. Because the economic development of Europe implied an increase in specialization, and because increased industrialization brought manufacturing to the Basque Country, small proprietors and tradesmen were faced with a choice of finding alternative employment or migration. Chain-migration information networks among Basques facilitated the latter. Migrants' choices of when and where to go thus were influenced by the amount and type of information they had regarding a possible host country community where other Basques had settled previously.

MOBILIZATION AND ORGANIZATIONS

THROUGHOUT the centuries, the immigrants of the Basque diaspora have created organizations that served their particular economic, religious, social, psychological, and cultural needs. Mutual aid societies were common in Basque diaspora communities in Mexico, Argentina, Uruguay, Peru, and the United States. In 1905, for example, in a pattern repeated throughout the Americas, a group of Basques in New York formed a mutual aid society and paid medical expenses, funeral expenses, and repatriations for needy Basques and their families. The shock and displacement of international migration were buffered by the numerous fellow Basques and the political, economic, and cultural involvement available to emigrants. Links were firmly in place among

The Arbaion or Arbayún gorge near the town of Lumbier is part of a nature reserve and also is designated a special conservation area for birds due to the protections offered by cracks, holes, and overhanging cliffs. It is 6 kilometers long, with canyon walls reaching 385 meters high. It was home to one of Nafarroa's wild boar populations, which were traditionally hunted, although this is no longer permitted.

Photograph by the author.

Basques in each host society and between Basques and their homeland.

In addition to these forms of mutual support and solidarity, Basques began to develop forms of cultural and political expression as a self-conscious diaspora. Beginning with the work of Basque political exiles leaving Euskal Herria in the 1820s, these forms can be seen in various cultural expressions such as songwriting and literary publications. Also, from Argentina's *La Baskonia* and *Irrintzi* to California's two Basque-language newspapers, *Escualdun Gazeta* and *California'ko Eskual Herria*, by the late 1800s, there were several different Basque periodicals consistently published in the Americas that promoted the Basque *fueros*, or local legal charters, and ethnonationalist ideas. Several shared their readership lists and distribution addresses through established international Basque networks. Although mostly disseminated to and read by an educated elite, in these publications, the imagining of an interconnected Basque diaspora had taken form and would play a significant role in aiding the Basque government-in-exile later in the century.

INSTITUTIONALIZED BASQUENESS

BASQUE ASSOCIATION networks enhanced migrants' capacities to adapt to new circumstances. The diaspora associations, and especially those that have a physical office or cultural Basque center, today still help fortify inter-Basque networking for friendship, employment, information, and news of the homeland. Newcomers from Euskal Herria, whether visiting or studying, still are likely to go directly to the community's Basque center for instant companionship and information. In 2004, there were more than one hundred and eighty Basque ethnic organizations known in twenty-two different countries.

Basque collectivities have progressed over time in very similar ways. Since the 1612 founding of the Fraternity of Our Lady of Aranzazu of the Basque Nation in Lima and the Confraternity of the Basque Nation in Arequipa, Peru, in 1630, through the 1800s in Argentina, Uruguay, and 1900s in the United States, as mentioned above, a *socorros mútuos*, a mutual aid society for defraying the costs of medical care, funerals, and repatriation has been present in nearly every country we will study. They also have provided local Basques with familial type networks and financial aid for health care. The centers have organized choirs, dance troupes, language and history classes, cooking seminars, homeland tours, and sports teams.

THE NEW IMMIGRANTS' incorporation into the established diaspora community could pose various problems, which we will be exploring in depth. They have recurred throughout the diaspora as immigrants have experienced tensions between homeland and hostland cultures and as cultural changes in the homeland over time have provoked tensions between older and more recent immigrants. In addition, the end of continuous Basque immigration has changed the functions of today's collective organizations, from agents of accommodation to the economic, social, and political realities of the hostland to preservers of homeland cultural identity in the diaspora by a variety of means, ranging from the preservation and transmission of Basque music, dancing, food, ethnic games, and sports to providing lessons in the Basque language, circulating newsletters that tie together the disapora community around its ethnic roots, and serving as informal travel agencies facilitating travel back to the Basque Country. We will explore these changes in depth, as well.

As we will also investigate, in recent years, globalization and its effects have played a part in transforming the Basque diaspora, its relations with the homeland, its conceptions of ethnicity, and the culture of the homeland itself. The progression of Basque center activities, from assisting Basque immigrants to integrate into the host societies, to functioning as ethnic organizations and regenerative sources of ethnicity by creating and recreating ties to the homeland, to serving as tourist agencies and vacation guides, however, has less to do with globalization, or with geography, or for that matter with changes in gender roles in the diaspora, which we will also examine, than with evolution in migration patterns, in addition to changes in the categories of people traveling and the purpose of their visits. The later generations now tend to experience their ethnicity by voluntary individual choice. Those who choose to do so continue to preserve a collective identity. Basque centers are becoming the unofficial embassies of Euskal Herria, promoting all of the unique and positive themes of the seven provinces. However, we should note that not all Basques living outside the Basque Country consider themselves as members of a diaspora. Many do not identify themselves as Basques and have assimilated completely into their host societies, whether they are of the first generation of immigrants or the fifth generation. Still others do define themselves as Basque, but do not exhibit the behaviors and psychology of diasporic consciousness.

IN RECOGNITION of the financial, political, and cultural contributions that supported the Basque government-in-exile for forty years, since the 1980s, the Basque Autonomous Government of Euskadi has collaborated with the diaspora communities via a policy of subsidies and grants, giving aid for their internal operating costs and educational and cultural activities. The Basque government has presented Basque organizations abroad with computer communications equipment, audio-visual materials with themes of the homeland such as sports, history, anthropology, tourism, cooking, and so on, and audio tapes and printed materials for studying Euskara, the Basque language. The Basque government is interested in using the centers for promotion and development and for disseminating the contemporary reality of the Basque Country. Particularly today, in an environment of continuous globalization and the internationalization of modern societies, Basque communities can play the part of stimulator for positive social, cultural, economic, and political relations.

MAKING SURE WE UNDERSTAND EACH OTHER

THIS TEXT is being used by students from various levels—from undergraduate students being introduced to Basque Studies to masters and PhD students and national government officials responsible for diaspora policy in their countries' legislative or executive branches. There may be times when some of you are frustrated by the specialist's level of vocabulary, and you may find the readings extremely challenging—especially to those who are not native speakers of English. Others of you may find the history and homeland references especially elementary and simplistic. You can overcome this with a more analytical essay response to the essay questions that appear at the end of each lesson. Please use any personal experiences as examples when appropriate, especially if you are a person who identifies with a certain ethnicity, but do not live in your ancestral homeland, or if you are an indigenous person (Native American, Aborigine, etc.) and your homeland has been colonized by "others."

As early as the Neolithic Age, megalithic monuments, dolmens, cromlechs, and grave mounds consisted of communal burial plots, some with personal artifacts that were buried with the corpses. The largest dolmens in the Basque Country are in Araba: Aizkomendi in Egilaz, Sorginetxeta in Arrizala, San Martin in La Guardia, and Hechizeria in Elvillar. Communal burial mounds are found around the world, and over 50 percent of all known dolmens are located in Korea.
Photograph by the author.

CHOICE OF WORDS AND PLACE-NAMES

In the complex reality of the Basque Country, there are Spanish names for Basque places and Basque names for Spanish places, to say nothing of the North, which is bestowed with the equivalent puzzle in French. How one determines the correct name for an appropriate place depends much on one's own identity and political opinions. When possible, I will use English terminology and language. Where there is no separate English-language term, I will use the standardized Batua Basque language and the official toponyms decreed by the Resolution of December 17, 2001, which lists the official place-names and spellings selected by the municipal councils (*Boletín Oficial del País Vasco*, no. 1, January 2, 2002, with the latest update from September 30, 2002). The legislative branches of Bizkaia (1986) and Gipuzkoa (1990) voted to use the Basque spelling as the official form in their provinces, and Alava voted to use "Álava" as the official spelling of the province for materials published in Spanish, and "Araba" for materials published in Basque. I therefore use "Araba," "Bizkaia," and "Gipuzkoa" when referring to these areas. For this work, I use the current geopolitical boundaries as stipulated in the Spanish Constitution of 1978, the Statutes of Autonomy of Euskadi of 1979, and the Statutes of Autonomy of Navarre of 1979, and by the French Department of Pyrénées-Atlantiques. Pyrénées-Atlantiques encompasses the Basque provinces of Lapurdi (Labourd), Behe Nafarroa (Basse Navarre), and Zuberoa (Soule). "Euskadi" is the political name for the politically and economically autonomous region of Spain that includes the provinces of Araba, Bizkaia, and Gipuzkoa, and "Nafarroa" is the separate autonomous community of Navarre. The glossary provides the Spanish or French equivalent for the names of Basque towns.

IN THE TRADITIONAL Basque language, Euskara, there are various orthographies, and the spelling of entire words differs depending on regional variations. I will apply the spellings of the standardized Basque language, which is the official version of the Basque Autonomous Government, the Basque public media, and the Basque Language Academy. Especially important are uses of "Basque Country" and "Euskal Herria," by which I mean all seven provinces described above, "Euskadi," which denotes only the three provinces of Araba, Bizkaia, and Gipuzkoa; and "Nafarroa," which includes only the territory in today's Spain that is ruled by its own statutes of autonomy.

BIBLIOGRAPHY

Douglass, William A., and Jon Bilbao. 1975. *Amerikanuak: Basques in the New World*. Reno: University of Nevada Press.

Edlefsen, John B. 1948. "A Sociological Study of the Basques of Southwest Idaho." PhD diss., State College of Washington.

Jacob, James E. 1994. *Hills of Conflict: Basque Nationalism in France*. Reno: University of Nevada Press.

Moya, Jose C. 1998. *Cousins and Strangers: Spanish Immigrants in Buenos Aires, 1850–1930*. Berkeley: University of California Press.

Totoricagüena, Gloria. 2004. *Identity, Culture, and Politics in the Basque Diaspora*. Reno: University of Nevada Press.

———. 2001. "Una aproximación al desarrollo de la diáspora vasca." In *Kanpoko Etxe berria: Emigración vasca a América siglos XIX–XX*. Bilbao: Museo Arqueológico, Etnográfico, e Histórico Vasco.

Totoricagüena, Gloria. 2001. "La identidad contemporánea de los vascos en la diáspora." Eusko Ikaskuntza *Euskonews and Media Electronic*

Journal, no. 121 (May). Donostia-San Sebastián. http://www.euskonews.com.

————. 2000. "Comparing the Basque Diaspora: Ethnonationalism, Transnationalism, and Identity Maintenance in Argentina, Australia, Belgium, Peru, the United States of America, and Uruguay. PhD diss., the London School of Economics and Political Science, University of London.

Waters, Mary C. 1990. *Ethnic Options: Choosing Identities in America*. Berkeley: University of California Press.

1 · Defining "diaspora"

ALTHOUGH for some people the term "diaspora" has a negative connotation connected to the scattering and dispersion as punishment mentioned in the Old Testament, specialists such as Robin Cohen write that the term was used to describe the Greek colonization in 800 to 600 B.C., with its positive connotation of sowing or spreading related to military conquest, trade, and settlement.

Although various diaspora experts argue about the categorization and definition of "diaspora," we will adopt these commonly shared factors of ethnic populations living outside their ancestral and historical homelands and categorized as indeed diaspora, which include:

1. Dispersal from an original homeland, often traumatically.
2. Alternatively, the expansion from a homeland in search of work, in pursuit of trade or to further colonial ambitions.
3. A collective memory and myth about the homeland.
4. An idealization of the supposed ancestral homeland.
5. A return movement.
6. A strong ethnic group consciousness sustained over a long period of time.
7. A troubled relationship with host societies.
8. A sense of solidarity with co-ethnic members in other countries.
9. The possibility of a distinctive, enriching life in tolerant host countries. (Cohen 1997:180)

Let us consider each of these factors in turn, amplifying and qualifying them as need be.

The Otxagabia Bridge crosses the small Anduña river
at the bottom of the Muskilda hill. The town of Otxagabia is the largest in the Salazar Valley of Nafarroa.
The December 27 festival of St. John the Evangelist was
traditionally celebrated here with the "Day for Dining
Together," when families were paired off by the parish
priest and then shared a meal. He attempted to pair rich
and poor families or families who had feuded during the
year, giving an opportunity for apologies.
Photograph by the author.

W HEN DIFFERENTIATING "diaspora" populations
from "immigrant" groups we specifically look for
maintained networks of exchange and an ethnic consciousness that spans temporal and spatial constraints.
As Cohen notes, there are different types and initiating
factors of diasporas in general. One can trace expansion
from a Basque homeland territory in search of work,
trade, or to further colonial pursuits, as Basques did

since the 1200s. We will use the plural terminology of
the Basque "diasporas" to denote differing time periods
and factors involved in the creation of various waves of
Basque emigration. Basques have journeyed out of the
Pyrenees in the repopulation movements of medieval
times, for whaling in the North Atlantic, for the colonization of the Americas, and into the political exile of the
Franco years, 1936–75. Basques have experienced a trade
and entrepreneurial phase, a colonization phase, a labor
phase, and a political phase, and each will be discussed
in future lessons and in our readings.

ALTHOUGH diasporic groups who have experienced
traumatic expulsions and dispersals from their
original homeland may physically adjust to life as
refugees, the emotional and psychological crisis of a
ruptured existence is extremely difficult to manage.
Individuals in existing Basque communities often served
as unofficial counselors to newly arrived Basques, and
women often have mentioned that being able to socialize with their Basque girlfriends served as an emotional
and psychological outlet. We thus can see that, in addition to assisting newcomers with housing, employment,
the education of children, and so on, the mental health
of immigrants needs to be a significant priority for the
receiving communities, although this is a new concept
and not one that is usually given the significance that it
merits.

Like other diasporic groups, Basques share a collective
memory, myths, and idealization of the seven provinces.
Many also maintain a "return to homeland" movement
that helps foster diaspora communities. The Irish promote the return to Ireland, the Jews promise "next year
in Jerusalem," and the Basques encourage their young to
participate in programs for youth initiated by the Basque
government, such as Gaztemundu, the World of Youth,

in order to "meet their homeland." The rite of passage to visit Jerusalem, the Emerald Isle, or the family *baserri*—for each respective group—symbolizes the completion of a circle. However, for most, a permanent "return" is no longer possible, or even necessary. Perhaps regular "virtual returns" using the Internet, e-mail, and chat rooms to imagine themselves in the Basque territories are just as meaningful. A permanent return is possible for others, such as the thousands of Argentine Basques who have applied for repatriation and the hundreds who have been repatriated to the Basque Country with aid from the Basque Government during this latest economic crisis of the new millennium. Visiting the cultural centers and participating in ethnic activities can also serve as psychological returns.

ANONYMOUS QUESTIONNAIRE data that I have collected in over fifty Basque diaspora communities demonstrates that the youth who returned from a "pilgrimage" to the Basque Country had indeed recharged their ethnic batteries. They had educated themselves, and they updated their respective Basque communities with news and stories from the homeland. It is fundamental for diaspora communities to fund travel to the homeland for youth, if this is possible. One person's experiences update the entire group and simultaneously may serve to strengthen ties with homeland family and institutions.

Cohen notes that diasporas exhibit a strong ethnic group consciousness sustained over a long period of time. Basques began establishing ethnic organizations in the 1600s in Peru and Mexico, and then throughout Latin America, and later in the 1900s in the new migration destinations of the United States, Canada, Australia, and Belgium.

However, this group consciousness is not easy to achieve or to maintain. The processes of settling include acquisition of a new language, finding employment, changing gender roles, and constructing new social spaces for the maintenance of ethnicity. Each successive wave of new migrants arrives to confront an existing ethnic institutional structure and has to adjust not only to the new host society, but also usually to the modified culture of an existing diasporic community, which promulgates a different kind of Basque identity than was known in the homeland.

THE "AUTHENTICITY" of the existing diasporic culture in the host country is questioned by the newcomer, and the newcomers' Basque authenticity is questioned by the existing community. "These young ones are not really Basque like we used to be," said one older emigrant living in Argentina. "They don't speak Basque, they never lived on the *baserri*, they don't even know how to play *mus*. What kind of a Basque is that?" And a recent Basque emigrant to San Francisco said,

> Why would I ever go to the Basque Cultural Center? They are living in the 1950s! Basques in the Basque Country don't go around wearing *txapelas* and singing songs from decades ago. Do young Americans go out square dancing on a Saturday night? Do they dress up like Thomas Jefferson, or do they teach their children to do dances from the Roaring Twenties? I don't think so. These Basques have to get with it and update their ideas of what it means to be Basque.

The development of a strong ethnic group consciousness, however, raises the issue of possible conflicts of interest with the host country, and indeed, issues of dual loyalties to host and home countries and tensions with host societies are raised often in diaspora studies. However, they are not as relevant in these Basque diasporic communities. Field research conducted with Basques living in Great Britain, Argentina, Chile, Uruguay, Brazil, Peru, Venezuela, Guatemala, Mexico, the Dominican Republic, Australia, Belgium, Canada, and the United States demonstrated that Basques tend to separate their civic identities with their host countries from their ethnic identity of being Basque. They have a "double consciousness" of being both, but the relationship is not hierarchical.

For example, Basques in Uruguay are very proud to be Uruguayan, and they see no conflict in being Basque *and* Uruguayan. Basques in the United States are also likely to be patriotic and thankful that they, or their ancestors, immigrated to the United States. Basques are able to define themselves as Belgian, Australian, or Canadian, and also as a Basque. Although participants defined themselves as hyphenated Basques—Basque-Uruguayans, or Belgian-Basques—they did not tend to conceptualize these two as competing identities, but as completely different categories of identity in the same way that I am female, Basque, mother, a university instructor, and live in the United States, which are all different factors in my identity.

THE QUESTION of dual loyalty is a often a question of patriotism to a state. Diasporas shatter the concept that citizenship equates to loyalty and belonging to one state and replace that with multiple layers of orientation and participation in ethnicity and cultural identity that are not grounded in territory. Diasporic Basques see no conflict of interest because their loyalties have not been tested, with none of these host societies declaring war on the Basque Country and with none having any serious trade or treaty conflicts. The same is not true for Ger-

The church of the Holy Sepulcher in Estella, Nafarroa. Estella is situated on the Catholic pilgrimage Way of St. James, which leads west to the Galician city of Santiago de Compostela. Prior to the founding of Estella, there was a Frankish and Jewish neighborhood known as Lizarra that had existed since at least Roman times. Estella was a fortified settlement and was important in the fight against Islam in the Middle Ages.
Photograph by the author.

man-Americans, Japanese-Americans, Italian-Americans, and so on. We will eventually examine how Basques have attempted to influence their host countries' governmental policies toward the central Spanish government and how these activities were received by their local communities and host society governments.

Indeed, although traditional characteristics of diasporas have included a troubled relationship between the diasporic communities and their host societies, the tendency among Basques has been the opposite. We will see that Basques have often been the societal leaders of politics and business in Argentina, Uruguay, Chile, Mexico, and Venezuela, and this aspect of diasporic communities will be discussed throughout the text.

It is true that nearly all immigrants to a new area experience some sort of a troubled relationship or questioned loyalty from their host society, and this often serves to consolidate the ethnic group even more and motivates individuals to protect each other. Basques are generally white-skinned Catholics who migrated to Caucasian societies dominated by Christians, many of those being Spanish-speaking, and Basques have not experienced mass overt discrimination based on their origin. There are isolated circumstances in the United States of Basque interviewees stating that they were discriminated against because of their Catholicism, and that they were called "dirty black Bascos," but there are not multiple examples of Basques being refused employment, housing, or equal treatment in the society because of their being Basque. However, they have constantly been questioned about their opinions of the Basque armed struggle movement, ETA, Euskadi 'ta Askatasuna, Basque Homeland and Liberty, and their relations to it.

MEMBERS OF A diaspora also exhibit a sense of community and feeling a part of an "us" that goes beyond the host state's borders. Armenians, Indians, Jews, Koreans, Chinese, and increasingly, Basques, are among the ethnic groups scattered around the world that feel a connection to others in their group, no matter the state in which they live.

There can be limits to this sense of solidarity. Diaspora populations often describe themselves as "not fitting" here or there. "En el limbo." In Euskal Herria, one is known as "the American," or the South American, *la Sudamericana*, or *la sudaca*, and not fully accepted as

Basque. In Caracas, she is "that Basque lady with the funny accent" and not fully accepted as Venezuelan. Despite this sense of not fully fitting in, the majority of Basques outside of the Basque Country admit that their families are now established in their new host societies and they are not likely to uproot and begin another process of emigration, settlement and adaptation. This realization can be agonizing for those who admit that their dreams of return have ended, and they have wakened to find that they feel more at home in their host country. "I have wasted all those years," one woman cried,

> "pretending to be somewhere else and someone else— trying to keep the "me" that I was before leaving my home and parents, always living for "someday." I have never even bothered to really learn any English, know anything about this city, or even make any non-Basque friends. Now look at me. Who am I—this seventy-year-old woman who is no longer fully Basque and never was American. Who am I? Where do *I* belong?"

ON THE OTHER hand, several younger and more formally educated Basques are describing a transnational identity of fitting here *and* there. Diaspora populations are selecting, mixing, and constructing a specific Basque diasporic identity. They fit into many physical and virtual places. Ethnic identity becomes transnational when physical geography is no longer a factor. Benedict Anderson's concept of "imagined communities" is related to the emerging community of the Basque diaspora. For example, Basques in Argentina describe themselves as connected to Basques in Belgium, Australia, and the homeland. They imagine themselves as a part of a single community because of the communications, culture, traditions, philosophies, history, and

Known as the father of contemporary Basque nationalism, Sabino Arana y Goiri (1865-1903) was the son of a
fervent Carlist. After studying in Barcelona and being influenced by the Catalan Renaissance and the nationalist
ideas of his brother Luis, he published Basque linguistic, historical, literary, and cultural works. In 1895, he
founded the Basque Nationalist Party. Arana proposed
the independence of Bizkaia and subsequently of all the
Basque territories.

situations they share. Transportable and mobile identity are not tied to physical territory, and therefore one can be Basque whether one lives in San Sebastián, Sydney, Sao Paulo, or San Francisco.

The diaspora experience in general problematizes modernity's linear account of time and space and rhetoric such as "integration," "assimilation," and "inclusion." Those who live a diasporic and transnational identity occupy the multidimensional, asymmetrical, and flexible world system to which they contribute. Their goals often are the opposite of assimilation and inclusion in a new society, although they do desire acceptance and respect for their identity. Diasporic populations display multiple and partial allegiances and feelings of belonging (their allegiance is toward their host countries, their belonging is from their host societies) to states, to ethnicity, and to various cultures and societies. It is a complex reconfiguration of meaning and power.

ONE DOES NOT have to replace one identity with another. A person can add identities to the original foundation, and ethnicity need not be hierarchical of being "more" or "less" Basque, Japanese, Jewish, Blackfoot, and so on. One can be Basque in this way or that way. A transnational identity has numerous layers and need not be threatening.

Finally, as Cohen notes, diasporas in general may achieve acceptance in welcoming host countries and have a distinctive, rich life of their own away from the homeland. The diasporic condition, in general, is not necessarily negative, as some erroneously designate it to be. Many ethnic groups have reconstructed a specific transnational identity and benefited intellectually, psychologically, economically, and artistically from sculpting their own futures and acting as ethnic pioneers. In that process, however, diaspora communities

_____

often find themselves negotiating their identities with the host cultures—not defining their identities themselves, finding answers to the question "Who are we?" but having to ask "Who are we allowed to be?" Not all aspects of culture, tradition, customs, and politics are acceptable to the host community, as we can witness with Muslims in the U.S.A. today.

CONVERSELY, citizenship and denizenship, or being an inhabitant or subject of an ethnic social space, entail rights and belonging, and also carry responsibility and obligation. Participation in a diaspora includes defending the rights of diaspora members in their own community and in their homeland. It also includes perpetuating a group that gives a sense of self-worth, uniqueness and group protection at the same time. This is extremely important to create for teenagers in communities who are struggling to shape their personalities and identities. This entails responsibility and obligation to one's self and to the group, to ancestors and to descendants. In Boise, Idaho the fiftieth anniversary motto for the Euzkaldunak, Inc. was: "Because of them we are. Because of us they will be." The implications to diasporic identification connect to a common past, a present, and a collective future. Transnational groups try to instill feelings of loyalty or sense of duty and responsibility to the greater ethnic community. In future lessons, we will be addressing these general themes of identity, ethnicity, and diaspora categorization of Basques around the world.

Lesson one

BIBLIOGRAPHY

Appadurai, Arjun. 1996. *Modernity at Large: Cultural Dimensions of Globalization*. Minneapolis: University of Minnesota Press.

Basch, Linda, Nina Glick Schiller, and Cristina Szanton Blanc. 1994. *Nations Unbound: Transnational Projects, Postcolonial Predicaments, and Deterritorialized Nation-States*. Amsterdam: Gordon and Breach Science Publishers S.A.

Lavie, Smadar, and Ted Swedenburg, eds. 1996. *Displacement, Diaspora, and Geographies of Identity*. Durham, North Carolina:: Duke University Press.

Shain, Yossi. 1989. *The Frontiers of Loyalty: Political Exiles in the Age of the Nation-State*. Middleton, Connecticut: Wesleyan University Press.

Sheffer, Gabriel, ed. 1984. *Modern Diasporas in International Politics*. London: Croom Helm.

———. 1994 "Ethno-National Diasporas and Security." *Survival* 36, no. 1 (Spring): 60–79.

———. 1996. "Wither the Study of Ethnic Diasporas? Some Theoretical, Definitional, Analytical, and Comparative Considerations." In *The Network of Diasporas*, ed. Georges Prévélakis. Paris: Cyprus Research Center Kykem.

Tölölyan, Khachig. 1996. "Rethinking Diaspora(s): Stateless Power in the Transnational Moment." *Diaspora* 5, no. 1: 3–36.

Totoricagüena, Gloria. 2004. *Identity, Culture, and Politics in the Basque Diaspora*. Reno: University of Nevada Press.

———. Inaugural Keynote Address to the Third World Congress of Basque Collectivities. July 14, 2003. Vitoria-Gasteiz.

Totoricagüena, Gloria. 2001. "La Identidad Contemporánea de los vascos en la Diáspora." Eusko Ikaskuntza *Euskonews and Media Electronic Journal*, no. 121 (May). Donostia-San Sebastián: www.euskonews.com.

REQUIRED READING
Robin Cohen, "Diasporas, the Nation-State, and Globalization," in *Global History and Migrations*, ed. Wang Gungwu (Boulder: Westview Press, 1997).
Gloria Totoricagüena. "Comparing the Basque Diaspora: Ethnonationalism, Transnationalism, and Identity Maintenance in Argentina, Australia, Belgium, Peru, the United States of America, and Uruguay." PhD diss., The London School of Economics and Political Science, University of London, 2000, chapter 2.

WRITTEN LESSON FOR SUBMISSION
In what kinds of social, cultural, political, or economic situations can you imagine that a conflict of dual loyalty would arise for a person who identifies with their ethnicity, but does not live in their homeland? (If you are such a person give personal examples if you choose.) Cohen argues that the factors of globalization have effected an increase in the number of individuals with multiple identities (ethnic, civic, religious, gender, occupational, etc.). Using the information you have so far, would you agree or disagree with him? Explain why.

2 · The history of human migrations

EXAMPLES OF patterns of forced and voluntary human migration in the contemporary era are not a new phenomenon, with the forced exile of the Jews to Babylon dating back to the Old Testament. Although the factors and dynamics of each migratory movement of Basques may be unique to a certain time and to particular social, economic, or political circumstances, the processes of migration often have remained similar. Migration tends to be a function of distance—the longer the distance, the fewer the migrants. Migrants also tend to move in stages—from village to town, from town to city. For each stream of migrants, there is a counterstream of people returning. People in urban areas are less likely to migrate than those in rural areas, and women make up the majority of short-distance migrants. Economic motives dominate the decision to migrate.

The people of Western Europe have never been sedentary. Many individuals were constantly on the move between farm and village, and then between villages. Some departed for seasonal work, others to partake in the building of the cities, where many stayed and then never returned to their ancestral towns or farms.

Leslie Page Moch discusses four periods of migration of Western Europeans during the last three centuries: 1650 to 1750, 1750 to 1815, 1815 to 1914, and 1914 to the present. She calls the century from 1650 to 1750 the "pre-industrial" period, which falls between the Thirty Years' War in Germany and the beginning of population increase and small rural industry. The period between 1750 and 1815 is marked by prolonged population increase and rural industry employing adult males and their families. Dependence on wage work necessitated the movement of men and women to find jobs in the growing urban areas. The countryside could not support the expanding populations there, and the result was an increase in temporary and seasonal migrations of people seeking temporary work away from home.

The period from 1815 to 1914 experienced the premier age of urbanization, characterized by growing cities resulting from the centralization of industry by machine production and from an increase in commerce and urban services. Rural areas were deindustrialized, and artisans and craftsmen could not compete with machine-produced goods. The continued population increase in the rural areas meant that again, workers would resort to seasonal migration and also often vacillated between city and countryside.

The period from 1914 to the present began with the commencement of World War I and the halt to international migration. European state policies discouraged international migrations, and later the United States also restricted migration by introducing quotas. However, the world wars and economic upheaval forced displacements and human population movements that were unprecedented in European history.

INTERNATIONAL migration patterns between states are related to the development of conditions in each state, which can also be categorized as "push" and "pull" factors. Factors that could influence a person's feeling as though he or she is being "pushed out" could include an economic depression, war, military conscription, expulsion, political oppression, lack of civil rights, and lack of religious freedom. We have discussed "push" factors when we noted that many Basques emigrated to escape the depredations of the wars of the eighteenth and nineteenth centuries. These are influences for leaving a place. "Pull" factors are the reasons that a person

Basque maritime pilots used maps such as this for navigating the Pacific Ocean. In 1606, Pedro Fernandez de Quiros sailed on behalf of Spain and discovered what he named Terra Australis del Espiritu Santu, the Great Southland of the Holy Spirit, today's Australia.

3

chooses a community as a migration destination, such as reuniting with family, seeking employment and improved economic opportunities, free passage or free land, and political freedoms. We have discussed pull factors when we noted that the Uruguayan government tried to recruit Basques to foster economic development in the nineteenth century. In the 1950s, the Australian government actually established a program and a recruiter to select over two hundred mostly Bizkaians to work three-year contracts cutting sugarcane in North Queensland. Assured work was a far cry from the close to 40 percent unemployment in some Basque towns.

In feudal Europe, a large percentage of the people were tied to a landlord and his economic interests. With the expansion of monarchical power, kings and queens took control over the economy and strategic interests, which included the production of goods and services by the kingdom's subjects, and the more people there were, the better. With the development of the state system in the fifteenth century, leaders continued to welcome immigration in order to increase their labor forces and military strength.

ONE OF THE FIRST large-scale expulsions of a population in this time period occurred in Spain with the 1492 campaign against the Sephardic Jews. A decree was ordered for all Jews to convert to Christianity or leave Spain, and the overwhelming majority fled the conversion and persecution. In 1609, the Moorish Muslims were forcefully expelled from the Iberian Peninsula. At the end of the sixteenth century, Philip II forced Protestants out of the Spanish lowlands. In the mid-seventeenth century, Oliver Cromwell's campaign against Irish Catholics caused many to flee to France and Spain. However, by this time, the New World was another option for a migration destination, and the pull factors of economic opportunities were strong. Sarah Collinson notes that between the fifteenth and eighteenth centuries, over two million Europeans departed to settle in the Americas, and nearly ten million West Africans were forced into slave labor in the New World. Inside the British Empire of the 1800s, an estimated sixteen million Indians were moved and forced to work in plantation slave labor in southern and eastern Africa and Southeast Asia.

The French Constitution of 1791 included the "freedom of everyone to go, to stay, or to leave, without being halted or arrested unless in accordance with procedures established by the Constitution" (cited in Collinson 1993, 29). However, although the freedoms were written in the French Constitutions, in reality, French citizens, including Basques in Iparralde, were not guaranteed these opportunities. Adam Smith's liberal economic thinking stressed the importance of individual economic actions and the withdrawal of government control over production and labor. In 1798, Thomas Malthus published his treatise regarding the growth of population leading to inevitable famine, and by the 1820s, most European countries had effectively removed most of their emigration controls, allowing people to leave for the New World. France was the exception, maintaining prohibitions on emigration, and actually was second only to the United States in immigration by the mid-nineteenth century. They had not yet experienced the economic dislocation of an industrializing Europe.

SPAIN ALSO IMPOSED strict rules for migration during certain periods. It required each emigrant to apply for a license and to depart through government-established channels. Violations were numerous, however, and the majority of emigrants left Spain illegally and did not register into the administration's official count for departures. Many Basques simply went to Iparralde, the three northern provinces of Euskal Herria, and departed from the French side, benefiting from Basque preferential treatment and aid. In their book *Amerikanuak*, William Douglass and Jon Bilbao quote a seventeenth-century document that states, "In 1640, three-fourths of the population of Vizcaya is composed of women due to the number of men who leave to never return" (Jorge Nadal, quoted in Douglass and Bilbao 1975, 72).

Emigration has always served to diffuse religious, political, social, and economic tensions, and many of those who were discontented and had the means and the information to leave did so. Migration to the Americas was actually the result of factors in Europe that were local, and we will see that Basque migration has often

Standing in the doorway of her own business is Juanachu Zamacona, next to her daughter and with neighbors of the area in the Plaza de Villaro, Bilbao, Bizkaia.
Photograph by Eulalia Abaitua Allende Salazar.
Courtesy of the Basque Archaeological, Ethnographic, and Historical Museum, Bilbao.

---

been from one specific area to another specific area in the receiving host country. Advocates of what is called the "new economics" of migration argue that the true decision-making unit is the collective unit of the household, and not the individual. Today's network theorists recognize that for many people in the developing countries, network connections are an important factor of economic strategies, including migration. Each theory, or a combination of them, helps to explain the rates and probabilities of Basque movement from certain areas of Euskal Herria to certain areas in the New World that have been affected by these family and village networks. For example, the high rates of emigration from northern Bizkaia to southwestern Idaho is significant, as are the links from the town of Arnegi to Wyoming, Iparralde in general to California, or from coastal Bizkaia to North Queensland in northern Australia.

EUROPEAN populations continued to grow, with an overall increase from 194 million in 1840 to 463 million in 1930. By 1915, about fifty-two million Europeans had emigrated toward the New World, with approximately thirty-four million going to the United States. In the nineteenth century, the largest number of people left underdeveloped Southern and Eastern Europe. Previously, the flows had been from developed areas of Europe to the underdeveloped regions of the colonies and newly independent states. Now, populations from underdeveloped Europe were departing for the developing areas of the New World, and Basques did both. The majority of Basque emigrants were rural, and they migrated to rural areas and rural employment throughout the Americas. However, a small number of the commercial elite, well-educated Basques, and other upper-class individuals left Basque cities, especially from the Bilbao area and other cities for the capitals of South America. Many thousands of Basques who had experience in maritime commerce found employment in the ports of New York, Havana, Buenos Aires, Callao, and Valparaiso.

Just as earlier rulers of the Middle Ages were concerned with the religious integration of European societies, leaders in the late nineteenth and twentieth

centuries became concerned with the problem of integration based on national or ethnic identity. Collinson
quotes Ernest Gellner: "'Industrial society presupposes a
mobile population with a shared literate culture .... The
state supervises the transmission of that culture .... It is
hostile to deep ... culturally marked chasms between its
own sub-groups'" (Collinson 1993, 33).

GOVERNMENTS were beginning to think about
controlling not only the number of individuals
who entered, but the type of individuals they desired for
entry. In 1892, the United States Supreme Court ruled in
Nishimura Ekiu v. United States that every nation has
the sovereign right and power to forbid the entrance
of foreigners in order to maintain self-preservation.
Congress began by imposing a literacy requirement for
new immigrants and in 1911 recommended the prohibition of immigration from most of Asia. Basques found
themselves in the desirable category because of the
positive social status and economic status they enjoyed
in many of the new American states. They had earned
reputations as good workers, responsible, trustworthy,
thrifty, energetic, and capable. As we have seen, many
countries such as Uruguay and Argentina actually
actively recruited Basque immigration to their countries, and Basques were recruited to cut sugarcane in
North Queensland in the twentieth century. Later, in the
United States, Basques would be given special Congressional recognition and entry advantages in order to hire
them as sheepherders. The effects of World War I, however, included the imposition of passport controls, and
by 1919 there was widespread regulation of immigration
and governmental control of human movement.

The question remains why some people migrated and
others did not. The neoclassical theory of migration is
based upon the economic decision making of individu-

als—seen as rational actors—attempting to maximize their gains from personal relocation. In this theory, migration is viewed as a self-regulating mechanism to restore labor equilibrium between sending and receiving areas. However, this assumes that all have access to the same information and that all actually have the choice whether or not to migrate and the means to do so, which of course is not the case. It also excludes emotional, gender, psychological, and religious reasons for migration, and as discussed previously in the case of the Basque primogeniture system, would not explain the departures of those who were to inherit the family *baserri*.

THE REASONS why disapora populations migrate and the circumstances of their migrations are extremely influential in the maintenance of their ethnicity, in what types of collective memories they share, and what types of networks they maintain with their homeland. For example, the Soviet occupation of eastern Poland and the collective deportation of one and a half million Poles and Jews as refugees to the Soviet interior in 1939 left these peoples and their descendants inside today's Russia, but many desire to return to their homeland. After World War II, approximately fourteen million ethnic Germans were expelled from Eastern Europe. Turks fled Bulgaria, Finns fled the annexation by the Soviet Union, Hungarians fled the Budapest revolution, and Czechs left Prague in the spring of 1968. Collinson cites a figure of roughly thirty million people who were forced to leave their homes during the war, and we have to remember that half of these were never allowed to return. In 1946, the International Refugee Organization was established by the United Nations, and in 1949, it established the United Nations High Commission for Refugees, which unfortunately is now a permanent body working with

---

millions of displaced persons as a result of war, ethnic conflict, famine, and disease.

TODAY WE have many, many examples of newly forming diaspora populations: Armenians who fled the Turkish genocide, Kurds escaping from Turkey and Iraq, Afghanis and Iraqis fleeing postwar repercussions, Hutus and Tutsis fleeing massacres in Rwanda and Burundi, Mexicans avoiding economic depression, Haitians leaving political repression, Liberians seeking political freedoms ....

Lesson two

BIBLIOGRAPHY

Baines, Dudley. 1991. *Emigration from Europe 1815– 1930*. London: Macmillan Education.

Collinson, Sarah. 1994. *Europe and International Migration*. London: Royal Institute of International Affairs.

Castles, Stephen, and Mark J. Miller. 1993. *The Age of Migration: International Population Movements in the Modern World*. New York: The Guilford Press.

Douglass, William A., and Jon Bilbao. 1975. *Amerikanuak: Basques in the New World*. Reno: University of Nevada Press.

REQUIRED READING

Leslie Page Moch, *Moving Europeans: Migration in Western Europe since 1650* (Bloomington: Indiana University Press, 1992), pp 1–21.

Sarah Collinson, *Europe and International Migration* (London: Pinter Publishers for the Royal Institute of International Affairs, 1993), pp 25–42.

WRITTEN LESSON FOR SUBMISSION
Discuss the significance of chain migration, networks of migration, and Moch's "personal information field" and their importance in a migrant's choice of a destination. Also, compare the four stages of migration set out by Page Moch.

A N ETHNIC GROUP'S history, both real and romanticized, is an active force in determining its present behavior and attitudes. It is important to examine various representations of Basques and their homeland, even though many are simplified and distorted. Especially in the diaspora, a nationalist representation is the impression kept in the collective memory of those who idealize Euskal Herria and their ancestors who lived there. Transmission of this idealized history and of narratives that represent Basques as victims of outside aggression characterize the prevalent ideology of Basque diaspora communities around the world, although in each community there are those who exhibit a more critical view of Basque history and its relationships with Spain and France.

What is important for an ethnic group's persistence is an interpretation of historical events that is personally meaningful to the individual and to the group, even though this interpretation of the past may not coincide with views of other historians. Many Basques in diaspora communities focus specifically on the relationship between Basque and Castilian political and economic control and have formed a view of the "Spanish" (understood in terms of the political structures of Madrid) as the permanent opposition—although most do not know why. Readers should keep in mind that each ethnic group typically records its own history favorably, speaking of themselves as distinguished by their "great warriors," as a proud, brave, and principled, and/or as an innocent people. The Basques are no different, although the first recorded histories of the Basques written by Basques did not appear until the fifteenth century.

Therefore, the chronicles of the Basque territories dating prior to that are from an outsider's perspective.

Contemporary Basques have put their own spin on the historical record, emphasizing that Basques have constantly been invaded, that they have forever been defending their homeland and rights, and that no power has been able to defeat the Basques (not the Romans, Goths, Franks, Arabs, the Castilian crown, and not Franco, either). Diaspora Basques, who usually have not formerly studied Basque history, propagate the typical phrases heard at the Basque centers and mentioned at ethnic functions, highlighting the biological differences and historical record that would indicate ethnic originality and even superiority. This is common to most peoples who want to maintain a feeling of ethnic uniqueness with a positive social status tied to that identity.

VASCONIA

The physical borders of Euskal Herria, the Basque Country, have helped to shelter it from invasion and infiltration by other cultures and military forces, as well as having provided a gateway to the rest of the world. Its major physical border is the sea, an element that has played an influential role in the history of Basque emigration and has fostered a relative ease of mobility for the population. The Basque Country is small in both territory and population. The total population, which has the lowest per capita birth rate in the European Union, is nearly three million.

THROUGHOUT its history, the Basque Country— referred to as "Vasconia" by the Romans—has been a nation and a kingdom, although not a state, thus the confusion for some when initiating their studies. The area is not a "country" or "state" as people tend to think of Canada, Japan or Argentina. It is a geographical region with a shared ethnicity, which, since the creation of the 1512 border divide, includes three territories under the political domain of France and four territories under the political control of Spain. Euskal Herria (literally "land of the Basques") is currently politically divided, with the provinces of Lapurdi, Behe Nafarroa, and Zuberoa under French administration and Nafarroa (Navarre in French and English), Bizkaia, Araba, and Gipuzkoa as territories in Spain.

I<small>N TODAY'S</small> political terminology, when Basques refer to "the North," Iparralde, they are referring to the three provinces that are in France, to the north of what many see as an artificial political border. "In the South," Hegoalde, denotes all four provinces that lie in Spain. Because these are also politically and administratively differentiated in the current Spanish state created with the Constitution of 1978, the Statute of Autonomy—also known as the Statute of Gernika passed in a 1979 referendum—established that together, Bizkaia, Gipuzkoa, and Araba make up the Basque Autonomous Community of Euskadi. Nafarroa, or Navarre, has its own separate autonomous statutes negotiated between the Diputación of Navarre (the executive branch) and the central government in Madrid. Nafarroa maintains a permanent right to join politically and administratively with the Basque Autonomous Community and vice versa. Political realities have affected culture, language development, and Basque identity in each of the seven provinces, and many Basques in Nafarroa identify themselves as specifically Nafarroan.

Homeland and diaspora Basques refer to themselves as "Euskaldunak" or "speakers of Euskara," the Basque language, although the majority of both do not speak Euskara. Despite five centuries of speculation by linguists and philologists concerning the possible relationships

From childhood, Basque girls in Euskal Herria learned
and worked doing their daily chores.
Photograph by Eulalia Abaitua Allende Salazar.
Courtesy of the Basque Archaeological, Ethnographic,
and Historical Museum, Bilbao.

between Basque and other languages, no studies have
indicated a conclusive relationship between Basque and
any other language (Michelena 1985; Tovar 1957; Collins
1986, 8–12). This makes Euskara unique among Western
and Central European languages and is often pointed out
by diaspora Basques as a sign of difference and prestige.
  Ethnic claims to physiognomic distinctiveness are not
specific to Basques, and certain features of physiological

makeup point to uniqueness and are used in Basque
nationalist rhetoric. Basques differ from their surrounding populations in their blood types, for example. They
manifest the highest rate in any European population
of the blood type O, and the lowest occurrence of blood
type B. They also have the highest occurrence of any population in the world of the Rh-negative factor (Cavalli-
Sforza and Cavalli-Sforza 1995; Collins 1986, 4–8). This
evidence suggests that the Basque people have remained,
over a long period of time, a small and isolated breed-
ing population. These factors are salient because of their
perceived importance to Basques themselves. They are
elements used to argue that Basques are biologically distinct from any other population and therefore deserving
of political recognition and status.

BASQUE COLLECTIVE myth includes the possibility of
a history that stretches to cave populations and
human occupation since the Stone Age (Caro Baroja
1958). Some authorities suggest that the Basques are the
direct descendants of cave painters who created the sites
at Lascaux and Santimamiñe. Basque legends and myths
celebrating supranatural powers, such as the feminine
force of Ilargia, or the moon, which emerged from a
world of unseen forces, are common and maintained
in song, dance, and literature today. Skeptics place the
modern Basques in the Pyrenees from approximately
5,000 to 3,000 B.C. Even with this most conservative interpretation, Basques would have arrived in the western
Pyrenees well before the invasions of the Indo-European
speaking tribes into Western Europe in the second millennium B.C.

What is certain is that there are no recorded histories
or information describing the Basques specifically until
the Romans targeted the Iberian Peninsula and wrote
that the Basque population was organized into small

tribal units inhabiting the valleys of the western Pyrenees—and beyond, according to later linguistic studies. They originally did not form a single civic unit and spoke a variety of tribal dialects of Euskara, whose diversity persists to the present day. Although until recently Basques have believed otherwise, the latest scientific research demonstrates that the Basque territory was indeed subject to Roman administrative, political, and military influence until approximately the fourth century A.D. Other questions arise regarding the linguistic and cultural Romanization of the existing populations. It seems the agricultural mentality of the colonizers led the agriculturally richer lower lands in Nafarroa and Araba nearer the rivers to experience more Roman administrative influences than did the more mountainous and forested areas in Bizkaia and Gipuzkoa (Sayas Abengoechea 1999). The Christian religion was introduced into the Basque region during these Roman times, but it scarcely spread beyond the southern fringes of lower Araba and Nafarroa.

THE DEBUT of the Basques as a separate entity in the history of Western Europe followed the fall of the Roman Empire and the establishment of the Germanic kingdoms. The era's chronicles describe the staunch resistance by Basques to the Visigothic powers in Toledo, in southern Iberia, and to the attempts at assimilation by the Franks from the north (Sayas Abengoechea 1999). The perseverance of the early Basque resistance through the seventh and eighth centuries indicates that some kind of civic cooperation may have been established among these tribes. The reality of the resistance and lack of assimilation had a salient effect on the political philosophy of the Basques at the end of the Middle Ages and in the following centuries.

The written texts of the 1452 Fuero Viejo de Vizcaya recorded the traditions, customs, rights, and privileges of Basque society. These included political, economic, and social liberties, plus exemptions, and responsibilities. Basque communities and valleys had their own similar versions of the *fors* or *fueros*, with the earliest dating from the tenth century in the Valley of the Roncal, Nafarroa.

During the eighth century, the independent and Christian populations in the northern sections of the peninsula, such as the Basques, began to organize around regional nuclei determined by three main factors: geography, ethnic identity, and prevailing politico-military pressures. Later, contemporary Spain arose from an unstable alliance of independent Christian kingdoms defending against Islamic invaders. The initial unifying idea behind Spain was Christian opposition to the Muslim threat. Unlike León, Aragon, and Catalonia, Castile had no previous political existence and was basically a product of the long *Reconquista* (718–1492). The historic Spanish kingdoms did not have their roots in Roman or Visigothic origins, but in the defensive reaction against Muslims in the early Middle Ages that led to the process of regaining lands.

HISTORIANS WRITE that Basques in the area of Pamplona constituted their own kingdom by the eighth century. By the twelfth century, as a result of gradually joining other lands free of Muslim occupations (as were Bizkaia, Gipuzkoa, and Araba), this region became to be known as the Kingdom of Navarre. For the next years, all of the Basque-inhabited territory south of the Pyrenees recognized a single Basque political sovereignty for the first and last time in its history thus far. Although remote in time, this period of political unification has had a significant effect on the development of Basque nationalism in the homeland and in the diaspora. These centuries of political unification ended in 1200 when the three western Basque territories were militarily occupied by Alfonso VIII of Castile. From this point on, their development was tied to the powerful kingdom of Castile, and historians tend to agree that their incorporation was interpreted as a bilateral pact, with Basque liberties respected as the status quo.

Gradually, the self-government of Basque communities
grew as recorded in the Basque *fueros* and *fors*, or local
laws resulting from custom and tradition. For centuries,
the Basque territories maintained exclusively separate
legal codes and created their own autonomous political
institutions. Under the *fueros*, the popular assemblies,
or *biltzarrak* in Basque, were granted legislative authority, and the Castilian kings and lords were subject to its
laws. Basques had the right of *pase foral*, which meant
they could veto crown laws, exercising both some
control over the central authority and local control.
Although both the Basque church leaders and lords
were excluded from the legislative debate and deliberations, upon accession to the throne, the Castilian king
was required to appear before the Basque assemblies to
swear to respect their authority. Some examples of the
citizens' rights enjoyed from the 1452 Fuero Viejo de
Vizcaya (Bizkaia) included: the freedom of every Bizkaian
to engage in commerce, rights of due process in all legal
proceedings, ownership of land in Bizkaia reserved for
Bizkaians, exemption from taxes on any maritime activity, and exemption from obligatory military service outside of the Basque territory.

ANOTHER important aspect of distinction between
regions in Spain was the concept of universal nobility, which can be traced back to 1053 and the Basque
valley of the Roncal in Nafarroa. In the Basque region,
there was a legislated collective nobility, and all Basques
were considered "noble." Thus, all citizens of the Basque
region, regardless of class origins or gender, enjoyed
political and economic rights and could aspire to noble
privileges and offices. And despite the fact that, with
the consolidation of Spain, throughout most of Castile,
the peasantry was crushed by taxes and the social and
economic predominance of the aristocracy, Bizkaia

(1526) and Gipuzkoa (1610), won royal recognition of
the "noble" status of all their native inhabitants. They
were the two juridically freest and most egalitarian areas
in all of Spain. Every person would enjoy equality before
the law and freedom from most common taxes. In Araba
and Nafarroa, different communities were protected by
their different *fueros*, and some had already established
this collective nobility for their residents. Other towns
and villages continued this process of emancipation and
social mobility through the seventeenth century.

THE BASQUE *fueros* and the practice of collective
nobility played influential roles in establishing
further-reaching regional identities beyond one's connection with village or town. The Basques set themselves
apart from the Castilian population and Castilian control
because of this separate political structure, reinforced by
their linguistic and ethnocultural uniqueness.

The importance and influence of the concept of the collective in Basque culture and society is extremely significant to understanding Basque people, politics, and community structure. From the reality of collective nobility
extended to all Basques born in the Basque historic
territories and to those born to Basques abroad, to the
traditional laws of rights and privileges, to economic and
political self-rule, and to codes of behavior and customs
and gender equality, Basque society exemplifies a rever-
ence for democratic values.

The integration of the Basques and their political culture into the Spanish monarchy entered a crisis at the
beginning of the eighteenth century with a change of
dynasty. The Bourbons consolidated the Spanish crown,
and, following the French tradition, unified it by dismantling the confederal structure. They implanted a
centralized state system with a single parliament, the
Cortes, and with ministers whose powers extended over

all territories. Nevertheless, there remained an exception to the unification: the four Basque territories. The *fueros* of the four territories remained valid and were enforced. This maintained the political differentiation of Vasconia, but simultaneously ushered in a period of tension between the administrations in Araba, Bizkaia, Gipuzkoa, and Nafarroa with the central administration in Madrid that, for many Basques, remains to this day.

Since the 1200s, Basque emigrants have spread throughout the Iberian Peninsula, and then later to Europe, the Americas, the Philippines, and Australia. Douglasss and Bilbao (1975) first opined that it would not be an exaggeration to state that no major Spanish expeditionary force and no ecclesiastical or secular administration in the New World did not have Basques.

THE BASQUE region entered advanced economic development during the eleventh and twelfth centuries with the growth of maritime and commercial activities. The fifteenth century proved to be another time of notable economic development, especially for Bizkaia and Gipuzkoa. The Bay of Biscay, and particularly Bizkaian shipping, dominated the peninsula's trade with northern ports in Europe. The sixteenth century was a period of continually expanding economy and social change in the Basque territories. Basque, and especially Bizkaian, interests controlled shipping and other trade interests, and several of the previously established Basque commercial interests in Spain opened branch operations with kinsmen in the Indies, especially in Santo Domingo (Bilbao 1958, 192–209). Iparralde Basques also participated in the American ventures, and vessels from Donibane Lohitzun (St-Jean-de-Luz) were registered with authorities as Bizkaian. John Lynch estimates that Basques controlled almost 80 percent of the New World traffic between 1520 and 1580, and between

The acceptance of Ferdinand, the Catholic king, as Lord of Bizkaia in 1476 was sealed when Bizkaian representatives kissed his hand after Ferdinand had sworn to uphold the *fueros* of Bizkaia. Ritual required that the king remove his shoes (which were of extreme importance and status in popular culture) and toss his lance or blade toward the Tree of Gernika when swearing to protect the rights and privileges of the Basques.

Painting by Francisco de Mendieta, 1609.

1580 and 1610, Basques interests represented at least 50 percent of the total.

THIS ACCOUNTS for nearly one hundred years of Basque domination in Spanish colonial efforts, pushing Basque maritime specialists toward the New World, where they established trade links back to their homeland. The Basque presence in Madrid and in the American colonies continued to be significant in the eighteenth century. The creation of the Gipuzkoan Company of Caracas demonstrated the involvement of the great Basque mercantile society in the colonization of Venezuela, and the Consulate of Bilbao produced the

---

ordinances that served as the model for all commercial trade in Spain and in the Americas.

Lesson three

BIBLIOGRAPHY

Bilbao Azkarreta, Jon. 1958. *Vascos en Cuba, 1492–1511*. Buenos Aires: Editorial Vasca Ekin.

Caro Baroja, Julio. 1998. *Ser o no ser vasco*. Trans. Antonio Carreira. Madrid: Editorial Espasa Calpe.

———. 1971. *Los vascos*. 4th ed. Madrid: Ediciones ISTMO.

Carr, Raymond. 1982. *Spain, 1808–1975*. Oxford: Clarendon Press.

Cavalli-Sforza, Luigi Luca, and Francesco Cavalli-Sforza. 1995. *The Great Human Diasporas: The History of Diversity and Evolution*. Trans. Sarah Thorne. Reading, Mass.: Addison-Wesley.

Collins, Roger. 1986. *The Basques*. Oxford: Basil Blackwell.

———. 1983. *Early Medieval Spain: Unity in Diversity, 400–1000*. New York: St. Martin's Press.

Jacob, James E. 1994. *Hills of Conflict: Basque Nationalism in France*. Reno: University of Nevada Press.

———. 1985. "Politics, Ideology, and the Fueros in Vizcaya during the Initial Phase of the Liberal Triennium (1820)." In *Basque Politics: A Case Study in Ethnic Nationalism*, ed. William A. Douglass. Reno: Associated Faculty Press, Basque Studies Program, University of Nevada, Reno.

Lynch, John. 1965. *Spain Under the Habsburgs*. Vol. 1. *Empire and Absolutism, 1516–1598*. Oxford: Basil Blackwell.

Michelena, Luís. 1985. *Lengua e historia*. Madrid: Paraninfo.

Monreal Zia, Gregorio. 1992. "Larramendi: Madurez y crisis del régimen foral." In *Manuel de Larramendi: Hirugarren Mendeurrena 1690–1990*, ed. Joseba Andoni Lakarra. Andoain: Andoain Udala.

————. 1989. "Annotations Regarding Basque Traditional Political Thought in the Sixteenth Century." In *Essays in Basque Social Anthropology and History*, ed. William A. Douglass. Basque Studies Program Occasional Papers Series, no. 4. Reno: University of Nevada, Reno, Basque Studies Program.

Sayas Abengoechea, Juan José. 1999. "De vascones a romanos para volver a ser vascones." *Revista Internacional de Estudios Vascos* 44, no. 1: 147–84.

————. 1994. *Los vascos en la antigüedad*. Madrid: Ediciones Cátedra.

Totoricagüena, Gloria. 2000. "Comparing the Basque Diaspora: Ethnonationalism, Transnationalism and Identity Maintenance in Argentina, Australia, Belgium, Peru, the United States of America, and Uruguay." PhD diss., the London School of Economics and Political Science, University of London.

Tovar, Antonio. 1950. *La lengua vasca*. Donostia–San Sebastián, Biblioteca Vascongada.

REQUIRED READING

Douglass, William A. and Bilbao, Jon, *Amerikanuak: Basques in the New World* (Reno: University of Nevada Press, 1975), chapter 1, pp 9–60.

Clark, Robert P., *The Basques: The Franco Years and Beyond* (Reno: University of Nevada Press, 1979), chapter 1, pp 3–32.

Totoricagüena, Gloria, *Identity, Culture, and Politics in the Basque Diaspora* (Reno: University of Nevada Press, 2004), chapter 2, pp 19–54.

Sayas Abengoechea, Juan José, *Los vascos en la antigüedad* (Madrid: Ediciones Cátedra, 1994).

WRITTEN LESSON FOR SUBMISSION

Create a detailed outline and chronological timeline of the eras of domination in the Basque region of the Pyrenees, noting the economic, religious, and political interests of those who populated the area. Include the six centuries of Roman rule, the Goths and Franks, the Arabs, the importance of the kingdom of Navarre, and Basque maritime interests.

4 · Iparralde
The three Basque provinces in France

MANY INTERNATIONAL academics new to Basque Studies exhibit a complete lack of knowledge and understanding of the northern provinces and their history, culture, politics, economics, and so on. Often, this is the result of a lack of available literature, with even less published in English for the international audience. However, Basques themselves in the South and in the diaspora are also quite ignorant in regard to the history of the northern provinces. Because of the political activity in the Basque territories in Spain, academic studies and media representations have tended to focus on Araba, Bizkaia, Gipuzkoa, and Nafarroa. James E. Jacob's analysis in *Hills of Conflict: Basque Nationalism in France* is the first contemporary work in English to give a detailed account of Basques in present-day France from the *ancien régime* to contemporary Lapurdi (Labourd), Behe Nafarroa (Basse-Navarre), and Zuberoa (Soule), which are a part of the administrative Department of the Pyrénées-Atlantiques.

Scholars believe that at one time, lands as far north as present-day Poitiers were inhabited by the Basques. At the close of the Upper Paleolithic Age, 15,000 to 10,000 B.C., the people of the Basque region sought caves for shelter and left us fantastic cave art and remains of human activity at Altamira, near Santander; at Arieges, Lourdes, Arudy, Etxeberri, and Sasiziloaga in Zuberoa; at Arxilondo, Haristoy, and Isturitz in Behe Nafarroa; at Alkerdi and Berroberria in Nafarroa, at Ekain in Gipuzkoa; at Santimamiñe and others in Bizkaia; and at Lascaux, near the Dorgone River, in France. Painted figures of horses, fish, bulls, bison, bears, and deer decorate the walls. During the Neolithic Age (to about 2500 B.C.),

Representations of the Holy Trinity are manifest
throughout Zuberoa in architecture from the seventeenth century, as seen here at the church in Gotein.
Historians argue that there was a specific Basque style
that differed from that of adjacent territories. Basques
built simple structures with similar designs throughout
Lapurdi, Behe Nafarroa, and Zuberoa.
Photograph by the author.

Basques began to build their own shelters for living and to construct dolmens, funerary markers of stone walls and a stone slab across the top above ground, for the dead. Rachel Bard writes that more than four hundred burial structures have been identified in the Basque Country (Bard 1982, 3). These burial sites included copper and bronze objects, as well as human remains.

Neolithic Basques were hunters, and they survived on bison, horses, goats, fish, fox, pigs, and bears. They sewed their clothing with needles made of animal bones. They decorated their bodies with seashells, pearls, and animal teeth. They made hunting implements of bone and rock (Goyhenetxe 1985, 22–23). Mountain peoples grazed their animals collectively and freely through the forests, and the valley peoples were more likely to cultivate and grow crops individually, much later with private ownership.

From 700 B.C. on, the Celts settled in areas around the Basque Country, but not in the actual Basque lands. Basque tribes such as the Tarbelli in Dax and Baiona, the Sibusates or Sibullates in Zuberoa, the Osquidates in Ossau, the Bigerriones in Bigorra, the Elusates in Eauze, the Vasates in Bazas, and the Auscii in Auch controlled the mountains and valleys in the Basque region. Bard describes small Basque communities in the North and larger communities in the central and southern regions of the Basque Country. Women were in positions of power, because inheritance of land and honors were through the female line, and women were responsible for the farming (Bard 1982, 7).

GREEK AND ROMAN geographers, including Strabo (63 B.C.) and Ptolemy (second century A.D.) described four different tribes speaking various dialects of Euskara. "Lapurdum" was the Roman name for Baiona. The Romanization of Iparralde seems to have been only peripheral and was stronger between the areas of the Adour and Garona Rivers. Iparralde shows few traces of Roman settlement compared with the rest of Aquitaine. Eukeni Goyhenetxe reports that in all of Iparralde, there are only two remaining inscriptions left by the Romans, one in Tardets and one in Hasparren (Goyhenetxe 1985, 28).

LATER, DURING the sixth century, there was considerable migration of the Vascones (or Gascones) tribe into today's southwestern France. This area would be called Gascoñes, from the Roman word for Basque, "Gascón." Vasconia was also later called "Gasconia." Maritime expertise prevailed on the coast of Lapurdi, and Basques were known as leaders in the medieval whaling industry, in cod fishing, and in ship design and production. Iron ore deposits also facilitated the production of tools. Basques developed coastal, mountain, and plains cultures and were also exposed to many different peoples coming through the area on their way north or south. Three of the four routes on the Catholic pilgrimage known as the Way of Saint James to Santiago de Compostela in northwestern Spain, where the saint's relics repose, passed through Iparralde, and the pilgrims also exposed Basques to many different languages and cultures.

The religious habits in Iparralde before the tenth century have not been established specifically, but it may be that Basques there were introduced to Christianity from the south first, as evidenced by the Castilian names of churches, and later from the north as a result of the influx of religious pilgrims. Goyhenetxe notes that there were three main dioceses from 1050 to 1566: Baiona, Dax, and Oloron. The pilgrimage routes that brought the population into contact with many foreigners also affected the economy, with Iparralde Basques providing accommodations, necessities, and hospital care for the individuals making the religious trek.

Basque homesteads, the *baserris*, were, and are still, typically modest, but give an identity to the family who inhabit them via the use of place names as family names. Because a Basque home was considered equal to all other Basque homes, the families were also equal to each other, and this was a founding principle of family law in the Basque territories. Basque family law was based on the absolute law of primogeniture, without definite distinction of gender. Vestiges of the primogeniture system exist to this day, as we have noted.

Because the family farm was too small to be divided as an inheritance upon the death of the owner, the first born in a family had total legal authority to make decisions regarding the property and goods of the farm. This person was to be known as the *etxeko-jaun*, "lord of the house," or *etxeko-andra*, "woman of the house."

ANIMALS NEEDED grazing lands, and because of the small farms, grazing lands were communal and used equally by all families in the parish or valley. By collective agreement, inhabitants also managed the lands and protected each family's grazing rights. Basques also collectively managed the forests and replanted them as a source of wood for construction and for heating and cooking. The idea of democratic communal responsibility for communal goods to be used for individual family needs is historic in the Basque Country. The collective management and use of the community's lands and resources led to the formation of representative assemblies for administrative and financial decision making, and each house sent its *etxeko-andra* or *etxeko-jaun* as its spokesperson. Behe Nafarroans and Zuberoans also gathered the leaders of the *baserris* in assemblies, and Zuberoans even elected other community posts, such as

the tax collector. Servitude never existed in the Basque
Country, and there were no special privileges for clerics.
In Lapurdi, clerics were actually excluded from the popular assemblies for decision making in order to prevent
undue church influence. In 1311 in Lapurdi, all persons
were officially declared as equals. All Basques had to
right to bear arms and to hunt and to fish and had freedom of assembly and speech.

The English occupied the area of today's province of
Lapurdi in 1152 with the marriage of Eleanor of Aquitaine to Henry Plantagenet, and later Richard the Lion
Hearted declared Ustaritz as the capital. In 1215, Baiona
received a royal charter, and the Bilçar, or council of
mayors from the parishes, met in a certain oak grove
above Ustaritz to create their public policies. Other parish councils met in the church porticos, and the mayors
were even sometimes called abbés. The English ruled
Aquitaine from 1152 to 1451. P. S. Ormond wrote that
"one of the greatest English governors of Aquitaine was
Simon de Montfort, who was later to be the champion of
representative government in England. It might be that
his dealings with the Labourd and the Soule gave him an
idea of what the constitution of a free country should be"
(Ormond 1926, 142).

AFTER THE HUNDRED Years' War—begun between
England and France in 1355—Lapurdi and Zuberoa
were officially annexed to France in 1451 with the Treaty
of Ayherre. Behe Nafarroa, which is the northern portion
of the former Kingdom of Navarre, was passed to France
officially in 1589 as Basse-Navarre with the accession of
Henri III, duke of Béarn and king of Navarre, when he
become Henri IV, king of France. In each case throughout the centuries, the ruling monarchs respected and
upheld the local Basque laws.

LINGVAE VASCONVM PRIMI-
tiæ per Dominum Bernardum Dechepare
Rectorem sancti michælis veteris.

Early Basque-language publications were scarce. The first known complete work in Euskara was a book of poetry produced by a Behe Nafarroan cleric, Bernat D'Etchepare. His 1545 publication was printed and distributed in Bordeaux. Religious works in Euskara followed in the coming decades by Sancho de Elso, Ioannes Leiçarraga, Joan Perez Betolaza, Esteban Materre, and Juan de Beriain.

These laws based on custom and tradition, were actually different in each of the three provinces, and they coexisted with specific local *fors*, which dictated daily communal life in the Basque villages. As the basis of the social and political organization in the three provinces, they covered economic transactions and obligations to the monarchy, as well as the rules of political representation and behavior, and listed the privileges and exemptions of the Basque provinces from the rule of the central French sovereign.

THE FRENCH National Assembly, in the last six months of 1789, began to dismantle the provincial liberties and particularisms enjoyed by the Basque provinces. Despite the Basque delegates' protests, the assembly suppressed Zuberoa's and Lapurdi's autonomy and then annexed Navarre to France. In 1790, the administrative Department of the Basse-Pyrénées was created, despite the joint opposition of the Basque and Bearn delegates, who asked for two separated departments. The conservative reaction of Basques to the French Revolution and resistance to Jacobin republicanism, which would dismantle the *fors*, is important to Basque history. James E. Jacob argues that linguistic particularism, clericalism, the economic defense of provincial privileges, and the defense of traditional democratic Basque institutions all played a role in the Basque reaction to the French Revolution.

The Terror of 1793 included capital punishment for complicity in illegal emigration or correspondence with priests in exile. Attempts at French nation building included changing the names of Basque towns to French names and mandating that priests serve their clergy in French, and not in Euskara. In 1793, after King Louis XVI's execution, Spain declared war on revolutionary France, and in 1794, four thousand Basques from

Lapurdi were deported to Gers and Landes for having refused to fight against the southern Basques, and thousands more were deported to Spain. Jacob cites a specific account of forty-seven Basque soldiers from Itxassou who deserted the universal, forced conscription and who were suspected of having followed an exiled priest's suggestions to do so. In 1795, the Bâle Treaty ended the war between Spain and France. The Basques had fought against the revolutionary ideas and wanted to protect local *fors*, privileges, and customary laws.

This included the notion of "collective nobility." "The privilege of nobility attributed to the Souletins [Zuberoans] in the written custom, recognized by the kings of France and assimilating each of these mountain men as gentlemen and owners of fiefs in the kingdom, was common to the Basques of the seven provinces, as much in France as in Spain" (Charles de Belsunce, quoted in Jacob 1994, 8). This system of granting noble status to all later facilitated emigration to the New World and often led to a superior status in the receiving lands, as well. It also served to differentiate the Basques from others in France and the Basques from others in Spain. In Behe Nafarroa, which was not a French province, but a separate kingdom, ruled by the king of Navarre, who had also been king of France, Basques maintained a different political status from other French subjects.

AS POLITICAL leaders of emerging states attempted to unify their populations, in 1539, the French sovereign, François I, ordered that all official documents be written in French. However, Basque culture has always had a strong oral tradition, and in the fifteenth century, public folk outdoor theaters, performed in Euskara, known as the annual *pastoral*, emerged in Iparralde and are still enormously popular today. In 1707, the French language became the single official language in the three

As titled by photographer Eulalia Abaitua Allende
Salazar, *Images of the Past* illustrates the home
environment living conditions and typical baserri
construction. Homes were built with available materials
of mostly stone, cement, and wood.
*Photograph by Eulalia Abaitua Allende Salazar. Cour-
tesy of the Basque Archaeological, Ethnographic, and
Historical Museum, Bilbao.*

northern Basque provinces. In the 1990s, approximately one-third of the population living in the three provinces—about seventy-five thousand people—spoke Basque and another fifty-five thousand had some knowledge of the language.

During the nineteenth century, Iparralde was passed over by industrialization due to its lack of raw materials and to its peripheral geographical location. Its economy remained based mainly on agriculture, artisanship, and cottage industries. When the Spanish customs border was changed from the Ebro River in the south of the Basque region to the actual 1512 Spanish-French political border in 1841, the tariffs dismantled the economic cohesiveness of the Basque Country. While previously Basques were able to trade and sell goods among the seven Basque territories without a tax until traveling into other parts of Spain, now those trade tariffs were placed on the goods upon crossing the border with Nafarroa and Gipuzkoa on the Spanish side of Euskal Herria. This seriously hurt small businesses in Iparralde. Many lost their profitability, and workers were displaced to other areas of France, while others chose to emigrate to look for employment.

JACOB DISCUSSES the depopulation problem of Iparralde: Although the population of Zuberoa was 21,693 in 1817, in 1982, it was only 15,404. In Behe Nafarroa in 1817, the census counted 43,684, but in 1982, it was almost half that—26,148. Lapurdi, with its coastal population, has indeed grown from 69,498 in 1817 to 194,937 in 1982 (Jacob 1994, xvi).

Economic cooperation among the northern and southern Basques is historic, and Basque leaders have recently strengthened ties by signing the Bayonne Treaty of 1995. As a result of European Union politics, the French and Spanish governments have recognized the rights of towns and cities to directly participate in cooperative structures across the border and to create additional collaborative projects. The coastal ports, towns, and villages between Baiona and Donostia–San Sebastián (the official name of the city includes the name in both languages, with the Basque name first) have joined to form the Bayonne-San Sebastián Eurocity. Estimates put the population in this corridor at over six hundred thousand people. The area of Baiona and Donostia–San Sebastián is a critical international transportation corridor between Northern Europe, the Iberian Peninsula, and North Africa. Automobile traffic has multiplied by more than 300 percent in just the last ten years, and thousands of long-haul trucks transporting goods travel through the Basque Country annually. During the summer tourist season, the population of the northern Basque coast grows to tenfold its normal stable population of approximately two hundred and sixty thousand.

Lesson four

BIBLIOGRAPHY

Bard, Rachel. 1982. *Navarra: The Durable Kingdom.* Reno: University of Nevada Press.

Goyhenetxe, Eukeni. 1985. *Historia de Iparralde: Desde los orígenes a nuestros días.* Donostia–San Sebastián: Editorial Txertoa.

Jacob, James E. 1994. *Hills of Conflict: Basque Nationalism in France.* Reno: University of Nevada Press.

Ormond, P. S. 1926. *The Basques and Their Country: Dealing Chiefly with the French Provinces.* London: Simpkin, Marshall, Hamilton, Kent and Company.

REQUIRED READING
James E. Jacob, *Hills of Conflict: Basque Nationalism in France* (Reno: University of Nevada Press, 1994), chapters 1 and 2, pp 1–62.

WRITTEN LESSON FOR SUBMISSION
Analyze the effects of nation building, the French Revolution, and the division of France into departments on the historical *fors* and "collective nobility" of the Basque provinces and people. What are the reasons for the severity of the French antagonisms toward the Basques in this time period?

THROUGHOUT the centuries, one can trace the global expansion of the Basques from their homeland territory in search of work, trade, or to further colonial pursuits, as they have since the Middle Ages' *Reconquista* to fight back the Muslims of al-Andalus (Andalusia). Many Basques colonized southern regions of today's Spain, leaving towns named Báscones and Villabáscones in Castile. In the thirteenth and fourteenth centuries, colonies of Basque merchants were located in Iberian cities and ports, especially in Seville, where their commercial networks were essential to later Basque participation in the conquest of the Americas. Maritime whaling expeditions brought Basques to the coasts of Newfoundland, where we know of indigenous peoples who have Basque words in their vocabulary.

Basque whalers left the Bizkaian and Gipuzkoan coasts as early as the seventh century for their North Atlantic hunts, and documents from 1540 demonstrate that they most likely had been fishing off the coasts of Greenland for a considerable number of years. Basque cod fisherman conferred Basque names on the bays of Newfoundland and traded with indigenous groups from Labrador. Throughout the late Middle Ages, the Bay of Biscay's marine economy and trade required Basques to travel and contact other cultures and societies. The Flemish city of Bruges, Belgium, retains archives from the commercial consulate established there in the fifteenth century recording Bizkaian and Gipuzkoan merchants, demonstrating the existence of trade networks between Basques in the Basque Country, the Low Countries, and England.

William A. Douglass points out that the "sixteenth and seventeenth century access to Spanish colonial enterprise proved attractive and stimulated Basque emigration." Indeed, notable numbers of Basques did not begin to leave the Basque Country permanently until the colonial pursuits of the 1500s in Central and South America under the crown of Castile and, later, Spain. Basque mariners played important roles in most of Spain's voyages of discovery, influencing outcomes with their expertise at navigation and ship building and their experience in whaling and off-shore fishing. Basques manned and directed expeditions of Christopher Columbus, Amerigo Vespucci, Vasco Nuñez de Balboa, and Magellan. Juan Sebastián Elcano was the first person to captain a circumnavigation of the globe when he assumed leadership after Magellan was killed in the Philippines in 1521.

It would not be an exaggeration to state that every major Spanish expeditionary force and every ecclesiastical or secular administration in the New World had Basques. Spain achieved several generations of colonial expansion in the Americas with Basque leadership, Basque capital, and Basque manpower. Basque interests, and especially Bizkaian interests, controlled more than shipping. They "supplied capital, equipment and goods for trade as well as many of its personnel" (Lynch 1964, 35).

IPARRALDE BASQUES from the North did not participate in the French colonization or in the administration of their colonies because they did not have the relative influence in France that Basques in Spain had in the dominant cities of Burgos, Madrid, Cadiz, and Seville. Maritime exploits in Iparralde had not developed to the degree that they had in neighboring Gipuzkoa or Bizkaia. During the 1400s, the port of St. Jean-de-Luz, or Donibane Lohitzune, harbored coastal fishing boats and later began to send ships to the ports of other European cities. Marine activity specifically from Lapurdi is documented in whaling and cod fishing in Newfoundland since at least 1520 and from 1537 to the Antilles and the coasts of Venezuela and Mexico (Goyhenetxe 1985, 55), but not to the extent of Bizkaian shipping activity.

The Basque presence in Madrid, the Philippines, and in the South American colonies continued to be significant in the eighteenth century. The cultural influence of the Basques in the colonial diaspora extended throughout the new territories, and the Royal Basque Society of the Friends of the Basque Country, created in 1765, had hundreds of illustrious Basque members throughout the Americas and also a branch in Madrid. Basques consistently assisted each other and created networks with other Basques in order to fill almost every need of their lives in the new colonial societies (Totoricagüena 2004b).

 IN 1808, THE FRENCH also became aware of the influence of elite Basques in the New World. Napoleon had gained control of the Iberian Peninsula that year and had decided to endow Spain with a new constitution. He planned to submit the text and amendments to the Assembly of Notables in Baiona, or Bayonne, in the province of Lapurdi. The attending representatives of the Basque territories in France reminded the emperor that the four Basque territories in Spain already had their own constitutions and therefore should be exempt from the new charter developed for Spain. They also reminded Napoleon that Basques from the four provinces controlled the colonial administration in the New World and that these people could be decisive in the emancipation and independence of the American territories if Napoleon deprived their homeland of its original historical

High fertility and live-birth rates in the Basque Country resulted in large families living on the *baserri*. Only one child would inherit the family farmstead, according to the rules of primogeniture, and the others were forced to look elsewhere for their futures, including migration to the Americas.

Photograph by Eulalia Abaitua Allende Salazar. Courtesy of the Basque Archaeological, Ethnographic, and Historical Museum, Bilbao.

---

constitutions, or *fueros* (Gregorio Monreal Zia, quoted in Totoricagüena 2004b, 26).

Spanish and French conquests provided new alternatives to Basques for overseas migration. However, both

France and Spain at various times imposed strict controls on population movements. Prior to 1853, Spain
required each emigrant to apply for a license and to
depart through government-established channels. Violations were numerous, however, and the majority of
emigrants left Spain illegally and did not register in the
administration's official count. As we have seen, many
Basques simply went to the north of Euskal Herria and
departed from the French side, benefiting from fellow
Basques' preferential treatment and aid. Conversely,
when France imposed strict laws and Spain did not,
Basques accordingly went south in order to depart from
southern ports.

A S WE HAVE noted before, the economic and political opportunities in the New World societies, with
the immediate demand for clerics, military personnel,
and tradesmen created by colonization, pulled emigrants
from the Basque Country. At the same time, the political
turmoil, wars, and the religious, social, and economic
upheaval of Europe provided the general stimulus that
pushed Basques to emigrate to the Americas, the Philippines, and Australia.

More specifically, as we also have previously noted,
factors pulling Basques toward a decision to emigrate
included the Basques' practice of extending collective
nobility, which aided each individual's prospects for
emigrating under favorable circumstances. Basques
also discovered that their noble status upon arrival in
the new host country facilitated their economic opportunities. Later, with the arrival of industrialization in
certain regions in or near the Basque Country, artisans
who could not compete in Europe found ample favorable circumstances in the South American countries,
whose developing economies in need of their expertise
and craftsmanship exerted a pull on many potential

emigrants. Conversely, the restricted economic opportunities in the homeland served as "push" factors, as did the physical position of Euskal Herria between Spain and France. The region was strategic for Napoleonic military campaigns, and because Basques tended to fight for the maintenance of the existing order and for the preservation of their local *fors* or *fueros*, war reparations and political and economic repression followed each campaign. As noted, in the southern Basque territories in Spain, the First Carlist War (1833–39), the Second Carlist War (1872–76), the Spanish Civil War (1936–39), and the Franco dictatorship all served as push factors sending Basques around the world in search of human rights and political freedoms, as well as economic stability.

IN THE nineteenth century, evading mandatory conscripted service to the Spanish military or the French military was one reason pushing young Basque men to decide to leave the country. As we have noted, on the southern side of Euskal Herria, in the Carlist Wars of the 1830s and 1870s, Basques fought on the losing sides both times and then endured war reparations.

In between wars, they suffered a corn crop failure and the famine of 1846–47, another factor pushing Basques to emigrate. Pulling them to do so were family and friends who had personally experienced emigration and the knowledge that they had the good possibility of being received by a relative or fellow villager.

As we saw in the Introduction, South America's newly independent states encouraged immigration to Uruguay and Argentina. In fact, there were more than twenty-five travel agencies in the Basque provinces alone, and free land and free transportation passage pulled Basque families to emigrate together and settle permanently. However, countless families were divided between continents. For example, Angel Bidasolo Zuluaga emigrated

Marriage dowries were common and could include animals, furniture, linens, and crockery, all practical and useful items for establishing a new household.
Photograph by Eulalia Abaitua Allende Salazar. Courtesy of the Basque Archaeological, Ethnographic, and Historical Museum, Bilbao.

---

to New York; brother Hilario stayed in Ibarrangelua, Bizkaia; brother Vicente left to Argentina; and brother Ricardo departed for "somewhere in South America, we don't know for sure, but maybe Venezuela," and no one from the family ever heard from him again. In other cases, father and sons left wife and mother to "make it big in America" (Totoricagüena 2004a, 47).

HOWEVER, THE overall system of primogeniture inheritance may have carried the most weight in pushing an individual to leave the Basque Country. Basque anthropologist Julio Caro Baroja argued that the most important element affecting emigration out of Euskal Herria emanated from the rules of inheritance followed in traditional rural Basque society (Caro Baroja 1971; Bilbao Azkarreta 1992). Typically, each traditional rural farmstead could support only a single family in agriculture. Those who owned their property and animals kept their holdings in the same family, and Basque common law discouraged fragmentation or division through sales or inheritance. Consequently, most Basque farmsteads remained unchanged for many centuries, with each generation having one single heir. This meant that in every family there were most likely at least three or four siblings who knew since childhood that they would not inherit the family farm and who were then candidates for jobs in other villages or cities in the Basque Country. However, population density, high fertility, and high live-birth rates, coupled with the scarcity of available agricultural lands and low agricultural output, resulted in limited potential for young Basques disinherited by the practice of primogeniture to make a living in agriculture. The lack of industrial and urban growth until the late 1800s also limited possible options for employment and movement within Euskal Herria. As a result, they became prime candidates for emigration to new lands (Douglass and Bilbao 1975, 131–33; Totoricagüena 2004b, 67).

Even today, in certain villages, the traditional rules of male primogeniture are followed. In other areas, a female heir is selected, while in parts of Nafarroa, the heir or heiress is chosen according to individual merit without reference to gender or birth order (Lafourcade

1999, 167–74). Until recently, the remaining siblings have had to depend upon the new owner for employment, accommodation, and care, but there usually has not been enough work to finance the entire extended family. Unmarried siblings had the right to remain and live on the family farmstead as long as they stayed single. Some married other heads of household and moved away, and others turned to religious professions or to military service. For thousands, however, a more viable alternative to alleviate hardship remained the possibility of emigration.

In 1853, the Spanish liberalization of a right to emigration encouraged thousands of persons to depart for Latin America annually without fear of reprisals. Many of the families of emigrants from the Basque Country believed that anyone who was willing to work hard could strike it rich in the Americas. They witnessed the changes in their local villages that resulted from remittances sent by *indianos*, the name given to people who emigrated to the Americas—the Indies. Remittances paid for church restorations, new altars or chapels, and for reconstruction, renovation, and/or additions to *baserris*. Earnings sent to the Basque Country also paid for dowries for sisters to marry into another *baserri*. There did not seem to be sufficient attention paid to the larger number of people who could not afford the passage price to return or who did not have profits to send back home.

ACCURATE NUMBERS of emigrants by year or by destination do not exist because of the lack of exact record keeping by departure port authorities as well as the lack of detailed records kept by receiving authorities in the host territories, who lumped Basque, Galician, Catalan and others together as simply "Spanish." The lack of consistency in data makes it unwise to infer total percentages or numbers of people leaving the Basque

Country itself. More contemporary records are no better. For example, Spanish official statistics give 1,042,775 emigrants leaving Spain between 1882 and 1930. However, the totals from the various receiving states show numerous millions of immigrants from Spain for the same years (Ruíz de Azua 1992, 266).

From the north side of the Basque Country, it is estimated that between 1832 and 1907, the provinces of Zuberoa and Behe Nafarroa lost between 20 and 25-five percent of their total population, and as we have noted, the entire population growth in Iparralde for the last half of the nineteenth century was completely canceled by emigration (Jacob 1994, 46). By this time, a part of this exodus was heading to North America. For example, in 1874, the steamship Lafayette left from Le Havre, near Paris, and voyaged to New York with the Amestoy family: Mrs. Marie Amestoy, Jean Amestoy, Antoine Amestoy, J. B. Amestoy, Jules Amestoy, Louisa Amestoy, and also the Aguerre, Haizaguerre, Daguere, Arrambide, Hirigoyen, and Etchepare families (Totoricagüena 2004a, 45–46).

THEORIES OF chain migration argue that social and familial networks play a significant part in migration decision making. In the Basque case, we see fathers sending for sons, brothers and sisters receiving their siblings, and aunts and uncles receiving nieces and nephews. There is also a prevalent region-to-region migration. For example, the overwhelming majority of Basques in the southwestern Idaho area originate from Bizkaia, and specifically from approximately a fifteen-mile radius around the town of Gernika, or Guernica. In December 2000, the town of Okondo, Araba, celebrated and paid homage to the figure of the Basque sheepherder. When I was asked to prepare a list of living past sheepherders who had worked in the Boise area and had returned to the Basque Country, I produced a list of forty-eight names. All but one still lived within that fifteen-mile radius, and the exception lived in Bilbao, which is very near Gernika. In North Queensland, Australia, we find almost the same circumstances. The overwhelming majority of Basques in the area surrounding Townsville, Ayr, Ingham, and Trebonne are of Bizkaian descent from the small region of Markina, Aulesti, Ispaster, Lekeitio, and inland toward Gernika.

SOCIAL IDENTITY theory argues that individuals strive to create a positive social identity in relation to other groups while retaining individual uniqueness. Maintaining an ethnic identity can serve both purposes in all of these Basque communities. Basques actually have a high social status (not necessarily a high economic status), and they benefit from that positive social identity and respect in their local communities. Although they did not receive any particular government benefits, over the years, many of my interviewees and research respondents have reported that being Basque has helped them earn employment and make friends because of their reputation for being honest, trustworthy, and especially hard working.

Basques thus have actually benefited from positive discrimination and positive prejudice in the communities where they have achieved a critical mass. I have found in ethnic community after ethnic community that the determinative group for positive communal relations is not the current contemporary immigrant population, but the original founders, the first immigrants from that group to settle. Those with positive social status derived from work habits (such as the Basques, Germans, Polish, Japanese, and Koreans) are able to maintain that positive identity generations later, and the host society perpetuates that historical view. Unfortunately for Latinos, Italians, or the Irish, their reputations in various countries

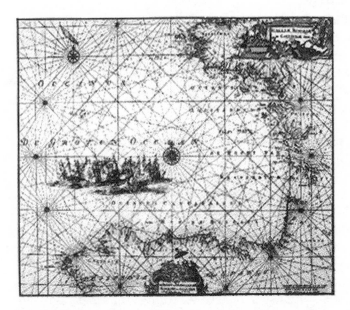

Basque maritime expertise extended to cartography, as depicted in this 1700 map of the Gulf of Biscay.

were established with low or negative social status, and the outside community has also perpetuated that negative view.

THE POSITIVE transnational networks resulting from chain migration were well established in South American countries, and Basques initiated trading, religious, and employment networks based on ethnicity (Quiroz Paz-Soldán 1996; Douglass and Bilbao 1975). Certainly, individual Basques used ethnicity instrumentally to gain political favors or employment from each other. Basques thus often acted as a self-aware ethnic group, maintaining ties to each other and to their homeland. This resulted in trade networks, collective action, mutual assistance programs, schools for Basque children, and associations and societies for the maintenance of Basque language, culture, and traditions.

NEW DESTINATIONS

BY THE LATE 1800s, Basque seamen from Bizkaia and Gipuzkoa were quite familiar with the ports of New York and the eastern seaboard of the United States as a result of their constant commerce with the Americas. Many Basque seamen from Latin American countries had also frequently visited the ports of Norfolk, Boston, Philadelphia, New York, and New Jersey. Before 1869 and the connection of the transcontinental railroad at Promontory Point, Utah, Basques interested in immigrating and settling to work in the United States were most likely to choose the West Coast as a result of the California Gold Rush of 1848. This actually began as secondary migration of Basques from Latin America moving to California, although thousands were already there as colonizing forces of the Spanish, and later as Mexican-Basques. They departed the South American capitals and the vast stretches of farmland in the pampas and traveled by ship up the Pacific coastline to reach California. Basques migrating directly from Euskal Herria endured many weeks consumed by the passage from Europe to the West Coast, crossing the Atlantic, then following the Atlantic coasts of Central and South America to the Strait of Magellan and round Cape Horn before heading north past the coasts of Chile, Peru, Ecuador, Colombia, past Central America and Mexico, finally reaching their destination of California. It was dangerous, expensive, and what must have seemed like a never-ending voyage.

It is often forgotten that the trip from the Basque Country to the United States was not only the crossing of the Atlantic, but actually began days earlier with travel by horse or train from a rural town to the cities of Bilbao,

Donostia–San Sebastián, Biarritz, or Baiona. Another entire day would be required for a train trip north to the French ports of Bordeaux or Le Havre. There, emigrants were kept additional days completing paperwork and eventually boarded passenger ships, if they were lucky or wealthy, and some were made to travel on cargo ships, if they were not.

EVEN AT THE beginning of the 1900s, the transatlantic journey for most Basques was lengthy and frightening. Crossing to the United States' East Coast could take anywhere from fourteen to twenty days, depending on the itinerary, weather and storms, and the power of the ship. Hundreds of Basque immigrants interviewed in the United States remember the fear of the voyage and the seasickness they experienced. Advancing the remaining miles to Ellis Island, and after a few days of inspections, to the entrance of the port of New York, was overwhelming for many. It also augmented a new fear of the metropolis, which was far larger than any of them could have ever imagined from their experiences in the rural Basque Country (Totoricagüena 2004b).

A formal education in the Basque Country was a luxury at nearly every time period before the 1940s. Classes usually included a heavy dose of Catholic religion, were taught in Spanish with a curriculum glorifying Spain, and in Iparralde in French, glorifying centralize France, and most were segregated by gender. The quality of instruction varied radically, and often children did not finish more than a few years of formal schooling. Spanish Basque emigrants with higher education were more likely to select Latin American destinations, where they could use their Spanish-language skills and continue their professions. Basques with little formal schooling and much rural agricultural experience could find agricultural work in the United States and Australia

Basque maritime expert Juan de la Cosa, also known as Juan Vizcaíno, was a Basque cartographer and explorer. Born in 1460 in Santoña, he was the owner of the *Santa María*, lead vessel of the discovery of the Americas by Christopher Columbus. His famous *Carta-mapamundi*, or world map, created in 1500, included the geographic details learned during of his many voyages. Juan de la Cosa was killed in 1510 on a voyage of discovery in Cartagena de Indias during a confrontation with indigenous populations.

This painting hangs in the Museo Naval in Madrid, as does his Carta-mapamundi.

much the same as what they would find in Uruguay or
Argentina, and by the early 1900s, the United States,
Canada, and Australia promised many more economic
opportunities than did the Latin American countries.

ALTHOUGH ACCESS to information was critical in the
selection of the destination, misinformation was
equally determinate. Emigrants were likely to send only
 good news home, not wanting to worry their family
members. Basques who could afford photography sent
images of themselves in suits and tailored garments, the
women in feathered hats and silk gloves. The majority
of Basques in the home provinces had no such clothing,
and the photographic images of San Francisco's or New
York's tall buildings and manicured parks with landscaping epitomized modernity—the opposite of what
seemed to characterize the Basque countryside and fishing villages. Modernity was equated with what was good
and desirable. Homeland families also likely did not
know that photography studios often provided clothing
for people to borrow for the photographs (and perhaps
did not notice the tattered shoes that did belong to the
subjects). Often missing from the letters sent home was
the information regarding the expensive cost of living,
the stresses of urban life or the lonely life in the sheep
industry and the reality of workdays twelve to fifteen
hours long.

Today, in diaspora communities, most of the immigrant generation are in their seventies, eighties, and
nineties. They departed the Basque Country in the
1930s and 1940s, immediately before, during, or after
the Spanish Civil War. Their perceptions of what they
lived through have been taught to their children and
grandchildren and have prominently influenced those
diaspora communities that received this latest heavy
flow of Basque emigration. Although the emigrants may

perpetuate limited historical facts, what is pertinent
are the emotions, attitudes, and opinions that correlate
with diaspora rhetoric of traumatic dispersal: collective
memory of ills to the Basque population, solidarity with
co-ethnics in the homeland and in the diaspora, the possibility of an enriched ethnic life in the host society, and
the maintenance of links with the Basque Country.

WE SHOULD remember that diasporas are groups
of people who have experienced traumatic expulsions and dispersals from their original homeland as a
result of war, famine, poverty, and political persecution.
In the Basque case, rural society, changing urban society, unemployment, unrest, labor strikes, and arrests
and imprisonments throughout the Basque territories
related to a lack of civil rights all preceded the cataclysm
of the Spanish Civil War (1936–39). None of the previous battles with the Castilian or Spanish central governments over regionalism versus centralism had prepared
the southern Basque Country for the repercussions it
would endure in the aftermath of fighting to preserve
an elected republican form of government. Neither had
Iparralde ever received such a profuse influx of exiles
requiring immediate medical and humanitarian aid.

After the elected Republican military forces were
defeated in 1939, Franco's victory guaranteed a central
policy of Spanish nation building and Basque nation
destroying. Throughout Spain, ethnic minorities were
expected to render their cultural identities. Basques suffered horrendous indignities, such as the dismantling of
their public institutions, the outlawing of manifestations
of Basque culture and even language, dictatorial repression, and lack of human and civil rights. Urban and
rural dwellers, widowed mothers and children, orphaned
teenagers, and Republican soldiers—thousands who had
the connections and the means to escape political and

military repression—did so. Most evacuated initially to Iparralde, where Basques from the North cared for almost one hundred and fifty thousand refugees from the South, in addition to exiles from other regions of Spain. War refugees then chose their final destinations, usually based upon family ties to regions in the New World or on information they had obtained from family and village networks. Many stayed permanently in Lapurdi and Behe Nafarroa, and later, those who were able to do so returned to the southern provinces, to Catalonia, or to other regions of Spain (Totoricagüena 2004b, 68–72).

Lesson five

BIBLIOGRAPHY

Bilbao Azkarreta, Jon. 1992. *América y los vascos*. Vitoria-Gasteiz: Eusko Jaurlaritza.

Caro Baroja, Julio. 1971. *Los vascos*. 4th edition. Madrid: Ediciones ISTMO.

Douglass, William A., and Jon Bilbao. 1975. *Amerikanuak: Basques in the New World*. Reno: University of Nevada Press.

Goyhenetxe, Eukeni. 1985. *Historia de Iparralde: Desde los orígenes a nuestros días*. Donostia–San Sebastián: Editorial Txertoa.

Huxley Barkham, Selma. 1989. *The Basque Coast of Newfoundland*. Plum Point, Newf.: Great Northern Peninsula Development Corporation.

Jacob, James E. 1994. *Hills of Conflict: Basque Nationalism in France*. Reno: University of Nevada Press.

Lafourcade, Maite. 1999. "Sistemas de herencia y transmisión de la propiedad en Iparralde bajo el antiguo régimen." In *Vasconia: Cuadernos de historia-geografía*. Donostia–San Sebastián: Eusko Ikaskuntza.

Lynch, John. 1964. *Spain Under the Habsburgs*. Vol. 1. *Empire and Absolutism, 1516–1598*. Oxford: Basil Blackwell.

Monreal Zia, Gregorio. Universidad Pública de Navarra. Pamplona. Interviews, July 1998, October 1999, August 2000, December 2001, September 2002, July 2003.

Quiroz Paz-Soldán, Eusebio. 1996. "Los vascos en la ciudad de Arequipa." In *Emigración y redes sociales de los vascos en América*, ed. Ronald Escobedo Mansilla, Ana de Zabala Beascoechea, and Oscar Alvarez Gila. Vitoria-Gasteiz: Universidad del País Vasco.

Ruíz de Azua, Estibaliz. 1992. *Vascongadas y América*. Madrid: Editorial MAPFRE.

Totoricagüena, Gloria. 2004a. *The Basques of New York: A Cosmopolitan Experience*. 2d ed. Basque Migration and Diaspora Studies Series, no. 2. Reno: Center for Basque Studies, University of Nevada, Reno.

———. 2004b. *Identity, Culture, and Politics in the Basque Diaspora*. Reno: University of Nevada Press.

———. 2003. "El País Vasco visto desde la diáspora: Análisis de las relaciones institucionales entre el País Vasco y la diáspora vasca." *Eusko Ikaskuntza XV Congreso Internacional Select Papers*. Donostia–San Sebastián: Eusko Ikaskuntza.

REQUIRED READING

Gloria Totoricagüena, *Identity, Culture, and Politics in the Basque Diaspora* (Reno: University of Nevada Press, 2004), chapter 3, pp 55–80.

Gloria Totoricagüena, "Una aproximación al desarrollo de la diáspora vasca," in *Kanpoko Etxe berria: Emigración vasca a América siglos XIX–XX* (Bilbao:

Museo Arqueológico, Etnográfico e Histórico Vasco, 2001).

Gloria Totoricagüena, "Comparing the Basque Diaspora: Ethnonationalism, Transnationalism, and Identity Maintenance in Argentina, Australia, Belgium, Peru, the United States of America, and Uruguay" (PhD diss., the London School of Economics and Political Science, University of London, 2000), chapter 4, pp 91–158.

William A. Douglass, "Factors in the Formation of the New-World Basque Emigrant Diaspora," in *Essays in Basque Social Anthropology*, ed. William A. Douglass (Reno: Basque Studies Program, 1989), pp 251–67.

WRITTEN LESSON FOR SUBMISSION

Compare the push-pull model to the chain-migration analysis of migration theory, using examples presented in the readings from the Basque diaspora. Give examples of factors that have served to push Basques out of Euskal Herria and examples that have served to pull Basques to specific host countries.

6 · Ethnic identity
The maintenance of ethnicity

IN ORDER TO understand the maintenance of Basque
ethnicity in the diaspora communities around the
world, we need to investigate and evaluate the theories
that attempt to explain why ethnic identity persists with
salience for some people, yet not for others. In various
historical settings, ethnic identity has shown itself to be
a stronger indicator of personal allegiance and loyalty
than class, gender, and sometimes even religion. Ethnic
diversity as a social reality remains a significant aspect of
society whether states are preindustrial or postindustrial,
socialist or capitalist, and social scientists continue to
ask and attempt to answer the following questions: How
can the persistence and reemergence of ethnic factors
best be explained? Why has ethnicity become a vehicle
for political mobilization in many regions? Has ethnic
conflict become more pronounced in recent years, or are
academics simply finally noticing and researching the
phenomenon? Why do Basques living in the diaspora,
in some circumstances after six generations, continue
to identify with their Basque ethnicity? Overall, we must
remember that the phenomena of ethnicity maintenance
and ethnic identity are not synonymous with racism
or ethnocentrism. The term "ethnic" derives from the
Greek term *ethnos* and was used to refer to peoples who
shared cultural and biological characteristics. "Ethnic
origin" refers to a person's biological and cultural ancestry.

When researching "ethnicity," we are looking at combinations of a sense of kinship, connection, and bonds
to a like people, group solidarity, and common language,
customs, traditions, religion, and shared ancestry, history, and territory. Ethnic communities have historically

served as the basic mode of group identification and individual organization in communities. Ethnic communities, such as in the Basque homeland and in the diaspora communities, interact consistently with each other and work together for common ethnic goals, with common ethnic and cultural interests for the group. Anthony D. Smith categorizes the *ethnie* or ethnic community as a collective that possesses six main features.

1. a common *proper name*, to identify and express the 'essence' of the community;
2. a myth of *common ancestry*, a myth rather than a fact, a myth that includes the idea of a common origin in time and place and that gives an *ethnie* a sense of fictive kinship, what Horowitz terms a 'super-family' (Horowitz 1985);
3. shared *historical memories*, or better, shared memories of a common past or pasts, including heroes, events, and their commemoration;
4. one or more *elements of common culture*, which need not be specified but normally include religion, customs, or language;
5. a *link with the homeland*, not necessarily its physical occupation by the *ethnie*, only its symbolic attachment to the ancestral land, as with diaspora peoples;
6. *a sense of solidarity* on the part of at least some sections of the *ethnie*'s population. (Smith 1986, ch. 2)

SMITH POINTS OUT the importance of the orientation to the past and to the historical origins of a community. Others, such as Fredrik Barth, focus on the boundaries established by social groups, arguing that it is the boundary itself, and not necessarily the cultural content of a group, that keeps it separate with a specific identity. Barth designates an ethnic group as a population that:

1. is largely biologically self-perpetuating;

2. shares fundamental cultural values, realized in overt cultural unity in cultural forms;
3. makes up a field of communication and interaction;
4. has a membership that identifies itself, and is identified by others, as constituting a category distinguishable from other categories of the same order. (Barth 1969, 10)

BARTH'S ARGUMENTS assert that clear boundaries persist and are maintained despite changing participation and membership in the groups. Important social relations are maintained across boundaries, cultural differences can persist despite interethnic contact and interdependence, and ethnic groups are categories of ascription and identification by the persons themselves (Barth 1969).

Ethnic groups have interests, but to define ethnic groups *as* interest groups would be erroneous and misleading. For example: Basques in Sydney, Melbourne, and North Queensland have interests in promoting their culture, maintaining ties with the Basque Country, and preserving Euskara. However, the Basques of Australia do not regularly organize themselves to influence the host country political or economic policies. They are not an interest group per se. Yet those of Greek descent do organize politically and lobby the Australian national parliament in Canberra. Is it only a matter of numbers, of having a critical mass of people large enough to "make a difference" to politicians? Perhaps in every group there are those who are interested in politics and those who are not, and in the majority of the Basque communities abroad there are not sufficient numbers of Basques who are interested in mobilizing with the intent to influence public policy.

The president of the Basque government-in-exile, José Antonio Aguirre y Lecube, regularly visited the New York Centro Vasco-Americano and their social events. He is seen here with the women dancers of the Ezpata Dantzaris at his welcoming Gala soon after his arrival to the United States in 1941.
Photograph courtesy of the New York Euzko Etxea.

PRIMORDIALISM

THE NATURAL, affective attachments of identity are categorized as "primordialist," a concept first introduced by Edward Shils in 1957 when examining the effect of "primordial qualities" on social interaction. According to Shils, race and ethnicity are primary sources of loyalty and the essence of the manner in which people group themselves. The primordial perspective focuses attention on the great emotional strength of ethnic bonds because primordial "givens" are not seen to change. Subsequently, Milton M. da Silva (1975) argued that the continued vitality of Basque ethnicity maintenance and nationalism are a result of this emotional power of the Basques' group identity. Primordialists generally argue that ethnic identity is a function of strong emotional ties based upon common descent and the distinctive common past of a group.

Primordialist theorists of ethnicity highlight shared kin, territory, language, religion, and traditions as the factors that often give people a sense of intense solidarity, passion, sacredness, and loyalty to each other. The current tide of ethnonationalism sweeping the world demonstrates that an "intuitive bond felt toward an informal and unstructured subdivision of mankind is far more profound and potent than are the ties that bind them to the formal legalistic state structure in which they find themselves" (Connor 1978, 377). This could describe the loyalty of diaspora Basques to their Basque culture and identity over time and distance, even though they are a part of a "formal legalistic state structure" elsewhere in Canada, Belgium, or Peru, among other hostlands.

THE APPLICATION of Shils's concept is expanded by Clifford Geertz (1973) beyond kinship to larger-scale groups based on territory, religion, language, and other customs. These attachments are the "givens" of the human condition, rooted in the nonrational foundations of the personality, and they provide a basis for affinity with others from the same background. In a more controversial usage, Pierre van den Berghe (1981 and 1996, 62) connects primordial ethnic feelings to sociobiology, which rests on genetic tendencies derived from the kinship process, and to the practice of "in-group amity and out-group enmity." According to primordialists, the attachments forming the core of ethnicity are biological and genetic in nature, and consequently they suggest that ethnicity is based upon descent and ancestry.

The primordial approach to Basque identity would refute the idea that identity is changeable, rational, or calculated. This approach seeks a psychological or biological explanation for the behavioral phenomenon of continued ethnic solidarity and the persistence of ethnic identity. It focuses on the important emotional strength of ethnic bonds that persist over time in radically different environments and adds a historical dimension by highlighting a group's distinctive past. Research in this area has shown that some ethnic attachments persist for hundreds of years and in certain cases override loyalties and affiliations to other significant groups. Edward Spicer (1971) observed that Basque ethnic populations have demonstrated a remarkable capacity to adapt to new environments, which has enabled them to maintain their traditional cultural systems. This could help us understand the persistence of Basque identity in the diaspora five and six generations after emigration.

HOWEVER, SCHOLARS are skeptical about this hypothesis. Why, some ask, is it that only certain Basques in some communities have these primordial attachments, and others do not? If they are natural, biological, and genetic, everyone should experience these attachments, should they not? Why have some Basques dropped their ethnic identity after emigrating and established themselves as Argentineans, or Venezuelans, or Mexicans? Why would many Basques in Euskal Herria identify themselves as Spanish or French, and not Basque? They argue that identities are subject to change. People change religious beliefs, learn new languages, leave their homelands, and settle elsewhere. If ethnic identity is founded on beliefs and practices shared through time, what about new identities that are constructed or reconstructed, or have undergone transformations and adaptations? Truly primordial

The Txantxangorriak, or Red-Breasted Robins, of Boise, Idaho. The group was formed in 2001 by Dan Ansotegui, Gina Ansotegui Urquidi, and Ana Mendiola. Children and adults learn together to play Basque traditional folk music on the tambourine and the accordion, preserving Basque music for future generations.
Photograph by the author.

sentiments would be naturally fixed and static, would they not? Perhaps it would be more beneficial and enlightening for us to examine ethnic identity in different situations. The primordial approach does not explain changing group solidarity or why some people feel loyalty to their ethnicity and their ethnic group, yet others do not.

INSTRUMENTALISM AND CIRCUMSTANTIALISM
Many social scientists categorize ethnicity as an instru-

ment to be used in order to gain certain social, political, economic, and cultural resources in the community. This manner of conceptualizing ethnicity is known as "instrumentalism." Instrumentalists argue that ethnicity is a social construct whereby individuals can add and mix different identities in order to suit themselves and in order to gain resources such as preferential treatment, special scholarships, societal status, or economic benefits. Although instrumentalists often argue that ethnicity must have a practical function in order to be viable, and they depict ethnicity as an instrument in the competition for scarce resources, T. H. Eriksen focuses on ethnic identity as the nexus of those distinctions that are socially relevant to the individual who maintains them (Eriksen 1993, 61). Although not necessarily an instrument of competition, for example, Basques' social status can be extremely relevant psychologically and emotionally, even if not used for material gain. Several authors have argued that utility is the most important factor in accounting for the maintenance of ethnic identity. They thus would ask, For what purposes—material, emotional, psychological—can Basques abroad use their "Basqueness"? The instrumentalist argument regards identity as contingent on political mobilization. However, perceptions of utility are themselves cultural creations, and the boundary between what is useful and what is meaningful for an individual is blurred. Basques in the diaspora may understand their ethnicity as being meaningful, but there is not sufficient convincing evidence to argue that they view it as useful for anything material.

The social identity theory argued by Henri Tajfel's claims that the process of social categorization enables the individual to define his or her own position in society as a member of the groups to which he or she

Table 6-1

Percentages of Respondents Who Perceived "Favorable or "Unfavorable" Treatment Because of Their Basque Ethnicity

Treatment	Joining a club	Admission to school or university	Selection for award or scholarship	Buying or renting accommodation	Receiving a government benefit	Getting a job
Uruguay						
Favorable	15%	10%	4%	7%	2%	7%
Unfavorable	8%	9%	8%	8%	10%	11%
Peru						
Favorable	50%	21%	0%	14%	0%	28%
Unfavorable	7%	7%	14%	14%	14%	0%
Australia						
Favorable	18%	13%	12%	10%	11%	22%
Unfavorable	2%	4%	2%	2%	2%	2%
United States						
Favorable	23%	7%	9%	9%	5%	26%
Unfavorable	1%	1%	2%	1%	2%	1%
Argentina						
Favorable	19%	21%	7%	9%	5%	19%
Unfavorable	5%	5%	4%	4%	5%	4%
Belgium						
Favorable	4%	8%	0%	0%	5%	25%
Unfavorable	0%	4%	0%	4%	0%	0%

Total of 832 responses from written anonymous questionnaires in Argentina, Uruguay, Peru, United States, Australia, and Belgium. (Totoricagüena 2004).

belongs. Social identity is defined as that part of a person's self-concept that derives from one's knowledge of membership in a social group, together with the value and emotional significance attached to that particular membership. People strive for a positive social identity (Tajfel 1978 and 1984; Tajfel and Turner 1979). Socioeconomic status is usually a reliable indicator of social categorization. Although Basques think of themselves positively, they do not tend to do so at the expense of other ethnic groups. Their perceived positive social status does not translate to a higher socio*economic* status. Sociological fieldwork questionnaire responses from self-defining Basques in Argentina, Australia, Belgium, Peru, the United States, and Uruguay from 1995 to 2004 indicate that in the United States, approximately one-third of those queried agreed that Basques enjoy a higher socioeconomic status than other immigrants, however another one-third disagreed.

PERHAPS BEING Basque is personally and individually relevant in the countries of these Basque communities abroad. If the chosen ethnic identity is determined by an individual's perception of its meaning to different audiences in one's community, along with its salience

Diaspora Basques tend to understand their Basqueness as being neither significantly favorable nor unfavorable in these selected social and economic circumstances. This points to a lack of instrumentality, or using Basqueness in order to obtain a specific benefit in society. Peru's 50% favorable response for joining a club may have pertained to their joining the Euskal Etxea of Lima.

in different social contexts and its utility in different settings, then joining and participating in Basque ethnic activities or joining a Basque center would have an individual and social effect. Diaspora Basques might also use the positive status of their ethnicity for personal material and/or psychological benefit. They do strive for a positive social identity and tend to believe they are perceived positively in each of their host societies in comparison with other ethnic groups, even if their socioeconomic status may not be higher. Personal interviews with Basques living in more than twenty countries demonstrate that a majority of them admitted that their own maintenance of Basque identity was related to the Basques' positive work-ethic reputation. Indeed, in the United States, 90 percent of those interviewed admitted that one of the reasons that they preserved their Basque identity was specifically because they were proud of the Basques' reputation as honest, hard-working people. In Peru, 85 percent of my respondents made this admission; in Australia, 81 percent; in Uruguay, 72 percent; in Argentina, 71 percent. In Belgium, 59 percent of those queried indicated that they valued this aspect of the Basques' reputation—a somewhat high number when taking into consideration that the Basques have had much less time to establish any reputation at all among the Belgians (Totoricagüena 2004).

THE POSITIVE association between "Basque" and "honest and industrious" is equivalent to social praise, and Basques said that they are proud when telling new acquaintances that they are Basque. Some individuals in Argentina, Uruguay, Venezuela, Chile, and the United States even admitted that they *expect* the person's reaction to be actual words of praise. In Sydney and Melbourne, Australia, they expect to give an explanation of what Basque ethnicity is and a short geography and

New Basque immigrant sheepherders arriving to the United States were often shocked to learn that they would be living in a covered wagon similar to the one shown here. The sheep wagon included a pipe stove for cooking and heating, a bunk bed, and shelving for storage of crockery, clothing, canned and dry goods. *Photograph by the author.*

history lesson, although most people in the North Queensland area are more familiar with Basques. Basques in Belgium and France reported that they usually have to disassociate themselves from the political violence of ETA, and also to abstain from political conversations. The majority of Basques I have spoken with still agreed that Basques have a positive social status in their host society, where they are known and recognized as a group in the community. Future research should test this by asking non-Basques what they think of Basques.

BASQUE ETHNIC festivals and communal activities serve to fulfill a psychological need to belong, and at the same time they offer the individual aspiration to uniqueness through Basque ethnicity. Basques are able to manifest their unique ethnic identity to the outside host society and simultaneously form a part of a group of fellow ethnics. Given a list of fourteen statements made by other diaspora Basques explaining why they maintain their ethnicity, 58 percent of the males and 62 percent of the female participants in the six-country study agreed that one of the main reasons they preserve their Basque identity is specifically because it makes them feel they "have a special connection to each other," and 53 percent of both groups agreed that their Basque identity makes them "feel special and unique" (Totoricagüena 2004).

As shown in Table 6-1, respondents were also asked if they had ever been treated favorably or unfavorably "specifically because you are Basque." Although instrumentalists contend that ethnicity is circumstantial and often used for gaining resources or services, in the case of Basques living in the diaspora, the evidence does not consistently support this argument. The table presents the percentages of respondents who believe their ethnicity has definitely affected the outcomes of certain situations, either favorably or unfavorably. If the respondents thought their Basqueness had no effect on the outcome of the situation, they were instructed to leave their responses to this section of the questionnaire blank.

The results for employment are difficult to interpret, because in interviews, some men explained that although they believe Basques tend to have a positive reputation in comparison with many other immigrants in their societies, if their Basque ethnicity had aided them in gaining employment, it was often because another Basque had hired them, not necessarily because a non-Basque had hired them. In interviews in the United States, several respondents did not want to admit that they had received special treatment because they "did not want to get anyone in trouble." One former miner stated that once, in the 1940s, while he was waiting in a line to apply for employment, the foreman walked down the queue asking if there were any Basques, and those who answered "Yes" were taken to the front and hired immediately. Although this incident was fifty years past, he had never admitted to what he thought was unfair treatment because of positive discrimination. What is important in social identity theory is the Basques' perception of themselves and whether or not they believe their ethnicity is a help or hindrance for actual instrumental benefit. The data reveal that in the circumstances mentioned, a majority perceived it as neither.

BASQUES MAXIMIZE the option of negotiating their identities depending on the situation. This situational or circumstantial identity does not mean that they are "Basque" sometimes and "Mexican" at other times. Rather, depending on the environment and people with whom they are associating, diaspora Basques

The 1931 Ezpata Dantzaris of the New York Centro Vasco-Americano were one of the first formal Basque dance groups in the United States. They performed in the Centro Vasco-Americano social club building for member events and also for the general public. All dancers at this time were Bizkaian emigrants or members of the first- generation born in the United States.

Bilbao newspaper La Tarde.

often emphasize one identity *more* than another, ethnic identity more than civic identity. "What ethnicity are than "In which country do you live?" or "What passport do you carry?"

THIS IDENTITY switching is often mistaken for and misunderstood as instrumental behavior for personal gain. However, often it is merely a response clarifying one's identity to an "other" person in a like category. For example: In Australia, describing oneself as "Australian" is not as useful as defining oneself to another Australian (of Greek ancestry) as a Basque. A Basque-Australian defines herself to a Greek-Australian as a Basque in order to differentiate herself and clarify their differences. They are both "Australian," or at least live in Australia. If a Basque from Uruguay is communicating with a person from Brazil, he would more than likely identify himself as a Uruguayan. These are equivalent comparisons: Brazilian to Uruguayan and Basque-Australian to Greek-Australian. Societal contexts and processes influence the self-definition and self-consciousness of diasporan identities in issues of self-representation.

IN REFINING these ideas of choosing identities, some sociologists argue what amounts to a "circumstantialist" position, emphasizing that ethnic identity is amenable to fluctuations (Matsuo 1992, 507) and that in certain cases, ethnicity involves a great deal of choice, as demonstrated in Mary Waters's research on European ethnics in the United States (Waters 1990). George M. Scott argues that primordial sentiments have to be elicited by some experience, and thus they are tied to circumstances (Scott 1990, 167, quoted in Eller and Coughlan 1993, 190). Circumstantialists, like instrumentalists, suggest that ethnic identities have a social source and are not natural givens from birth.

Stanford M. Lyman and William A. Douglass (1973) argued originally that ethnic group boundaries are not only selected and permeable, but that individuals use ethnicity differently in varying situations. The "us" and the "them" change according to circumstances, and different identities are called upon according to their appropriateness for each situation, as the Greek and Basque Australians did in their self-identifications. What is "appropriate" may also be whatever is instrumental in achieving a goal or specific objective. In the early stages

of Basque immigration to Argentina, Uruguay, and the
United States, for example, Basques were likely to help
other Basques setting up bakeries, working in tanning
operations, buying livestock and land, dairying, establishing sheep businesses, or in a few other pursuits,
which meant that this ethnic group, like others, evolved
with certain labor specialties. If members of an ethnic
group tend to be relatively homogeneous with respect
to occupation and residence when they settle in a new
host society, they are affected in much the same way
by government actions and policies. Ethnic groups are
therefore likely to become interest groups, and this fact
breathes new life into Old World social groups and identities (Glazer and Moynihan 1970). In societies lacking
sharp class divisions, ethnicity may tend to be under-
scored for social-class positioning and then becomes the
"appropriate" instrument used to obtain government
resources and benefits or a positive social status and
identity in the community. We have seen that the data
regarding Basques in the diaspora do not definitively
support or refute this argument.

THEORISTS WHO adopt the circumstantialist view-
point agree on at least one essential feature:
Renewed ethnic tensions and conflict are not only the
result of a primordial need to belong, but are the "conscious efforts of individuals and groups mobilizing ethnic symbols in order to obtain access to social, political,
and material resources" (McKay 1982, 399). Note how
these theories tend to emphasize (or assume) that identity is a matter of rational choice undertaken by individuals for instrumental reasons. Nathan Glazer and Daniel
Patrick Moynihan (1970) write about the "strategic
efficacy of ethnicity"; van den Berghe (1978) claims that
the use of ethnic symbols for gaining access to economic
and political resources is an "ethnic game" played in

nearly all multiethnic societies; and William D. Bernard (1971) and Frances Henry (1976) argue that ethnic identities and ideologies are maintained and highlighted in order to influence political and social policies, although ethnic identity is situationally variable and involves both revivals and creative constructions (Nagel 1994). However, the public profile and degree of participation in politics that ethnic groups achieve in their host countries is related to the wider questions of assimilation and integration and is tied to the "host country's legal, political, administrative and cultural-ideological apparatus" (Tölölyan 1996, 20). The rational-choice account of the persistence of ethnic identity focuses on group loyalty and the congruence of self-interest and group identification as well as on the costs and benefits of ethnic identity maintenance as opposed to total assimilation (Hardin 1995; Congleton 1995; Hechter 1996).

A S MENTIONED above, the fact that a group has common interests does not mean it will act collectively as an interest group. Explanations dealing exclusively with political and economic factors underrate the emotional power of ethnic bonds and exaggerate the influence of materialism on human behavior (Connor 1972; Epstein 1978). The instrumentalist approach tends to ignore the affective ethnic ties and the feelings and emotion that ethnic identity creates in individuals. Indeed, as we in fact have seen in this survey, instrumentalist (strategic) and primordialist (cultural) approaches to ethnicity need not be mutually exclusive and could be combined. The fact that some ethnic groups pursue domestic and transnational political and economic interests does not mean that all ethnic groups take identical actions, and the groups that do pursue resources and certain policy outcomes are not ipso facto political interest groups.

OPPOSITIONAL ETHNICITY

Why are economic interests sometimes pursued through ethnic cohesion and networks? Is it a result of primordial tendencies to practice in-group amity and out-group enmity? Do groups automatically react to the circumstances and banding together to win resources? Or are ethnic groups uniting to protect themselves from an opposition?

Edward Spicer argues that an "oppositional process frequently produces intense collective consciousness and a high degree of internal solidarity" (Spicer, quoted in Scott 1990, 158). In this view, which is a combination of the primordial and circumstantialist approaches, the maintenance of Basque ethnic identity has been aided by reacting to the "oppositional" forces of invading Romans, Visigoths, Franks, and Muslims, to French and Castilian political power, to the creation of Spain, to protection of the *fueros* and *fors*, to Franco, and so on.

HOWEVER, FRANCO died three decades ago, and the Basque Country enjoys various levels of autonomous political and economic powers. If we regard the maintenance of Basque ethnicity from this point of view, what is the current opposition? Do Basques in the diaspora truly consider the current central government in Spain as "the opposition" and therefore continue to protect themselves and their endangered culture? Perhaps this theory does not explain the growth in Basque ethnic identity outside of the homeland.

Walker Connor often reminds his readers that nationalism and patriotism are two very "distinct loyalties: the former is to one's national group; the latter to one's state (country) and its institutions" (Connor 1996, 69). In a world where there are thousands of ethnic groups, but fewer than two hundred states, we can see that for many groups, there is no allegiance to the state in which they

Basque boardinghouses and hotels were often recognized by the general public for the outstanding quality and quantity of their cuisine. Although the restaurants were usually open only to boarding customers, in later years, as migration dwindled, the restaurants became at least an equal part of the revenue stream. In New York, Benita Orbe's meals at the Jai-Alai Restaurant and Bar—which did serve the public—were famous throughout the city, and many of her customers included public officials and business tycoons.

find themselves, but rather a stronger allegiance to their ethnicity and ethnonational bonds, and such is the case for many Basque nationalists who find their own loyalties in conflict with a Spanish patriotism.

SINCE WORLD WAR II, it is estimated that over twenty million people have died in ethnic conflicts. Ethnoregional movements especially flourish in Europe, Africa, and Asia. Perhaps this is a result of the effects of globalization and growing isolation. Individualizing and specializing almost every aspect of life may actually cause a negative reaction to those forces and cause individuals to seek out social companionship and activities that are celebrated with others who are similar. Although there are conflicting theories attempting to explain why, there are new Basque organizations sprouting in Argentina, Uruguay, Canada, Italy, Columbia, the United States, and Australia.

Lesson six

BIBLIOGRAPHY

Barth, Fredrik, ed. 1969. *Ethnic Groups and Boundaries: The Social Organization of Culture Difference.* London: George Allen and Unwin.

Bernard, William S. 1971."New Directions in Integration and Ethnicity." *International Migration Review* 5, no. 4 (Winter): 464–73.

Congleton, Roger D. 1995. "Ethnic Clubs, Ethnic Conflict, and Ethnic Nationalism." In *Nationalism and Rationality*, ed. Albert Breton et al. Cambridge: Cambridge University Press.

Connor, Walker. 1996. "Beyond Reason: The Nature of the Ethnonational Bond." In *Ethnicity*, ed. John Hutchinson and Anthony D. Smith. Oxford: Oxford University Press.

———. 1994. *Ethnonationalism: The Quest for Understanding*. Princeton: Princeton University Press.

Connor, Walker. 1978. "A Nation Is a Nation, Is a State, Is an Ethnic Group, Is a ..." *Ethnic and Racial Studies* 1 (October): 377–400.

————. 1972. "Nation-Building or Nation-Destroying?" *World Politics* 24: 319–55.

Da Silva, Milton M. 1975. "Modernization and Ethnic Conflict: The Case of the Basques." *Comparative Politics* 7 (January): 227–51.

Eller, Jack David, and Reed M. Coughlan. 1993. "The Poverty of Primordialism: The Demystification of Ethnic Attachments." *Ethnic and Racial Studies* 16 (April): 183–202.

Epstein, A.L. 1978. *Ethos and Identity: Three Studies in Ethnicity*. London: Tavistock.

Eriksen, Thomas Hylland. 1993. *Ethnicity and Nationalism: Anthropological Perspectives*. London: Pluto Press.

Geertz, Clifford. 1973. "The Integrative Revolution: Primordial Sentiments and Civil Politics in the New States." In *The Interpretation of Cultures: Selected Essays*. New York: Basic Books.

Glazer, Nathan, and Daniel P. Moynihan. 1975. *Ethnicity: Theory and Experience*. Cambridge, Mass.: Harvard University Press.

————, eds. 1970. *Beyond the Melting Pot: The Negroes, Puerto Ricans, Jews, Italians, and Irish of New York City*. 2d ed. Cambridge, Mass.: MIT Press.

Hardin, Russell. 1995. "Self-Interest, Group Identity." In *Nationalism and Rationality* ed. Albert Breton et al. Cambridge: Cambridge University Press.

Hechter, Michael. 1996. "Ethnicity and Rational Choice Theory." In *Ethnicity*, ed. John Hutchinson and Anthony D. Smith. Oxford: Oxford University Press.

Henry, Frances, ed. 1976. *Ethnicity in the Americas*. The Hague: Mouton.

Horowitz, Donald L. 1985. *Ethnic Groups in Conflict.* Berkeley: University of California Press.

Jenkins, Richard. 1997. *Rethinking Ethnicity: Arguments and Explorations.* London: Sage.

Lyman, Stanford M., and William A. Douglass. 1973. "Ethnicity: Strategies of Collective and Individual Impression Management." *Social Research* 40 (Summer): 344–65.

Matsuo, Hisako. 1992. "Identificational Assimilation of Japanese Americans: A Reassessment of Primordial and Circumstantialism." *Sociological Perspectives* 35: 505–52.

McKay, James. 1982. "An Explanatory Synthesis of Primordial and Mobilizationist Approaches to Ethnic Phenomena." *Ethnic and Racial Studies* 5 (October): 395–420.

McKay, James, and Frank Lewins. 1978. "Ethnicity and the Ethnic Group: A Conceptual Analysis and Reformulation." *Ethnic and Racial Studies* 1 (October): 412–27.

Nagel, Joanne. 1994. "Constructing Ethnicity: Creating and Recreating Ethnic Identity and Culture." *Social Problems* 41 (February): 152–76.

Okamura, Jonathan Y. 1998. *Imagining the Filipino American Diaspora: Transnational Relations, Identities, and Communities.* London: Garland.

Scott, George M., Jr. 1990. "A Resynthesis of the Primordial and Circumstantial Approaches to Ethnic Group Solidarity: Towards an Explanatory Model." *Ethnic and Racial Studies* 13 (April): 147–71.

Smith, Anthony D. 1986. *The Ethnic Origins of Nations.* Oxford: Blackwell.

———. 1984. "Negotiating Ethnicity in an Uncertain Environment." *Ethnic and Racial Studies* 7: 360–72.

Smith, Anthony D. 1981. *The Ethnic Revival*. Cambridge: Cambridge University Press.

Spicer, Edward. 1971. "Persistent Identity Systems." *Science* 174: 795–800.

Tajfel, Henri. 1982. *Social Identity and Intergroup Relations*. Cambridge: Cambridge University Press.

———. 1981. *Human Groups and Social Categories*. Cambridge: Cambridge University Press.

———, ed. 1984. *The Social Dimension: European Development in Social Psychology*. Vol. 2. Cambridge: Cambridge University Press.

———, ed. 1978. *Differentiation Between Social Groups: Studies in the Social Psychology of Intergroup Relations*. London: Academic Press.

Tajfel, Henri, and Turner, J. C. 1979. "An Integrative Theory of Intergroup Conflict." In *The Social Psychology of Intergroup Relations*, ed. S. Worchel and W. G. Austin. Monterey, Calif.: Brooks-Cole.

Tölölyan, Khachig. 1996. "Rethinking Diaspora(s): Stateless Power in the Transnation Moment." *Diaspora* 5: 3–36.

Totoricagüena, Gloria. 2004. *Identity, Culture, and Politics in the Basque Diaspora*. Reno: University of Nevada Press.

Van den Berghe, Pierre L. 1996. "Does Race Matter?" In *Ethnicity*, ed. John Hutchinson and Anthony D. Smith. Oxford: Oxford University Press.

———. 1981. *The Ethnic Phenomenon*. New York: Elsevier.

———. 1978. "Race and Ethnicity: A Sociobiological Perspective." *Ethnic and Racial Studies* 1 (October): 401–11.

Waters, Mary C. 1990. *Ethnic Options: Choosing Identities in America*. Berkeley: University of California Press.

REQUIRED READING

John Hutchinson and Anthony D. Smith, eds., *Ethnicity*
(Oxford: Oxford University Press, 1996), introduction,
pp 3–14.

George M. Scott, Jr., "A Resynthesis of the Primordial
and Circumstantial Approaches to Ethnic Group Solidarity: Towards an Exploratory model," *Ethnic and
Racial Studies* 13, no. 2 (April 1990): 147–71.

James McKay, "An Explanatory Synthesis of Primordial
and Mobilizationist Approaches to Ethnic Phenomena," *Ethnic and Racial Studies* 5, no. 4 (October
1982): 395-420.

WRITTEN LESSON FOR SUBMISSION

Compare the "primordialist," "circumstantialist," and
"oppositional" approaches to ethnicity. Which do you
favor for explaining ethnic identity and group solidarity
and why? Give examples from the readings or from personal observations of ethnic groups in the society where
you live. Also, do you personally feel any "loyalty,"
"intense solidarity," or "responsibility" to others in your
own ethnic group? Explain why or why not.

7 · Basque emigration
Inside the Castilian and Spanish empire

FOR MANY centuries, Basques migrated—from the lowlands to the mountains, grazing livestock; in Europe, during military land conquests on the Iberian Peninsula; and at sea, with maritime adventures, whaling, and cod fishing. Basque society experienced many cultural and commercial contacts with outsiders, and many historians argue that Basques' knowledge of other lands and other peoples was extensive. Basques participated in the military colonization of Iberia with the Romans, and Basque names appear in Roman inscriptions and literature. There is also written documentation of three hundred years of Basque participation in the Roman military colonization of northern Europe, up to the Rhine river in Germany and to Hadrian's Wall between England and Scotland, and these documents record that Basques were also administrators in these colonization efforts (Bilbao 1992, 5).

Prior to the fifteenth century, most long-distance trade with the Basque Country revolved around wool, wines, and iron, especially as exports to England, which at the end of the 1400s named Bizkaia as the place with the most iron for export in the world. The English even gave the name "bilbo" to their finest swords in reference to the quality iron produced in and near the port of Bilbao, which is "Bilbo" in Euskara. With the increase in the use of iron for the construction of maritime vessels and large buildings such as cathedrals, England was importing 85 percent of its total iron from Bizkaia, mainly on Bizkaian vessels carrying it from Lekeitio to London and from Gipuzkoan ports to Bristol and Southampton. Basque shipbuilders increased their efficiency and the carrying capacity of their vessels by learning from and adopting

A painting of Simón de Bolívar, born in Caracas,
Venezuela, in 1783. The child of Basque immigrants,
Bolívar was known as the liberator and father of
independence of South America. His victories over
the Spaniards won independence for Bolivia, Panama,
Colombia, Ecuador, Peru, and Venezuela. Upper Peru
became a separate state, named Bolivia in Bolivar's
honor, in 1825. The constitution that he drew up for
Bolivia is considered one of his most important political
pronouncements.

---

certain aspects of Scandinavian and Italian shipbuilding.
Lapurdi and Zuberoa were still under the English crown
in the mid-1400s, and although Gipuzkoa, Bizkaia, and
Araba were related to the kingdom of Castile, England
easily benefited from its proximity to these other Basque
territories in order to enhance its own trade.

The growth of political and economic power of Castile led to expansionism and colonial pursuits in North
Africa and the Mediterranean, and the monarchy eventually sponsored the voyages of discovery that led to the

opening of the New World. The monarchy depended on sea power and a supply of iron products in order to maintain its military and commercial maritime interests. Although Castile lacked surplus quantities of both necessities, "maritime activities and the mining and manufacture of iron constituted two major underpinnings of the economy of the Basque country" (Douglass and Bilbao 1975, 67).

AFTER THE "discovery" of the Americas funded by Queen Isabella and King Ferdinand, the monarchy requested that Basque shipbuilders triple their output of vessels for the colonization of the Americas, and this implied larger, heavier and longer-distance ships. The Basques of the ports of Bizkaia and Gipuzkoa achieved this goal within only four years. This phenomenal accomplishment demonstrates that there had to be an existing sophisticated infrastructure and a developed technology in order to organize the labor, transportation, and administration involved. Administrative expertise was necessary to manage the many aspects of the relations with Castile, the preparation of human labor, the collection and movement of materials, , and the construction and finally the launching and manning of the ships themselves. Bilbao served as a financial center for the noblemen, artisans, landowners, merchants, and commercial agents who invested in the creative ventures of the New World.

The Basque territories were under three different political administrations at this time. Lapurdi and Zuberoa had been passed from the English to the French crown, today's Nafarroa and Behe Nafarroa were continued as one united Kingdom of Navarre, and Gipuzkoa, Bizkaia, and Araba were territories allied with the kingdom of Castile. Castile was the colonizer of American territories, therefore the Basques of Araba, Bizkaia, and Gipuzkoa enjoyed more favorable economic and political circumstances if they were interested in the opportunities of the New World. Later, when the Kingdom of Navarre was conquered by Castile, the Basques of Nafarroa had the same opportunities for migration inside the Spanish colonization as did those of the three other territories. The Basques of Lapurdi, Behe Nafarroa, and Zuberoa began to migrate in higher numbers after the American colonies gained their independence from Spain during the 1800s.

Juan de la Cosa, of mixed Bizkaian and Cantabrian background, but referred to as "Juancho Vizcaíno" by Queen Isabela (Bilbao 1992, 19), was second in command on the *Santa María* (built by Basques) and answered directly to its captain, Christopher Columbus. De la Cosa was an expert cartographer who in 1500 created the first complete map of the world. When the *Santa María* was shipwrecked, the crew constructed the fort of Fuerte de la Navidad on the island of Hispaniola, and thirty-nine men stayed behind to initiate the first establishment of the Hispanic colonization. When Columbus returned on his second voyage to the Americas, he discovered the colony had been destroyed. The cause seems to have been that the Basques and the "others" had divided between themselves and were then killed by the native population (Douglass and Bilbao 1975, 74).

WITHIN A FEW decades, Castilian and Basque investors were in competition with Portuguese interests for the investment possibilities of the New World and the riches that were expected. Shipbuilders and cartography experts were in great demand, and Basques were both. In 1505, the monarchy of Castile designated a representative of Bilbao to direct the necessary shipbuilding and preparation of men to be sent to the West Indies. Basques, already established in the city of Seville, began to create commercial networks between Seville in Spain and Santo Domingo in the Caribbean. The next expeditions under the Castilian crown focused on the Caribbean and lands that are today Panama, Columbia, and Venezuela, and in addition to maritime and military experts, the pioneers included Catholic missionaries, many of whom were Basque. Francisco de Garay is known to have conducted the Catholic conversion of the entire island of Jamaica in the first decades of the 1500s and also administered the creation of business networks with Puerto Rico.

SPANISH COLONIZATION of Central and South America and French control of Canada and parts of the Caribbean and Louisiana created emigration opportunities for Basques, and many were sent abroad with high administrative posts. We see examples of ethnic preference when Basques chose to do business with each other, to intermarry, and to give preference in many aspects of colonial administration, in commercial interests, in shipping, and in banking. Ships from St.-Jean-de-Luz were registered as Bizkaian and also participated in transportation to the Americas, facilitating early emigration from Zuberoa, Lapurdi, and Behe Nafarroa also.

Juan de la Cosa would lead at least seven voyages to the Americas, and Columbus led four. On Columbus's forth voyage, approximately 15 percent of the men were Basque, and one of the ships was named the *Vizcaina*. Luís de Arriaga created a plan to colonize the island of Santo Domingo with 200 Basque families divided into four different villages of fifty families each, with the expectation to stay for at least five years in exchange for ownership of the land. Queen Isabella agreed, however there were not sufficient Basque families who were committed to the plan, and this venture was not successful.

In 1518, Ferdinand Magellan presented his plan to circumnavigate the globe to the Castilian king, Charles V, and with the help of a Basque, Juan Sebastián Elcano, and 264 other men, 36 of them Basque, they set out in 1519. Magellan was killed in 1521 in the Philippine Islands, but Elcano continued on, and almost three years to the day of departure, Elcano's ship reached its home, having been the first vessel ever to make a trip around the entire Earth. This historic feat opened the imagination to future possibilities of world commerce and colonization.

THERE IS NO doubt that Basques manned the ships of colonization and that they participated in the agriculture, mining, and excavating of the New World. Segundo de Ispizua wrote in his six-volume study of the Basque emigration to the Americas during sixteenth century, "If we except the Andalusian-Extremaduran group that formed around Cortez and his relatives, there was not another group more numerous, arriving collectively, and with respect to their place of origin, than the Basques" (Ispizua, quoted in Douglass and Bilbao 1975, 76). Chain-migration networks reached full force as Basques called upon other Basques to help colonize, administer, and proselytize and to create commerce, both within the new colonies and between the colonies and the homeland. The conquest of Nueva España, New Spain, which is today's Mexico and southwestern United States, created the need for thousands of farmers, ranchers, and artisans. Other Basques, however, went beyond the Americas and in 1527 manned Cortez's ships to find the route to the Orient. In 1564, two Basque captains, Andrés de Urdaneta and Miguel López de Legazpi sailed from Nueva España to the Philippines.

Because Basques in the homeland maintained their *fueros* and universal nobility, they retained an exemp-

Basque maritime expertise resulted in Basque leadership and participation in the early voyages of discovery that led Columbus to the Americas. Depicted here in the painting of José Gamelo Alda, Christopher Columbus reaches the Western Hemisphere with three ships, including the *Santa María*, owned, captained, and manned by Basques.

---

tion from taxes on maritime activity and freedom for every Bizkaian to engage in commerce. As we will see in the next lesson, their universal nobility gave them access to administrative and authoritative positions that facilitated their New World socioeconomic status and prestige.

IN 1500, JUAN de la Cosa had drawn a map of Venezuela and named the area "Venecieula" because the native dwellings there had reminded him of Venice, Italy, "Venecia" in Spanish. During the first half of the century, various Basque captains and explorers, commercial agents, and colonizers made their way to the Venezuelan coastline and later in 1567 founded the capital,

Santiago de León de Caracas. The colonizers of what would be Venezuela actually attempted the first mobilization for independence from Castile in 1561. It was led by a Basque, Lope de Aguirre, against King Phillip II. Immigration to Venezuela was slow, and most families created large agricultural estates using imported slaves to harvest cacao for export to Europe.

IN 1728, BASQUES formed the Royal Guipuzcoan Company of Caracas (Real Compañía Guipuzcoana de Caracas) in a joint venture between Basque homeland private interests and the government of Gipuzkoa. With the permission of the Spanish king, this trading company eventually would colonize Venezuela and then organize and control its exports. After initial problems, for fifty years, the Basque trading company was financially successful, and its activities significantly influenced Basque immigration to the colony. Douglass and Bilbao discuss in detail the commercial enmities and problems between Basques, Canary Islanders, and other non-Basques, who accused the Basques of favoritism toward each other to the extent that they completely controlled the commerce of Venezuela.

In 1765, the Royal Basque Society of the Friends of the Country (Real Sociedad Bascongada de los Amigos del País) was created in Euskal Herria. This organization's purpose included "to cultivate the inclination and the tastes of the Basque Nation [*Nación Bascongada*] towards the Sciences, Letters and Arts, and to further increase the unity of the Three Basque Provinces of Alava, Vizcaya, and Guipúzcoa" (Douglass and Bilbao 1975, 105). They attempted to network Basque commercial, religious, and administrative interests, desiring to use ethnic-group loyalties to aid Basque researchers, entrepreneurs, and the Basque economy in the homeland. The majority of the society's members lived outside of the Basque Country, in the American colonies, and maintained ties to the homeland and to each other. DOUGLASS AND Bilbao illustrate how Basques were prevalent in the highest social and business circles the Spanish Empire, a position that provided the foundation for diasporic consciousness. This special status also prompted charges of elitism, clannishness, and favoritism in colonial activities, which often made Basques suspect, although this is also a typical charge by "outsiders" competing with other ethnic groups for limited resources.

Lesson seven

BIBLIOGRAPHY

Bilbao Azkarreta, Jon, ed. 1992. *América y los vascos.* Bilbao: Eusko Jaurlaritza.

Douglass, William A., and Jon Bilbao. 1975. *Amerikanuak: Basques in the New World.* Reno: University of Nevada Press.

REQUIRED READING

William A. Douglass, and Jon Bilbao, *Amerikanuak: Basques in the New World* (Reno: University of Nevada Press, 1975), chapter 2, pp 61–115.

Jon Bilbao Azkarreta, ed., *America y los vascos: 1492–1992* (Vitoria-Gasteiz: Gobierno Vasco, Departamento de Cultura, 1992).

WRITTEN LESSON FOR SUBMISSION

In the light of Robin Cohen's definition of "diaspora" from the first lesson, do you think the Basques do indeed constitute a diaspora population according to his terminology? Use examples from Lessons 5, 6, and 7

to construct your argument. From the information you
have so far, which of the Cohen's defining factors pertain
to the Basque experience in the Americas? Which do
not?

8 · Basque beginnings in Nueva Vizcaya
Initial colonization of the Americas

T HERE ARE abundant examples of trade networks in
the Basque diaspora that functioned successfully and
profitably during the colonization of the Americas and
the Philippines. As we have noted, favoritism and preferential treatment from Basques toward other Basques was
prevalent in military expeditions, religious missions,
and commercial pursuits. Basques attempted to maintain their ethnic ties to each other in their new host societies and to their families and institutions in the homeland. William A. Douglass and Jon Bilbao (1975) point
to several villages in Navarre where families worked
together through financial networks and chain migration to control entire aspects of New World trade. The
authors mention the 1683 founding of the Royal Congregation of San Fermín of the Navarrese in Madrid, which
in 1685 extended an invitation to other Navarrese living
around the world in various colonies to join their cause
and collect alms for their charity. This exhibits the diaspora mentality of solidarity with other co-ethnics around
the world. In 1713, Basques from the provinces of Araba,
Bizkaia, and Gipuzkoa also formed their own Congregation of Natives and Those Originated in the Three Provinces of Alava, Guipúzcoa, and Vizcaya and later changed
the name to the Royal Congregation of Saint Ignatius.
These Basques also asked for membership from Basques
living in the American colonies. The Real Sociedad Bascongada de los Amigos del País, the Royal Basque Society
of Friends of the Country, is another example of Basque
ethnic ties maintained across the continents—and
through the centuries—and of the use of ethnicity for
organizational purposes that included goals of education,
scientific investigation, literature, and commerce. When

The coronation of the Basque Agustín Itúrbide y
Arámburu (1783–1824) as the first emperor of Mexico.
Itúrbide crowned himself Emperor Agustin I on July
21, 1822. As emperor, Itúrbide controlled the area that
ranged from Oregon to Panama and included today's
states of California, Texas, Arizona, and New Mexico. He
was deposed by General Antonio López de Santa Anna in
1823, but returned from exile to Mexico in 1824 and was
executed.

Francisco de Ibarra founded Nueva Vizcaya in 1562, the
first province of northern Mexico in what is now the
states of Durango and Chihuahua, he declared that the
Fuero Viejo de Vizcaya would be the law of the province,
including the Bizkaian concept of an exemption from
non-local taxes, although this did not last for long after

information reached the Spanish authorities in Mexico City. So extensive was Basque involvement in the Americas that this lesson can be no more than a basic introduction to Basque participation in the initial colonization of the New World.

THE INITIAL European colonization of today's Mexico began in 1506 with several explorations of its Atlantic coastline. Hernán Cortés was sent to Nueva España from Cuba in 1519 on an expedition to search for gold and to continue the colonization from the Caribbean islands to the mainland. Jon Bilbao lists thirty-five names of known Basques accompanying Cortés on this trip (Bilbao 1992, 36). In 1520, Basques also fortified another expedition, which was led by Pánfilo de Narváez. Many early Basques were in Mexico as public scribes, civil servants and bureaucrats, government administrators, military men, construction experts, makers of military armaments, and even translators who had learned the language of the indigenous Aztecs. Basques participated in the explorations of the coasts and interior lands, and as payment for their services, they received plots of land taken from the Aztecs, which they were to cultivate.

They formed groups of colonizing settlers in various regions and eventually became miners, ranchers, and merchants. Many of the ranchers introduced cattle and sheep into the northern regions of Nueva España and today's New Mexico, Arizona, and California. Other Basque mariners returned to Euskal Herria for their families, and together they set out for the New World and the Mexican settlements and colonies of Iberians. Others continued their voyages back and forth across the globe while their families stayed in the Basque Country. As a result of the many voyages, eventually different products from American agriculture were brought to Europe and cultivated with much success. For example, by the 1520s,

maize and beans had been introduced into Basque agricultural production in the homeland, which affected
its agricultural expansion and improved the diet of the
population.

Once the indigenous population of Mexico was militarily conquered, colonizers were needed as artisans, craftsmen, builders, farmers, and ranchers, and numerous
Basques participated in this settlement, with several of
them becoming wealthy and historical figures. Basque
migration to Mexico over the centuries has included
persons of all socioeconomic classes, mainly from the
Spanish territories of Hegoalde as a result of the Spanish
colonization, their Spanish language, and early preferential treatment resulting from their universal nobility.

NUMEROUS EXAMPLES demonstrate that Basques
favored each other during the settlement process
and in commercial efforts throughout the conquest
of New Spain. Familial networks assisted information
exchange, and chain migration resulted from relatives
sending for relatives and villagers receiving fellow villagers in the new colonies. Mexico City was the capital
of the entire Spanish empire north of Panama and
was later a stop-off point for goods and people moving
between Europe and the Philippines. It was also a center
for Catholic missions and an important region for commercial trade. Mexico City served as the Spanish colonial
center for the North American and Central American
conquests. The military conquests were closely followed
by missionaries and then agriculturalists, ranchers, and
commercial merchants, who would spread along the
west coast of Nueva Vizcaya, taking possession of the
California coast and claiming missions for the king of
Spain. Among the naval engineers and maritime specialists were numerous Basques, and Basques played a

leading role in exploratory coastal voyages to present-day Alaska.

Basques tended to live together in their residential arrangements, and although there were relatively fewer Basques than other ethnic groups, the Basques were prominent. Many were well-known explorers, conquerors, and commercial giants. Basques were chosen for positions of responsibility as administrators, miners, colonists, missionaries, and merchants. They intermarried and created very potent family structures with significant political and economic clout and prestige. They founded cities such as San Miguel, Espíritu Santo de Guadalajara, and Durango, served as mayors and governors of territories, and founded new provinces such as Zacatecas, and Nueva Vizcaya. Francisco de Urdiñola, from Oiarzun, arrived to Nueva Vizcaya in 1575 and became one of its most effective governors. Basque Juan de Zumárraga was the first bishop of Mexico. Juan de Zumárraga was named as the bishop of all Nueva España in 1527, and he proceeded to surround himself with fellow Basques for the creation, construction, and manning of Catholic missions. Basque missionaries of the Basque Saint Ignatius of Loyola Jesuit order advanced to Durango, Nueva Vizcaya, in 1589.

CRISTÓBAL DE OÑATE arrived in Mexico City in 1524, and with his brother Juan and friend Miguel de Ibarra, served in the military colonization forces of Nuño de Guzmán—a non-Basque. In 1529, explorations were begun into the areas of today's Michoacán, Jalisco, Zacatecas, Durango, Sinaloa, and Nayarit. Juan and Cristóbal de Oñate governed the indigenous population of Jalisco, and later they founded Guadalajara with the assistance of many Basques in their forces. Cristóbal initiated several expeditionary forces in Nueva España and what would become the southern United States.

Cristóbal de Oñate's son, Juan de Oñate, also was an explorer and in 1598 embarked on an expedition including civilian settlers and subsequently founded a colony in today's New Mexico. Bilbao's *America y los vascos, 1492–1992* describes Oñate's group as including 129 soldiers, some with their families, nine Franciscan missionaries, eighty-three wagons full of tools and necessary provisions, and seven thousand head of cattle. In 1601, Oñate continued on into today's southern Kansas, searching for the famous mythical city of gold, while his co-captain, Vicente de Zaldívar, continued to present-day Texas and Oklahoma. In 1604, Juan de Oñate explored the Colorado River, Arizona, and the Pacific coast of Baja California.

Juan de Tolosa discovered silver at Zacatecas in 1546 and founded the city of that name, which would become one of the most significant sites of silver production in all of the Americas. Diego de Ibarra, from Eibar, Bizkaia cofounded Zacatecas and served as its first mayor.

Basques Andrés de Urdaneta and Miguel López de Legazpi opened the sea route between Nueva España and the Philippines in 1564, and thereafter, goods and people traveled between Spain and the Philippines via Mexico. The Pacific naval base of San Blas de Nayarit was not founded until 1767, but once it was established, Basque mariners and explorers investigated the northern Pacific coastline to today's Alaska, and Basque shipbuilders were brought from Euskal Herria to create a construction and repair site for Spanish ships.

AFTER A CENTURY of Basque immigration to New Spain, some Basques were already worried about the maintenance of their language and ethnic identity. In 1607, in Mexico City, Basque Baltasar de Echave Orio published his work, *Discursos de la antigüedad de la lengua cántabra Bascongada* (Treatise on the

D. XAVIER MARIA DE MUNIVE,
Conde de Peñaflorida Primer Direc
tor de la Sociedad Bascongada.

Xabier María de Munibe, Count of Peñaflorida, founded
the Royal Basque Society of Friends of the Country in
1763, with governmental approval in 1765, from his
home, the Palace of Insausti in Azkoitia, Gipuzkoa.
Regular meetings among intellectuals, economists,
agriculturalists, and mining specialists led to the
conclusion that the Basque Country needed to update
and modernize its economy. The primary focus was
educational, social, and commercial development.

antiquity of the Basque language), pleading with Basques to maintain their language, ethnicity and cultural heritage. Although there were networks for encouraging migration, employment, and commerce, Echave was preoccupied with encouraging the preservation of the cultural aspects of being Basque. There is evidence that latter Basques heeded his advice. They created their own religious brotherhood, the Hermandad de Nuestra Señora de Aránzazu, the Brotherhood of Our Lady of Aránzazu, in the Franciscan convent in Mexico City in 1671 with the requirement that the chaplain always be a Basque. In 1688, they created their own chapel, which also served as a crypt where Basques and their families could be interred with each other. In 1696, Basques decided to apply to extend their brotherhood to a confraternity, an organization of higher importance and status. Later they built the College of Saint Ignatius—founded by Francisco de Echeveste—commonly known as the Colegio de los Vizcaínos, or College of the Vizcayans, as an asylum for Basque daughters and widows of Basque families. In 1731, there were 181 donors to the college, and the construction began in 1734, with the final inauguration in 1767 after many problems with church leadership.

THE ROYAL Basque Society of the Friends of the Country, la Bascongada, had 171 members from Mexico by 1777. The Bascongada's seminary in Bergara, Gipuzkoa, had hundreds of students annually who returned to their ancestors' homeland for their educations. Of the society's over one thousand members at the end of the 1700s, nearly half were living in the New World (Douglass and Bilbao 1975, 108–9).

The estimated population of Mexico in 1742 was over three million people, and by the beginning of the 1800s, it had doubled to over six million. The increase in population necessitated an expansion of agricultural production and commercial activity, led by the export of silver to Europe. By the end of the 1700s, there were nearly three thousand mines in colonial Mexico. In 1786, Fausto de Elhuyart was selected to fill the position of general director for all technical development and education for mining programs. He was a former professor at the Basque Royal Seminary of Bergara, and in Mexico, he created a center for the study of metallurgy and mineralogy.

DOUGLASS AND Bilbao provide us with a historical snapshot of personalities who were powerful in the colonial development of Mexico, Basque missionaries serving the Catholic Church, Basque commercial merchants, Basques with maritime expertise, and Basque military administrators. We see that there were clearly interweaving colonial interests along ethnic lines. These ethnic networks are examples of what we deem so important to diaspora consciousness. They support the maintenance of ethnic identity and solidarity outside of an ethnic group's homeland. Basque descent was of both social and legal importance in relations with Castile and in the New World, and we know that Basque descent became a claim to a noble status, a requisite for high posts in the Spanish military system. Many who emigrated thus did so knowing that the Basque collective nobility would also aid them in the New World competition for advancement. Basques were in key posts in the religious, military, and political administrations of Mexico, and many used their ethnic loyalties to assist and show preference for fellow Basques for appointments and contracts. All of Alta California's governors during its period of Spanish control were Basque, and Douglass reports that new Basque immigrants entering California during the Gold Rush, beginning in 1849, sought to make connections

The 1810 insurrection by colonists in today's Argentina eventually led to its independence in 1816. Here, leaders debate in the Buenos Aires City Hall where many of the participants were Basque.

---

and to network with the established Basque elite (Douglass 1995, 10).

IN 1804, THE Basques in Mexico raised sufficient funds to publish the works of Pedro Pablo de Astarloa regarding the Basque language, and later in 1883 a collection of his works on Basque grammar and a Basque dictionary. Brother Joseph Francisco Irigoyen published a book in Mexico in 1809 that gathered Basque surnames and gave the reader their significance and meanings. By this time, many Basques in Mexico were fifth and sixth generation, and the community obviously felt a need to educate the later generations regarding their own history and culture, much as we find today in the later destinations of Canada, the United States, and Australia.

All of these are examples of Basques forming ethnic associations and ethnic networks for migration, settlement, commerce, education, religious worship, and endogamy. After the independence of Mexico from Spain, Basque immigration continued through family and ethnic networks of chain migration, although it was not the contemporary destination of choice, since the new promised lands were now Argentina and Uruguay. Later, during and after the Spanish Civil War (1936–39), Mexico once again became a preferred destination for Basque political refugees and also the home of the elected Spanish Republican government-in-exile.

IN THE EARLY 1900s, there were five different Basque periodical publications being distributed in Mexico: three in regard to politics, one reporting on sports and athletics, and the bulletin of the Basque Center of Mexico. After the Spanish Civil War there were twelve publications being published in Spanish, Basque, French, and English (Garritz and Sanchiz 1999, 175–76).

The Basque Center of Mexico City was founded in 1907 by thirteen Basques, who coincidentally also represented by their birthplaces and ancestry all seven provinces. It continues as a democratic organization with annual elections for officers to a board of directors. In 1935, the organization sought a different legal status within Mexican law and reestablished itself as a formal civil association. In 1937, there was a political split in the membership as a result of differing ideologies regarding the Spanish Civil War and the reaction to incoming Basque and Republican political refugees. While the Basque nationalists and those interested in Republican politics remained at the Basque center, others departed the association and formed their own Círculo Vasco Español, the Spanish Basque Circle. These individuals eventually rejoined the original Basque center or departed from institutional ethnic activities, and only their restaurant remains, without any type of organizational program.

EARLY BASQUE INVOLVEMENT IN OTHER NEW WORLD REGIONS

Basque commercial and maritime interests were also prominent in Guatemala, as were ethnic tensions. In the seventeenth century, Juan Martínez de Landecho, a Basque, was deposed as president of the Audiencia de Guatemala, a subdivision of the Viceroyalty of New Spain, literally an audience or court, because of fear that he would convert the Guatemala into a New Bizkaia with foral rights (Sáenz de Santa María 1969, quoted in Douglass and Bilbao 1975, 80).

BY THE BEGINNING of the seventeenth century, the Basque presence in Chile was extensive. Luis Thayer y Ojeda concluded that, following the pattern we have seen elsewhere, immigration in Chile was characterized by "the father bringing over his son, the brother sending for the brother, the cousin inducing his cousin to come, the friend inducing the friend …. This Basque immigration, improperly called *Vizcaíno*, was nothing more than a change of residence of various related families." The transnational networks of chain migration were also well established in Chile. "By the nineteenth century half of all illustrious persons in Chilean history and society were of Basque descent" (Thayer y Ojeda 1904, 32–35, quoted in Douglass and Bilbao 1975, 81). However, anti-Basque sentiments were likewise prevalent in Chile. In the capital, Santiago de Chile, Bishop Francisco de Salcedo warned the king of Spain that the royal treasury was not receiving all it was due from the area. According to Salcedo, the reason was that all of the traders, or at least most of them, were Bizkaians, and the harbor authority and the registrar who examined the cargos were both Bizkaian, as was the chief police authority. In all of the warehouses, Salcedo wrote, "the Bizkaians guarded their goods, which were great in quantity" (Thayer y Ojeda 1904, 13–14, quoted in Douglass and Bilbao 1975, 80).

THE END OF the 1500s to the mid-1600s witnessed much ethnic conflict between Basques and non-Basques in present-day Bolivia and Peru. Beginning in 1582, Basque emigrants and other emigrants from the Extremadura region of Spain fought each other in the mining districts of Potosí (Martín Rubio 1996). Dwellings were destroyed, and the ensuing forty years of violence was ethnically based. Salvador de Madariaga cites evidence that jealous tensions and anti-Basque sentiment were in part due to Basque indiscretion in the display and use of their economic and political power. There was constant civil war, with one leader even advising his followers, "let all nations be united with the Creoles. This will quicken the destruction of these Vizcaínos" (Madariaga 1950, 629).

In Peru, where the Brotherhood of Our Lady of Aránzazu in Lima dates from 1612, Basques and non-Basques remained antagonistic, and between 1661 and 1665 there were bloody incidents in La Paz. In 1665, at the mining camp of Icazota, there was an aborted plot on the part of non-Basques to eliminate the Basque population. Again in 1666, eight hundred non-Basque men returned to Icazota and set fire to Basque businesses and houses, killing three hundred and fifty persons (Idoate 1957, quoted in Douglass and Bilbao 1975, 83).

_____

It is possible that envy of Basque economic and political success, as well as Basque clannishness and exclusiveness, were factors in the anti-Basque violence. Or perhaps the Basques remained close-knit and ethnically united out of self-protection from anti-Basque sentiments and acts. Regardless, Basques were prone to collective action in the New World, and they constituted a self-aware ethnic group in colonial societies—an ethnic group that was perceived as such by outsiders. Upon arriving in the American and Filipino colonies, they continued to define themselves as Basques and tried in many cases to recreate their Basque homeland's social, economic, and political structures, such as the Fuero Viejo de Vizcaya in Mexico. There were many examples of individualism and competition between Basques, too, but Basque activities were usually interpreted by non-Basques as being collective and bordering on an ethnic-group conspiracy. Certainly, individual Basques used ethnicity to gain political favors or employment with each other, although not necessarily using their Basqueness to secure partiality from non-Basques.

THE MANY Basque place-names in New Spain record not just the successful efforts of the Basque colonists, but their tendency to cluster together. And the Spanish, for their part, often viewed the Basques as potential subverters of Spain's interests, although in their roles as administrators, clerics, and mercantilists they also served the crown's policies, which may have affected sentiments toward them. Ethnic rivalries were certainly prevalent, but in some cases anti-Basque activities could have been fundamentally opposed to the crown, yet aimed at the Basques because they were the controlling representatives of crown interests. Yet in the cases presented here, usually the non-Basques favored the ruling king.

Lesson eight

BIBLIOGRAPHY

Alday, Alberto. 1999. "Vasco-navarros en el Nuevo Mundo: Una identidad dual." In *The Basque Diaspora/La diáspora vasca*, ed. William A. Douglass , Carmelo Urza, Linda White, and Joseba Zulaika. Reno: Basque Studies Program, University of Nevada, Reno.

Bilbao Azkarreta, Jon, ed. 1992. *América y los vascos*. Bilbao: Eusko Jaurlaritza.

Douglass, William A. 1995. "Studying the Basque Presence in North America." Unpublished paper, Basques in Mexico Conference, 1995.

Douglass, William A., and Jon Bilbao. 1975. *Amerikanuak: Basques in the New World*. Reno: University of Nevada Press.

Gaarder, Lorin R. 1976. *The Basques of Mexico: An Historical and Contemporary Portrait*. PhD diss., University of Utah.

Garritz, Amaya, and Javier Sanchiz. 1999. "Estudios vascos en México." In *The Basque Diaspora/La diáspora vasca*, ed. William A. Douglass, Carmelo Urza, Linda White, and Joseba Zulaika. Reno: Basque Studies Program, University of Nevada, Reno.

Madariaga, Salvador de. 1950. *Cuadro histórico de las Indias: Introducción a Bolívar*. Buenos Aires: Editorial Sudamericana.

Martín Rubio, Carmen. 1996. "Vascos en Potosí: Minas y mineros según una fuente inédita de Arzans y Vela." In *Emigración y redes sociales de los vascos en América*, ed. Ronald Escobedo Mansilla, Ana de Zabala Beascoechea, and Oscar Alvarez Gila. Vitoria-Gasteiz: Universidad del País Vasco.

Pérez de Arenaza Múgica, José Maria, and Javier Lasagabaster Olazábal, eds. 1991. *América y los vascos: Presencia vasca en América*. Gasteiz: Departamento de Cultura, Gobierno Vasco.

Totoricagüena, Gloria. 2004. *Identity, Culture, and Politics in the Basque Diaspora*. Reno: University of Nevada Press.

REQUIRED READING

William A. Douglass, and Jon Bilbao, *Amerikanuak: Basques in the New World* (Reno: University of Nevada Press, 1975), chapter 4, pp 177–201.

William A. Douglass, "Studying the Basque Presence in North America," unpublished paper, Basques in Mexico Conference, 1995.

SUGGESTED READING

Comisión América y los Vascos, *Presencia vasca en América* (Vitoria-Gasteiz: Gobierno Vasco, Departamento de Cultura, 1991).

Jon Bilbao Azkarreta, ed,, *America y los vascos, 1492–1992* (Vitoria-Gasteiz: Gobierno Vasco, Departamento de Cultura, 1992).

WRITTEN LESSON FOR SUBMISSION

In Douglass and Bilbao's research, is there enough evidence to argue that the Basques constituted a trade diaspora in the New World? Give examples. How do you think this illustrious history affects present-day Basque maintenance of ethnic identity in Mexico? Or does it? Is the golden age of the Basques in Mexico too far from the minds of present-day Mexicans to make a difference?

9 · New destinations in the New World

SPAIN'S EMPIRE was stretched thin between its holdings in the Americas, in the Philippines, and in a few additional colonies in Asia and Africa. Although it was arguably the hegemonic leader in Europe during the fifteenth and sixteenth centuries, the monetary and human costs of maintaining such power were enormous. Regionalism and favoritism seemed inevitable, as were a chaotic lack of organization, coordination, and control over human and material resource economics. There simply were too many lands and too many populations with a multitude of differences to coordinate and to govern. Not only was the administration of the New World spinning out of control, but the heterogeneity of the Iberian Peninsula itself and the many ethnicities represented there also presented challenges for Madrid. Castile had never succeeded in "colonizing" or "nation building" in its own sphere of influence at home. The Golden Age for Spain was coming to an abrupt end, and the 1800s would bring two civil wars within Spain, wars of independence with the American colonies, and war with the United States.

Commercial networks linking the Basques in the seven provinces with Basques established in the Spanish cities of Seville and Cádiz and with Basques who were in the Americas were well established, formidable, and generally exclusive to Basques. During the seventeenth century, Cádiz and Seville enjoyed a monopoly over American commerce because of regulations that all imports and all exports from the peninsula had to enter or depart from one of these two ports. Therefore, the Basques established themselves in these two cities early on.

Many of the Basque elites in the homeland territories sent their sons for formal education to the University of Mariners and the Royal Seminarian College of San Telmo in Seville. These students would go on to become the explorers and commercial giants in the colonies. Often, Basque families would relocate to Cádiz or Seville while their sons earned their titles, and the families would establish additional commercial connections, and even contract marriages, with other Basques for their daughters and sons. Basque ethnic connections worked among family members, among co-villagers, and among people of the same province. Bizkaians assisted Bizkaians, Nafarroans assisted Nafarroans, and so on.

At the end of the 1700s, Basques from Peru and the Río de la Plata regions, among others, were sending their sons to the Basque Country for their educations at the Seminario de Vergara. By this time, of the nearly twelve hundred members of the Royal Basque Society of the Friends of the Country, almost five hundred lived in the New World. Early historians of the New World colonies mention the language factor in communications, with Basques tending to group themselves with others in the host community who spoke the same language. Evidence of commercial and trade networks along with human migration patterns demonstrate that the Basques did indeed manifest diasporic behavior of solidarity with co-ethnics, maintaining ties to the homeland, and preserving their ethnic language and identity.

BASQUES WERE prominent in the independence movements of Chile, Uruguay, and Argentina, and to this day, the positive social status attributed to Basques in these countries is related to the positive correlation with participation in the battles for emancipation. Once in their new environments, Basque immigrants were likely to define themselves specifically as Basques, and their

The Centro Vasco de Santiago, or Basque Center of
Santiago, Chile, was established informally in 1913 and
legally in 1914, with the Euzko Gaztedija, or Basque
Youth, following in 1932. In 1949, they joined forces to
create today's Eusko Etxea. Chilean historians estimate
that by the end of the eighteenth century, approximately
17 percent of the Chilean population was of Basque descent. Today there are Basque associations in Santiago,
Viña del Mar-Valparaiso, Linares, and Valdivia.
*Photograph courtesy of the Basque Government publica-
tion* Euskal Etxea.

---

numbers in Uruguay, Argentina, and Chile brought recognition to the Basque identity as something different
from Spanish. In these countries (as in Mexico), Basques
had distinguished themselves as leaders of independence movements, commercial giants, military heroes,
missionaries, and political administrators. For example,
the Basque mayor of Buenos Aires, Martín de Alzaga,

was one of the initial politicians to call for independence from Spain. Bernardo O'Higgins of Chile, known as the father of Chilean independence, was the grandson of a Basque. Mauricio de Zabala, born in Durango, Bizkaia, is known as the founder of Uruguay.

ALTHOUGH THE prominence of Basque men in the colonization of South America is well documented, there is great difficulty in determining the many roles of women in early South American societies, including the roles played by Basque women, because so little was recorded. However, it is generally agreed upon by historians and anthropologists that women worked right alongside the men in agricultural employment, such as managing small family farms and estates. Basque women were more likely to be responsible for raising the animals near the farmhouse that were meant for the family's consumption, such as chickens and hogs, and they managed gardens and small orchards, cultivating fruits and vegetables. Women were expected to administer the household and to maintain inventories of foodstuffs, clothing, and linens for their own families and for the workers who may have also lived at the family dwelling. Women worked in the dairying world in the production and distribution of milk and cheeses, especially in Uruguay and Argentina. In Uruguay, women managed Basque hotels and also worked as cooks and chambermaids. If they were members of the elite upper economic class, Basque women assisted in financial accounting and family banking. Those who were educated and were literate served as the communicators between family nodes in various geographic locations, and they wrote and read letters and disseminated information from relatives and friends.

The Vatican had given the Castilian monarchy, known as the "Catholic Kings," Queen Isabella and King Ferdinand, a monopoly to colonize and convert the indigenous population of the New World to Catholicism, and Spain had decided that they also had the power to limit immigration in their colonies to Spaniards only. Therefore, it was very complicated and even dangerous for Basques from Iparralde to immigrate to the New World until the revolutionary movements for independence there were successful in breaking away from Spain. Prior to this time, Basques from Iparralde entered the Americas disguised as Navarros, and the evidence shows that there must have been substantial numbers. There was even a dictionary and grammar guide published in 1850 in Buenos Aires by the Imprenta Errepublicanuan for Basque speakers from the North to learn Spanish. The *Gramera berria, ikasteco Eskualnec mintzatzen españoles* (The new grammar for Basques to study the Spanish language; Sarramone 1999, 94) used the Euskara spellings and vocabulary employed in Iparralde. Investigating Argentine church records of certificates of matrimony from the 1700s, we find in the listings of places of birth, that there are Basques from Saint-Etienne de Baigorry, Atardazuri, the Valley of Uriarte, Hasparren, Urdax, Ainhoa, and Espellete, all of Iparralde.

PERU

AFTER FRANCISCO Pizarro and his men defeated the Incas and one of their leaders, Atahualpa, in 1533, there were at least fourteen men with Basque surnames and places of birth in the Basque territories who were documented as beneficiaries of the spoils of the confrontation. Antonio Navarro was one of the signatories of Pizarro's founding act, which in 1534 converted the city of Cuzco, Peru, from the capital of the Incan Empire to a city of the Spanish conquerors. There were hundreds of Basques who lent their skills and professions to the

Basque sheepherders in the American West led an extremely lonely and solitary life. With the responsibility for between 1500 to 2000 head of sheep, one or two men would trail the animals everyday, moving to new grounds for better feed.
Photograph courtesy of the Basque Library, University of Nevada, Reno.

---

establishment of Lima in 1535 (originally named the Ciudad de los Reyes, or City of the Kings), and the first mayor, Rafael Ribera, was a Basque.

SCRIBES, ACCOUNTANTS, merchants, commercial shop owners, clerics, and soldiers all had Basques as cohorts. Numerous Basques in Peru in the 1600s worked in mining, such as Martín de Arriola Balerdi, who effectively took over the management of mercury mines in 1643 in Huancavelica. Many of the original Basque explorers were sea captains and mariners who probed present-day Columbia, Peru, Chile and Argentina.

AT THE beginning of the seventeenth century, a group of prominent Basques began to meet regularly at the convent of Saint Augustine in Lima. In 1612, the many Basques who were resident in Lima organized themselves in order to create the Brotherhood of Our Lady of Aránzazu, which would guide and administer charitable works and offer to conduct the burials of Lima's Basques. They acquired a chapel and crypt in the Church of San Francisco, and by 1635 they had more than one hundred members. They developed into a confraternity and later commissioned an artist to create an exact copy of the statue of Aránzazu that is in Oñati. The piece arrived at their chapel in 1646. Their goals were to unite peoples from Araba, Bizkaia, Gipuzkoa, Nafarroa, and the Cuatro Villas of Santander, Castro Urdiales, San Vicente de la Barquera, and Laredo. Members visited and cared for their own sick members, gave financial aid to members and their families in need, received and housed new Basque immigrants, paid for the marriages of orphans, and gave dowries to women who chose a life of religious dedication if they or their parents were members or if they were of Basque origin. They also barred anyone from membership who had married a black or indigenous woman. Although in 1857 the Confraternity of Our Lady of Aránzazu had 278 members of its own, in 1865 it was joined to the Public Charity of Lima and was no longer supervised by Basques.

CHILE

The first Spanish explorers in Chile traveled in search of the wondrous mines of silver and gold and in pursuit of mythical Incan treasures. Various Basques joined Lieutenant Governor Pedro de Valdivia in his explorations

during the 1540s. The capital city, Santiago del Nuevo
Extremo, now Santiago de Chile, was founded in 1541
with at least fifteen Basques participating, and the first
mayor was the Basque Francisco de Aguirre. Basques
from Bizkaia initiated links of migration after the first
to enter Chile were Basques in the military service of
the Castilian crown. The colonization of the Americas
included taking over land tracts and attempting to cultivate the soil with crops and to corral animals for meat,
skins, and wool. There was much resistance from the
indigenous populations to the Iberian colonization of the
Pacific coastline. The longest and most damaging war
recorded in the history of the Spanish colonization was
with the Arauco, beginning in 1550. Historians argue
that it was not considered ended until 1881.

COUNTLESS BASQUE clerics worked in Chile to convert the native population and to minister to the
spiritual needs of the colonizing population. In 1656, Sor
Ursula Araos from Oñati, Gipuzkoa, founded the royal
monastery of Nuestra Señora de la Victoria, Our Lady of
Victory. Many Basque clerics initially arrived in Santiago
and were later sent inland to Catholic missions throughout Chile.

Because the search for silver and gold was not successful in Chile, agricultural production and animal hus-
bandry were soon to become the major source of wealth
in this colony. The first known grain mills constructed in
Chile were those of the Basque Rodrigo de Araya. By the
end of the 1700s, Basque families were arriving to Chile
as one unit, and no longer was the colony completely
dominated by men. Around 1840, the Basque emigration to Chile outnumbered the movement to Uruguay
because of the ensuing war there, with high numbers
coming from Iparralde. Lands taken from the Arauco
needed cultivation by European immigrants, however

Basques migrating to Chile were more likely to work in the ports, in small shops, and in trade, manufacturing, and commerce than in agriculture.

In Chile, Basques from Iparralde founded many small businesses and established small manufacturing enterprises. Immigrants from Hasparren established leather tanneries and shoe factories. Others from Ustaritz, Itxassou, and Ainhoa managed mills, hotels, and food industries. Remittances sent back to the old country helped pay for the construction of new homes named "Lota" or Arauco," "Valparaiso" or "Talcahuano" (Sarramone 1999, 165) after New World geography. Just as emigrants left the Basque country and named New World sites after their hometowns and home territories, Old World Basques named new homes after the New World towns where the fortunes that paid for them had been earned.

Luis Thayer y Ojeda's study of Basques in Chile highlighted the chain migration evident in the Basque populations, and he even calculated that during the seventeenth and eighteenth centuries, 45 percent of all Chilean immigrants were Basques. He also estimated that half of the elite of Chilean society during the 1800s were of Basque descent (Thayer y Ojeda, quoted in Douglass and Bilbao 1975, 80–81).

AS WILL BE discussed in coming lessons, Basque populations in the South American communities eventually organized cultural centers known as the *euskal etxea*, or, literally, "Basque house" or "Basque center." The Basque Center of Santiago de Chile was reestablished in 1922–23, and at the inaugural ceremonies in January 1923, there were 105 founding members.

RÍO DE LA PLATA

Bruno Mauricio de Zabala (also written as "Zavala") was born in Durango, Bizkaia, in 1682, and by 1717 was named the general captain and governor of the region known as the Río de la Plata. In 1724, Zabala established the fortress of Montevideo, which developed to a municipality in 1730 and later was declared the capital city of the country, and he is considered the founding father of Uruguay. In 1725, he worked to strengthen the fort of Buenos Aires and also that of Asunción, Paraguay. Zabala was then named as the captain general of Chile in 1735. However, he died in 1736.

In 1737, immigrants from Bilbao living in Buenos Aires attempted to create a Basque trade-route monopoly between Buenos Aires and Cádiz similar to the Royal Guipuzcoan Company of Caracas's monopoly over trade in the Venezuelan colony. The plan was never approved by the authorities in Madrid, however.

THE YEAR 1810 witnessed the independence of Argentina, a country the size of continental Europe with a population of fewer than 500,000. Its rich soil favored growing foodstuffs, which at the time were needed by European societies unable to meet the demands of their growing populations. Argentine, Uruguayan, and Chilean land was abundant, but with a scant population, much-needed farm labor was scarce. In Europe, labor was abundant, and the population was growing. The majority of Basques migrating to the Southern Cone had rural backgrounds, and they traded the *baserri* for the *estancia* or *hacienda*. Life in rural Argentina or Uruguay was not so different from rural life in the Basque Country at this time. Argentina, Uruguay, and Chile were about to become the natural destinations and host societies for millions of immigrants. As we have noted before, the Argentine and Uruguayan governments even sent agents specifically to the Basque Country to encourage migration to their countries in attempts to populate the interior lands.

Immigrant departures often began with people walking several miles to a road before moving by wagon or bus to the nearest train station. Thousands of Basques traveled on passenger ships to the Americas, departing from Baiona and Le Havre, France, often carrying only one trunk with all of their possessions.
Photograph as published by DEIA.

AFTER THE beginning of the independence movements of the new Latin American states, Spain prohibited emigration of its own citizens to the former colonies until 1853. As we also have noted previously, prior to this date, Basques from the North had crossed into the South and departed from southern ports, but now southerners crossed into the northern Pyrenees and embarked on their voyages from the ports in Lapurdi. Hundreds of Basques disembarked at the port of Montevideo and then traveled into Brazil and Paraguay by land. The pampas of Argentina and the rich interior of Uruguay were much more inviting for Basque agriculturalists than the Amazon regions of Brazil, Venezuela, or Colombia. By the 1840s, Basques had established themselves as sheepherders in the south of Buenos Aires Province.

THE BASQUES immigrating to the Southern Cone in the nineteenth century were part of the second phase of Basque immigration. They were no longer government administrators for the Spanish or trained lawyers, military leaders, or professionals with formal educations. Now the typical Basque immigrant was a young rural male with almost no formal schooling, a male escaping mandatory military service for Spain or to France, a political refugee fleeing persecution after the Carlist Wars, or a brother or sister who would not inherit the family *baserri*. Particularly in Argentina and Uruguay, the second wave of Basques worked in agriculture, in animal-skin tanning factories, in the sheep raising business, in shoe factories, in dairying, in small groceries, in brick factories, and in transportation, moving foods and goods inside the cities and between the towns and the cities. Basques—especially those from Lapurdi and Gipuzkoa—almost had a monopoly on the salting and preserving of foods and later on the refrigeration business. Basques worked building the infrastructure of the countries, as well, constructing the port of Buenos Aires and the roads, railways, bridges, and canals of the interior. Basque dairies and dairy products were famous, and hundreds were employed selling milk in the neighborhoods and in town markets. Basques published journals, newspapers, and bulletins, as well as books, in Euskara and in Spanish, such as *La Baskonia, Laurak Bat, Eusko-Deya, Boletín del Instituto Americano de Estudios Vascos, Eusko-Gogoa, Irrintzi, Tierra Vasca,* and *Galeusca*.

While under the Spanish crown, Argentina's overall immigration was controlled by rules Madrid's rules prohibiting immigration by those of non-Spanish descent and restricting departures from Spain. After independence, South American political leaders opened the doors to all non-Spanish immigrants, although still preferring those of European descent. Governmental programs even arranged for transporting Europeans free of charge, and preferably entire families, so that people would stay permanently, exemplified, in Juan Bautista Alberdi's famous words, that in Argentina, "to govern is to populate." By the mid-1800s, Malthusian theories regarding the idea that overpopulation would create unsustainable economies had taken hold in Spain, which is why in 1853, the restrictions on Spanish emigration to South America were lifted. Migration became a business, with specialists providing loans, dealing with legal paperwork, and providing transportation to ports, inns, and places to eat and stay while waiting for ships and transatlantic voyages. The business of migration required the services of notaries public, of administrators for governmental offices, and of travel agencies for passage and items needed for the voyage. All were significant in expediting the constant flow of Basques—out of Bizkaia mainly, but also from the other six territories. In addition, migration between the Basque Country and the Southern Cone was actually bidirectional by the end of the 1800s. Temporary laborers returned to their homeland, and records from 1857 to 1924 show that nearly one million Spanish and French nationals departed Argentina.

As we have seen elsewhere, Basques in the Southern Cone continued to use ethnic transnational networks when selecting their destinations for migration, and former acquaintances and the abundant information that

A plaza in Bilbao during the 1890s depicts typical urban life, which would have been similar for those emigrating to Buenos Aires, Montevideo, or New York. However, the majority of Basque emigrants were from rural areas, with the largest numbers departing from Nafarroa and Bizkaia.

---

made its way back to the Old Country facilitated the arrivals. At the time, Irish and Basque immigrants dominated the sheep industries of Argentina, and when European demand for wool and lamb increased in the mid-1800s, numerous Basque families made fortunes. In the 1840s, the majority of hotels in the Uruguayan capital were owned by Basques, who had helped each other become established entrepreneurs (Azcona Pastor 1992). There were twenty-three travel agencies in Bordeaux alone that serviced Basque emigration to Uruguay (Douglass and Bilbao 1975, 122–23). In the National General

Archives of Argentina there are letters, sent as early as 1826, between an agent, Loreilhe, in Bordeaux, and the Argentine director for promoting immigration, discussing the advertising and advocacy for convincing people to depart for the Americas, and as we have noted before, the entire population growth in Iparralde during the last half of the nineteenth century was canceled by emigration (Jacob 1994, 46). Alberto Sarramone lists many hundreds of Basque surnames represented in Argentina and Uruguay that originated in Iparralde (Sarramone 1999, 154–64).

MANY OF THE Basques from Nafarroa and Behe Nafarroa who fled the armed forces of Spain and France, upon their arrival in the Río de la Plata region were forced to serve in a military capacity. War being waged in the Montevideo region from 1838 to 1852 witnessed Basque immigrants fighting for their new host society. In 1846, a special battalion named the Cazadores Vascos, or, Basque Hunters, was led by Juan Baptiste Brie of St. Jean Pied-de-Port. Unfortunately, the Basque immigrants who had fled the aftermath of the First Carlist War now found themselves fighting in another conflict in Uruguay. Punishments for Basques escaping mandatory military service in Spain were applied to the remaining families of those who departed.

While exiles were fleeing to Argentina and Uruguay in the wake of the Carlist Wars, emigration agents in the Basque Country were punished with severe fines for assisting any military escapees, and departures were very dangerous. The famine of 1846–47 aggravated already poor circumstances and drove many more to seek new lives in the Americas.

Argentina, Chile, and Uruguay were new countries with new, emerging political and economic structures, and the political ideologies of liberalism appealed to many who had suffered in France and Spain with central control of society. Following the Second Carlist War (1872–76), the more substantive aspects to the Basque local customary laws or *fueros* were abolished in Spain by the Abolitionary Foral Law of July 21, 1876. The uprising and protest among Basques extended to the Americas, and the first and the largest Basque centers—in Uruguay, the Laurak Bat, and in Argentina, the Laurac Bat—were formed in 1876 and 1877 respectively. The Laurac Bat, or Four are One, referred to the unity of the four Basque provinces.

A N ECONOMIC crisis in the 1890s forced the wages of workers and the profits of agriculturalists down to half of their previous totals, and harsh exclusive immigration laws were passed and implemented, discouraging Basques from continuing their consistent flows of chain migrations to the Southern Cone. Except for the fifteen thousand Basque political refugees who fled to Argentina in the aftermath of the Spanish Civil War (1936–39) and the Franco dictatorship (1939–75), the constant emigration of Basques to the Southern Cone nearly ended. Simultaneously, events and changing circumstances in the United States created ample opportunities that pointed to as North America another viable option for one's choice of destination.

Lesson nine

BIBLIOGRAPHY

Azcona Pastór, José Manuel. 1992. *Los paraisos posibles: Historia de la inmigración Vasca a Argentina y Uruguay en el siglo XIX*. Bilbao: Universidad de Duesto.

Douglass, William A., and Jon Bilbao. 1975. *Amerikanuak: Basques in the New World*. Reno: University of Nevada Press.

Jacob, James E. 1994. *Hills of Conflict: Basque Nationalism in France*. Reno: University of Nevada Press.

Moya, Jose C. 1998. *Cousins and Strangers: Spanish Immigrants in Buenos Aires, 1850–1930*. Berkeley: University of California Press. 1998. Pérez de Arenaza Múgica, José Maria, and Javier Lasagabaster Olazábal, eds. 1991. *América y los vascos: Presencia vasca en América*. Gasteiz: Departamento de Cultura, Gobierno Vasco.

Perez-Agote, Alfonso, Jesus Azkona, and Ander Gurrutxaga. 1997. *Mantener la identidad: Los vascos del río Carabelas*. Bilbao: Servicio Editorial Universidad del País Vasco.

Sarramone, Alberto. 1995. *Los abuelos vascos en el Río de la Plata*. Buenos Aires: Editorial Biblos Azul.

———. 1999. *Los abuelos vascos que vinieron de Francia*. Buenos Aires: Editorial Biblos Azul.

Totoricagüena, Gloria. 2001. "Una aproximación al desarrollo de la diáspora vasca." In *Kanpoko Etxe berria: Emigración vasca a América Siglos XIX–XX*. Bilbao: Museo Arqueológico, Etnográfico e Histórico Vasco.

REQUIRED READING
Jose C. Moya, *Cousins and Strangers: Spanish Immigrants in Buenos Aires, 1850–1930* (Berkeley: University of California Press, 1998), chapter 1, pp 13–44; chapter 3, pp 76–120.
William A. Douglass, and Jon Bilbao, *Amerikanuak: Basques in the New World* (Reno: University of Nevada Press, 1975), chapter 3, pp 117–76.

WRITTEN LESSON FOR SUBMISSION
Describe the differences and similarities in the push and pull factors affecting Basques who migrated to Mexico and those who later went to South America. What arguments do Douglass and Bilbao and Moya, propose to explain Basque emigration overseas when there was abundant industrial growth and employment in Baiona, Mauléon, Bilbao, and other industrial districts of Bizkaia and Gipuzkoa and prosperity in the Valle del Baztán of Navarre? Would these not serve as factors to keep Basques in the homeland?

10 · Destination Argentina
Then and now

THE LATIN American colonies began declaring their individual independence from the Spanish empire in the early 1800s. An exact accounting of Basque emigration in this time period does not exist—the pertinent agency, the Geographical and Statistical Institute in the Ministry of Agriculture of Spain, was not created until 1882. We do know that there were agencies in Iparralde devoted exclusively to recruiting and transporting Basque emigrants to the Río de la Plata region. In 1852 alone, the Argentine consul in Baiona processed 2,800 emigrants—destination Buenos Aires. According to the official passenger lists for boats leaving from Baiona, between 1832 and 1884, 64,227 persons emigrated from the Department of the Basse-Pyrénées. From the French side of the Basque Country, it is estimated that between 1832 and 1907 over one hundred thousand persons emigrated to Argentina and that the provinces of Zuberoa and Behe Nafarroa lost between twenty and twenty-five percent of their total populations. And as we noted in the Introduction, the entire population growth in Iparralde for the last half of the nineteenth century was canceled by emigration (Jacob 1994, 46).

Although Argentine immigration data for the period between 1857 to 1930 record 2,070,874 "Spanish" immigrants (Moya 1998, 1), some went back and forth and some returned to Spain. For others there are no records that contain data to enable a separation and calculation of exactly who was or was not Basque." José Maria Pérez de Arenaza and Javier Lasagabaster (1991) conservatively put the number of Basque-only emigrants to Argentina in the same period at two hundred thousand because of the illegality of emigration, the repercussions and fines that fell to the families of emigrants, the lack of record keeping, and the nonspecific records that were kept.

What is certain is that the preferred earlier destinations of Mexico, Venezuela, and Peru had taken a back seat to Argentina and Uruguay, although later in the twentieth century, as the post–World War II Argentine economy declined, so did the number of people choosing Argentina for a destination. Basque immigration to the Río de la Plata region then was reduced to a trickle and was replaced with emigration to oil-rich Venezuela and to the English-speaking countries and booming economies of the United States and Australia.

As a result of the postcolonization shift in emigration to the so-called Southern Cone, however, the Basques in Peruvian history are usually connected to Spanish conquerors and colonizers and are categorized by the general population as "Spanish," while the Basques in Río de la Plata's history are distinguished as immigrant pioneers who fought for independence and built the new countries. "Basque" in Peru is a relatively unknown and misunderstood description of either a far-off history of the colonization of the Americas or of a very few more recent immigrants from the 1900s. However, "Basque" in Argentina and Uruguay carries a positive connotation from more recent history and the creation of their respective societies, promoting a positive social status of creators.

THE FIRST expeditions to the Río de la Plata region were led by Basques representing the Spanish crown. Basque Juan de Garay, who crossed the Andes from Peru and named the territory from the Paraná River to the ocean "New Bizkaia," went on to found Buenos Aires in 1580. Thirty-four governors of the territory and then the province of Buenos Aires have been Basque, and of the province's founding council in 1810, 40 percent were

Carlist forces were overcome for the second time in the Second Carlist War (1873–76), ending the hopes for Basque regional political and economic power and for the maintenance of the existing system of *fueros*, or traditional laws. Many of the war refugees departed for Chile, Argentina, and Uruguay.

Basque. Argentina's Declaration of Independence of 1816 was signed by twenty-nine deputies, ten of whom were Basque, and four of the five priests giving the blessing were Basque. For centuries, Argentina's commercial regulatory codes were those of the Ordinance of Bilbao until 1859, when Argentina created its own commercial codes. Sociologist and economist Juan José Guaresti has noted that Argentine law is based upon the tenets of the Basque *fueros* (Guaresti 1950). The Basque foral laws were an integral part of Basque identity in the New World because of their salience in the homeland, and their protection was the most significant factor in the Carlist Wars of the nineteenth century. Basque emigration to Argentina and Uruguay thus included not only the transfer of persons, but also of their attitudes, values, and institutional principles.

Pulling potential immigrants toward Argentina were decades replete with success stories of riches and the early 1800s welcoming policies of the Argentine state. European settlers were desired and specifically mentioned in Article 25 of the Argentine Constitution of 1853, when Spain's Royal Order of September 16, 1853, coincidentally relaxed emigration restrictions: "The Federal Government will foment European immigration and will be prohibited from restraining, limiting, and taxing the entrance to the Argentine territory any foreigners who enter with the intent to till the soil, improve industries, and introduce and teach the sciences and arts." All categories of handicraftsmen, professionals, and laborers were needed for these expanding economies and societies.

FACTORS PUSHING Basques to emigrate now included the effects of the Industrial Revolution of the nineteenth century in Europe. The Industrial Revolution disrupted traditional agricultural economic activities and displaced workers from both rural and urban areas. Although it may have provided new jobs for existing urban Basques, it simultaneously displaced many as floods of migrants from the south of Spain made their way to the more industrialized Basque Country seeking employment. Basques had to compete with this cheaper labor in their home territory. At the same time, the demand for labor in South America was soaring. The cheaper manufacture of products left European artisans searching for markets, which waited open-armed in the Americas.

The 1879 military action by General Julio Argentino Roca (elected president the next year) against the Araucanian natives opened vast areas of the pampas for control by the Argentine government and increased the demand for European settlers. Updated immigration laws authorized advancing the costs of passage for certain newcomers, and particularly Basques. The Argentine government used established Basque ethnic ties and sent recruiters to Euskal Herria to advertise economic opportunities and encourage the emigration of entire families. It subsidized transatlantic passages, made land grants, established facilities for free room and board, and provided transportation and employment for the new immigrants. These favorable factors convinced thousands to leave their crowded homesteads and to head for South America.

Upon arrival in Buenos Aires, the latest Basque immigrants would most likely remain in the capital city or in a coastal town, where the majority of the population of Argentina lived. Others moved on to the Uruguayan capital and its interior. Those who were from Basque cities and were accustomed to urban administrative, factory, and commercial regimes stayed in the Argentine cities, while those Basques originating from villages and rural homesteads were attracted to the rural, agricultural life they knew.

CONSTRUCTION LABORERS, longshoremen, craftsmen, brickmakers, loggers, charcoal makers, and especially dairy producers and meat-salting-plant operators all provided employment and social connections for Basque settlers, who dominated these industries in the latter half of the nineteenth century. Euskara was the working language spoken by laborers and entrepreneurs. Basques owned many of the stores and markets in Buenos Aires and Montevideo, and their economic success strengthened their influence in Río de la Plata financial circles. There were Basque ethnic neighborhoods, barrios, such as the Barrio de la Constitución in

The Hotel Vasconia in Buenos Aires catered mostly to newly arrived immigrant Basque guests. Like Basque hotels and boardinghouses in Uruguay and the United States, the Hotel Vasconia served as an information center for employment and provided assistance with housing and family necessities, as well as a place for Basque social gatherings.

Buenos Aires, where Basques enjoyed their own markets, shops, housing, schooling, and churches and where Basque was the language of communication. Certain Catholic churches were known as Basque churches, and there was a sufficient number of Basque priests to hold masses, weddings, baptisms, and confirmations in Euskara. All of these factors point to a sustained ethnic consciousness and solidarity with other Basques three hundred years after the founding of Buenos Aires.

In the interior, a few Basques became land barons, and others earned tremendous fortunes in the livestock industries. Initially, new Basque immigrants worked in teams as sheepherders and sheep shearers, barbed-wire-fence stringers, oxcart drivers, and ranch hands and farmhands. Successful ranchers needed additional hands and often sent passage for relatives from Euskal Herria, especially younger disinherited males from the rural regions. Basques opened hotels, restaurants, and bakeries in the interior. Artisans and handicraftsmen sent word to unemployed family and friends in the homeland that their specialties were needed, appreciated, and profitable in the Americas. Hundreds of links, forged one at a time, produced a chain of transnationalism and bonds between the Southern Cone of South America and the Basque Country.

BASQUE INSTITUTIONALISM

BASQUE IMMIGRANTS in various host societies had organized themselves for economic, religious, social, and cultural reasons throughout the seventeenth, eighteenth, and nineteenth centuries, and one of the first known political organizations was created by Buenos Aires Basques. As we noted in the last lesson, in 1877, outraged by the abolition of the *fueros* after the Second Carlist War, they established the first Basque immigrant association in Argentina, the Laurac Bat, for the united four Basque provinces in Spain. Its purpose was to unite Basques in the area, to provide aid to new immigrants, and to establish improved contacts with the Basque Country. The Laurac Bat organized political protests against the Spanish government's abolition of their ancestral rights in the homeland, keeping in mind their hopes of returning to Euskal Herria with amassed fortunes. The organization created a library, an orchestra and choir, and a dancing troupe and arranged numerous cultural and political events. It also provided assistance to needy Basques in Argentina, and because many did not strike it rich in the Americas, Laurac Bat also aided funding for repatriations to the homeland.

Concurrently, additional institutions for ethnic cultural maintenance continued to sprout in Argentina. In 1882, a Basque sporting club for handball, Plaza Euskara, was inaugurated. The Basque magazine *La Vasconia* began publication in 1893, which in 1903 changed to a Basque spelling of *La Baskonia*, educating its readers in regard to current political news and cultural issues in the Basque Country, as well as disseminating news of Basque immigrant activities and events, until the outbreak of the Spanish Civil War in 1936. The Basques of Bahia Blanca, Argentina, formed the Unión Vasca de Socorros Mútuos, the Basque Union of Mutual Aid, in 1899. In 1901, the Asociación Cultural y de Beneficiéncia Euskal Echea, the Cultural and Charitable Association, Home of the Basques, was created as an asylum for indigent elderly persons of Basque descent and was combined with a boarding school for Basque orphans.

SOME BASQUE organizations in the Southern Cone and elsewhere were explicitly political. In the mid-1900s, right-wing politics in Latin American states made speaking out against the Franco regime extremely dangerous. The Basque communities in the United States, Argentina, Uruguay, Chile, Venezuela, Cuba, and Mexico, however, raised private funds to be sent to the Basque government-in-exile during the Spanish Civil War, and later, they enthusiastically received the Basque government-in-exile's president, delegations, and thousands of political exiles. The final collapse of the Spanish Republic in 1939 produced an estimated one hundred and fifty thousand exiled Spanish Basques in Iparralde alone, plus several thousand children placed throughout Europe and Mexico for their safety. There are no Basque government official statistics for Basques who entered other host countries as political refugees.

DURING THE Spanish Civil War, Argentine-Basque women formed Argentine chapters of the women's nationalist organization of the PNV, the Partido Nacionalista Vasco or Basque Nationalist Party, Emakume Abertzale Batza, or United Patriotic Women. They sent financial and material aid to the Basque Country, and received thousands of Basque political refugees in Argentina. Although the world economic depression had strengthened xenophobic and anti-immigrant legislation, one particular wave of approximately fourteen hundred Basques arrived in 1939 with the formation of the Comité Pro Inmigración, Committee for Immigration, which obtained two decrees from Argentina's president, Roberto M. Ortíz, facilitating the entry of Basque refugees to the republic. The Basque government-in-exile sent delegations to France, Belgium, Uruguay, Argentina, Venezuela, the Dominican Republic, Cuba, Mexico, and the United States, among other countries, to help organize relief and promote the Basque cause.

TODAY'S ARGENTINE BASQUES

Inasmuch as any diaspora population differs from its host society and continues to maintain networks and connections to its homeland, often problems of coexistence with, and integration into, the host population arise. However, this does not seem to have been the case in Argentina. Perhaps because of the numbers of Basque immigrants surpassed the critical mass necessary for the maintenance of Basque ethnic identity through institutional organizations and because of the positive social identity earned by earlier Basque immigrants, today's

Basques in Argentina generally do not consider it necessary to choose one identity or another.

IN PERSONAL interviews and written questionnaires of
269 self-identifying Basques from fourteen different
communities in Argentina, most stressed that their identity as "Argentine" is a political definition or one that
would define official citizenship, rather than an ethnic or
cultural category. This is understood to create and enrich
the total person, rather than to produce conflict or opposition. "I am both Basque and Argentinean simultaneously, just as I am female and Catholic simultaneously,"
illustrated one respondent. Most Basque immigrants
interviewed affirm that they had not experienced social
problems or discrimination and were actually more
likely to be highly esteemed. As exemplified above,
earlier generations of Basque immigrants had earned
the reputations of being honorable, loyal, responsible,
thrifty, and hard-working employees and this positive
social status has been preserved.

Political exiles after the Spanish Civil War and later
generations have benefited from this distinction, and
those who participate in Argentina's Basque cultural
institutions overwhelmingly respond that one of the reasons for maintaining their ethnicity has to do with the
pride associated with this positive social status. This is
not to be interpreted as contemporary instrumental use
of Basque ethnic identity, but rather as a felt responsibility both to their ancestors and to future descendants to
"retain the good name of Basques," plural, rather than
to claim a good name for oneself by being a Basque.
Unlike at the beginning of this century, when diaspora
Basques often classified themselves as French-Basque
or Spanish-Basque, at the close of the century, they rarely
even mention this qualification, and not one single ques-

In Argentina, the Emakume Abertzale Batza, the United Patriotic Women, were instrumental in the reception of Spanish Civil War exiles in their country in 1940. They gathered and then disseminated to the new immigrants information regarding employment, housing, child care, religious services, transportation, and medical services. All of the women served as volunteers. This organization continues today in Argentina with a general cultural focus.

------

tionnaire respondent chose to distinguish himself or herself as "French-Basque" or "Spanish-Basque."

THIS COLLECTIVE, as opposed to individual interpretation of identity is reiterated often by the Basque cultural centers in Argentina. The program printed for the 120th anniversary celebration of the Laurak Bat Center in Buenos Aires (held in conjunction the Semana Vasca Nacional, or the National Basque Week) in 1997 demonstrates this attitude: "For all human groups (collectivities, for the cases we are referring to), collective action is the most essential .... Collective action is what develops the group, what generates spaces of adequate coexistence, what favors personal, social, and cultural growth of its members .... In synthesis, it is what makes the whole stronger than the sum of its individual strengths."

Interviews conducted between 1996 and 2004 affirmed that although singular pronouns were used in questioning, responses generally were made in a plural form of "we Basques." Respondents did not perceive their patriotic feelings for Argentina to be in conflict with equivalent *abertzalismo*, or active Basque nationalism, for Euskal Herria, and they regularly defined both in terms of love of the culture, history, land, and people—but not of politics or the state.

TODAY, THE COLLECTIVE action of Basques in Argentina is generally directed by the eighty-nine Basque associations spread throughout the country. As of 2004, over sixty of the centers were officially integrated into the Federación de Entidades Vascos Argentinos (FEVA), the Federation of Basque Argentine Entities, and numbered approximately thirteen thousand members. The total of recognized members of the centers in Argentina refers only to the officially listed, paid member, usually the head of a household. It does not include other family members who participate or other Basques who attend center functions, but do not pay for a membership. There are another approximately thirty Basque associations not affiliated with FEVA.

The Basque centers are democratic organizations with elected boards of directors serving usually from three to five years. All are voluntary posts entailing numerous hours spent arranging events and caring for finances.

Those interviewed scoffed at the suggestion that there might be an instrumental reason behind their participation, because the donated time spent assuring that events, folk dancing instruction, choirs, language classes, dinners, festivals, libraries, and so on are successful. When asked directly if being an administrator of a Basque center, or if being Basque, has specifically helped them materially or economically in any way, all respondents answered "No."

WHY THIS DEVOTION to the preservation of Basque ethnicity? They do not view their interest as necessarily requiring a reason—because it is not rational. To the participants, "being Basque" is an emotional and spiritual part of identity. Repeatedly, Basques from all over Argentina, of all ages and generations, both genders, and all levels of education and economic class tend to be speechless when responding to questions regarding why they maintain their Basque culture after so many years or generations. Their heritage is internalized and so much a defining factor of their personae that they do not generally think about it. Instead, they feel it. For many interviewees, this "why" question is perceived as ridiculous and most unnatural, and they simply respond, "Well, of course I maintain it because it is who and what I am." Theirs is a primordialist response to the question of ethnic identity.

Who and what Argentine Basques are is difficult to analyze without biased judgment, comparison, and evaluation. Describing the preservation of ethnicity in Argentina as simply "symbolic" or connected to "leisure time," or as an "instrumental" or "primordial" ethnicity would be a gross misunderstanding and would be a use of non-Argentine and non-Basque societal, cultural, and personal paradigms. A description of these Basque immigrants' and their descendants' behaviors may give

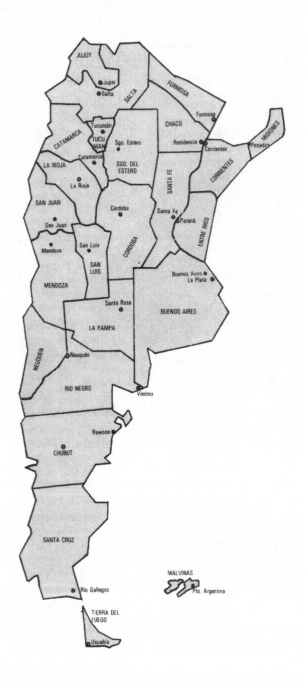

breadth to a study of what and how ethnic preservation continues. However, personal interviews and detailed observations give depth to our understanding of why it persists.

AFTER THE economic decline of Argentina in the 1950s, the dictatorships of the 1970s and 1980s, and the 1982 Malvinas War (the Falklands War), general demoralization and shame affected Argentineans over a government and a society that tolerated widespread corruption and inefficiency. It was at this time that nearly sixty new Basque organizations were created, perhaps out of Basques' desire to identify more with their Basqueness and thereby distinguish themselves from being entirely Argentine. Only 12 percent of the surveyed population used "Argentinean" to identify themselves, while others used "Argentinean-Basque," "Basque-Argentinean," or "Basque" as a self-descriptor. It may be that Basques felt a psychological need to distance themselves from the negative Argentine image and to associate more with the positive Basque reputation by publicly demonstrating that, "Yes, we live in Argentina, but we are Basque." After the Malvinas War, the new Basque associations were not created because of any new Basque immigration or internal migration of Basques already in the country. These new organizations were created

Rebelling colonists in Argentina set up their own government in 1810 and formally declared independence from Spain on July 9, 1816. Today, Argentina is the second-largest country in South America after Brazil. Its estimated population in 2004 is 39,144,753, with the capital city of Buenos Aires boasting 13,000,000. The cities of Córdoba, Rosario, and Mendoza each have over 1,000,000 residents.

in the interior regions in already existing communities
and within historic Basque populations. From Chubut to
Jujuy, Mendoza to Entre Rios, and from urban Cordoba
to rural Trenque Lauquen, Basques have been forming
societies to practice and preserve their cultural traditions
collectively.

COINCIDING WITH this period was the death of the
Spanish dictator Francisco Franco and the movement toward democracy in Spain, the creation of the
Basque Autonomous Government, its establishment of a
specific department for relations with the diaspora, and
new communications between the Basque Government
and FEVA, as well as with individual Basque centers.
Basque government appropriations—equal to 0.03 percent of the total government budget—have been made
available for diaspora Basque cultural projects. In 1996,
it gave 66.8 million Spanish pesetas (530,000.00 U.S.
dollars) to the Basque centers in Argentina, and in 1997
increased the grants to 75 million pesetas (595,000.00
U.S. dollars). The Instituto Vasco Argentino de Cooper-
ación y Desarrollo, the Basque Argentine Institute for
Cooperation and Development, headquartered in Buenos
Aires, which focuses on business and international joint
ventures between the Basque Country and Argentina,
was given an additional 12 million pesetas (95,000.00
U.S. dollars) in 1996 and 10 million (79,000.00 U.S. dollars) in 1997.

This raises the possibility that the new centers are
being formed mainly in order to receive Basque Government grant monies. The boom in interest seems to be
continuing. However, these funds are not assured from
year to year, nor do they come close to covering opera-
tional costs for any organization. There is absolutely
no financial profit for any center or individual. Most
of the associations have actually operated at a loss or

have barely broken even during the economic crises of the 1990s and the new millennium. These combined facts argue against a material motive for the creation of the new centers. The "roots" movement for Basques in Argentina has emerged at the intersection of low status for Argentine identity, comparatively high and positive position and reputation of Basque ethnicity in Argentina, intensified by euphoria over the political autonomy of the Basque Country, and an embrace of technology and globalization that affords many opportunities for communication.

THE CONTEMPORARY DYNAMICS OF ETHNICITY MAINTENANCE

THE ARGENTINE-Basque population's communications with the homeland historically were retained through the chain migration of thousands of individuals from the late 1800s to the 1950s. Personal letters and newspaper clippings sent from family and friends likewise kept immigrants linked to Euskal Herria. Those families that have lost contact over the years may rely on the Basque centers and other Basques for information. Recently, though, technological advances, includ-ing telephones, faxes, e-mail, and Internet communications, have dramatically changed the dynamics of the Basque communities in Argentina. Many of the centers now receive Basque newspapers and other timely publications regularly from the Basque Autonomous Government, which officially represents the provinces of Araba, Bizkaia, and Guipuzkoa. The government of the autonomous region of Nafarroa has also answered communications requests initiated by the Basques in Argentina, and several nongovernmental cultural organizations in the northern French provinces of Iparralde have introduced themselves and their objectives by means of publications, videos, audiocassettes, Internet Web sites, and so on. The *Euskal Etxeak* journal, published quarterly by the Basque government for distribution to diaspora Basques in twenty countries, informs readers about each other's activities in their respective communities and highlights the importance of the diaspora's efforts in maintaining traditional Basque culture.

THE BASQUE Autonomous Government has funded the purchase of computers with Internet hook-ups for every government-recognized Basque center and encourages the intercommunication of Argentine-Basques as well as their connection to other Basques and sources of information in the homeland and in other diaspora centers. Basques in Argentina are communicating by Internet with Basques in Uruguay, Chile, Venezuela, Mexico, Australia, Canada, Puerto Rico, the United States, and Belgium. The imagining of the ethnic community is now stretched to a worldwide fellowship in which each individual can be an integral part. Being Basque no longer means being born in Euskal Herria, speaking Basque, or having eight Basque surnames, as it did in the turn-of-the-nineteenth-century nationalism of Sabino de Arana. When asked about the salience of "accepting as Basques all those who feel and identify themselves as Basques," 80 percent of the respondents answered this was of "great" or "very great importance." There are no hierarchies or degrees of Basqueness in cyberidentities. The shrinking world has ceased to be a barrier to the maintenance of ethnicity because the homeland is much quicker and cheaper to access by airplane and by the above-mentioned instant communications. This translates into less nostalgic and less mythical interpretations of Basque Country lifestyles and culture and has resulted in a Basque population in Argentina that is relatively well informed, or at least

In 1946, Enrique de Umaran, of Mar del Plata, officially
proposed that the Basque centers in Argentina should
unite to form a federation with the goals of promoting
Basque activities and the maintenance of Basque identity
in Argentina. In 1953, delegates of the various centers
met to discuss proposed statutes for the federation, and
in 1954, they approved a constitution, forming the Federación de Entidades Vasco Argentina, FEVA. Shown here
is FEVA's first meeting in 1954.
*Photograph courtesy of Basque Government Urazandi
Collection.*

---

better informed, about Basque homeland issues and
realities.

IN THE new millennium, travel and even migration
have actually reversed directions as, increasingly,
Basques from Argentina are returning to Euskal Herria or visiting it for the first time. The new programs
established between FEVA and the Basque government

include return tours for senior citizens who cannot afford the trip themselves; a Gaztemundu World of Youth program for diaspora Basques between twenty and thirty years of age, brought together in the Basque Country from around the world for exposure to culture, for business, and for educational purposes; and university exchanges of professors and students. These interactions have fomented institutional networks of communication between the Basque Government and FEVA, as well as personal exchanges and strengthening of Argentine-Basque bonds with the seven provinces. Apart from FEVA and the Basque cultural centers is the Instituto Vasco-Argentino de Cooperacion y Desarrollo, the Basque-Argentine Institute for Cooperation and Development, which carries out economic and commercial research for businesses from the Basque Country interested in joint ventures with Argentine enterprises.

TODAY'S YOUNG adults in the Argentine Basque communities are less likely to think of Euskal Herria as a faraway land that will forever be idealized and never visited, as many of their parents thought. Now the main hurdle is financial and no longer military, legal, or familial. Of the 269 people I questioned, 18 percent had visited or lived in Euskal Herria between 1975 and 1985, 38 percent between 1986 and 1996, and 45 percent planned a visit before 2000. Only 33 percent had never visited or lived in the Basque Country.

Constant personal and institutional communication works to increase understanding and interest, especially in the younger participants. Whereas previously being Basque may have meant recreating a past, complete with music, dance, food, and traditions, and recreating the collective memories of a legendary homeland out of grandparents' recollections, today the manifestations of Basqueness prevailing among Argentine-Basque youth include abstract art, rock music and videos, nouvelle cuisine, aerospace engineering, and technology. Being Basque is not a folk costume to be donned a few days of the year and closeted away, any more than being Argentinean is wearing gaucho clothing on Independence Day.

M ANY OF those who have traveled to the Basque Country admitted in their interviews that their first trip began in a disappointing manner. Expectations of reenacting grandparental memories, of living the familiar nostalgic paintings and photography of yesteryear, were illusory and unrealistic. Some admitted that they felt isolated and almost pariahlike following their visits. In Argentina, they feel disconnected because they choose to focus on their ethnic identity and often define themselves as Basque. In Euskal Herria, there is also a feeling of detachment when they are defined by the homeland Basques as Argentinean. Some have felt as though they were not accepted as "true" Basques by those living in the homeland.

This is a common theme in self-analysis by immigrants, as well as in the literature of diaspora studies— the sense of not belonging exactly anywhere, physically being in one land while always thinking about the other. Respondents reported that while in Argentina, they are constantly thinking about the homeland, and when they visit the homeland, they are continually thinking about Argentina. "En el limbo" is the description given repeatedly. This physical rootlessness seems to intensify the emotional and psychological importance of ethnic identity divorced from environmental surroundings.

After returning to Argentina from the Basque Country, most are able to ridicule their own previous naïveté, imagining how unrealistic the expectation would be to see people on horseback in Buenos Aires or Rosario, expecting to hear songs from the 1920s and 1930s while

Juan Sebastián Elkano, of Getaria, Gipuzkoa, circumnavigated the Earth on the ship *Victoria*. This statue, located above the port of Getaria, was sculpted by Victorio Macho in 1922, at the 400-year anniversary of Elkano's return.
Photograph by the author.

patronizing a bar in Mendoza or Jujuy, or traveling to Mar del Plata to look for the farmhouse in which one's great-grandmother was born. The Basque Country for the most part has developed politically and economically and has changed socially along with the rest of the world, and at a much faster pace. Today's travelers experience today's Basque Country and share its population's modern impressions, although often unexpected, with other Basques upon returning to Argentina.

For those unable to visit the homeland, current news is available over the Internet, from printed materials at the Basque centers, and now from their own television sets. Galeusca TV, originally created as a consortium of Galicia, Euskadi, and Catalunya, but now a partnership between Euskal Telebista (Basque Television, with Spanish and Spanish-subtitled Basque programming) and Catalunya Television, has been transmitting twenty-four hours a day by satellite to Argentina since 1997. Programming can be downlinked by cable television only, and only audiences in certain areas of Argentina receive this channel. Its success could be a major factor in shaping attitudes about the Basque Country in all Argentineans, because currently the only news reported about issues in the Basque Country comes from the relatively right-wing Madrid press, which is then published in the Argentine national newspapers. Access to Basque television could give all who watch another version of events.

THOSE FRUSTRATED with explaining and sometimes defending Basque nationalist politics in the homeland against a flood of Spanish media are especially enthusiastic about the Basque television station as a source of information, as a means of cultural preservation, and as an equalizing force against what they perceive to be a biased Spanish nationalist media that defines Basques as "ETA-loving explosives specialists."

Most interviewees reported that they regularly correct and educate other Argentineans regarding their
perceptions of reality in the seven provinces. Although
bothersome for several, this did not seem to seriously
detract from the overall high social status that Basque
immigrants and their descendants enjoy. Basques in
Argentina want their fellow Argentineans exposed to
the homeland's view of its own history, anthropology,
science, technology, art, literature, music, gastronomy,
and tourism, as well as to its politics, so that when one
introduces oneself as a Basque, the opening conversation will not dwell exclusively on contemporary media
coverage
of ETA.

BASQUE NATIONALISM IN ARGENTINA

WHILE SOME diaspora individuals shy away from
discussing homeland politics, others do not. In
my research I have asked for opinions regarding the
most desirable future for the political administration of
the seven provinces. Although the majority of Basques
responding to my anonymous questionnaire answered
that they favor complete political autonomy through
independence for the seven provinces in Spain and
France, they do not favor the use of violence to achieve
that end. While only 1 percent responded that the current political divisions between the three provinces in
France, the three of Euskadi in Spain, and the one of
Nafarroa in Spain are the most desirable, 62 percent
favored the "seven provinces declaring independence
and unifying to form one separate country." Approximately only 28 percent agreed or strongly agreed that the
use of political violence would be effective for achieving
this goal, and in a separate question, 72 percent of the
participants thought it of "great" or "very great impor-

tance" to "support the movements for peace and anti-terrorism." In personal interviews, many also responded that they believe the importance of the state to be diminishing, especially within the European Union, and that a consociational political autonomy with recognition of the seven provinces as the Basque Country would not be "compromising" or "giving in." It would acknowledge that the current economic and political power structure in Europe is evolving toward the region, not the state.

THE MORE recent one's immigration, the more likely a person is to be knowledgeable about the politics of the Basque situation and Europe. Basques in Buenos Aires were also more likely than those of the interior to be politically active, maintain dual citizenship, and hold strong opinions regarding Basque politics. One-quarter of those few Basques who hold dual citizenship and are allowed to vote in the Spanish and Basque Country elections tend to favor the Partido Nacionalista Vasco, the Basque Nationalist Party (PNV), the most conservative of the Basque nationalist parties. However, when asked to describe the PNV platform or to give the reasons why they support this political party and not the others, respondents tend to affirm their party choice because their parents had been members of the PNV or because it was the original Basque nationalist party. Few are able to detail specific differences between the several Basque nationalist parties presenting candidates in elections.

The separate Basque centers and FEVA, as institutions, do not formally back one or another party specifically, stating in their legal statutes that they are "apolitical" organizations. Individual questionnaire responses showed 40 percent answered they did "not know enough about Basque Country political parties" to select a party that best represented their political views for Euskal

Herria. The greatest number of those interviewed tended to agree with one female political exile:

> Homeland politics would divide the people in the Basque centers and therefore it is not an issue discussed openly. Of course, friends know each other's political leanings and discuss events appropriately. Otherwise, it is better to leave Euskadi politics to those Basques that live in Euskadi. We Basques who live in Argentina have enough to worry about with Argentina, and those Basques who live in Uruguay should worry about Uruguay, etc.

THIS DOES NOT mean that Basques lack opinions regarding the circumstances of their homeland. There are significant numbers of Basques in Argentina who worry about the Basque Country's politics and economy, from fourth-generation teenagers to Franco-era exiles. There is a prominent history of aid to the Basque government-in-exile and to the homeland during the Spanish civil war of 1936–39. Argentina opened its borders to Basque political refugees due to the influence of the Comité de Pro-Inmigración Vasca de 1940, designating Buenos Aires and the Laurak Bat Center as the port of entry and host, respectively. The Argentine-Basque women of Emakume Abertzale Batza, the United Patriotic Women, commanded an impressive effort to organize all the essential aspects of preparing the new exiles with accommodation, employment information, Catholic masses in Basque, details of daily family life, and fundamental emotional and social support through constant communication and contact with the new arrivals at the Laurak Bat. Many interviewed exiles pointed to the efforts and dedication of the Basque women in Argentina

A Basque family in Wyoming poses for a photograph to be sent home to the family in Euskal Herria. The information received in the Basque Country was often only good news, with photographs of immigrants in suits and luxury clothing, strengthening the somewhat mythical image of their "rich American brothers." *Photograph courtesy of the Basque Library, University of Nevada, Reno.*

political associations, and "a part of an international network of Basques helping Basques."

ARGENTINA'S Basques also provided international leadership that clandestinely made its way to other diaspora Basques in Uruguay, Venezuela, and Mexico, keeping homeland Basques informed about the Basque government-in-exile's activities and providing crucial emotional support against the Franco repression. However, because Argentina's Peronist and subsequent military governments were pro-Franco and Basques in

Euskal Herria were depicted as atheistic Communists, political involvement took refuge in more private forums.

BECAUSE SO MANY of these refugees were political, rather than economic immigrants, and scores had been condemned to death should they return to Spain, their ideological convictions are deeply held. Some Basque-Argentine interviewees agreed that ETA's tactics had been successful and even justifiable against the Spanish Guardia Civil, the Civil Guard, and mentioned that state violence against the Basques warranted the violent response in self-defense. Others, 7 percent, applauded the left-wing party Herri Batasuna/Euskal Herritarrok's more radical nationalist economic and social party platform, but differed with its refusal to denounce the current violence of ETA. Those few respondents who support ETA's ideology still tend to decry the means it employs and argue that while there were epoch-specific justifications for ETA's tactics against the "other" of Spanish dictatorial domination, they denounce the ETA that today appears to be targeting Basques themselves. At this point, many interviewees prefer to change the topic and focus on the cultural, rather than political expressions of their identity. This negative aspect to Basque identity, while salient to those in Argentina, tends to be a secondary factor, outweighed by centuries of influential Basque pioneers, politicians, military leaders, businessmen, and artists.

The choices for participation in the preferred cultural realm are numerous. Eighteen Basque centers have organized Basque language classes with a total of approximately one hundred students and certified instructors who have lived in Euskal Herria and have participated in a three-year language-methods course. Hundreds more are taking on-line Euskara classes. Thirty-four centers have Basque folk-dancing troupes, nine have choirs, and thirteen have *frontons* and continue teaching and playing the Basque sports of *pelota*, handball, and *pala*. Most have bars and restaurants, and private *txokos* (physical quarters) for members where cooking classes and dinners take place. There are two Argentine rock music groups that sing in Basque and scattered visual artists who portray Basque themes. There are assorted Basque volleyball and football (soccer) teams that compete on behalf of their centers. Card players are a given bar fixture at any time of day and every year vie for the opportunity to represent Argentina at the world championships of the Basque card game *mus*. All of the established centers, as well as the other Basque associations and foundations, have dinners, dances, and Basque fiestas. The most celebrated festivals are those of San Fermin, on July 7; San Ignacio, on July 31; Aberri Eguna, on or near Easter Sunday; and the Argentine National Basque Week, in November.

BASQUE IDENTITY in Argentina is now transfiguring itself into a more inclusive category than the biological one previously heeded. Although many older Basques are still likely to define being Basque in connection with having descended from people born in the Basque territories who spoke Basque and had Basque surnames, Basques as a group are also evolving in their many ways of defining "us." Argentine law mandates that the Basque centers be open in membership to all Argentinean citizens. Hence, people of any heritage may join, and with the generations of intermarriage and changing surnames, it is easy to confuse who is of Basque ancestry and who is not. Ancestry thus is less a determining factor in the definition of who "we" are. Basque centers welcome those who "feel and work for the Basque culture and Basque cause."

B ASQUES IN Argentina are following the homeland's lead in changing their perspectives on what it means to be Basque. Describing some things as "more Basque than" or "less Basque than" is giving way to describing individuals and activities as "Basque in this way" or "Basque in that way." The interpretation of Basqueness is undergoing transformation from a continuum or spectrum defined in terms of hereditary and primordial constructions of ancestry, language, and place of birth to a collective answer to questions presented by the world, to put the outcome in terms of José Miguel de Barandiaran's concept of culture. Luis "Koldo" Mitxelena's writings are also recently popular with Basques in Argentina because of their pertinence to contemporary globalization and cultural reactions to modernization. "Everything changes." One epoch finishes and another commences. To preserve is not as important as it is to progress and adapt to societal change. Basques have been adapting and progressing while attempting to preserve what is most significant and consequential. At the same time, Argentine-Basques realize that it is not necessary to be Basque in a turn-of-the-nineteenth-century, Old World, Basque homeland fashion. Rather, they can be Basque in a turn-of-the-millennium, Argentine way.

Lesson ten

BIBLIOGRAPHY

Douglass, William A., and Jon Bilbao. 1975. *Amerikanuak: Basques in the New World*. Reno: University of Nevada Press.

Guaresti, Juan José. 1950. "Notas para un Apunte sobre : La influencia vasca en la Argentina." *Boletín del Insti-*

tuto Americano de Estudios Vascos 1, no. 1 (April–June).

Jacob, James E. 1994. *Hills of Conflict: Basque Nationalism in France.* Reno: University of Nevada Press.

Moya, Jose C. *Cousins and Strangers: Spanish Immigrants in Buenos Aires, 1850–1930.* Berkeley: University of California Press, 1998.

Pérez de Arenaza Múgica, José Maria, and Javier Lasagabaster Olazábal, eds. 1991. *América y los vascos: Presencia vasca en América.* Gasteiz: Departamento de Cultura, Gobierno Vasco.

REQUIRED READING

Jose C. Moya, *Cousins and Strangers: Spanish Immigrants in Buenos Aires, 1850–1930* (Berkeley: University of California Press, 1998), chapter 2, pp 45–59.

Marcelino Iriani, "El futuro de la 'cultura vasca' en Argentina," in *The Basque Diaspora/La diáspora vasca,* ed. William A. Douglass, Carmelo Urza, Linda White, and Joseba Zulaika (Reno: Basque Studies Program, 1999), pp 44–60.

Felipe Muguerza, "¿Qué es la Federación de Entidades Vasco Argentinas?" in *The Basque Diaspora/La diáspora vasca,* ed. William A. Douglass, Carmelo Urza, Linda White, and Joseba Zulaika (Reno: Basque Studies Program, 1999), pp 61–77.

William A. Douglass and Gloria Totoricagüena, "Los vascos en la Argentina," in *La Inmigración Española en la Argentina,* ed Alejandro Fernandez and Jose C. Moya (Buenos Aires: Editorial Biblos, 1999).

WRITTEN LESSON FOR SUBMISSION

The immigration of Basques to Argentina developed and continued from the 1600s through the 1950s. How do you imagine this history has affected their reputation in

Argentine society, and how do you think it has affected
their organized Basque associations? Include references
to language, politics, cultural maintenance, economic
and familial ties to the homeland, and so on.

11 · Basques Move North
Immigration and Identity in the United States

LARGE-SCALE BASQUE emigration to the United States has ceased, and new immigrants now entering the country are generally graduate students or well-educated professionals with artistic skills and/or corporate connections for employment. They leave a Basque Country that now has freely elected autonomous governments and a European Union with relative economic stability. This was not always the case, and in fact, initial Basque emigrants to the United States from the mid-1800s and the beginning of the 1900s escaped what could be described as almost the opposite circumstances. Following the two Carlist Wars, 1833–39 and 1872–76, economic stagnation, production declines, and political upheaval throughout the Basque Country produced many of the circumstances we have examined that pushed Basques out of their homeland. Access to information networks concerning possible economic opportunities and assistance was abundant. Emigration out of the Basque Country was nothing new, and, as we have seen, was quite a common option. What, then, were the new factors driving emigration to the United States at this time?

Two loom largest: the discovery of gold and silver in California, Nevada, Oregon, and Idaho in the 1850s, and the possibility of moving west across the United States by train, instead of traveling by boat around the American continent. The first Basques to migrate to the United States did so after initially emigrating to Argentina and Chile, and they traveled from South America to California in search of gold. For those coming after them, however, the completion of the Transcontinental Railroad in 1869 facilitated the movement of people across the

The Basque population of Wyoming is a result of chain migration, mostly from the area around the town of Arnegi, Behe Nafarroa, and led by this man, Jean Esponda. Esponda and his family were the first Basques to work in the sheep industry in Wyoming in the early 1900s. Because manual labor was scarce in the state at that time, Esponda requested relatives and friends from Arnegi to make the trip, and slowly, but consistently, hundreds of Basques made their way to Wyoming. *Photograph courtesy of the Basque Library, University of Nevada, Reno.*

territories to the West, where public lands were available free of charge for grazing animals, where populating the towns was a priority, and where the Basques who preceded them had put down roots.

In the rush for gold, not all of the miners would find valuable minerals, but they did need to eat every day, and the agricultural business of producing foodstuffs grew tremendously. Basque immigrants may have attempted their luck in the Gold Rush, but they soon turned their attention to raising cattle, and later to raising sheep, dairying, managing hotels and boarding houses, and farming. Brothers Pedro and Bernardo Altube, who had emigrated from Oñati, Gipuzkoa, to Argentina, and from Argentina to California in the 1850s, became livestock barons when in 1873 they created their Spanish Ranch in Independence Valley, Nevada, near Elko. In 2004, it remained one of the largest ranches in the United States. Several other Basques who had arrived in California's San Joaquin Valley moved their livestock herds east to New Mexico and Arizona and northeast into Nevada. Once the railroad connected the East Coast to the West Coast, the safer, faster, and cheaper travel enabled many more Basques to immigrate directly to the western United States after crossing the Atlantic and landing in New York. Men began to send for their sons, brothers, and cousins and then their wives, daughters, and sisters.

BASQUES WERE already spread throughout the southwestern United States as a result of the Spanish colonization of lands making up what was formerly Mexico. They were considered "Mexicans" before the land was ceded to the United States, and for generations had lived in the areas that are now California, Arizona, and New Mexico. Basques raised cattle and sheep inexpensively and with high profit margins on the public lands. English was not necessary for agribusiness, and the difficulty of mixing with other non-Spanish-speaking immigrants encouraged Basques to seek each other's business and social company.

Researching Basque surnames, we find several Basques working as gardeners at Mission Dolores, in San Francisco, as early as 1849, and the marriage-rites certificates of the Catholic churches at this time document

206 · CHAPTER ELEVEN

numerous weddings between Basques. The first Basque
hotel was constructed after the California Gold Rush on
Powell Street in San Francisco in 1866 by Juan Miguel
Aguirre. Aguirre also established the first *fronton*, or
handball court, in California. The Yparraguirre family
then built the Basque Hotel and *fronton* in the 1880s,
and soon after, other Basque hotels appeared, such as
the Hotel France, Hotel des Alpes, and the Hotel des
Basses Pyrenees. In the San Francisco earthquake and
fire of 1906, these businesses were destroyed, but others soon followed. The Hotel de España was constructed
in 1907 by the Lugea brothers, the Hotel des Pyrenees,
Hotel Iriarte, the Obrero, the Hotel Español, Hotel du
Midi, and Hotel Cosmopolitan were all prosperous in the
new century.

EARLY BASQUE emigrants pushed from their homelands by war, lack of economic opportunity, and
political repression could not resist the magnetism of
the welcoming and boisterous economies, the political
favoritism resulting from already established Basque
families in these territories, and the advantages of their
extended ethnic commercial networks. Urban life in San
Francisco was comparable to urban life in Donostia–San
Sebastián or Bilbao, and although the climate and ter-
rain of the interior were not similar, rural daily life and
agriculture in the North American West at that time were
analogous to that of Euskal Herria, just as we have seen
it was in South America. The chain migration and settlement of these immigrants typically brought Basques
from Nafarroa, Behe Nafarroa, Lapurdi, and Zuberoa to
California and southern and western Nevada, while those
from Bizkaia tended to choose Idaho, eastern Oregon,
and northern Nevada. New York, Utah, and Wyoming
received a mixture of Basques from all seven provinces.

Regardless of the geographical location, it is significant that the majority of the Basque immigrants to the West were involved in cattle ranching and especially sheepherding. The largest numbers of Basque emigrants to the United States were from rural towns and farmsteads, and they lived an underdeveloped agricultural lifestyle. The majority of the Bizkaians who chose New York and New Jersey as their destinations, by contrast, had maritime experience in their families, and they worked in the ports and on the docks of the eastern seaboard, many as merchant marines.

WHEN THE transcontinental railroad's tracks were united at Promontory Point, Utah, in 1869, Basques could make a fifteen-day voyage across the ocean to the East Coast of the United States, then continue on by rail across the continent, making the trip much safer, faster, and cheaper. Before this time, Basques from Euskal Herria who migrated directly from their homeland were forced to make the sea voyage across the Atlantic Ocean and around all of South America, and up the Pacific coast to California. It was a dangerous, expensive, and what must have seemed like a never-ending voyage. Numerous Basques in California, Idaho, and Nevada have mentioned in oral-history interviews that they do not believe their parents would have made the trip westward had it not been for the possibility of moving by train once they had reached New York. "In those days, going to the West was like going to Mars," a woman rancher mentioned. Interviewing Basques who stayed in New York, I found that numerous individuals did in fact have plans to continue west, but instead found employment in the ports of New York and New Jersey, and a few had reached the end of their tolerance for traveling and simply refused to move any further (Totoricagüena 2003).

In the mid to late 1800s, Stockton, California, near San Francisco, boasted one of the most important centers for cattle ranching, and there was an established Basque colony there. Between 1910 and 1970, there were nineteen Basque hotels in Stockton alone, including the first one constructed, the Basque Hotel. Basques established their own newspaper, *Escualdun Gazeta*, which was published in Euskara in Los Angeles, California, in the 1880s. The *Bakersfield Daily Californian* published infrequent articles in Euskara in the 1890s according to Mary Grace Paquette (1982).

THE YEARS between 1900 and 1914 registered the largest European migration to the United States in history, and Basques participated in this movement. Between 1897 and 1902, there were 636 persons with definite Basque surnames who entered the country legally through the immigration offices in New York. Eighty-six percent were male, and 77 percent were single. There most likely were many other Basques who also entered but were not counted in the 636 because their surnames were not so obviously recognizable and their hometowns were not recorded. They were listed simply as "French" or as "Spanish," with no further information. Marie Pierre Arrizabalaga's statistical study of Basques, using the census figures of 1900 and 1910, concluded that in 1900, there were approximately 986 Basques who answered census questionnaires in California, Nevada, Idaho, and Wyoming, but by 1910, that number had grown to 8,398. Many more individuals would not have known how to complete the form, or would not have known enough English to do so, or might have been completely illiterate. Other illegals would never have received the forms. Following the drought and low production years in the Basque Country from 1904 to 1906, the year of the largest Basque immigration was the next

Basques in Southern California were farmers, as well as ranchers and sheepherders. The Bastanchury Ranch in San Diego provided hay for livestock throughout the area. Upon reaching the homeland, photographs such as these perpetuated the image that everything in the United States was on a grand scale and that is was easy to become wealthy with access to such wide-open spaces. Photo 1920.
Photograph courtesy of the Basque Library, University of Nevada, Reno.

---

year, 1907. The next decade also brought a large Basque immigration to the Western states. The Spanish Council of Emigration notes that the legally registered emigrants departing between 1911 and 1915 from the four Basque provinces in Spain reached 18,547 young men. There likely were many others not included in these official government statistics.

EMIGRANTS ARRIVING in New York between 1855 and 1890 were processed at Castle Garden, among eight million other arrivals. Ellis Island officially opened as an immigrant processing station in 1892 and remained active until Congress passed the 1924 National Origins Act, which allowed potential immigrants to undergo their inspections before they left their country of origin, and not when they arrived in the United States. Until that change, there were medical inspections and hearings from a Board of Special Inquiry for those detained at the island. In 1900 alone, 3,500 people died at Ellis Island, including 1,400 children. Unescorted women and children were detained until their "safety" was assured by the arrival of a relative, a prepaid ticket to a final destination in the country (the 1930s Union Pacific train fare from New York to Boise was $54.20), or the arrival of a letter or telegram from a trusted official regarding the individual's financial ability to care for his or her own expenses. There were various other exams immigrants had to pass, such as drawing a diamond shape. This in reality tested if the individual knew how to hold a pencil, which inferred some level of education. Persons with physical deformities, sickness, or disease could be refused entry and sent back to their countries. As a result, and not surprisingly, there were also suicides at Ellis Island. Inspectors worked from 9:00 A.M. to 7:00 P.M., seven days a week, and generally questioned and inspected four hundred to five hundred immigrants each day. The relief of passing the inspection and receiving the entry permission card and stamp was emotionally overwhelming for most new entries to the United States (Totoricagüena 2003).

Once allowed to depart Ellis Island, numerous Basques were met at the docks of New York City by Valentín Aguirre or one of his sons, calling out in Basque, "Euskaldunak emen badira?" Hearing that simple question, "Are there any Basques here?" was an incredible moment, and a lifesaver for many. A Basque boardinghouse owner, Aguirre also arranged to have his sons meet the boats and search for Basques. Over the years, thousands of Basque immigrants to the United States would seek refuge at the Valentín and Benita Orbe Aguirre boarding-house, the Casa Vizcaína, and later the Santa Lucia Hotel and the Jai Alai Restaurant. Aguirre simultaneously oper-ated a travel agency and made all of his customers' travel arrangements to cross the United States, including the provision of baskets of food cooked and packed by his wife for the train journey. Other Basques just pointed to the food of passengers and hoped they were ordering the same thing. However, some were terrified of not being able to communicate in English and pretended not to want anything. They arrived to their destinations fam-ished (Totoricagüena 2002,).

CHOOSING THE United States as a destination instead of Argentina or Uruguay may seem a more trau-matic experience for these Basques because of their lack of English skills and inability to communicate, but the truth is that the majority exchanged a humid agricul-tural life for an arid agricultural and ranching lifestyle where, as we have noted before, speaking English was not necessarily crucial or compulsory. They were sur-rounded by Basques and helped each other as a result of chain migration and networking.

For example, migration to the Boise region, expanding to the Jordan Valley and Twin Falls areas, was basically the transplantation of rural Bizkaians from Santurtzi to Durango to Ondarroa. Various oral history projects con-ducted throughout the 1970s until 2003 show that the overwhelming number of Basques in the southwestern Idaho area immigrated after a relative did so, usually a

The Western Range Association of the United States organized several recruiting trips to the Basque Country in the 1950s to entice Basques to come to the American West and work three-year contracts as sheepherders. This group of new recruits traveled together from Euskal Herria to Reno, Nevada. The photograph records their day of arrival before being dispersed to various Basque businesses.
Photograph courtesy of Mary Lou Urrutia.

_____

father or an uncle. Those very first Basque immigrants to the area in the 1890s set the scene, facilitating the entry of Bizkaians to the Boise area's Treasure Valley. Early Basques went to Idaho after the discoveries of silver in De Lamar in 1889 and Silver City in 1890. Repeating the patterns of Basques in California, Oregon, and Nevada, they stayed in mining only temporarily and shifted their labors to providing foodstuffs to the mining camps. Preparing beef and lamb products meant that Basque ranchers had steady customers.

THE SHEEP INDUSTRY

For the majority of Basques arriving in the United States in the late 1800s and early 1900s, the economic means to provide for their families thus were related to agriculture and the cattle and sheep industry. The largest migration of Basques with intentions to work in the sheep industry occurred between 1900 and 1930. The demand for lamb and wool was strong, and the profit margin was substantial. Ranchers could graze their sheep free of charge on massive tracts of public lands and sheepherding in the United States became synonymous with itinerant grazing, moving herds constantly to new pastures and new regions where there were nutrients. In the high desert, this was often difficult, and sheepherders were required to move their herds every single day looking for feed, as well as for water. For the sheepherder, this lifestyle was extremely taxing and lonely.

 TYPICALLY, a recently arrived Basque sheepherder worked for another already established Basque business and was paid annually. Many chose to have their pay in sheep rather than in salary in order to establish their own herds. An average band of sheep ranged in number from nearly fifteen hundred animals to twenty-five hundred. This was not the sort of sheepherding to which any of these Basques might have been accustomed or had ever even seen. Basque sheepherders interviewed decades later still remember their fright on arriving to the United States and reaching their destinations, only to be taken to the mountains and left with supplies and a band of two thousand sheep, then told, "See you in a month at the next mountain range—just head that way." Most were completely untrained and unprepared for the physical endurance required to care for so many animals and were certainly ill equipped to deal with the psychological and emotional loneliness of the range.

Table 11-1
Census 2000

Alabama	107	Montana	564
Alaska	276	Nebraska	85
Arizona	1,655	Nevada	6,096
Arkansas	71	New Hampshire	158
California	20,868	New Jersey	643
Colorado	1,674	New Mexico	600
Connecticut	262	New York	1,252
Delaware	12	North Carolina	330
District of Columbia	180	North Dakota	39
Florida	2,127	Ohio	230
Georgia	282	Oklahoma	126
Hawaii	175	Oregon	2,627
Idaho	6,637	Pennsylvania	278
Illinois	533	Puerto Rico	187
Indiana	168	Rhode Island	23
Iowa	50	South Carolina	76
Kansas	146	South Dakota	64
Kentucky	55	Tennessee	145
Louisiana	354	Texas	1,691
Maine	57	Utah	1,361
Maryland	399	Vermont	34
Massachusetts	383	Virginia	515
Michigan	306	Washington	2,665
Minnesota	195	West Virginia	8
Mississippi	64	Wisconsin	98
Missouri	180	Wyoming	869
		TOTAL	57,793

California is clearly the state with the largest number of Basques in the United States. Erroneously, Idaho is often touted as the region having the "most Basques

During the winter months, when the sheep were down in the valleys and the men were in town, they stayed at the various Basque boarding houses, reveling in Euskara and Basque music and dance, receiving news from the Old Country, and hoping to meet Basque women. The boardinghouses played varying roles in the Basque communities and filled needs for the sheepherders in addition to supplying their lodging and meals, including social networking and economic assistance if necessary, the maintenance of ethnic identity, and the exchange of information.

PROBLEMS eventually emerged between the itinerant sheepherders moving their bands constantly on public grazing lands and the cattlemen doing the same. Cattlemen complained that the itinerant Basques allowed their sheep to overgraze the lands, ruining the chances for quick regrowth of the grasses. The Idaho territorial legislature passed legislation preventing sheepherders from bringing their sheep within two miles of any cattle range or any human habitation. A 1917 Idaho Supreme Court case, *Omaechevarria v. State of Idaho*, upheld the earlier law separating the sheep and cattle status, and the United States Supreme Court affirmed the decision to give preference to the cattle owners in prior occupancy of the public lands. Cattlemen also complained that the

---

outside of Euskal Herria," which we see here is factually incorrect. Data show that each decade larger numbers of individuals are defining themselves as Basque to the Census Bureau, even though there is no new immigration. This leads researchers to believe that Basques are just becoming aware that they have this choice on the Census form, and that additional people are choosing to manifest their Basque ethnicity.

majority of Basques were not United States citizens and were benefiting from U.S. lands and public policies, then sending their profits to their homeland and not reinvesting or buying property in the United States.

IN 1934, THE United States Congress passed the Taylor Grazing Act with the objective of protecting Western public lands from overgrazing by itinerant sheepherders. It placed an additional 173 million acres of land into federally controlled grazing districts. The new requirements for grazing on these public lands included paying fees and following a specified schedule for all of those using the land, but most importantly, it created the requirement that all of those wishing to use the federal lands had to establish a base property that they privately owned in order to be eligible for the public-lands grazing rights. Land allocation was determined by the government officials and cattle ranchers who were serving on the advisory boards, who were keen to deny access to the itinerant Basque sheepmen. As a result, Basques who migrated to the American West in search of quick riches and profitable sheep grazing were faced with the problem of making long-term investments involved in purchasing land. The 1924 Immigration Act or National Origins Act established quotas for new immigration based on a country's total number of people already in the United States, and the low numbers of Spanish residents or citizens in the United States resulted in low numbers allowed in for new migration. This act, together with the economic depression beginning with the stock market crash in 1929, when added to the Taylor Grazing Act of 1934, curbed economic opportunities for Basques migrating to the United States. However, although the flow from Euskal Herria decreased, it did not stop.

During and after the World War II, there was an agricultural labor shortage in the United States, and sheep-

In addition to learning how to live on the range
with the responsibility for many hundreds of sheep,
sheepherders had to learn to cook for themselves and for
others, if they were camp tenders. A foreman generally
brought supplies and foodstuffs once a month to the
sheepherder, who then had to invent his own recipes
for range cooking. Many first-time herders had great
difficulties, because they had had no experience with
food preparation before leaving home.
*Photograph courtesy of the Basque Library, University of
Nevada, Reno.*

---

herders were scarce. Sheep-business owners offered a
contract guaranteeing payment for the voyage from Euskal Herria to the American West in exchange for a commitment of three to five years of work with the same
outfit. Many Basques went back and forth, working until
their three-year or five-year contracts were up, then
returning to the Basque Country, only to come back
to the United States after a few years. However, in
other cases, once the sheepherder's three-to-five-year

obligation was paid off, he left the business, looking
for other employment closer to the cities, in construction, in farming, or in any other field that allowed him a
more fulfilling lifestyle. Senators from the Western States
passed amnesty legislation giving permanent residency
to Basques who had illegally entered the United States,
in hopes of luring them back to the sheep industry.

In 1950, the United States senator from Nevada, Patrick McCarran, and the Congressional representative of
Nevada, Walter Baring, worked together to pass legislation known as the Sheepherder Bills. These laws brought
about changes to immigration laws that allowed skilled
laborers to enter the country if employers specified that
this job could not be filled by anyone else already in the
United States. Sheep-industry employers argued that
no one could perform the sheepherding tasks the way
that the Basques had, and could, and that they needed
to facilitate the entry of Basques for the success of the
sheep industry. They were allowed three-year contracts,
which were renewable, but once the contract had been
completed, the herder was free to seek other employment, and the United States government allowed the
herder to apply for permanent residency, if he desired
it. By 1955, Spain's annual quota of allowed immigrants
was a very low total of only 250 persons. Under the
immigration law, the first 50 percent of the quota was
available for a preferred person with certain skills, and
the wool industry was lobbying for this to be given to
sheepherders.

IN 1960, THE California Range Association established
the Western Range Association, which would function
at the national level. Joshe Mendiburu was the president,
and the principal representative was Germán Pizarro.
The association pushed the goal of recruiting Basques
to come to the American West to work as sheepherders.

During the 1960s, sheepherders were paid an average of $200 per month for inexperienced males and $300 per month for experienced workers. The Western Range Association negotiated with the central government of Spain and established an office at the American consulate in Bilbao, from which they recruited hundreds of Basques. Between 1957 and 1970, the Western Range Association received 5,495 applications for sheepherding, and 95 percent of those were from Basques from Nafarroa and Bizkaia. However, as the economy of the Basque Country improved, fewer Basques wanted or needed to emigrate for economic reasons. During the 1970s, in addition to the appearance of competitive salaries in the Basque Country itself, Basque immigration related to sheepherding waned because of an overall decrease in the demand for sheepherders in the United States and the existence of cheaper labor available from South America. The Western Range Association therefore began to recruit sheepherders in Peru (1971) and in Mexico (1973).

IN 1966, THERE were approximately twelve hundred Basque sheepherders working in the United States, but by 1976, there were only 106 Basques with sheepherding contracts. Basques had dominated the sheep industry in the United States for almost exactly one hundred years, beginning with the establishment of the Altube brothers' Spanish Ranch in Nevada in 1873. By the 1970s, however, most of the second-generation and third-generation Basques had moved into different industries, occupations, and professions, leaving agricultural labor behind. Nevertheless, Basque ethnic identity in the United States remains tied to the collective past they share. Sheepherding and the sheep business provided opportunities to move to the United States, and even those Basques whose families were never a part of

From the 1930s to the 1950s, the New York Centro
Vasco-Americano raised funds for its organization with
individual membership dues and with the proceeds
of several annual dances. The calendar of the society
included dinners, picnics, meetings, dances, gatherings
for weekend outings, soccer matches, card playing, and
Basque folk dancing. From 1928 to 1946, the New York
community enjoyed its own "social building", but it was
razed by the New York Public Housing Authority to make
way for a new housing project.
Photograph courtesy of Anna M. Aguirre.

the sheep business still preserve this significant aspect of collective identity and the common history of Basque development in the West.

EAST COAST COSMOPOLITAN BASQUES

Basques immigrating to New York not only endured the frustrations of changing from one continent, culture, and language to another, but also the frustrations of changing from a traditional to a modern lifestyle. They not only exchanged one country for another, they exchanged country life for city life.

VALENTÍN AGUIRRE was one of those first Basque pioneers to reach New York City. He arrived from Bizkaia in 1895 and eventually become one of the most significant Basques in the United States. He and his wife, Benita Orbe, had eight children, and, as we have noted, together they established the Basque boardinghouse known as the Santa Lucia Hotel (also at one time named the Casa Vizcaína) and the Jai Alai Restaurant. Although the exact records that Aguirre meticulously kept were unfortunately later thrown away carelessly, it is estimated that several thousand Basque immigrants stayed at the hotel and benefited from the Aguirres' care and assistance in continuing on their journey to the American West.

In addition to making arrangements to get Basque immigrants their train tickets to their final destinations in the West, the Aguirres' travel agency provided information about employment and Basque boardinghouses along the way. After staying in New York for a few days to recover from their sea voyages, the majority of Basques continued on to meet the relatives and fellow villagers. Other Basques with no family commitments in the West were thrilled with the energy of the city and decided to stay. Many were from coastal towns in the Basque

Country and wanted to remain living in a coastal environment. Others had years of experience working on the docks and in maritime commerce and found jobs in the ports and docks immediately.

THE ORIGINAL Basque community took root at the foot of the Brooklyn Bridge, along the docks of Cherry and Water Streets. Besides the Aguirre hotel, there were Basque families that gave room and board to Basque immigrants in their own homes. There were Basque grocery stores and restaurants, Basque delivery businesses, and Basque wine and beer distributors. Carmen Moneo sold imported goods from the Basque Country and Spain for more than seventy-five years, until the 1980s. Most of the Basques in the Manhattan area attended Catholic mass at St. Joaquin's Church, St. Joseph's Church, and at the Our Lady of Guadalupe, where there was a Basque priest. Numerous Basque couples were married at Our Lady of Guadalupe.

A 1916 *New York Times* headline, "Basque Miners Here to Get Work," covered a rare occurrence in Basque migration. Although the century-old established pattern of Basque relocation to the United States had followed chain migration and departures of individuals to join their families or close friends, this story illustrated an aberration:

Among the 479 passengers landed yesterday from Bordeaux by the French liner Rochambeau were 100 miners from the Basque Provinces of Spain, who were on their way to work in the Pennsylvania fields, where they had been informed labor was in demand. It was suggested by an officer of the steamer that the miners might have had a hint that Spain was going to enter the war and that they wanted to be out of it.

No further information was given. However, it would be interesting to attempt to find and track these individuals' movements, because no known Basque community was ever established in Pennsylvania.

During the late 1940s and early 1950s, several of the youths in the New York Basque organization, the Centro Vasco-Americano, which had been organized in 1905 and chartered in 1913 as the Centro Vasco-Americano Sociedad de Beneficiencia y Recreo, the Basque American Society of Benevolence and Recreation, decided to form their own group called Juventud Vasca, or Basque Youth. At that time, Jon Oñatibia, the organist, *txistulari* (player of the Basque three-holed flute), dance choreographer, and Basque philologist, was living in New York, and he led Juventud Vasca and the way to forming the dance troupe Euzkadi, which eventually performed in the New York and East Coast area and also conducted a five-month tour of Canada, the western United States, Mexico, and Cuba. Oñatibia directed this group from 1950 to 1963 and later was selected by the Idaho Basque Studies Center and the North American Basque Organizations to teach Basque language, dance and *txistu* at their annual summer music camps for adolescents. In 1966, the women of the New York Basque community also formed their own group, named Andrak, or Women. During the 1960s, the attendance at Basque picnics, dinners, and dances increased from a usual one hundred and fifty to over six hundred persons.

IN THE DECADES after World War II, the Centro Vasco-Americano suffered from various problems and had to move the locale of the organization various times, renting in different places in Manhattan. In 1973, after many years of leasing and moving, the now-named Euzko-Etxea of New York bought its own building in what was a Polish neighborhood in Brooklyn. The building

was formerly a two-story church, and the Basques renovated it to include a large kitchen and bar, a dining
room, a small meeting room or classroom for language
classes, a small library, and, upstairs, a reception hall
for special events that can seat more than four hundred
persons. A stage and piano complete the second-floor
reception hall.

BECAUSE OF their involvement with the Basque government-in-exile offices located in the city during
in the 1930s–1960s, New York City Basques played a
significant role in political affairs, while the Connecticut, Rhode Island, and Florida Basque communities are
unique because of their promotion of *pelota* and *jai alai*
from the 1970s to the 1990s, when several professional
jai alai players and families were established in Hartford,
Bridgeport, Tampa, and Miami. Basque communities in
New York City and Miami were very influential in home-
land-diaspora relations because of these specific political
and sports networks.

Currently, a small group of influential Basques and
friends of Basques are leading an effort to establish an
International Basque Cultural Center in Manhattan at
the foot of the Brooklyn Bridge, where historically the
Basque immigrants lived and worked. Today it is a posh
area where millions of tourists enjoy the architecture
of the Brooklyn Bridge, the South Street Seaport and
its shops, and various other attractions. The idea is to
establish a three-story complex that will include offices
for Basque Country enterprises doing business in the
United States and vice versa, an art gallery for exhibitions, a library for research about Basques worldwide, a
restaurant and bar, and a reception-hall area for cultural
and educational activities. The Basques of New York may
very well accomplish the goal of returning to the old
neighborhood of their ancestors.

Basque immigrants to the United States registered with
the government as legal residents in order to obtain
employment and public services, which were scarce in
the 1930s. Basques often used their own ethnic networks
to obtain information regarding job openings and new
business opportunities. They also established their
own mutual aid societies to care for Basque indigents
who required help with medical bills and missed
employment.
*Photograph courtesy of the Esteban Aspiazu Family
Collection, New York.*

NABO: A NONGOVERNMENTAL ORGANIZATION TO GOV-
ERN THE ORGANIZATIONS
The North American Basque Organizations, Incorporated (NABO), was founded in 1974 with the objective
of promoting and preserving the cultural and social
activities of the Basque people, cultivating understanding and friendship among Basques and between
Basques and non-Basques, educating and enlightening
the public about Basque themes, and advancing open

communications between Basques in the United States
and Basques around the world. It is an organization serving the Basque associations in the United States that are
members of this collaborative union. Before the 1970s,
it was quite unusual for Basques in the American West
to create exchanges or to travel the long distances to
each other's functions. Today, because of the networks
established, it is not unusual for Basques from San Francisco to drive the twelve hours to arrive for Boise's Jaialdi
Festival, or for those from Fresno to drive several hours
to the Reno Basque Festival. NABO organizes Basque
cultural and educational activities and sports and card-
playing competitions between the members of the associations of the United States. It functions like a confederation because it may not infringe upon the autonomy
of any individual Basque center, and these organizations
can choose to participate in joint projects or may completely abstain.

EACH OF the member Basque organizations is self--
funded and does not depend on any public subsidy.
Each creates its own fund-raisers, charges a small fee to
members, and charges participants for activities. Basque
cultural functions are well attended by the non-Basque
populations throughout California, Oregon, Washington, Nevada, Idaho, Utah, Wyoming, and New York, and
the Basque center events are used as an educational tool
for non-Basques. However, because the latter generations are now further away from Basque culture than the
original emigrants from Euskal Herria, often the Basque
centers and clubs must educate their own members
concerning Basque topics from the homeland. Many
Basques in the United States do not know anything
about the history of their ancestors' emigration from
Europe, nor are they familiar with the history of Basques
in the United States.

THERE ARE nearly forty different Basque organizations in the United States that are members of NABO. The club in Vancouver, Canada, is also associated with NABO, and its members are invited to participate in collective functions and celebrations. In 2002, another group of Basques from Montreal inquired about joining NABO. Each center has its own history and particular interests, but all share in the common goal to preserve the Basque language and Basque culture. All have elected boards of directors who serve voluntarily, and all have various committees of volunteers that organize dinners, dances, Euskara classes, Basque cuisine classes, choirs, *dantzari taldeak* or dancing groups, tournaments of *mus* and *briska*, the card games, and *pelota*, or hand-ball championships.

NABO's function is to sponsor activities and events beyond the scope of the individual clubs and to pro-mote exchanges among Basque-Americans and with the Basque Country. The three major interclub events are the annual handball tournament, the annual *mus* tour-nament, and a two-week summer camp for Basque youth called Udaleku, or Summer Place. The first regional *pelota* tournament was held in 1976, and in 1981, play-ers representing NABO traveled to Mexico City for the amateur world championships. The *mus* tournament followed in 1977, and NABO soon hosted the world *mus* championship in San Francisco (1979) Las Vegas (1986), San Francisco again (1997), and Boise (2001).

NABO has also created networks with the Basque Autonomous Community's government and its various institutions, as well as those in Nafarroa and Iparralde, which have provided many clubs with educational mate-rials, performers from the Basque Country to enliven festivals, language teachers, scholarships for univer-sity studies, and grants for Basque center projects. It

Claudia Landa, with her husband, John, owned and managed the Basque boardinghouse called the Hogar Hotel, in Salt Lake City, Utah. She was known for her excellent cooking, and the Hogar was also recognized as a place where Basques could go if they had a long-term illness. Many boarders lived at the Hogar for years, including Basque university students and retired sheepherders. *Photograph courtesy of the Basque Library, University of Nevada, Reno.*

has good relations with the government of the Basque Autonomous Community and the Office of Relations with Basque Communities Abroad in the Lehendakaritza, or Office of the Presidency. Several institutions in Iparralde have relations with NABO clubs, mostly those in California, for sending *pelotaris*, chefs, language teachers, and dance instructors. There have been fewer contacts or exchanges with institutions in Nafarroa due to their domestic politics, but not from a lack of desire on the part of the United States organizations.

THE FINANCIAL support for NABO activities comes from membership dues, fees, from various fund-raising events, such as publishing and selling Basque calendars, from Basque Government grants, and from donations. Delegates representing each club meet three times per year to determine policy, and the annual convention for the election of officers is held during the summer, hosted by one of the clubs to coincide with their Basque festival.

NABO's most popular annual activity is the Udaleku summer music camp. The first NABO music camp was held in 1977. That year, three separate camps were organized: one in San Francisco, one in Reno, and one in Boise, under the spirited leadership of Jon Oñatibia. In 1978, the regional camps were combined into one, and the following year, Luis Manuel Pe-Menchaca arrived from Europe to teach the Basque flute, *txistu*, beginning many years of loyal and dedicated service to the Basques of the United States. In the 1990s, various instructors from Euskal Herria and from around the United States served as instructors for the participants. The NABO Udaleku program offers two weeks of instruction in Basque dancing, singing, accordion, tambourine, *mus*, *pelota*, history, cuisine, the *txalaparta* musical and percussion instrument, and the Basque language. Many of

the youngsters are third-generation or fourth generation
Basques who do not have much knowledge about Euskal Herria or about Basque culture except to know that
they are Basque by heritage. This camp gathers Basque
youths from around the United States and gives them
the opportunity to meet other Basques of their own
age and to learn new information and skills that they
can then take back to their own Basque communities
in order to disseminate the knowledge. The number of
Udaleku participants varies from fifty to –one hundred,
and the camp location is rotated between different clubs
in Wyoming, Utah, Idaho, Nevada, and California.

THE KANTARI EGUNA, or Day of the Singer, is held
in Gardnerville, Nevada, and is enjoyed by all music
lovers. *Bertsolaris*, or Basque troubadours, sing sponta-
neous poetry, and choirs and instrumental musicians
participate with pieces of original music and lyrics,
and also with established traditional Basque music. In
some years, there have been competitions with prizes,
and in others, the artists perform for exhibition only.
NABO organizes an annual *pelota* championship with
players from the centers in California, Idaho, and
Nevada. Although several of the centers in other states
have *frontons*, many are in disrepair, and there are not
enough players who can practice in order to compete.
Mus tournaments are the highlight of the year for many
members, with each club organizing their own card tournament to send their winners on to the NABO national
championships. The winners of the NABO tournament
then participate in the International World *Mus* Tournament.

An annual calendar project displays photography from
the homeland and from events in the United States. The
calendar mixes the French, Spanish, Euskara, and English languages and notifies readers of each club's events,

summer picnics, dances, and annual festivals. The newsletter *Hizketa* is published three times a year on paper and on the NABO Web site, www.basqueclubs.org, and in addition to giving current-events information regarding NABO and individual NABO clubs, it educates the reader regarding topics of Euskara, homeland history, anthropology, and culture. Individual diaspora Basques are interested in the movement for Euskara, and NABO promotes language classes in each of the member organizations. Several clubs have beginning Basque classes, and Boise has its own *ikastola*, or Basque language school, with nearly thirty children, ages three to seven.

The number of Basque organizations in the United States is actually increasing (in the 1980s there were twenty member clubs of NABO) as are the membership numbers of a few Basque centers and associations. Others, such as Gardnerville, are in decline and have considered disbanding the organization. Basques in the United States are enthusiastic about educating the public in regard to Basque language, culture, history, and traditions and they strive to promote the best of the Basque Country. When the Basque president, or *lehendakari*, José Antonio Ardanza stated that Basques in the diaspora are Euskal Herria's ambassadors, he spoke a truth with enormous, yet almost completely untapped potential.

ONE OF THE NABO member organizations is the Society of Basque Studies in America, which was founded by Dr. Emilia Sarriugarte Doyaga, Dr. Gloria Castresana Waid, and Dr. Juan Mendizabal in 1979 in San Francisco, California, with the goal of promoting Basque academic studies in the United States. A few years later, Waid and Mendizabal left the society to form their own Basque American Foundation in Fresno, California. The Society of Basque Studies in America has continued its mission with a steady international

membership and now also works to disseminate information regarding Basque culture, traditions, customs,
and folklore to the English-speaking audiences of the
world. The membership of the society is open to all who
are interested in such topics, and it does not function as
a traditional Basque center as the *euskal etxeak* do, but
instead is focused on academic research and investigations and the spreading of that information to the larger
English-speaking community. The society transcends
physical geography and adds to the imagination of a
Basque community that is not dependent on physical
interaction of its members, but instead on a common
interest in Basque studies.

THE SOCIETY of Basque Studies is engaged in many
activities throughout the year. They are represented
in NABO and at its conferences three times each year.
They serve as essential links for the Basque communities
from the eastern part of the United States to the Basque
communities and organizations in the American West.
The *Journal of the Society of Basque Studies in America*
is published annually by the society. Among other projects, the society has sponsored the First International
Basque Congress in North America in 1982, an exhibition in Chicago of three outstanding Basque sculptors
in 1984, a series of musical concerts, the creation of the
National Basque Sheepherders' Monument in Reno,
Nevada in 1989, academic conferences on Basque topics,
and the building and donation of an authentic *trainera*,
or traditional Basque fishing boat, from Basques in the
Americas to the Basques of Euskal Herria in 1998. The
society has also sponsored the Basque Hall of Fame
every year since 1981, recognizing individuals and
organizations that have contributed positively to the
image of Basques in the world.

The president of the Basque government-in-exile, José Antonio Aguirre, often attended social functions of the New York Basque community held at the Basque boardinghouse of Valentín Aguirre. The Casa Vizcaína, later named the Santa Lucia Hotel, was owned and operated by Benita Orbe and her husband, Valentín Aguirre, with five of their eight children also working in the hotel and later at the added Jai-Alai Restaurant. The Santa Lucia was a transit hotel for thousands of Basques coming into the United States and for those returning home. It gave them their first impression of America and also their last memories of "the promised land."

BASQUE ASSOCIATIONISM

In approximately 1905, Basque immigrants Valentín Aguirre, Elias Aguirre, Juan Cruz Aguirre, Escolástico Uriona, and Toribio Altuna gathered one night in a New

York apartment to discuss creating an association for Basques in New York. By 1913, they had formally incorporated the Central [sic] Vasco-Americano Sociedad de Beneficiencia y Recreo, the Basque American Center Society of Benevolence and Recreation, the first Basque center of the United States, and in 1928, they purchased their first building. Initially, this association was a mutual benefit and charity organization dedicated to helping those newly arrived and to aiding Basques living in New York who might be in financial difficulties. The Central Vasco-Americano, later renamed Centro Vasco-Americano, began as an all-male organization, although families participated in all events. This organization has continued without interruption and through many changes evolved into today's New York Euzko-Etxea.

BY THE 1920s, in Boise, Idaho, there were two private Basque insurance societies established for men only, which would pay for death benefits, hospital care, and the repatriation costs for those indigent and needing to return to the Basque Country. Escolástica Arriandiaga Ondarza saw the need for a Basque women's club similar to the Basque men's Sociedad de Socorros Mutuos (1908), or Mutual Aid Society, which had approximately two hundred members, and La Fraternidad Vasca Americana (1928), or American Basque Fraternity. She helped form the American Basque Fraternity Auxiliary group for Basque women in 1930 and served as its president for thirteen years. The Men's Mutual Aid Society, Socorros Mutuos, was a private insurance fund created in 1908 for medical emergencies, funeral costs for those unable to afford the expenses, and to insure cases of long-term disability. La Organización Independiente Sociale (sic), the Independent Social Organization, which was formed in 1933, was the women's counterpart of the Socorros Mutuos.

THE MEN'S Fraternidad Vasca Americana gave financial assistance to members, but also promoted United States citizenship, learning English, and the Americanization of Basques. The women's American Basque Fraternity Auxiliary encouraged the same goals of learning about the United States, becoming and being good citizens, and learning English.

Basques in the San Francisco area established their own mutual aid society in 1923, La Sociedad Vascongada de Beneficencia Mutua, the Basque Society of Mutual Assistance, and in 1924 created their first Basque club, the Zazpiak Bat, or Seven Are One, which lasted for ten years.

THE CHURCH OF THE GOOD SHEPHERD

Catholicism has historically been an influential aspect of Basque diasporic culture and has persisted as another sociological group marker differentiating "us" and "them." In Basque communities the United States today, contemporary Basque identity is less intertwined with religion, and many Basques interviewed mentioned they do not attend mass regularly. Others, in Boise, for example, mentioned they attend the Basque Saint Ignatius Mass because it is celebrated in the Basque language, Euskara, and others stated they "go to listen to the Biotzetik Basque choir, but ... don't really care about the religious meaning of the mass." After the 2001 Catholic celebration, several participants agreed, "It's such a beautiful mass. It's like going to a theater performance. But honestly, the religious part is not so important to me." However, in surveys of Basque communities in the United States, when asked if "continuing Catholic beliefs and traditions" was of great importance, 83 percent agreed that the "Catholic religion is consequential to Basque culture," and only 8 percent responded that

This stained glass artwork represents the king of Castile, Alfonso VIII, integrating the territory of Gipuzkoa into his own in 1200 and swearing to uphold the *fueros* of the separate Basque region. The segment is one of a series found in the executive branch's Gipuzkoan Foral Diputación building in Donostia-San Sebastián. *Photograph by the author.*

Catholicism is not of any importance. This has been evident in Basque ethnic celebrations such as Aberri Eguna, Santa Agueda, San Ignacio, and Omenaldia (Day of Remembrance) and in summer picnic festivals, which all have a Catholic mass component and have been well attended. The Boise mass for the annual Saint Ignatius feast day is standing room only, and for the Jaialdi 1995 and 2000 masses, hundreds of Basques were turned away from a brimming Saint John's Cathedral (Totoricagüena 2002a)

BASQUES HAVE been instrumental in supporting and building Catholic churches in several communities in the United States, but the Church of the Good Shepherd in Boise was the only one built with the intent of being a Basque parish with a Basque priest for a Basque congregation. In the early 1900s, there was a substantial, mobile, young population of single male sheepherders who tended to be fixated on making as much money as possible, and it was the already established Basque families that were responsible for the creation of the Good Shepherd parish. The sheepherder population certainly did not demand it. According to Father Ramon Echevarria, "They did not go to church. Sometimes masses were taken to the mountains, but when in town, young men did not go to church."

In 1910 the bishop of Boise, Alphonse Glorieux, communicated a need and desire for a priest to serve the Basque-speaking population of southern Idaho and eastern Oregon. The Bishop of Araba, in the Basque Country, responded by sending Father Bernardo Arregui to the American West. Father Arregui was born in 1866 in Tolosa, Gipuzkoa, ordained in 1889 in Vitoria-Gasteiz, Araba, and served his parish in Irura, Gipuzkoa, until 1911. During his studies, he learned to speak French and English (in addition to his Spanish and Basque) and even lived in London for six months during 1899. He arrived in Boise, Idaho, on July 11, 1911 and administered to Basque Catholics across southern Idaho, west to Jordan Valley, Oregon, and south to McDermitt, Nevada. He conducted marriages, baptisms, and confirmations, administered last rites, and celebrated funeral masses. Photographs at burial sites were often taken in order to mail the Basque Country relatives a proof that their loved one had indeed received a Christian burial.

IN 1916, THE Spanish king, Alfonso XIII, conferred upon Father Arregui the title of Vice Counsel of Spain to the United States, and he performed these responsibilities in addition to his religious duties. Father Arregui then became the pastor of the new Church of the Good Shepherd Basque parish in 1918, the only Basque church in United States history. Two buildings were purchased on the corner of Fifth and Idaho Streets, one to be converted to a church, and the other to function as the pastor's private home. The Church of the Good Shepherd was built with the financial contributions of many Basques, including substantial donations from John B. and Bene Archabal, and was completed and dedicated on March 2, 1919. Bishop Daniel M. Gorman blessed it. The church sat about one hundred worshippers and held daily masses, mostly attended by Basques. A new leader, Bishop Edward Kelly, closed the Basque Church of the Good Shepherd in 1928 with the goal of encouraging the unification of the United States Catholic Church and putting an end to separate ethnic parishes, and after the diocese used the building as a private chapel for the bishop for years, it now holds commercial offices.

Basques in the United States have enjoyed the services of many Basque priests on the East and West Coasts, and throughout the 1970s to the present, the bishop of Baiona has assigned one Basque priest to San Francisco,

California, to minister to the Basques of the United States.

COUNTING BASQUES

In the United States, the official government census results show that with each decade, higher numbers of people are claiming Basque identity. California has the largest Basque population of any state. However, Basques there are simply one more ethnic group and are not as noticeable as they are in Idaho or Nevada, where the overall population is much smaller. The 1980 census's total number for Basques was 43,140, and the 1990 census showed 47,956 Basques in the United States. The increasing numbers are more likely accounted for by already existing Basques who are just now claiming their ethnicity on this form and/or whose families are expanding, and not a result of new immigration.

ALTHOUGH BASQUES are a recognized and known ethnic group in Argentina, Uruguay, Venezuela, Chile, and Mexico, in the United States, because of the relatively smaller numbers of Basques, there is very little general knowledge among non-Basques. Even in smaller cities such as Reno, Nevada, which has a Basque club, two dance groups, three Basque restaurants, and the Center for Basque Studies at the University of Nevada, Reno, or, in Boise, Idaho, which has a Basque center, a museum and cultural center, three restaurants, two dance groups, and sporadic university courses dealing with Basque topics, there still remains a lack of recognition and understanding when a person in the United States says "I am Basque."

Lesson eleven

BIBLIOGRAPHY

Arrizabalaga, Marie Pierre. 1986. "A Statistical Study of Basque Immigration into California, Nevada, Idaho and Wyoming between 1900 and 1910." Microfilm MA thesis, University of Nevada, Reno.

Paquette, Mary Grace. 1982. *Basques to Bakersfield*. Bakersfield, Calif. : Kern County Historical Society, 1982.

Totoricagüena, Gloria. 2004. *Identity, Culture, and Politics in the Basque Diaspora*. Reno: University of Nevada Press.

———. 2003. *The Basques of New York: A Cosmopolitan Identity*. Serie Urazandi. Vitoria-Gasteiz: Eusko Jaurlaritza.

———. 2002a. *The Basques of Boise: Dreamers and Doers*. Serie Urazandi. Vitoria-Gasteiz: Eusko Jaurlaritza.

———. 2001 and 2002b. Euskonews and Media, KOSMOpolita Series. www.euskonews.com. Issues 119, 121, 184, 190, 193, 200, 206, 212, 214, 216. Donostia–San Sebastián: Eusko Ikaskuntza.

REQUIRED READING

Gloria Totoricagüena, "Celebrating Basque Diasporic Identity in Ethnic Festivals: Anatomy of a Basque Community," *Revista Internacional de Estudios Vascos* 45, no. 2 (Fall 2000): 569–98.

William A. Douglass and Jon Bilbao, *Amerikanuak: Basques in the New World* (Reno: University of Nevada Press, 1975), chapter 7, pp 327–95.

Koldo San Sebastian, *The Basque Archives: Vascos en Estados Unidos (1938–1943)* (Donostia–San Sebastian: Editorial Txertoa, 1991).

William A. Douglass, "Basque Ethnic Resurgence: Consolidation or Crisis of Heritage." Paper presented to the American Association of Anthropology, San Francisco, 1992.

WRITTEN LESSON FOR SUBMISSION
Compare Totoricagüena's analysis (2000) focusing on Boise, with Douglass's and Bilbao's (1975) observations and conclusions regarding the future for Basques in the United States diaspora communities. How accurate were Douglass and Bilbao's conclusions of thirty years ago? If a diaspora Basque in the United States does not practice homeland Basque culture, is the diaspora culture still Basque culture? Do you believe there is a continuum of Basqueness in which certain people or certain behavior is more Basque than other Basques? If diaspora Basques are not practicing homeland culture, then what makes them Basque? If a Basque living in Araba does not speak Euskara, is employed by a German company, eats frozen Italian foods regularly, drives a Toyota, watches Hollywood movies, and listens to British rock music ... what makes him or her Basque?

12 · "Home away from home"
Basque hotels and boardinghouses in the United States

B ASQUE BOARDINGHOUSES, hotels, and rooming
houses in the United States, from Valentín and
Benita Orbe Aguirre's establishment in New York City
to Juan Miguel and María Martina Aguirre's in San
Francisco, satisfied several functions for the Basque emigrants, as well as for their later-generation descendants.
The Basque boardinghouse and hotel can be understood
as a precursor to the Basque center: a physical place
where Basque immigrants could feel comfortable to
socialize with people of their own ethnicity, speak Euskara, eat recognizable foods, and know that there would
be several people willing to help them with medical,
legal, and employment issues. They were informal travel
agencies, medical offices, employment agencies, marital
match-making centers, language institutions for learning
and translating, post offices, storage units, dissemina-
tors of information, and even honeymoon destinations.
Jeronima Echeverria's masterful studies demonstrate
how these institutions facilitated connections and networks between New World and Old World Basques and
served as a "home away from home."
Echeverria points out that Old World regionalism was
evident in the choice of boardinghouses, in places where
there were more than one, for the Basque customers in
the United States. Bizkaian customers were more likely
to stay in a Bizkaian-owned or Bizkaian-operated establishment, Navarrese sought out Navarrese, and Basques
from Iparralde did the same. This seems logical, because
the language differences could be such that there might
be customers from the French Basque provinces who did
not speak Basque at all and those from the Spanish side
who spoke only Spanish. There are also differences in

the vocabulary and pronunciation of Euskara, sometimes from town to town, let alone from province to province. Of course it makes sense that lodgers would want to choose a Basque boardinghouse that would have other boarders from nearby their own villages, similar cuisine, and a similar language. Chain migration information also often determined that available details regarding the names and addresses of establishments were shared by fellow villagers, influencing one's choice of the same boardinghouse.

AS A RESULT of the U.S. Civil War (1861–65), there was a decline in industrial production, in textiles—especially wool products—in agriculture, and in livestock, and those individuals in the West who could produce these goods realized high profits. Public land grazing for sheep added to the profitability, and Basques took advantage of these opportunities by pouring into the western states. The earliest Basque boardinghouses of the 1860s and 1870s were constructed in the cities of disembarkation, and some were private homes along the overland trails for pioneer migration across the United States.

THE BEGINNINGS OF A BASQUE NETWORK
The first Basque hotel was constructed on Powell Street (near Broadway) in San Francisco in 1866 by Juan Miguel and Martina Aguirre and continued in business until the earthquake and fire of 1906. The Aguirres also built the first *fronton*, or handball court, in California. Douglass and Bilbao (1975, 418–20) describe early ship registries of passenger lists from Valparaiso to San Francisco showing 170 people with Basque surnames entering California after the announcement of the discovery of gold, from January 1849 to February 1852. Some of these Basques may have been the Aguirres' customers.

By the 1870s, the Aguirre's hotel was also known as a center for employment information regarding opportunities in California and then later for news from Nevada. Owners of California mines, ranches, and citrus groves knew they could go to the Basque boardinghouses and hotels to interview candidates for employment.

THE YPARRAGUIRRE family then built the Basque Hotel, also with its own *fronton*, in the 1880s, and soon after several other Basque hotels appeared, such as the Hotel France, Hotel des Alpes, and the Hotel des Basses Pyrenees. In the San Francisco earthquake and fire of 1906, these businesses were destroyed, but others soon followed. The Hotel de España was constructed in 1907 by the three Lugea brothers, the Hotel des Pyrenees, Hotel Iriarte, the Obrero, the Hotel Español, Hotel du Midi, and Hotel Cosmopolitan were all prosperous. The typical Basque migration pattern at this time was for newcomers to land in San Francisco and then, if they did not stay in the California cattle or sheep industry, they likely moved eastward into the Great Basin states. The peak years of Basque migration directly to California lasted until approximately the 1930s. However, as the railway system and transportation infrastructure matured, the migration pattern changed. As we have just seen, Basques then landed in New York and traveled by rail toward the West. In both cases, the majority in this migration movement was young, single, and male—individuals who needed room and board.

The San Francisco businesses attracted city workers in addition to travelers and recently arrived immigrants. Former sheepherders came to San Francisco and worked in bakeries, dairies, and in gardening, and they lived all year around in the Basque hotels and boardinghouses. Although the immigration to the smaller towns and to sheep-related employment nearly ceased in the 1950s,

Louie Elu owned and operated the Hotel de España in
San Francisco, California, from 1959 to 1983, first with
Fermin Huarte and later with Elu's wife, Marie. With
the end of heavy immigration and the establishment of
the San Francisco Basque Cultural Center in South San
Francisco, fewer Basques patronized the existing Basque
hotels and boardinghouses for accommodations or weekend social functions. Several of the San Francisco Basque
establishments now function as Basque restaurants only
or have been sold, often to Chinese families.
*Photograph courtesy of the Basque Library, University of
Nevada, Reno.*

Basque immigration to San Francisco continued. During World War II, when the Japanese-Americans were interned in war camps for questions of dual loyalty and suspected allegiance to Japan, their businesses were confiscated or simply abandoned, and gardeners of Japanese ancestry were almost nonexistent. Basques moved into this field and called for their relatives to come from Euskal Herria to work with them in their new California gardening and landscaping businesses. The San Francisco boardinghouses continued on robustly as a result of this continuous immigration until the 1990s.

The boardinghouses served Basque-style cuisine and offered a place for their lodgers as well as outside diners to enjoy a Basque meal. As we have already noted, many of the Basque establishments also built *frontons*, or outdoor *fronton* walls, in order to entice boarders to stay with them and to lure weekend customers to have dinner and drinks while watching the *pelota* matches. Owners organized regular dances that were exclusively for their Basque boarders and Basque customers. Customers could enjoy each other's company, often resulting in lasting friendships and romances. Weekends often saw more than one hundred Basques traveling to town or visiting the boardinghouses on Sundays in order to playing *mus* and enjoy a *pelota* match and an afternoon of discussions and gossip. Dances were held on Saturday nights, with live accordion music for dancing, singing, and socializing.

BOARDINGHOUSE owners and employees worked in many capacities outside their job descriptions. They were interpreters and translators for doctor's appointments and for visits to the bank, employment agents, psychological counselors attempting to decrease loneliness, and amanuenses, writing and reading letters for illiterates. They stored the belongings of sheepherders who would be on the range or in the mountains for months at a time. They gave lessons in the English language and United States history. Owners could never take a vacation, or sometimes even afford to be sick, because the boarders always needed to eat and have their linens cleaned. Boardinghouse "mothers" often arranged or chaperoned dates between their borders and their serving girls. When sheepherders left for the hills, often their wives stayed at the Basque boardinghouses, or if pregnant and living somewhere else, Basque women often came into town and stayed in a Basque establishment until the delivery of the child. These homes also functioned as accommodations for children who lived in remote areas and needed to attend school in town. Basques who were ill and alone often lodged at the boardinghouses, where they knew another Basque would take care of them. The institutions even substituted for churches in the small towns where there was no Catholic church. Weddings, baptisms, and rosaries were held in the hotel and boardinghouse lobbies.

STOCKTON, CALIFORNIA, near San Francisco, was an influential city in the cattle and sheep livestock industry and played a significant role in the development of California. Its location on the railroad tracks facilitated its eventually becoming one of the most important livestock centers in the world. By 1917, there were over twenty Basque families and numerous single males, and by 1920, there were five Basque accommodations establishments, three from Hegoalde and two from Iparralde. The California Hotel, the Central Hotel, the Royal, La Baskonia, La Coste, the Ospital, and the Wool Growers were a few of the establishments of the early 1900s. The majority of the existing Basque boardinghouses and hotels in Stockton were demolished in 1957

The Hogar Hotel, Salt Lake City, Utah, owned by John and Claudia Landa for fifty years. They established their business in 1927 in this building, which was constructed in 1877 in the city center near the train tracks. At this time, the rail lines transported people and goods to Los Angeles, or to Nampa, Idaho, near Boise. From 1960 to 1970, the Hogar Hotel was managed by Milagros y Gracian Etchepar. It was sold to non-Basques in 1977 after John Landa's death.
Photograph courtesy of the Basque Library, University of Nevada, Reno

---

when the city bought out the properties to raze them and then construct new apartment complexes.

BASQUE MINERS and sheepherders in the area of Fresno, California, have had the choice of the Basque Hotel and the Santa Fe Hotel and Restaurant since the 1920s. The businesses continue with mostly non-Basque clientele. In Bakersfield, California, Basques from the town of Aldudes were the majority, and by 1900 there were four Basque hotels. Even today in this county, almost 95 percent of the sheep raised are from Basque-owned businesses (Zubiri 1998, 154). We can count ten Basque boardinghouses in Los Angeles between 1878 and 1888, and the Basque newspapers, the *California'ko Eskual Herria* and the *Escualdun Gazeta*, carried advertisements from a few in the area. They advertised *frontons* and nearby businesses, and one hotel even had a corral for the sheepherders' sheepdogs, which came into the city with them.

BOARDINGHOUSES FOLLOWED THE SHEEPHERDERS
It is estimated that between 1870 and 1890, more than two million sheep were trailed from California into Nevada. Following this migration of sheep, the numbers of officially recorded Basques in Nevada grew from 180 in 1900 to 986 in 1910, and these people needed accommodations and meals. Echeverria suggests that after the first Basque entered an area and established a sheep business, generally, within five years a Basque boardinghouse was founded (Echeverria 1999b, 39). In Arrizabalaga's study, she notes that in 1900, thirty-two Basque individuals listed themselves as boardinghouse or hotel owners or workers, and that by 1910 the number of Basques employed in the boardinghouses had flourished to 329 people (Arrizabalaga 1986, 126). These Basque businesses were often constructed near the train stations of the town, and traveling passengers could see the signs from the train platform.

WINNEMUCCA, Nevada was one of the most important cities for Basque migration because the railroad from San Francisco had reached it in 1868, facilitating the movement of people, livestock, and goods. Elko also was connected to the railway in 1868, and the Basques followed, with several of the original Basque hotels continuing to this day, and others developed as restaurants. The Commercial Hotel was established in Reno, Nevada, in 1917 and soon was followed by the Star, the Santa Fe, the French Hotel, the Altona, the Indart, the Hotel Español, the Toscano, the Martin, and Louie's Basque Corner. Carson City and Garnerville have also had their Basque establishments, and those in Gardnerville continue as restaurants open to the general public.

Jordan Valley, Oregon, is situated between Winnemucca, Nevada, and Boise, Idaho, and it was also a historically significant point of Basque migration that needed boardinghouses for gold miners and sheepherders. In 1889, José Navarro and Antonio Azcuenaga left McDermitt, Nevada, with one loaded packhorse and walked north across the high desert until they reached Jordan Valley. Navarro and Azcuenaga are the first known Basques in that area, but others soon followed from California and Nevada and then directly from the Basque Country. Basques constructed a *fronton* in 1915, which was renovated in 1997. Agustín Azcuenaga built the Jordan Valley Hotel, and José Navarro later established the Monopoly Hotel. Domingo Yturri and his sister, Eustaquia Marquina, managed the Basque boardinghouse named the Yellow House. Eulogio and Trinidad Madariaga and the Elorriaga family also gave accommodation to Basques in their own private residences.

IN BOISE, Idaho, customers of Basque hotels, boardinghouses, and rooming houses were most likely in the sheep business, and they shared information about unfriendly and threatening cowboys and about public mandates outlawing public grazing. The work cycles of the year brought spring as the time for sheep shearing in the valley, and herders and shearers needed lodging after a day's work. Those who brought the wool into Boise to send it by train to market and to commercial centers also needed a place to stay. Their patterns of work helped establish the need for boardinghouses, and the hotel workers and owners could plan for their busy seasons.

BOARDINGHOUSE businesses changed hands often and also changed locations. For example, one of Boise's most famous boardinghouse owners was Mateo Arregui, from Berriatua, Bizkaia. Mateo and Adriana Arregui married in the Basque Country and upon arriving in Boise began managing the Oregon Hotel, built by Antonio Azcuenaga in 1900, which was across from the Oregon Short Line Railroad depot. Next, they managed the Capitol Rooms in 1905. They sold this enterprise in 1912 to José and Crusa Arostegui and Pedro and Maria Epeldi. The Arreguis then managed the Modern Rooming House, which in 1912 had 238 Basque herders who either lived there or left personal items, according to Arthur Hart (the *Idaho Statesman*, September 25, 1986). The Arreguis sold this to Ventro Urresti, who later sold it to Eustaquio and Guillerma Ysursa Ormaechea, who sold it in 1925 to her brothers, Benito and Asunción Ysursa, and Tomás and Antonia Ysursa. Mateo Arregui then ran the DeLamar with his second wife, Maria Dominga Goicoechea, and later they moved this business to another location until they left the lodging business completely in 1945. Laura and Hilario Arguinchona then managed the DeLamar from 1945 to 1961.

As was the case elsewhere. the Basque boardinghouses in Boise's downtown also served as hospitals, sports facilities, employment agencies, interpretation and translation centers, post offices and message centers, and depositories for herders' valuables. Many practiced their English and received help with citizenship information from Victoria Letemendi Urresti and Espe Alegria.

Between 1891 and 1920, there were seventeen different boardinghouses in Boise, managed at various times by different families. During the decade of the 1920s, there were thirteen. These ethnic institutions supplied precious economic opportunities for employment for Basque immigrants and first-generation women. They served myriad purposes including promoting functional, emotional, and psychological well-being for Basque women. The boardinghouses gave women opportunities for financial independence, and hundreds worked as supplies buyers, preparing and serving meals, finishing laundry, doing light house maintenance, cooking, cleaning, and caring for children. A few Basque women were hired as hostesses. However, for the majority of women, working at a boardinghouse equaled seven days of unrelenting physical work preparing meals, laundering by hand, ironing, and cleaning up after the boarders. Employment or ownership of the businesses also put them into contact with others in the community. In Nampa, Idaho, Tomasa Mallea Jausoro dealt with many non-Basque-speaking people because of her hotel business—for example the Chinese selling eggs, the Japanese selling vegetables, and the French at their bakeries.

Yakima, Washington, had its own twenty-five-room Hotel Bascongado, opened in 1912 by Espectación Elizalde and later owned and managed by her daughter, Elena Elizalde Arralde, until 1993.

BASQUES WHO chose to move to Utah had generally already tried other states and other employment before they tried mining there. The Church of Latter Day Saints, the Mormon Church, had almost completely monopolized farming, ranching, and livestock raising, and it was difficult for Basques to break into the market. Although mining jobs were dangerous, English was not a necessary skill, and many immigrants took these jobs.

The Hotel de France welcomed Basque immigrants, mainly from Iparralde, to San Francisco and the Bay Area. Although Basque immigration to other Western states began to diminish in the 1970s, consistent, although small numbers still immigrated to New York and San Francisco. Many in the Bay Area were employed as gardeners and, living in the city, needed accommodation. They also needed social interaction with fellow Basques, which they found at the boardinghouses. *Photograph courtesy of the Basque Library, University of Nevada, Reno.*

Basques needed accommodations, and soon Basque hotels and boardinghouses were established. Matilde Zabala operated a Basque boardinghouse in the copper mining region of Highland Boy from 1920 to 1950. John and Claudia Landa managed the Hogar Hotel in Salt Lake City beginning in 1927, and customers stayed anywhere from a few days to a few decades. Different owners managed this establishment, keeping the name Hogar Hotel until 1977. The Otasue Fonda Español and the Realty Hotel were also Basque hotels from the 1940s through the 1970s. Salt Lake City's location on the railroad between Boise and Los Angeles facilitated movement and the sharing of information between Basques in Salt Lake City and those in other Basque communities.

OGDEN, UTAH, was a crossroads of railways moving people and goods east and west as well as north and south. Various rail companies provided service through Ogden, and customers changed lines there to continue their journeys. However, in many circumstances, the journeys were days long, and travelers needed a rest before continuing on to a final destination. Whether they were sheepherders whose contracts had expired and were returning to Euskal Herria, first-time immigrants making their way from New York to Elko, or Basque honeymooners traveling to see the Wasatch Mountains, thousands of Basques passed through the boardinghouses of Ogden. In 1910, the Pyrenees French Basque Hotel and the Vizcaíno were built, and nearby were the French and the Allies Hotels, businesses run by Basques.

BASQUE BOARDINGHOUSES AND NEIGHBORHOODS IN NEW YORK

The United States Census of 1910 recorded 1,944,357 foreign-born persons resident in New York City. Adjusting to this inundation of immediate multiculturalism would have been extremely difficult without a retreat such as one's own small Basque neighborhood. It is likely that Basques forfeited personal and business relationships with others because they had to rely on each other. Many of those from Spain had the advantage of being able to communicate in Spanish with the many Galicians in the area and could reach a high level of understanding with the Italians. Basques from the French side were more dispersed throughout the city and more likely to use their French language skills, although they also gathered for social events at various hotels. William Douglass and Jon Bilbao wrote in their classic Basque diaspora book *Amerikanuak*, "Elderly informants estimate that by 1920 there might have been as many as eight to ten thousand Basques residing in New York City, with most concentrated in a thirty-square block area around Cherry Street" (Douglass and Bilbao 1975, 341). The majority at that time worked in marine commerce, either in the merchant marines, on passenger liners, or on the docks. The South Street Seaport was a stone's throw away, and for the Basques from the fishing villages of the Bizkaian coast, life on the New York waterfront encompassed familiar sights, sounds, and smells.

BASQUES ALSO owned and operated small businesses in this area from the 1900s to the 1950s. "Plencia" and Sabina Bajeneta Bilbao owned and managed a grocery store in the Basque neighborhood on Roosevelt Street. Pedro and Mary Toja lived on Water Street for decades, and were also frequent customers of the Spanish Grocery at 53 Cherry Street, where they could purchase familiar spices and fish and socialize with Basque friends at the same time. The P. Astarbi y Compañía, Inc. of Brooklyn sold *bacalao*, or codfish, imported from the Basque Country. La Competidora de Ituarte y Company was a Basque-owned delivery service on Cherry Street.

Between 1849 and 1852, several hundred Basques left Mexico to join the California Gold Rush. Many hundred more traveled from Chile, Argentina, and Uruguay, although they did not stay in mining and moved into farming and ranching. San Francisco served as the new immigrants' point of entry, and Basque boardinghouses were established to serve these customers. The Hotel Vasco gave room and board almost exclusively to Basque recent arrivals and also to those who traveled to the city for banking, medical appointments, and shopping. *Photograph courtesy of the Basque Library, University of Nevada, Reno.*

Near the Centro Vasco-Americano (C.V.A.), on the corner of Cherry at 100 Roosevelt Street, Manuel Fernandez owned La Ideal Carnicería butcher shop where he sold *bacalao* and made fresh chorizos. He also sold quality olive oils, which are fundamental to Basque cuisine. Catherine Street also had numerous businesses owned by Galician and Catalan immigrants (Totoricagüena 2003).

FROM MANHATTAN in New York City, Valentín Aguirre maintained communications with other Basque boardinghouse owners throughout the United States, with sheep and cattle ranching operations in the West, and with various travel agencies across the country. He knew where workers were needed, or when the managers of certain ranches in Idaho or of a construction project in Nevada wanted immediate help, and he would send his customers to where the job opportunities awaited. Owners of Basque boardinghouses across the West also kept in touch with each other, and the constant flow of Basques from east to west and from west to east on the way home kept communities informed about new businesses, changes in immigration rules, and employment openings. Aguirre consistently worked with shipping agents, passenger liners, and travel agents and shared his own customer information with other businesses.

In the early 1900s, when Ogden, Utah, was the end of the rail line for direct travel from New York to more northern and western parts of the United States, Aguirre would make arrangements for Basques to stay at Basque businesses in Ogden and then, according to their direction of destination, he might also make arrangements for a boarding stay at the final stop until relatives were available to come and collect the newly arrived immigrant. Jeronima Echeverria's study describes Aguirre's Santa Lucia Hotel as "the consummate transit hotel in that it served more Basques than any other boardinghouse known in the recorded history of these establishments, and in the United States, it was the only one that operated a travel agency as part of its business (Echeverria 1999b, 45).

The Aguirres made a fortune with their investment and hard work. The boardinghouse owners and managers helped thousands of Basque people, and they made significant earnings doing it. These were businesses like any other, and of course entrepreneurs wanted to make a profit. The Aguirre operation was on a much larger scale than others in the United States. It mainly attracted short-term patrons and could therefore charge a higher fee. It had higher numbers of customers, plus the travel agency, plus the restaurant and bar, and Basques both coming from and going to the Basque Country. Non-boarders, such as hundreds of Basque mariners, regularly frequented the bar in order to catch up on news they had missed while at sea and to socialize with other Basques. Benita Orbe's cooking was famous throughout the city, and New York celebrities and important public officials were regular customers at the Jai-Alai Restaurant. During Prohibition, Aguirre told Mario de Salegi, he brought his alcohol to New York from Canada, and the bar was never dry. There were customers from the Philippines, South America, and Europe docking in New York, and there was substantial ship traffic, which brought in Basque seamen and foreign goods. Basques from those ships also sometimes lodged at the Santa Lucia and dined at the Jai Alai Restaurant.

ALTHOUGH ON THE surface it may seem that an Aguirre monopoly controlled Basque immigrant traffic in New York, in reality, there were several other Basque boardinghouses. Relying upon the ledger books of the Centro Vasco-Americano, whose secretary of the 1920s through 1940s meticulously recorded the addresses of its members, and on the testimonies of elderly Basques who were still present in the New York community in 2003, I have concluded that there were approximately ten establishments that accommodated an estimated fifteen to twenty people—usually single males—in each business. However, what seemed to have been more prevalent in Manhattan and Brooklyn was for a family to rent out two or three rooms to other Basques in their own private residence.

AN ANALYSIS of the Centro Vasco-Americano members' official recorded addresses demonstrates that forty-one listed their 1919 residence as 43 Cherry Street, just a few doors away from what would become the first building location of the C.V.A. Juan Polo Pedernales originally established this business at 43 Cherry Street. In the 1934 program of the Centro Vasco-Americano and the Basque festival picnic, the then current owner, Francisco Santa María, advertised his Fonda y Posada boardinghouse at 43 Cherry Street as "the oldest of the Basque colony, with fastidious and careful service."

Twenty-four Basque men lived at 41 Cherry Street. Lily Fradua used to play there as a child, and she recalls the boarders being mainly seamen and men who worked on the ships or on the docks, loading and unloading. They would come and go based on the length of their ship's voyage. Several Basques worked as cooks on passenger liners that traveled to Cuba and other ports in the Caribbean. They would be away from New York for two weeks and then back for one week. Lily explained that her husband, Martin Fradua Sr., "worked on the *Oriente* of the Ward Lines when he was single. "When he came into port he'd be in for a week or so, and that's when we'd go out on our dates." Lily is also sure that Juan Polo Pedernales managed a boardinghouse at 32 Cherry Street, and it seems that he would have worked there after the establishment at 43 Cherry Street. In 1919, sixteen other Basque men lived at 38 Cherry Street. That brings the total to four known Basque-owned and Basque-operated boardinghouses at 43, 41, 38, and 32 Cherry Street.

In 1924, ten members of the Centro Vasco-Americano listed their permanent address as 106 Roosevelt Street. Escolástico Uriona, Felix Uriona, Eugenio Urrutia, Juan Zavala, Daniel Echevarria, Saturnino Legarreta, and José Larralde Aguirre all lived at 82 Bank Street in 1924, which was the Santa Lucia Hotel operated by Valentín and Benita Aguirre. In the 1930s, Aquilino Zubillaga owned and managed the boardinghouse and restaurant El Mundo Bar and Grill at 489 West Street. During 1943–46, nine Basque men lodged at 94 James Street, and 59 James Street was listed by four more members of the C.V.A. On July 1, 1948, nine new Basque members simultaneously signed up to join the Centro Vasco-Americano, and each gave 95 Madison Street as his home address. Nine existing members gave this same residence, showing a total of at least eighteen Basque men living there at the same time. A few blocks down, 77–79 Madison Street was the home for four Basque males from 1943 to 1946.

IN THE MID-1940s, the name and address register of the C.V.A. shows several Basque males living at 258 William Street in Manhattan: Francisco Santamaría (who very well could be the same Francisco Santa María who earlier owned the boardinghouse on Cherry Street with a slight error in how his name was recorded), José Ugalde, Amalio Elorriaga, Tomas Uribe, Luis Salazar, and Severo Ybarguen all lived there from 1943 to 1946 and possibly before and after, as well. The same registry shows that numerous Basques were clustered at different addresses on the following streets: Oliver Street, Roosevelt Street, Monroe Street, Madison Street, Atlantic Avenue, Cherry Street, James Street, Catherine Street, and William Street.

Angel Viña remembers that the "Spanish neighborhood" around State Street in Brooklyn was mixed with Galicians, Asturians, and Basques. The 1943–46 ledger shows twenty C.V.A. members lived at 14–15 State Street

In San Francisco, California, the Des Alpes Restaurant and Hotel was originally established on Broadway in 1916 and remained open until the 1990s. It was a favorite of recent Basque immigrants for home-style Basque cuisine and was also popular with non-Basques.
Photograph courtesy of the Basque Library, University of Nevada, Reno.

---

in Brooklyn. Fifteen lived at Columbia Place in Brooklyn. Angel Viña lived with his aunt and uncle, Gabriel and Segunda Gainsa Elustondo, in their Brooklyn boardinghouse at 187 Atlantic Avenue. He remembers at least seven or eight men eating dinner there nightly during the 1930s. "My *tía* [aunt] had a reputation for good food, and she always cooked good food and had lots of it. People paid fifty cents a meal."

BECAUSE BASQUES and Galicians worked together on the ships, patronized each other's businesses, and socialized together, it is likely that Galicians would also have stayed at these boardinghouses, and it is also possible that the boardinghouses were actually Galician owned. These are commonly called "Basque boardinghouses" because Basques stayed there, but there are no existing records that demonstrate who actually owned and operated the businesses. In White Plains, New York, it is certain that many Basques lodged at the Galician boardinghouse of Juana Migues. Her family emigrated first to Puerto Rico and stayed there during the Spanish Civil War, then moved to White Plains. Manny Zuluaga remembers that his "great-grandmother's boardinghouse had a player piano, and the Basque and Gallego boarders thoroughly enjoyed singing Basque and Spanish songs with pride. There were a lot of parties held in that house."

As in the West, the New York boardinghouses also employed Basque women as receptionists, in accounting, and preparing meals and linens, and cleaning bedrooms, parlors, and kitchens. They shopped for each day's groceries with early morning stops at the fish and meat markets, then cleaned, skinned, sliced, cut, and prepared the food for meals. Boarders usually had three meals each day at the hotel's dining room, and generally a few extra men who worked nearby also came in for lunches. After each meal was finished, the women washed and dried all of the cutlery, drinking glasses, plates, and cooking and serving pots and pans, then started all over again for the dinner menu. Linens had to be washed and hung out to dry and then ironed. However, it was often more economical to send out the laundry to a nearby service for cleaning and pressing. Women working in the boardinghouses who were in the first generation born in the United States also tended to act, without pay, as translators, interpreters, and companions in assorted offices where they completed official and legal paperwork in English for new arrivals.

THE END OF AN ERA

The end of the boardinghouse era is related to the end of new Basque emigration to the United States in the 1950s and 1960s. Without new immigrants arriving to the United States, there was less and less need for the boardinghouses' services. Earlier Basques had established themselves financially by then, had married, and had rented or purchased their own homes and no longer required lodging.

THE BOOM years for the boardinghouses had been between 1890 and 1930, but the 1924 National Origins Act, together with the Taylor Act of 1930, squeezed the opportunities for Basque sheep businesses and therefore immigration. The established boardinghouses and hotels were able to maintain their businesses with the existing Basque population, and when Basques traveled to areas away from home, they continued to seek out Basque hotels, boardinghouses, or rooming houses for their temporary lodging. By the early 1950s, however, owners were attempting to appeal to nonlodging customers by advertising their restaurants to Basques and non-Basques alike. One by one, the Basque boardinghouses closed due to a lack of customers.

As Basque families grew and established their own residences and no longer needed temporary room and board or a informal employment agencies, they nevertheless still had a need for the social functions that the *ostatuak*, or hotels or boardinghouses, had provided.

The need to congregate and share with other Basques remained strong, and Basques from the first to the third generations and their descendants found other ways to maintain their ethnic identity, to socialize, to communicate with others in their own language, and to practice their own traditions and culture. The institutions of the boardinghouse and the Basque hotel, abundant in the hundred years between 1850 to 1950, were replaced by the Basque centers as the focus of social gatherings and cultural maintenance.

Lesson twelve

BIBLIOGRAPHY

Arrizabalaga, Marie Pierre. 1986. "A Statistical Study of Basque Immigration into California, Nevada, Idaho and Wyoming between 1900 and 1910." Microfilm MA thesis, University of Nevada, Reno.

Douglass, William A., and Jon Bilbao. 1975. *Amerikanuak: Basques in the New World*. Reno: University of Nevada Press.

Echeverria, Jeronima. 2000. "Expansion and Eclipse of the Basque Boarding House in the American West." *Nevada Historical Society Quarterly* (Summer.

———. 1999a. "The Basque *Hotelera*: Implications for Broader Study." In *The Basque Diaspora/La diaspora vasca*, ed. William A. Douglass, Carmelo Urza, Linda White, and Joseba Zulaika. Reno: Basque Studies Program.

———. 1999b. *Home Away from Home: A History of Basque Boardinghouses*. Reno: University of Nevada Press.

Totoricagüena, Gloria. 2004. *Identity, Culture, and Politics in the Basque Diaspora*. Reno: University of Nevada Press.

———. 2003. *The Basques of New York: A Cosmopolitan Identity*. Serie Urazandi. Vitoria-Gasteiz: Eusko Jaurlaritza.

———. 2002. *The Basques of Boise: Dreamers and Doers*. Serie Urazandi. Vitoria-Gasteiz: Eusko Jaurlaritza.

Zubiri, Nancy. 1998. *A Travel Guide to Basque America: Families, Feasts, and Festivals*. Reno: University of Nevada Press.

REQUIRED READING

Jeronima Echeverria, "The Basque *Hotelera*: Implications for Broader Study," in *The Basque Diaspora/La diaspora vasca*, ed. William A. Douglass, Carmelo Urza, Linda White, and Joseba Zulaika (Reno: Basque Studies Program, 1999), pp 239–48.

———, "Expansion and Eclipse of the Basque Boarding House in the` American West" *Nevada Historical Society Quarterly* (Summer 2000): 127–39.

———, *Home Away from Home: A History of Basque Boardinghouses* (Reno: University of Nevada Press, 1999), chapter 3, pp 36–61.

WRITTEN LESSON FOR SUBMISSION

Imagine you are a Basque serving girl employed at one of the boardinghouses. Describe your typical day and its activities and the people with whom you might come into contact, from the time of waking at 6:30 A.M. to your last chore at 11:30 P.M.

Then imagine what it would be like to have crossed the Atlantic Ocean, leaving behind family, friends, romances, and your known life, and traveling to a

completely foreign culture and society to discover
Valentín Aguirre in New York and a network of Basque
boardinghouses in the American West to receive you.
What would your feelings likely be toward the *hotelero*
and *hotelera*? Give examples using the many functions
of the *ostatuak*. Finally, Echeverria claims that the *ostat-*
uak may have been the Basques' major social institution,
although an invisible one. Do you agree or disagree with
her? Why?

13 · Spanish nation building
Basque resistance

T HE TRAGEDY of the Spanish Civil War has to some
degree marked almost every Basque living in the
Basque Country, as well as those living abroad. Whether
one experienced it personally or through relatives and
friends, the collective memories of the war and the ensuing Franco era have been influential factors in the construction of a Basque identity in the homeland, as well
as a diasporic Basque identity. The greatest number of
diaspora Basques who are from the emigrant generation
departed the Basque Country in the 1930s and 1940s,
immediately before, during, or after the Civil War. Their
perceptions of what they lived through, now passed on
to their children and grandchildren, have prominently
influenced those diaspora communities that received
this phase of Basque emigration.

For many of those abroad, Basque identity took on
a distinctly anti-Spanish aspect. The members of the
majority of the Basque centers around the world promoted ideologies opposed to the fascism of Francisco
Franco and in favor of the Republican government, the
elected central government in Madrid with which the
Basque nationalists sided during the Civil War, ideologies that continue to this day. Although diaspora
Basques may not always recall the historical facts of the
Spanish Civil War correctly, the effect of the war on their
emotions, attitudes, and opinions correlates directly
with many of the defining characteristics of a diaspora as
elucidated by Robin Cohen: traumatic dispersal, a collective memory, solidarity with co-ethnics in the homeland
and in the diaspora, a return movement, both real and
mythical, an enriched ethnic life in the host society, and
the maintenance of links with the homeland.

Elu's Basque Restaurant, owned and operated by Louie and Marie Elu in San Francisco, California, was famous with elderly and young Basques alike. The popularity of the hotel and restaurant owners often drew customers for weekend socializing far beyond the daily accommodation of clients. Basques traveled to the city seeking ethnic companionship, cuisine, music, and song. Photo 1992.
Photograph courtesy of the Basque Library, University of Nevada, Reno.

THESE PRO-BASQUE nationalist attitudes emanate from the massive influx of political refugees to South American countries, Australia, the Philippines, Belgium, France, and less so to the United States and Canada, refugees who were escaping political oppression, war labor camps, and even death sentences. The Basques who fled to the communities abroad, especially to Belgium, Mexico, Argentina, and Venezuela, were generally

Basque republicans and Basque nationalists, and the populations in those existing communities would not likely otherwise have received the equivalent personalized information regarding Spanish nationalist ideas, although these were also supported by other Basques in the homeland.

THE SPANISH CIVIL WAR

IN 1923, Miguel Primo de Rivera staged a coup in Madrid establishing a military dictatorship that would last for the remainder of the decade. He suppressed non-Spanish nationalism in all forms, and imprisoned or drove into exile many Basque nationalists, with the exiles fleeing to Mexico, Venezuela, Chile, Argentina, and Uruguay. Primo de Rivera's policies attempted to restructure Spanish society and its economy along corporatist lines, most of which failed and resulted in a rise in anarchism. Primo de Rivera resigned in 1930, and after elections in the municipalities showed a desire for elected republican government, King Alfonso XIII abdicated his throne and left Spain in April 1931. The ensuing Second Republic (1931–36) undertook many anticlerical and leftist initiatives, which caused serious divisions in popular opinion. In the 1932 election results, the opposing rightist Radical Party won and formed a coalition government to manage the Spanish Cortes, or parliament, in Madrid. The Spanish Left grew increasingly alienated and experienced many divisions within and among its intellectuals and leaders, and their reactions to the right-wing government policies included a socialist insurrection in Asturias and a separatist attempt in Catalonia. By 1935, the ruling coalition was unable to agree on how to answer appeals from regionalists, unions, and those demanding land reform.

The leadership of the Partido Nacionalista Vasco, PNV, or Basque Nationalist Party, shelved its claims for independence and instead struggled to obtain a statute of autonomy similar to that of Catalonia. During the Second Republic, Basque nationalists demanded and worked almost exclusively for that statute. On July 14, 1931, in Estella-Lizarra, Nafarroa, the Basque people—through their representative delegates—had voted 90 percent in favor of proclaiming separation and accepting their Statutes of Autonomy. The Republic required that in order to obtain home rule, the region meet subsequent procedures: A majority of all the municipalities in the region had to vote yes, all four of the provinces had to agree, and in addition, a popular plebiscite had to pass in the four Basque provinces. Even after each of these conditions had been fulfilled, the Spanish parliament still reserved the right to accept or reject the proposal. In the Basque plebiscite held on November 5, 1933, 88 percent of the population voted in favor of the home rule. The Spanish republican parliament delayed their deliberations, and Basque autonomy was finally approved on October 1, 1936, only after the Spanish Civil War had already begun.

BY 1936, BASQUE nationalism had become the most powerful force in Bizkaia and Gipuzkoa by attracting support from the traditionalists and the local bourgeoisie. Theirs was a program of a conservative middle class aimed at establishing a society of small-scale industrial and agricultural producers in which religious principles would inform most aspects of life. However, electoral results and outcomes of the referenda for the approval of the drafts of the Statutes of Autonomy demonstrate that there was not great support in Araba or in Nafarroa. Support for right-wing parties in the 1936 elections in Nafarroa was 69.2 percent and only 9.5 percent for the PNV.

In Araba, the 1936 support for the right-wing parties was 57.7 percent and only 20.3 percent for the PNV (Clark 1979, 60).

THE REVOLT of the Spanish army against the existing elected republican government in Madrid was not unexpected, and certain politicians and military leaders had solicited support for a fascist coup in Spain as early as 1932. In March 1934, Spanish monarchists visited Mussolini in order to seek backing from the Italian government for an uprising against the republic. The February 1936 Spanish parliamentary elections produced a winning coalition of leftist and moderate republicans, socialists, communists, and anarchists called the Popular Front. However, many of the rightists refused to accept defeat. Overall in Spain, 34.3 percent had voted for the leftist Popular Front, a very close 33.2 percent for the rightist National Front, and 5.4 percent (including 125,714 Basque nationalists) for the Center (Thomas 2001, 147). The uncompromising rightist leader of the parliamentary opposition, José Calvo Sotelo, was assassinated on July 13, 1936 by assault guards of the newly elected republican government, and after sensationalist media accounts and additional street violence, this triggered a reaction with a military uprising.

The Spanish Civil War began July 18, 1936 with the rebellion of Spanish army units in Morocco. Conservative rebel forces led by Generals José Sanjurjo, Manuel Goded, Francisco Franco, and Emilio Mola (in Pamplona) had the support in the Basque Country of established conservative Carlists from the last century. In many ways, the Spanish Civil war was another replay of the First and Second Carlist Wars—the issues, revolving around a confrontation between modernity and tradition, were very similar. In the Falangist movement, for example, when it was taken over by Francisco Franco and the Spanish Nationalists, the regionalism espoused by Basque nationalists was seen as bad for Spain, and national unity was the highest goal at all costs. They insisted that all obstacles to radical modernization had to be overcome. The Falangists called for the dismantling of all voluntary associations and all intermediary institutions that stood between the individual and the state, emphasizing instead the corporative nature of the state, with all citizens bound together through state-directed official associations. Labor unions and regional institutions had to be suppressed and replaced with organizations run from Madrid. Other issues in the face-off between modernity and tradition included land reform, the role of the military in society, church-state relations, and cultural renaissance.

NAFARROA and Araba were controlled early on by the rebel forces of General Mola, and thousands of Basque Carlists volunteered to fight with the Spanish Nationalists against the Republicans. Many Basque Catholics were opposed to the anti-Catholic leftist rhetoric of the Republic and believed that the conservative forces would protect their *fueros*, their traditional customary laws. The Spanish nationalists persecuted those who were sympathetic to Basque nationalism or to the Republic and imprisoned thousands of Basques in labor camps or executed them. Mola's forces moved to capture Gipuzkoa and to close the border with France, cutting off aid from Basques in Iparralde and making escape extremely dangerous. By September 1936, tens of thousands of Basques attempted to flee to Bizkaia and to Bilbao, where they believed they would be safe after the fall of Donostia–San Sebastián on September 13.

In Bizkaia and Gipuzkoa, the Basque Nationalist Party enjoyed strong support (although not a majority of the population), and it aligned itself with the Republic as a

Spanish Civil War propaganda included artistic postcards with Basque nationalist themes. Notice the rays of the sun shining through the window, which depict the *ikur-riña*, or Basque flag. These postcards were received and circulated in the diaspora.
Postcard courtesy of the Peter Toja Jr. Family Collection.

result of the ruling parties' promise to support regional autonomy for the Basque territories. The conservative forces of the rebels promoted a unified and centralized authority in Spain, but had talked in Nafarroa about preserving the *fueros*. Basques fought against each other, and many families had brothers fighting against brothers and sons fighting against fathers. Insurgent army forces in Bizkaia and Gipuzkoa that fought with Franco to overthrow the elected republican form of government in Madrid were held down by the Republicans, although the uprisings in Nafarroa and Araba were successful.

It is significant to note that there never was a homogeneous Basque nationalism. The differences were various, pitting rural against urban, tradition against modernization, industrial interests against agricultural interests, liberals against Carlists, and autonomists against centralists. On certain issues, Basque nationalists had much in common with the Spanish Nationalists of Mola and Franco, sharing strong ties to Catholicism and an emphasis on social order, discipline, and traditional values.

ONCE THE WAR commenced, the Italians immediately sent men, air power, and one billion lira to aid the military rebellion of the Spanish forces. Additionally, the Germans sent the Condor Legion for air raids—never before seen in Spain—resulting in the destruction of Durango, Gernika, Santander, and Bilbao. The United Kingdom, France, and the United States declared neutrality and gave no aid to the elected government of the Republicans, necessitating its reliance on purchasing munitions from the Soviet Union. The fledgling coalition Basque Autonomous Government, only weeks old, began to assemble a Basque militia force, initially with civilians from Gipuzkoa and Bizkaia, creating a Basque military of between twenty-five thousand and thirty thousand individuals in just a few months, but fewer than twenty leaders who had any type of professional military training. Diaspora Basques sent financial aid to their families, and in the majority of communities in Argentina, Uruguay, and the United States, several Basques could recall at least a few men from their areas who had returned to Euskal Herria to fight with the republicans.

THE TOP PARTIDO Nacionalista Vasco leaders had denounced the military's revolt and interference in an elected constitutional government, and their pronouncements depicted the struggle as one between civil rights and fascism, the Republic and the monarchy. The Basque nationalist leadership declared that "its principles led it to come down on the side of civil rights and the Republic in consonance with the democratic and republican regime of our people during its centuries of liberty" (Payne 1975, 163). However, this civil war was not a conflict between two political ideas, it was also a civil war between Basques in the four provinces. In Nafarroa, the army rebels of General Mola were aided by former Carlists after he declared that the remaining foral privileges in the province would be completely upheld. The PNV leadership in Nafarroa issued its own declaration of support for the Spanish military, saying that it would not endorse or support the Republican government. In Araba, there was support for all sides, but the military insurgents seized control of the capital, Vitoria-Gasteiz, and sent troops to close the Basque Nationalist Party offices in the area. PNV leaders were arrested and forced to write declarations urging Basque Nationalists to support the military takeover, and a few months later in Nafarroa, General Mola completely dismantled the Basque Nationalist Party organizations.

October 1, 1936 the parliament of the Spanish Republic approved a fourth draft of the Basque autonomy statute,

Another example of Spanish Civil War Republican propaganda postcards with Basque nationalist themes. The destruction of the town of Gernika and its historic Tree of Gernika, where for centuries Basques met to discuss and debate the *fueros,* or traditional laws, is illustrated, including the use of German aircraft . These postcards were received and circulated in the diaspora.
Postcard courtesy of the Peter Toja Jr. Family Collection.

first presented in 1931, that did not include Nafar-roa. The statute established an autonomous regional government for the three provinces of Araba, Bizkaia, and Gipuzkoa, although all that remained free at this point was Bizkaia and a section of Gipuzkoa. The president of the new Basque government was elected by the municipal councils, and the unanimous choice was José Antonio de Aguirre y Lecube. Basque nationalists were divided in support of the statute, and many perceived it as a sellout to the Spanish government because of the lack of total independence. When Aguirre swore his oath of office under the traditional Tree of Gernika, as Basque representatives of *fuerista* governments had done for centuries before him, many onlookers jeered and protested for total independence. The same day, Luís Arana y Goiri, brother of Sabino Arana and one of the founders of the Basque Nationalist Party, officially resigned from the party in repudiation of its compromising of nationalist principles and objectives (Payne 1975, 179).

THE WAR IN THE north of Spain entailed Basque nationalists of various parties, republicans, and leftist supporters fighting against other Basque Carlists and against Spanish Nationalists and Falangists, Germans, and Italians. On April 26, 1937, the most famous incident of the war occurred with the saturation bombing and partial razing of the historic foral center of Gernika, Bizkaia. Worldwide condemnation of the civilian bombing, and consequently Pablo Picasso's work of art *Guernica*, illustrated the horrors suffered in this and all wars. Because the entire town of Gernika was destroyed, except for the church, the parliament building, and the Tree of Gernika, where representatives of Basque society had met for almost one thousand years, Basques have promulgated as a part of the common history and Basque myth that the symbolism of Basque nationalism, history, and identity can never be eliminated. Tree of Gernika symbols, posters, paintings, and sculptures decorate diaspora Basque centers and homes around the world.

An estimated thirty thousand children were evacuated from Bizkaia to refugee camps in safer locations in Iparralde and other parts of France, England, Belgium, the Soviet Union, Switzerland, Denmark, Mexico, and Cuba. Upon returning to the Basque Country after the war's end, many of the child refugees found their families to be the targets of persecution by Franco's government and again were forced to escape the oppression of the Spanish central government as political exiles to other countries (Legarreta 1984).

CIVIL WAR REFUGEES were received in Iparralde by the Basque government-in-exile agencies, which were allowed and basically ignored by the French government. From the three northern provinces, the waves of Basque refugees spread out to the other European countries, especially the Soviet Union, Belgium, and England. Others tried to unite with relatives who had emigrated earlier to Latin American states and an estimated fifty thousand persons departed for South America. Of those, thirty-five thousand refugees made their way to Mexico, Venezuela, and Argentina. The Basque exiles were received by already established Basque communities, which cared for them with medical attention, housing, and employment. Although the overwhelming majority of Basque political exiles thought this would be a temporary situation, interviews more than sixty years later revealed the repeated histories of refugees who could not return to the Basque Country for political or economic reasons. This forced separation from family and homeland caused an intense hatred for all things Spanish and an abhorrence of the memories of Franco.

Numerous Basque nationalist intellectuals, members of the business elite, industrialists, merchants, writers, lawyers, and other professionals fled to the Basque communities in the Americas, and as a consequence, these communities prospered and also became sources of important financial support for the Basque government-in-exile. Local radio programs in Euskara in Venezuela, and in the United States in Boise, Idaho, and Buffalo, Wyoming, as well as in combinations of Spanish, French, and English in other Basque communities in the United States, ran for decades with homeland news and information from the Basque diaspora network.

SEVERAL BASQUE centers in Argentina and Uruguay tried to influence their host-country governments by protesting Franco's censorship of speech and the press, often resulting in their own censorship. While official media reports concerning Spain were usually press releases from host-country governments and typically pro-Franco, the diaspora communities also received a conflicting flow of information from their own and other exiles' families and friends relaying the stark reality of life at home. This frequent access to information through personal contacts affected Basque identity in each community. In the Basque organizations that received political exiles from the Civil War, the contemporary ethnic identity of the Basque descendants is more political, more nationalist, and more separatist than communities that did not have exiles join their towns and cities (Totoricagüena 2003). The effect of only a few political exiles could outweigh the national and international media, the host society's culture and attitudes, and time and distance away from the circumstances and events of the Franco regime. As mentioned previously, the primacy and consequences of diaspora transnational communications, new immigration, and chain migration cannot be overstated for the Basques, regardless of geography and host country setting.

THE OFFICIAL end of military struggle for the Basque nationalists and republicans in the Basque provinces came with the fall of Bilbao on June 19, 1937, leaving nearly all of Bizkaia now in the hands of the Spanish Nationalists. The Spanish Republic finally collapsed in 1939 after several hundred thousand deaths, with thousands more left homeless and hundreds of thousands driven into exile. The majority on both sides were economically, psychologically, and emotionally devastated. Hugh Thomas quotes the following figures: The loss of life from all military causes, including those killed in action, by aerial bombardment, from wounds, from malnutrition, and those executed after the war (approximately one hundred thousand) totaled more than half a million. An additional permanent emigration of three hundred thousand individuals escaped and were then exiled from Spain and never returned (Thomas 2001, 900–901). This loss of eight hundred thousand persons is extraordinarily high for a relatively small country, and to it must be added the physical destruction of personal and public property, infrastructure, agricultural fields and livestock, small businesses, commerce, and manufacturing plants. Defeat of the Republicans halted the growing institutionalization of the Basque nationalist movement, but failed to eradicate nationalist sentiments. On the contrary, for many, it intensified them because of their suffering and losses during the war.

SPANISH NATION BUILDING AND BASQUE RESISTANCE DURING THE FRANCO DICTATORSHIP

The collective memory of victimization during the Franco dictatorship is shared by the diaspora with Basques in the homeland, and whether or not they

500 little Basque refugees coming to U.S.A.

OFFERS U.S. HAVEN TO 5,000 BASQUES

FOOD AND PEACE FOR LITTLE WAR VICTIMS

OFFER U.S. HAVEN TO 500 BASQUES

Washington May Admit 500 Basque Children On Visitors' Visas Granting Six-Month Stays

500 Children
Little Basque Victims to Be Brought Here

American Board of Guardians for Basque Refugee Children

20 Vesey Street   Suite 304   BArclay 7-4162   New York City

The American Board of Guardians for Basque Refugee Children, established in New York, attempted to organize foster homes for 500 Basque children fleeing the Spanish Civil War. Two thousand people in New York alone responded positively. However, the U.S. State Department reversed its policy and refused their entrance to the country after the Catholic Church suggested that Basques might have Communist ties.

personally experienced it, the narratives of Basques are extremely similar throughout the communities abroad. The occupation forces of a retaliatory and vengeful General Franco descended upon the Basque Country with the determination to erase all signs of a distinctive Basque culture and any remaining remnants of Basque nationalism. The anti-Basque nationalist purge extended from schools and churches to businesses and factories. Properties of Basque nationalists were confiscated, teachers and civil servants were fired and replaced, and Basque priests suffered imprisonment, deportation, and execution because of their support for Basque culture and language and nationalist politics. Because Basque nationalism relied so heavily on the linguistic, ancestral, and cultural, definitions *of* nation, Madrid placed a special emphasis on the destruction of this aspect of non-Spanish behavior.

THE MOST damaging threat to Basque culture was the outlawing of the use of the language as a functioning means of communication. Euskara was prohibited in all public places and even for conversation in the streets. All Basque-language newspapers, magazines, and radio programs were banned. However, the grandparents' generation still contained Basque monolinguals, and Basque was still spoken behind closed doors and in safe environments such as on hiking excursions in the mountains. However, the Basque language was removed from school curriculums and from public places. Civil registry names of newborns had to be Spanish, not Basque, and names, and surname spellings were Hispanicized to remove the Basque "tx" and replace it with "ch," to exchange the Basque "b" for the Spanish "v," and so on. Names of towns were changed to Spanish spellings and street and plaza names were changed to those of Spanish National-ist war heroes. Cemetery tombstone names were erased and in some cases reengraved with the Spanish equivalents, such as the Spanish "Maria" instead of the Basque "Miren." Masses were celebrated in Spanish only, and non-Basque clergy were brought in to administer to the now Spanish-speaking Catholics. Non-Basque teachers from the south of Spain were assigned to the provinces to instruct the now Spanish-speaking children. Most noticeably, Bizkaian and Gipuzkoan civil police and security forces, the *miqueletes*, disappeared, and non-Basque Guardia Civil, military civil guards, were imposed in the provinces for policing the population. Civil liberties were nonexistent.

FOLLOWING THE conclusion of the war in 1939, Franco promulgated the infamous Law on Political Responsibilities, which made it a crime for anyone over the age of fourteen to have "helped to undermine public order" at any time since October 1, 1934, "to have impeded the Spanish Nationalist movement" even by being passive at any time after the beginning day of the war, or to have belonged at any time to any leftist political parties, to any regional nationalist parties, to the Liberal Party, or to a Masonic lodge (Clark 1979, 82). Anyone convicted of any of these crimes could have all properties confiscated, be deprived of their nationality, be deported to Africa, or be sentenced to a prison term. Mixed military-Falangist tribunals conducted the trials, and there was no right to appeal the decisions.

In the fifteen years after the end of the Civil War and the exile and imprisonment of most of the Basque nationalist leaders, a durable Basque resistance emerged in spite of Franco's efforts to Hispanicize the Basque population. The Basque government-in-exile installed in Paris and New York was supported by a sympathetic French government and by the Basque diaspora. The oppressive measures utilized to create "Spaniards" out of

On October 7, 1936, José Antonio de Aguirre y Lekube
was sworn in as the first president of the newly autonomous Basque government at the age of thirty-two. The
first executive branch consisted of ten additional coun-
cilors or ministers, who represented the political parties
of the Basque Nationalist Party and the Popular Front.
Urgently, the first Basque government attended to Spanish Civil War issues such as the distribution of food and
medicine, public health, military defense, diplomacy
with Western powers, and the evacuation of war refugees.

Basques backfired, instead galvanizing anti-Spanish sentiments in Euskal Herria. Iparralde Basques were especially helpful during the war and were about to become
essential to the underground resistance and movement
of arms and people. Because of the French government's
unofficial blind-eye policy, Iparralde became a safe haven
for numerous activists and exiles, whose first stop before

embarking for the Americas, the Philippines, or Belgium was usually a Basque family in the North.

Basque resistance emerged in the mid-1940s with the creation of the Basque Consultative Council, which represented all of the Basque political parties and included delegates from the trade unions in the Basque provinces. The council was responsible for ensuring that the Basque government-in-exile in Paris would remain in close contact with the main forces and current events in the Basque Country and for coordinating the strategy for the Basque resistance. There was a Resistance Committee that operated primarily on the Spanish side of the border, and the role of the Basque Consultative Council was to ensure that the activities of the resistance coincided with the political strategy of the government-in-exile. Diaspora communities in Mexico and Argentina published newspapers and information bulletins that were then distributed in Euskal Herria, and clandestine radio broadcasts were transmitted to the south of the Basque Country from Iparralde, then later for thirteen years from Caracas, Venezuela to Euskal Herria.

THE UNDERGROUND PNV had reinforced its own reputation for being a parliamentarian and Christian Democratic party of the middle class. It continued to define itself within the Spanish state, and for many at this time, the goal of outright independence had decades ago been exchanged publicly for the goal of autonomy within the state. The Basque Nationalist Party even disassociated itself from nationalist movements in Iparralde (Jacob 1994). The prewar rifts and divisions between nationalists—temporarily fused by the war effort—surfaced again. Never considered separatist nationalists, the Basque bourgeoisie had continued their association with the Spanish system, and this economic elite enjoyed preferential treatment within Franco's established economy.

Many Basques defined the resistance as a fight for cultural identity and for preservation of the language, focusing their efforts on the clandestine ikastola or the Basque schools movement, and they pressured the Spanish government to allow the use of Euskara in public. There were those who saw this struggle as a political and partisan one. For them, the focus was the Basque Nationalist Party. Other Basques saw economic and class questions as of higher importance and joined the struggle through membership in one of the Basque unions. Yet another sector tired of waiting for the Basque government-in-exile to take decisive action and declared war on Spain, the Spanish language, and on capitalism, as well. Those who believed that Basques should mobilize to obtain independence, without regard to what was happening in Madrid, argued that no Spanish government would ever be willing to release the Basque provinces to form their own state, therefore the sooner the process began, the sooner it would be completed. Voices began to complain that the government-in-exile did not truly represent all Basques and had never actually been ratified by a popular vote. Many believed that confrontational politics would be more effective than working through established political channels.

THE ACTIVITIES of the PNV reflected its passive form of political struggle. Party leadership in the PNV was more concerned with long-range plans, keeping in contact with all anti-Franco forces, and preparing the ground for the emergence of democracy in Spain after the removal of Franco. Theirs was a defensive strategy, to wait it out and work with Madrid within an eventually democratic Spanish government. The party's energy and resources went into organizing in the diaspora and into the Basque government-in-exile, establishing ties to other underground anti-Franco groups in Spain, and raising money to support resistance activities. The more cautious and conservative PNV repelled many youths, who called for defensive and offensive political violence in response to Franco's state violence.

DIASPORA REACTIONS TO HOMELAND TROUBLES

DIASPORA communities received personal information from their family members, while the older communities in Argentina and Uruguay relied more on the Basque government's interpretations of desired future goals. But there were other sources of information. At the turn of the century in the diaspora, there was an already established nationalist press and information-circulation network. Articles enlightened and updated readers regarding the Basque Country's political and socioeconomic realities. In Argentina, the Basque periodicals *Revista Laurak Bat* (1878), *La Vasconia* (1893), and *Irrintzi* (1904) were published in Buenos Aires, as were books with Basque nationalist themes such as *Amí vasco, Inocéncia de un patriota, Aitor, Egi-Zale,* and *Patria*. In the United States, *Euzkotarra* originated from New Orleans (1907) and later, by the period of the Spanish Civil War, there were *Eusko Deia, Galeuzka, Euskaltzaleak,* and *Tierra Vasca* in Argentina, *Euskal Ordua* in Montevideo, and various others in Chile, Venezuela, and Mexico. These nationalist writings circulated throughout the Basque population in Uruguay, Argentina, Venezuela, Mexico, and the United States and then clandestinely in Euskal Herria. Their support of Luís Arana y Goiri and later their anti-Franco orientation influenced the Basques abroad and gave hope to those in the homeland that something was being accomplished in the international networks.

After the Spanish Civil War, in Uruguay, the distribution of *Ekin* and other informative bulletins sustained the political interest of those in Montevideo. Although the statutes of the Euskal Erria Basque Center refer to its being "apolitical," it supported Basque Nationalist Party activities. In addition, the PNV-dominated Basque government-in-exile appointed a party delegate specifically for Uruguay. Basques in Belgium, Argentina, Uruguay, and the United States all received the president of the Basque government-in-exile, José Antonio de Aguirre y Lecube, in some official and institutional capacity or other, and the Basque centers were often used as nuclei for mobilizing anti-Franco support and for lobbying their respective host-country governments for foreign policies sympathetic to the Basque cause.

THE BASQUE government-in-exile apportioned its delegates around the world to the largest diaspora communities and the most politically significant cities, sending spokespersons to France, Belgium, England, United States, Mexico, Cuba, Columbia, Venezuela, Chile, Uruguay, Argentina, and the Philippines. As the established Basque nationalist party, the PNV at the time enjoyed relatively unified political support in the diaspora, and although the delegates were expected to implement administrative undertakings, for most people, there was no separation between the PNV and the government-in-exile. The Basque Government *was* the PNV, and vice versa. Hence the lingering diaspora approval for the Partido Nacionalista Vasco, although those endorsing it in recent interviews could not describe its programs or specific policies. Diaspora nationalists are loyal to the PNV because they believe it was the party in government that enabled their escape from Spain and it was the party that received and cared for them in the host societies. Party loyalty has stamped the third generation

The Parliament of the Basque Autonomous Community first met in Bilbao April 29, 1980, and their first law, passed on May 23, declared the city of Vitoria-Gasteiz to be the capital city of the community. The search for chambers ended with the adoption of the former Institute of Secondary Education, first constructed in 1851, and the first session was celebrated in Gasteiz in 1982. *Photograph by the author.*

of immigrants, as well. Young adults relaying their party preferences mentioned that their grandparents were PNV, and therefore so were their parents, and so were they. Research in contemporary Basque communities shows that the PNV remains the most popular party with diaspora Basques who distinguish among homeland parties (Totoricagüena 2004).

An official Basque Delegation of the government-in-exile was established in New York City in 1938, and when the State Department granted a special visa to President

Aguirre y Lecube in 1941, he remained to lecture at Columbia University. However, despite United States government support for the exiled Basque government during World War II, Basques' anti-Franco rhetoric and republican ties to socialists and communists during the Spanish Civil War made them the target of interest for the U.S. Office of Security Services, the OSS, the predecessor of the CIA, and for the FBI. Beginning in 1942, there were investigations of officials in the Basque government-in-exile, of Basque immigrants in the New York area, and of those in California, Nevada, Oregon, Idaho, Wyoming, and Utah, as well as of the Basque organizations and the political activities they carried out in each community (Ordaz Romay, 1996, 230).

In the face of these suspicions, maintaining U.S. governmental endorsement for the Basque cause was imperative and the top priority objective for President Aguirre. But Basques were uncertain about U.S. support for their cause. In a letter that the FBI intercepted from Aguirre to another Basque in Havana, the Basque president illustrated his fears about a possible agreement between Franco and the democracies and suggested that Basques everywhere must present an image of political unity with other republicans, even at the cost of sacrificing Basque nationalist goals (Hoover, FBI Bureau File 10-14311-3, 1942).

HOWEVER, Basques in the diaspora also contributed to the U.S. war effort. Three Basque government-in-exile delegates, José María Lasarte Arana, Telesforo Monzón Ortiz de Uruela, and Antonio de Irala e Irala, organized Basques in the South American countries into counterespionage units to aid the United States with its World War II effort. The Basque delegations in Czechoslovakia, Bulgaria, and Yugoslavia also aided with espionage.

Yet U.S. suspicions of Basques remained. The FBI actually hired Basques as agents to help investigate the South American counterespionage plan. In a communication from the United States legal attaché in Buenos Aires to the FBI director, J. Edgar Hoover, it looks as though the FBI was spying on its own spies in the Organization of Basque Intelligence. The letter lists the categories of information that could be obtained regarding Argentine Basques' nationalist and/or communist activities, political ideologies, as well as religious affiliations (Totoricagüena 2004, 86–88).

IN THE DIASPORA communities, it was almost impossible for Basques to dam the pro-Spanish media's flood of misinformation defining Basques as Communists and anti-Catholic. The Catholic clergy in the United States and Australia praised Franco from the pulpit as the savior of religion in traditionally Catholic Spain, and Mexican, Chilean, Argentine, Uruguayan, and Peruvian Basque Catholics heard similar sermons. In Belgium, however, socialist and Catholic relief organizations received over 5,130 Basque children evacuated during the war years (Artís-Gener 1976, 176), and if children were orphaned, many families adopted them permanently. Young adults who returned to Euskal Herria after their formative years and education in Belgium often found they felt a stranger in their own land. Several returned to their Belgian families and have remained mainly in the Brussels and Antwerp areas.

As the United States was drawn into World War II, Franco's identification with Hitler and Mussolini finally prompted United States government support for the exiled Basque government. The Basque government maintained a delegation to the United Nations in New York City, and their presence influenced the local Basque center, the Centro Vasco-Americano, its Committee

Basques fighting for the democratically elected Republican government were outmanned and outgunned. They generally had no military training or military equipment, and because of the nonintervention pact signed by the Western powers, they were not allowed to buy weapons to defend themselves. Battalions such that seen here, Amayur, bravely fought into 1937, when they were defeated by the combination of Spanish, Italian, and German troops aiding Francisco Franco's Spanish rebels. *Photograph as published in DEIA.*

Pro-Euzkadi, and the publication of *Basques: Bulletin of the Basque Delegation in the USA.* Interviews with New York area Basques between 2001 and 2003 demonstrate that they remain more politically aware than Basques in the communities of the western United States. For example, many interviewees understood the nuances of the partisan differences in the Basque parliamentary elections and the significance of the PNV wins to maintain coalitions in Vitoria-Gasteiz.

THE REACTIONS in the American West were quite different. In 1937, the Basque government delegate to the United States, Ramón de la Sota, visited Boise in order to inform the Basque community and to attempt to raise money for the Basque war effort. Although many Basques attended events to hear news from the Basque Country, de la Sota was unable to create enough interest for financial support. In a 1938 letter to Basque government-in-exile's President Aguirre, the Basque government delegate to the United States, Antonio de Irala, wrote of the Basques of Idaho, "there is a lack of national consciousness ... and their mentality in regards to patriotism is American" (my translation from San Sebastián 1991, 236). In 1940, a Basque delegation emissary Juan "Jon" M. Bilbao was sent to Idaho and Nevada, but found no significant interest in political mobilization, and he maintained his Boise office for only a few months. Little aid came from the United States Basque communities in the West for the military cause, but they did provide humanitarian war relief.

EUSKADI 'TA ASKATASUNA BASQUE HOMELAND AND LIBERTY

Basque nationalist sentiments during the 1950s and 1960s in the homeland remained strong among the same groups as earlier: farmers, peasants, white-collar workers of the lower middle class, shopkeepers and small entrepreneurs, and a few skilled urban workers. During this time, the young liberal clergy and the Basque intelligentsia also became the most dissident sectors of the society, due in part to the slow but steady growth of secularism in what had been potently Catholic territory. The effects of increasing modernization also stirred crises of personal and collective identity and values. All of these factors, which when added to the repression of Basque culture, language, and traditions, resulted in an explosion of frustrations that are still being vented today.

IN THE 1950s, clandestine groups of Basque students were regularly meeting to write and publish magazines and newspapers, distributing Basque diaspora publications coming from Argentina, Venezuela, and Mexico, discussing examples of European contemporary political writings, and eventually, in Bilbao, forming a secret organization, EKIN, which in Euskara means "to act." The participants in EKIN were frustrated with the lack of commitment by the PNV to preserve Euskara, which was sidelined in its list of priorities. A student leader, José Luís Alvarez Emparanza, known by the political pseudonym "Txillardegui," argued that Euskara was on the verge of extinction, not only because of the massive immigration of Spaniards to the Basque Country, but because of laziness on the part of those who knew it and did not use it to communicate. Members of EKIN announced that a true Basque patriot should not be content until an independent state of all seven provinces was realized. Most of the older, established Basque nationalist leaders found such ideas utopian and feared such expectations would alienate potential allies in Spain, France, and elsewhere. In 1959, Txillardegui and other youth leaders decided to establish an independent group, Euskadi 'ta Askatasuna, ETA, Basque Homeland and Liberty.

In the early 1960s, ETA activity consisted mainly of educating new et*arras*, or ETA members, preparing ETA activists, and studying the nationalist ideological works of Sabino Arana and Elias Gallastegui. Because of the ongoing police repression and inability publicly to organize and spread information, from its inception, ETA lacked a centralized system of authority. Local groups often acted independently of each other, and there was a general lack of coordination of activities. Subsequently there was also an uncoordinated effort to educate the diaspora and to use its potential for the homeland struggle, although the institutionalized diaspora continued to take its cues from the Basque government-in-exile and from the PNV. Representatives of the ETA movement advertised that ETA was a "Basque Revolutionary Movement of National Liberation," not a political party, and that it would dedicate itself to securing political and cultural liberty for Basques in all seven provinces and to changing the existing society. It would promote mass propaganda, labor activism, internal publications and paramilitary preparations, grass-roots agitation, and popular demonstrations (Enrike Pagoaga Gallastegui interview, 1997).

E TA's "STATEMENT of Principles" proposed the creation of an independent, democratically elected political order for the region, one dominated not by any one party, but by the people at large. Basques would enjoy internationally recognized human rights such as freedom of speech, press, religion, and assembly, which were not a part of the society Franco allowed. Unions would have constitutionally protected rights, as would ethnic and linguistic minorities. The political framework would be decentralized, with as much power as possible reserved for municipalities. Although there was ambivalence about government planning and centralized power in general, the *etarras* advocated a modified market economy in which personal wealth and income inequality both would be limited. Various economic sectors and resources would be owned or managed by the government, and workers' cooperatives would be encouraged

(Zirakzadeh 1991, 152). Methods for achieving this Basque state were vague at this point, because there was much disagreement about them. Some favored following the principles of Ghandi's nonviolent resistance, others advocated Julen Madariaga's calculated use of defensive violence or perhaps offensive tactics and declarations of war, and others supported varieties and combinations of these strategies.

THE ECONOMY of the Basque territories continued to expand, and soon the memberships of ETA and the labor unions overlapped. Following constant arrests, imprisonments, and exile to France and Belgium of the ETA leaders, the less experienced labor-oriented activists soon inherited control of the leadership offices. Now university-educated urbanites, the new directors of ETA, entertained joining forces with immigrant workers and advancing proletarian demands while simultaneously pushing for Basque self-determination in an independent state. The previously emphasized themes of cultural and ethnic oppression were superseded by complaints of economic exploitation. Publications concerning traditions, values, and language were replaced by those referring to the proletariat, the misery of factory production, class struggle, and the destruction of the roots of capitalism. Leaders read and studied Europe's New Left theoreticians, who argued for a novel way of thinking about social revolution, deducing that socialism would not come from a dramatic economic collapse or from a coup, which the international community would not allow. Through patient labor activity and local policy-making centers, they argued, workers would gradually gain control over society. Other *etarras* read works of inspiring anticolonial struggles and wished to adapt the contemporary liberation movement models of Franz Fanon (*The Wretched of the Earth* was required reading for the orga-

During more than three hours on April 26, 1937, the Basque market town of Gernika, Bizkaia, was bombed by German and Italian airplanes dropping approximately thirty tons of explosives and incendiary bombs. Fleeing civilians were machine-gunned from the air, with the total number of killed approximately two thousand and another one thousand wounded. The horrors of Gernika were depicted by Pablo Picasso in his painting *Guernica*, created for the Paris art exhibition of 1937.
Photograph as published by DEIA.

---

nization), Ernesto "Che" Guevara, and Mao Tse-tung. Action, not the hibernation of the PNV, they believed, would bring about change.

Federico Krutwig, writing under the pseudonym Fernando Sarrailh de Ihartza, declared in his publication Vasconia (1964) that violence could be effectively used to set off widespread popular mobilizations against the government. Proposing a positive correlation between state violence and popular violence, Krutwig saw an accelerat-

ing spiral of violence between Basque protestors and the
Guardia Civil leading to greater popular anger and mili-
tancy to the point of revolution. Krutwig's arguments
were refined and detailed into how a guerilla should
move against a government, becoming a primer for ETA
guerilla warfare. During the first half of the decade of the
1960s, ETA's energies and resources had been devoted
primarily to cultural activism. The second half could be
exemplified by the following statement published in the
ETA newsletter, *Zutik* (Arise): "Violence is necessary—a
contagious, destructive violence that supports our struggle, a good struggle, one that the Israelis, Congolese, and
Algerians have taught us" (Zirakzadeh 1991, 162).

IN EUSKAL Herria, ETA participants of all the various
groups continued to disagree about objectives and
the methods for achieving such objectives, forming additional detached groups that promoted different paths
to different goals for the Basque Country. Opposition to
the focus on labor and to strategies of violence mounted.
Txillardegui and other senior ETA members, many of
whom were in exile in Belgium, France, and several Latin
American countries, packed a meeting of ETA's Fifth
Assembly and overthrew the labor leadership, expelling
them from the organization. The original ETA became
known as ETA-V, because of the significance of the Fifth
Assembly, while the expelled New Left members and
followers formed an ETA-berri, literally the New ETA.
The subsequent divisions within ETA confounded an
already extremely fragmented nationalist movement.
The original objectives of Txillardegui's ETA—territorial independence and cultural revitalization—were now
hardly recognizable and were greatly misunderstood in
the diaspora.

When Basque nationalism had slowly resurfaced in
the 1960s, its ideology thus had shifted dramatically.

Previously the nationalists had declared socialism and socialists to be anti-Christian and anti-Basque. However, the young nationalists who emerged with Euskadi 'ta Askatasuna proclaimed themselves to be socialists as well as nationalists, and many were members of the Catholic clergy. This conversion was inspired in part by the student demonstrations and movements in Europe, the Vatican II proclamations and changes in church relations with oppressed peoples, and Third World struggles against colonialism and imperialism. In defining Basqueness, the importance of Basque culture had replaced the Basque race, and Basque socialism had replaced Basque Catholicism. Opinions had gradually changed to agreement on the idea of a right to self-determination and therefore an inherent right to sovereignty—only Basques could and should rule Basques.

WHAT HAD not been altered was the significance of being *abertzale*, or patriotic, being a "good" or "true" Basque, according to ETA sympathizers. Only a nationalist could be an *abertzale*, and hence only an *abertzale* could be a nationalist. Basque society became polarized into *abertzales* and *españolistas*: One was either Basque or anti-Basque. Anti-Basques included the Spanish police, the Guardia Civil, plus the internationalist Communist and Socialist Parties in Euskadi and ancestrally Basque people who were not nationalists. Basque industrialists suffered tremendously at the hands of ETA, with kidnappings, extortion payments, and assassinations justified by the explanation that these industrialists were traitors to Basque society because of their ties to the Spanish economy.

As is often the case, it took sensational political events with international media attention to demonstrate to the Basques and all others in the outside world that Franco's Spain was still not democratic and that civil and human

News from the Basque Country to the immigrant communities was generally communicated by word of
mouth from recent immigrants and by letter. During
the Spanish Civil War, Basques could not rely on the biased articles being published in their local media, and
they shared their own personal letters from home with
others. Peter and Mary Altuna Toja received postcards
from the Basque Country depicting the 1937 bombing
of Gernika, or Guernica, and shared them with the New
York Basque community.
Postcard courtesy of the Peter Toja Jr. Family Collection.

rights in the Basque provinces were almost nonexistent. In 1968, Melitón Manzanas, a Spanish police commissioner with a reputation as a torturer, was assassinated, and ETA participants were fingered as the main suspects. The Spanish government imposed a state of exception, and over two thousand Basques were arrested, with many beaten and tortured for information. Sixteen nationalists (two of whom were priests and others who were admitted *etarras* and ETA sympathizers) were charged with the killing, although all pleaded innocent. Conviction was to result in capital punishment, and the city of Burgos— outside the Basque provinces—was chosen for the military tribunal site. Foreign journalists reported repeated violations of international human rights conventions and principles of due process and repeated in detail the suspects' descriptions of Spanish police torture.

DIASPORA communities in Australia, the United States, Uruguay, and Argentina mobilized in rare collective political action and attempted to influence their host country governments' foreign policies with Spain. Basques in Melbourne organized a dockworkers' strike in Canberra to protest at the seat of the national government. Radio interviews included Basque community leaders, such as Pablo Oribe, giving their perception of the Franco dictatorship and lack of civil rights in the Basque Country. In Sydney and in North Queensland, Basque communities sent hundreds of letters to the national parliament demanding that the Australian ambassador to Madrid object to the treatment of the Basque suspects (Pablo Oribe interview, 1997; Miren Garagarza interview, 1997). In Uruguay, Montevideo witnessed street demonstrations, letter-writing campaigns to parliamentarians, and public denouncements of Franco by the Basque community and the centenary Basque center, Euskal Erria. Dozens of centers in

Argentina demanded that their government react to the Spanish government actions, and immediate fund-raising activity for the families of those imprisoned in Burgos resurrected latent nationalist sentiments.

SURPRISINGLY, in the typically apolitical Basque communities of the United States, private individuals, not centers, organized dinners, dances, and donation drives to send money for the Basque cause. According to organizer Pete T. Cenarrusa, more than two hundred people met at the Boise Euzkaldunak Incorporated Basque Center to sign a telegram to Franco requesting clemency for the death sentences ordered by the military tribunal. The governors of Idaho, Nevada, and Oregon sent official letters of protest to Madrid. Belgian student groups in Brussels demonstrated against their government's support for or neutrality regarding Franco. After the sixteen guilty sentences were announced, six including orders for execution, even the Vatican entered the arena, asking the Spanish government to exercise clemency.

Within Euskal Herria, the unanticipated outpouring of international attention and support reinforced the commitment of activists within the ETA movement and catapulted others into action for the first time. Although six were found guilty, after the intercession by the pope, Franco granted stays of execution, reprieves, and lesser prison sentences. Although in the aftermath of the Manzanas killing the membership of the ETA had been decimated by arrests and flights from the homeland, now hundreds of new recruits were ready to take their places. Worldwide attention to the plight of the Basques as an oppressed people lent credence and justification for ETA actions for the first time, and Basque individuals in diaspora communities began to perceive a justification for ETA activity that previously had not been understood.

A recurring theme in interviews with Basques abroad is that although respondents may not support ETA operations today, they did favor Franco-era ETA activities as necessary defensive reactions to state terrorism. They used the Burgos trials as one more example of repeated victimization by central Spanish political powers.

Prior to Franco's death in 1975, conforming to Krutwig's spiral theory of violence, ETA unleashed a wave of violent political protests unlike anything ever experienced before in the Basque Country. It defended its armed robberies, bombings of personal, commercial, and military properties, kidnappings, and assassinations as necessary acts against the region's symbols of capitalist wealth. The kidnapping of industrialist Lorenzo Zabala in 1972 was perplexing, because he was ethnically and linguistically Basque. ETA-V argued that the kidnapping demonstrated how ETA's armed struggle and the demands of striking workers could be combined for success. A new justification for the violence emerged: Intense differences of opinion among government officials concerning responses to ETA violence would bring down the coalition of moderate reformers and hard-core Francoists (Zirakzadeh 1991,186).

CONTRARY TO ETA's expectations, there did not seem to be any fissures in the government or doubts about another harsh crackdown by the Guardia Civil when ETA assassinated Franco's chosen political successor, Carrero Blanco, by bombing his car sky-high in 1973. Another series of arrests, beatings, and tortures of suspected ETA sympathizers and labor dissidents, together with a mass exodus into exile in France, Belgium, and Venezuela, left organized Basque nationalist groups in the four southern provinces devoid of senior leadership. More infighting regarding the lack of communication and approval of acts to be undertaken, doubts about aligning with non-Basque labor groups, and immediate plans for action after Franco's imminent death further divided the already fragmented Basque nationalists. The label *etarras* now would include ETA-poli-milis, those who favored subordinating violent military action to the political task of mobilizing non-elites, and ETA militar, those who believed ETA's most important goal should be to continue the armed struggle and strategy in accordance with the spiral theory of violence. Military operations were out of control, and there was no oversight and no communications between field organizers. Operations backfired, and instead of inspiring popular action, repelled many by the Basque use of terror against other Basques. Former ETA members and sympathizers watched from Euskal Herria and from exile as Basque nationalists became each other's worst enemies.

THE POLITICAL and economic ideological fragmentation in the homeland nationalist movement during the 1970s confused those in Euskal Herria and most of those in the diaspora who were being asked to support the Basque government-in-exile, ETA, ETA-V, ETA-berri, and ETA-poli-milis. "What is going on in our country?" and "Which group believes in what theories?" became the exasperated questions of discussions, as well as the cause of many debates and problems in Basque communities around the world. Lacking information, and often worse, receiving conflicting descriptions and explanations of events, Basques abroad whom I interviewed stated that they began to lose interest because they could not keep straight all of the arguments, factions, and movements within what they judged should be a unified Basque nationalist movement for independence.

The creation of ETA and the subsequent splits within ETA thus confounded an already extremely complex nationalist movement. The change in rhetoric of the

Although Basque centers as institutions have not usually become involved in the political issues of the host country or the homeland, individual Basques have shown interest in issues and events in Euskal Herria, from protests against the abolition of the *fueros* in the late 1800s to anti-Franco protests in the 1970s. Here, Basques in Los Angeles, California, demonstrated at the Spanish Consulate on October 12, 1975 against the lack of civil rights and due process of law under the Spanish government.

Photo as published in Voice of the Basques.

New Left to class struggle and class identity rather than ethnic and cultural struggle and identity was not well received by Basques who had not lived in the provinces perhaps for decades. At the same time, except in Australia, the PNV had the advantage of a developed network and already established communications with diaspora Basque centers. The majority of Civil War exiles were familiar with the PNV leadership's names, strategy, and goals.

During the 1970s, most of the Basque centers in the diaspora modified their organizational statutes and practices and began describing themselves as apolitical, fearful of experiencing the same divisiveness that was descending upon their homeland. Politics slowly moved to the arena of home and private conversation, and the cultural activities of maintaining the Basque Country's language and its music, dance, gastronomy, literature, art, and sports moved to the forefront of diaspora institutional activity. The political layer of the Basque diaspora would be thin and short-lived on top of its trade and colonial substrata.

SPANISH STATE violence and repression triggered more Basque violent reactions. Although murders carried out by ETA units had never exceeded seventeen per year between 1968 and 1977, in *each* of the years 1978, 1979, and 1980, over sixty-five killings were attributed to ETA groups (Clark 1984, 133). Franco's widely celebrated death in November 1975 did nothing to diminish ETA activities. Worldwide attention to the plight of the Basques as an oppressed people initially had lent credence and justification for ETA actions. However, soon the media coverage focused on the activities themselves, not the rationale or objectives behind them, leading host-country populations to equate "Basque" with "violence" and "terrorism"—a burden that homeland and diaspora Basques everywhere have had to carry. The spiral theory of violence was accurate for ETA and Spanish state actions, but a popular uprising against the regime never materialized. The opposite attitude seemed to have affected most in the middle and upper classes, and the lower working class was tiring of bearing the brunt of Spanish state repression against them. They believed ETA tactics had been unsuccessful in igniting popular revolution and that with a new prime minister and king, improvements should be on the way. They had waited forty years, what would five or six more matter?

Not only did Basques in the diaspora oppose nationalist talk of workers' struggle, coalitions with Spanish labor unions, and abandoning an independent Euskal Herria, but they rejected outright the proposals of armed revolution and arbitrary violence advanced by Federico Krutwig. However, because the Basque government-in-exile had been unsuccessful in achieving any change or improvement for the southern provinces, its status and that of the PNV also waned, and diaspora Basques were willing to listen to the original ETA goals. However, too many mutations of political ideologies and strategies, a lack of information and communication, and a general misunderstanding of the fragmentation in the nationalist movement caused many exiles to begin questioning whether or not there would ever be a Basque Country to which they could return, the Basque Country that they remembered. More upsetting for them, they began to question whether or not they would *want* to return.

Many in the Basque communities abroad had been exiled for at least forty years, and the majority had married and started families in their host countries. Some had taken adolescent children with them into exile, and those had now married with host-country residents and were producing grandchildren, making it yet more distressing for immigrants to leave their families in the host country for a return to an uncertain Euskal Herria. As would be expected, immediate daily pressures and exigencies in the host society demanded attention, and Basques in their communities abroad began to lose interest in and understanding of political events in the

Traditional agricultural Basque society was based upon
family manual labor, which used rudimentary planting
and harvesting implements such as the picks seen here,
up until the 1960s and 1970s.
*Photograph by Eulalia Abaitua Allende Salazar. Cour-
tesy of the Basque Archaeological, Ethnographic, and
Historical Museum, Bilbao.*

---

homeland. Ties to each other were still strong, with
associations and ethnic social networks that provided
pieces of information—although specifics occasionally
conflicted. What is significant is that the transnational
ties of Basques in their separate host countries con--

tinued with individuals and organizations in the Basque homeland.

AT THE END of the 1970s, the Spanish prime minister, Adolfo Suarez, approved a representative body, the Basque General Council, to facilitate the expected limited transfer of power from Madrid to the Basque region, and all sectors of Basque society wished to have their opinions voiced. Exhausted by government repression and arrests, frustrated by the failure of the spiral theory of violence and the inability of ETA to ignite popular resistance, and subject to the increasingly strong disfavor of the public and other Basque nationalist groups, most of the units of ETA-político-militar dissolved in the 1980s, leaving only a small sector of ETA-militar still engaged in armed struggle. Former participants decided to use nonviolent means of change and the new legal opportunities presented in the increasingly democratic institutions of post-Franco era. A number of ETA leaders also endorsed the idea of negotiating while there was still something to negotiate before a new French government policy of cooperation with the Spanish wiped out their safe houses, weapons, and money. A new coalition of former and current *etarras* and their sympathizers developed, calling itself Herri Batasuna, HB, One United People or One United Land. It was a loose coalition that agreed to promote what is known as the KAS Alternative, Koordinadora Abertzale Sozialista, the Democratic Alternative for the Basque Country, which included immediate withdrawal of Spanish polices forces from the Basque provinces, release of all Basque political prisoners, and political independence for the four Basque provinces. The Herri Batasuna coalition would not participate in the newly developed political institutions, and with the legalization of political parties and unions and limited autonomy and self-governance

for the Basque regions, the KAS Alternative lost importance for other nationalists, who were willing to play by
the rules of the new constitution.

IN THE SUMMER of 1979, the Suarez government
debated an autonomy statute allowing the provinces
of Araba, Bizkaia, and Gipuzkoa to establish a regional
parliament with limited fiscal, educational, and a few
other policy-making rights, and importantly, to allow the
Basque provinces their own police force. Many citizens
vividly remember the parades of the original Ertzaintza,
the Basque police, in front of the cheering and emotional
crowds throughout the provinces. Nafarroa negotiated
a separate autonomy apart from the other three, which
are now politically Euskadi, the Basque Autonomous
Community, and it created its own autonomous community. The PNV and Euskadi'ko Ezkerra, the Basque Left,
endorsed the proposal for Euskadi and urged Basque
citizens to approve it through the referendum process.
HB opposed the statute and favored abstention, com-
plaining that the powers granted were too limited, that
Nafarroa had been separated on purpose to divide the
power of the Basques and should be included with the
other three, and that demands for removing the Spanish
military police and granting amnesty to political prisoners had not been addressed. The voter turnout was only
57 percent. However, 94.6 percent of those voted in favor
of the proposed statute, and therefore the referendum
passed.

CONCLUSION
In order to understand the intense hatred of Franco,
which extends to the Spanish central government, the
military, and for others the Catholic Church because
of its silence and later pro-Francoism, it is imperative
to read many works about the Spanish Civil War and

the Franco years. The reader is strongly encouraged
to investigate this complex topic with additional readings and perspectives. However, here, we will focus
on the fundamentals and the overarching perceptions
that are manifested by Basques abroad. In my years of
fieldwork with Basques living outside of Euskal Herria,
I have found that the older a person is, the more likely
they know more about the circumstances of the turmoil
and tragedy, but also the more likely they are emotionally involved and are unable or unwilling to see any
other side to the story besides the conservative Basque
nationalist version. In later generations of Basques, the
younger the person is, the less likely he or she is to have
any clear knowledge or understanding of the Civil War
and of the following Franco dictatorship. In interviews
I conducted from 1986 to 2004 with Basque teenagers
from twenty-one different countries, the results have
been similar: Many do not know exactly who Franco was,
many are confused about the dates of the Spanish Civil
War, and others *do* know there was a long dictatorship
in Spain by someone—or something—named "Franco,"
but they are not sure in which century this took place.

IN SEVERAL of the Basque communities abroad I was
asked by one adolescent or another, *"What was*
Franco?" or *"What* is that?"—*"What?"* not *"Who?"* Perhaps this lack of knowledge stems from being a teenager
and generally insufficient formal studies thus far in life.
However, this information is not in the formal education
curricula in any of their countries, but is the sort that
was passed down in oral histories from parent to child
and grandparent to grandchild. It seems that perhaps
this tradition is no longer being kept or has begun to
lose its importance in these communities.

Lesson thirteen

BIBLIOGRAPHY

Artís-Gener, Avelí. 1976. *La Diáspora Republicana*. Barcelona: Editorial Euros.

Clark, Robert P.1984. *The Basque Insurgents: ETA, 1952–1980*. Madison: University of Wisconsin Press.———. 1979. *The Basques: The Franco Years and Beyond*. Reno: University of Nevada Press.

Jacob, James E. 1994. *Hills of Conflict: Basque Nationalism in France*. Reno: University of Nevada Press.

Legarreta, Dorothy. 1984. *The Guernica Generation: Basque Refugee Children of the Spanish Civil War*. Reno: University of Nevada Press.

Ordaz Romay, Mari Ángeles. 1996. "El FBI y los vascos del exílio de 1939 en Estados Unidos." In *Emigración y redes sociales de los vascos en América*, ed. Ronald Escobedo Mansilla, Ana de Zabala Beascoechea, and Oscar Alvarez Gila. Vitoria-Gasteiz: Universidad del País Vasco.

Payne, Stanley G. 1975. *Basque Nationalism*. Reno: University of Nevada Press.

San Sebastián, Koldo. 1991. *The Basque Archives: Vascos en Estados Unidos (1939–1943)*. Donostia–San Sebastián: Editorial Txertoa.

Sarrailh de Ihartza, Fernando. 1964. *Vasconia*. Buenos Aires: Ediciones Norbait.

Thomas, Hugh. 2001. *The Spanish Civil War*. New York: The Modern Library.

Totoricagüena, Gloria. 2004. *Identity, Culture, and Politics in the Basque Diaspora*. Reno: University of Nevada Press.
———. 2003. *La Diáspora Comparada*. Serie Urazandi. Vitoria-Gasteiz: Eusko Jaurlaritza.

Zirakzadeh, Cyrus Ernesto. 1991. *A Rebellious People: Basques, Protests, and Politics*. Reno: University of Nevada Press.

REQUIRED READING
Robert P. Clark, *The Basques: The Franco Years and Beyond* (Reno: University of Nevada Press, 1979), chapter 2, pp 49–55; chapter 3, pp 57–76, and notes, pp 398–99.

Hugh Thomas, *The Spanish Civil War* (New York: Modern Library, 2001), pp 12–186.

Cyrus Ernesto Zirakzadeh, *A Rebellious People: Basques, Protests, and Politics* (Reno: University of Nevada Press, 1991).

WRITTEN LESSON FOR SUBMISSION
Compare the ideals and issues of the Carlist Wars in the 1800s to those of the Spanish Civil War, 1936–1939 Describe the importance of the Basque Statutes of Autonomy and its significance in gaining and keeping loyalty to the elected Spanish Republican government under siege, and give a brief account of the immediate duties of the first Basque government Also describe the causes and effects of the use of political violence by the Spanish state and by the Basque resistance Do you believe that the apparent decline of communication from generation to generation of the memories of the Spanish Civil war and the Franco era via oral transmission is a positive or negative development? Why?

14 · The Basque government-in-exile
The political diaspora

WE HAVE DISCUSSED the fact that the newly elected Spanish republican government had promised to grant autonomy to those regions voting with a clear majority in favor of their own autonomy. In 1931, in Estella-Lizarra, Nafarroa, elected representatives of Basque society voted 90 percent in favor of proclaiming separation and accepting their Statutes of Autonomy. After meeting additional conditions the actual population voted in favor of the home rule in 1933. The Spanish republican parliament delayed their deliberations, and Basque autonomy was finally approved on October 1, 1936, only after the Spanish Civil War had already begun.

Members of the government-in-exile were appointed by the *lehendakari*, or president, of the Basque Country, who was elected by delegates of the Basque population on October 7, 1936, in accordance with the law for Basque home rule. President José Antonio de Aguirre y Lecube took his oath of office under the Tree of Gernika, at the site of the historical Basque parliament. However, after the Spanish nationalists' military victories in the Basque provinces, the Basque government was forced into exile. The cabinet of this first Basque government consisted of five members from the Partido Nacionalista Vasco, two from the Basque Republican Party, two from the Basque Socialist Party, and one from the Communist Party—who actually was expelled from the Communist Party because he had followed the Basque nationalist policy. There were others who were caught and forced to surrender to Franco and who were later executed and one who died while escaping the German invaders. The government was able to benefit from the diaspora networks of established *euskal etxeak*, or Basque centers, and from economically and politically elite Basque individuals who attempted to influence their host-society governments in favor of the Republic.

Because the border with France was controlled by the Spanish nationalist forces, the Basque government negotiated an agreement with the British to use their military vessels for an evacuation of thousands of civilian war refugees from the port of Bilbao, and France agreed to accept the Spanish citizens and to provide care for them. The Basque government oversaw more than sixty trips by Basque, French, and British ships taking exiles to safety to more than twenty locations in France and Belgium. With the fall of Catalonia another half a million persons attempted to move into France. The Basque government worked fervently to arrange for transportation, especially for the wounded and elderly, and they even established a system of Basque schools for the children. During the Civil War there were Basque delegations in Baiona, Madrid, and Barcelona, and by 1938, there were more than fifty different Basque organizations in Barcelona. With the military fall of Catalonia, the Basque government-in-exile moved its operation to Paris, where between 1936 and 1939 Rafael Picavea had created an information network in favor of the Basques and the republican cause, including the publication of the newspaper *Euzko Deya* beginning in November 1936. Delegates worked diligently to get the support of the political leaders and Catholic elite in Europe and in the Americas.

As early as August 1937, the Basque government sent officials to France to construct a framework for a government-in-exile and to begin urgent organization for the immediate care of thousands of refugees pouring into Iparralde. President Aguirre and other Basque officials also established an office of the Basque government in Barcelona in order to maintain communications

The president of the Basque government-in-exile, José
Antonio Aguirre (center of photograph) worked with
his cabinet and delegates in the New York offices of the
Basque government, which were officially established
in 1938. The New York Basque delegation attempted to
influence the United States government and representatives of the Catholic Church in favor of the Basque Autonomous Government, the ouster the dictator Francisco
Franco, and the return to the elected representative government in Spain. From left are government ministers
Ramón María Aldasoro, Santiago Aznar, José Antonio
Aguirre, Telesforo Monzón, and Gonzalo Nardiz.

---

with the government of the Spanish Republic. When
Barcelona fell, Aguirre also fled, eventually establishing
his location in Paris as the headquarters of the Basque
government-in-exile. This was the home of the Basque
government-in-exile until the outbreak of World War II.

The same year, war refugees from Nafarroa, Gipuzkoa,
Araba, Bizkaia, and other areas in Spain began fleeing

to Cuba, Mexico, Venezuela, Chile, Uruguay, and Argentina. In 1938, a Basque government's Delegate Commission visited several of the established Basque centers throughout the Americas in order to investigate the possibilities of the *euskal etxeak* being used as official reception centers for the coming immigration. Numerous Basques in South America volunteered their services and their homes. Already established Basque communities provided information and knowledge for migration networks to their relatives and friends. This reinforced relations between the government-in-exile and the diaspora because many of the political officials were now in these communities abroad and were able to mobilize people at the Basque centers to aid other refugees and to collect financial contributions for the office in Paris.

BETWEEN 1939 and 1945, approximately fifteen hundred Basque exiles fled to Venezuela alone. In 1940, these Basques established the charity Asociación Vasca de Socorros Mutuos, the Basque Association of Mutual Aid, and in 1942 founded the first Basque center in Caracas. As we have noted before, Argentine-Basque women formed Argentine chapters of the PNV's women's nationalist organization, Emakume Abertzale Batza, United Patriotic Women, which transferred financial and material aid to the Basque Country and received Basque political refugees into Argentine society. And as we have also noted, Basque communities in Argentina, Uruguay, Chile, Venezuela, Cuba, and Mexico sent private funds and accommodated and sustained the Basque government-in-exile, its delegations, and fugitive families. Basques assisted in creating the delegations of the Basque government-in-exile in several different countries in Europe, South America, and in the United States, in New York City. The same level of support cannot be claimed for Basque communities on the West Coast of

the United States, as we have also noted. There, attempts
to raise money for the Basque government-in-exile fell
on deaf ears.

THE BASQUE DELEGATION IN NEW YORK

PRIOR TO ANY Basque government suggestion, the
Basques in New York established the Committee Pro-
Euzkadi in 1937 in order to create and disseminate information about the current war situation in the Basque
Country and to search for humanitarian aid for the
refugees. The Committee Pro-Euzkadi used the offices
of the New York Basque center, the Centro Vasco-Americano, or C.V.A., and together the organizations mailed
information to members encouraging them to join the
cause. The Centro Vasco-Americano donated the profits
from dances to the Committee Pro-Euzkadi. The C.V.A.
received letters from the Argentine Basque organization
Zazpiak-Bat of Rosario in the province of Santa Fe, from
the Department of Justice of the Basque government,
and from the Euzkadi Buru Batzara, or National Council
of Euzkadi, which governed the PNV. In 1938, the C.V.A.
communicated with the Basque delegation in Mexico
City, asking for information about their activities in support of needy Basques exiled from the Basque Country.
It is evident from these and many more examples that
the New York and other organizations were participating
in nonstate international affairs, with questions regarding the Spanish Civil War, refugee safety and placement,
and funding for the government-in-exile, as well as in
an international network of information sharing among
Basque communities.

The C.V.A. in New York maintained communications
with the Basque government while it was headquartered
in Valencia, Spain, in the summer of 1937. The collector
of C.V.A. membership dues was directed by the organiza-

tion's board of directors to share all of the books, letters, and documents sent by the Basque government with the Basque families and persons he visited when collecting fees. Assorted individuals also privately received information bulletins from the Basque government's general delegation located in Barcelona after the fall of Bilbao. In July of 1937, the president of the Basque government went into exile after the bombings of Durango and Gernika and the fall of Bilbao, just one year into the Spanish Civil War. As we noted in the preceding lesson, José Antonio de Aguirre escaped to Paris, and from there his officers organized the exile of over one hundred and fifty thousand Basques, including approximately thirty thousand orphans and children traveling without their parents—none of whom were ever admitted into the United States.

A s WE ALSO noted in the preceding lesson, it is not surprising that many people around the world were confused with the politics of post–Civil-War Spain. There were three elected governments representing the people: the government of the Spanish Republic, representing all of Spain, but not the Basque and Catalan provinces; the new government of Euzkadi, representing the recently autonomous Basque provinces; and the government of Catalonia, whose president, Lluis Companys, was executed by Spanish Nationalist forces, representing the now autonomous provinces of Catalonia, and each government had gone into exile by the end of the war in 1939. Besides the government of Euzkadi, both the Spanish Republican government and the government of Catalonia had representatives in South America, Europe, and New York who maintained relations with the Basque communities. The Basque delegation tried to distance itself from the government of the Spanish Republic in order to create their own identity among U.S. politicians and elites in New York, as well as among the existing New York Basque population. The Basque government-in-exile used its base in New York as its central office for its relations with the U.S. government and later with the United Nations.

WHEN THE Basque government-in-exile established the Basque delegation in New York in 1938, it opened its offices in the New Weston Hotel and later in the Hotel Elyseé, both in Manhattan. The initial delegates were Antón de Irala e Irala, Manuel de la Sota y Aburto, Ramón de la Sota Mac Mahon, José Urresti, Juan Aramburu and Eustacio Arrítola. Later came Jesús de Galíndez, Jon Bilbao, Jon Oñatibia, and Cipriano Larrañaga. With the help of the C.V.A. and especially the help of boardinghouse and restaurant owner Valentín Aguirre, they created a list of names and addresses of people who would likely be interested in their cause and able to help it. By February 1939, 271 Basques in New York had donated money and pledged a contribution each month. Amounts ranged from twenty-five cents to three dollars per month. They also had created a list of nineteen donors from Reno, Nevada, and twenty-four from Elko, Nevada. Manuel María de Ynchausti, a principle actor in both the evacuation of children from the Basque Country and the advancement of Basque interests in diplomatic circles, founder of the International League of Friends of the Basques, and a wealthy temporary immigrant to White Plains, New York, also funded several thousand dollars to the Basque delegation. Ynchausti and his family had come to New York on their way to the Philippines, where their family fortune had been made, planning a short stay just long enough to establish a committee and a New York office of the International League of Friends of the Basques. However, World War II

Dr. José Antonio Aguirre was elected as President of the newly formed Basque Autonomous Government on October 7, 1936 by delegates of the Basque people. The government fled the Spanish Civil War bombings and eventually moved offices from Bilbao to Santander, Barcelona, Paris, London, New York and back to Paris. During his time in New York, President Aguirre was selected as a special lecturer at Columbia University. He left New York for Paris in 1946 where he remained as President until his death in 1960.

intervened, and the Ynchaustis stayed for eight years in White Plains, from 1939 to 1947.

In the early years, the main efforts of the Basque government-in-exile's New York delegation were focused on the Catholic community of intellectuals and clergy, with the hopes of influencing their policies and attitudes toward the Franco dictatorship and the media propaganda, which branded Basques as anti-Catholic and as Communists. The U.S. Catholic Church had been the intervening factor in not allowing Basque refugee children into the United States.

AFTER MANUEL de la Sota and Antón de Irala toured the American West meeting Basques, they decided to send Jon Bilbao to Boise, Idaho, to open a subdelegation in March 1940. He had recently finished a master's degree at Columbia University and was enthusiastic about the Boise possibilities. However, because of the lack of interest in homeland politics from the Idaho Basque community, the Boise office closed after only a few months, and Jon Bilbao departed for Berkeley, California, to begin his studies toward a PhD. New York remained the only office of the Basque delegation in the United States.

Lehendakari Aguirre left the Paris offices for Belgium and a family visit in May 1940 and was consequently trapped when Hitler's troops invaded the Low Countries in the very next days. The Nazi occupation in France and the Vichy government served as push factors for Basques to migrate again and to leave their somewhat safe havens in Iparralde for the Americas. Although the previous Pétain government had permitted hundreds of thousands of refugees from the Spanish Civil War to enter France and had allowed the installation of the Basque government-in-exile in Paris, after pro-Nazi French officials gained power in northern France, the Basque government-in-exile moved to London, and the Basque National Council was created there in 1940 by Manuel de Irujo and José Ignacio Lizaso to serve as the decision-making hub during the disappearance of *Lehendakari* Aguirre. Basques in London were translating the Parisian Basque Government newspaper *Euzko Deya* into English and distributing it to opinion leaders and diplomats in Britain. There were additional Basque dele-gations of the Basque government in Czechoslovakia, Bulgaria, and Yugoslavia, and, as we have seen, these networks were later also used by the U.S. government in agreements between the Basque government-in-exile and the United States State Department for espionage assistance during World War II.

AGUIRRE OBTAINED a false passport from the Panamanian consulate in Antwerp, Belgium, and disguised himself as "Dr. Álvarez Lastra." He determined that his best hiding place from the Germans would be right in Berlin, where they would never suspect him living, and he hid there from January to April 1941. He managed to travel from Berlin to Gothenburg, Sweden, and to get himself, his wife, and two children aboard a cargo ship headed for Rio de Janeiro, where they arrived in August 1941. They continued on to Uruguay, where he was able to reveal his true identity safely. During a few weeks in Argentina and Uruguay, *Lehendakari* Aguirre was received as a head of state and met with Catholic Church leaders and politicians of the highest levels. The Basque communities' *euskal etxeak* also prepared special celebratory dinners and conferences. The U.S. State Department received and approved a petition requesting a special visa for President Aguirre y Lecube in 1941, and from South America, the Aguirre family traveled to New York, where they were given permanent resident visas

The Basque Government-in-exile's Basque Delegation of Mexico worked in tandem with delegations in New York and throughout Europe and Central and South America in order to influence western aid for the return to democracy in Spain. Here, President José Antonio Aguirre, at the head of the table, meets with his delegate in Mexico, Alberto de Azua, second from left, and other Mexican representatives of the Basque Nationalist Party.
Photo courtesy of the Alberto Azua family collection.

---

and arrangements had been made for a special lecturer's position at Columbia University.

IRENE Renteria Aguirre was hired as the personal secretary to the president. She worked for eight years in the Basque delegation and also as the secretary to the *lehendakari*. Her knowledge of Basque, Spanish, English, and business management, coupled with her understanding and experience of New York and U.S. politics and protocol, made her indispensable and a much-desired expert for the Basque government. Andoni Aguirre (no relation to the president) arrived in New York in 1945 from the Philippines. He was hired by the Basque government as a commercial attaché, and later he and Irene Renteria married.

The offices in New York dealt with many diverse issues. They created lists of supporters in the United States with the intention of obtaining financial aid for the war victims. Many of the requests that were originally sent to the Centro Vasco-Americano, were eventually passed on to the delegation. Manuel de la Sota, one of delegates, agreed to offer the C.V.A. four consecutive Saturday conferences of presentations regarding the history of the Basque Country. During September 1942, Antón de Irala was also invited to give conferences for the Basque community. The delegation also attempted to support Basques from other regions of the world who requested assistance in obtaining special visas to enter the United States.

THE BASQUE delegation in New York published a news organ for the public, *Basques: Bulletin of the Basque Delegation in the USA*. The first issue was published in March 1943 and ran six issues until August 1944. The bulletin tried to inform its readers regarding the misinterpretation and omissions by the American press covering the current events in Spain and its military and political institutions. Every issue was published in perfect English and began with an editorial by Manuel de la Sota. Bulletins varied in length from eight to twenty-three pages and were distributed to the New York Basque community, Catholic elites and influential lay and clergy, and to academics and journalists. The largest number of articles concerned foreign-policy issues, the history of the Basque Country, and attempts to educate readers about the Basque point of view regarding the Franco dictatorship. Attempting to influence the

Catholic clergy, the November 1943 issue, number 5, was devoted to religion and the Basque people. The articles gave the names of Basque priests executed in Spain and information surrounding their executions, examined the relationship of Basques to the Catholic Church, and explained how the Basque *fueros* had already established a separation of church and state by the fourteenth century. Issue number 6 was devoted to law, the *fueros*, and the future of Basque democracy.

PROFESSOR José Antonio de Aguirre was officially invited to serve as a lecturer by Columbia University professors Carlton J. H. Hayes and Joseph P. Chamberlain. Hayes was a personal friend of President Franklin D. Roosevelt and later an ambassador to Spain. Manuel María de Ynchausti had worked with Hayes in 1939 in an attempt to have the renowned Basque anthropologist José Miguel de Barandiarán granted exile and given a position at Columbia, but the endeavor was unsuccessful. His friendship with Hayes likely influenced the invitation for Aguirre, as did his willingness to make donations to the university. In a letter sent September 23, 1941, Ynchausti pledged to pay Aguirre's salary through anonymous donations to Columbia, with the understanding that the funds were to be used specifically for Dr. Aguirre's salary for lecturing and giving courses at the university, but without Aguirre knowing that Ynchausti was funding the position.

Aguirre taught in the History Department from 1941 to 1946, in addition to his myriad responsibilities as president of the Basque government. Ynchausti helped President Aguirre translate his course lectures into English and did everything possible to facilitate the work of the Basque delegation and its representatives. Columbia University repeated their annual invitation to Aguirre to remain as a lecturer, and the institution's president exclaimed in several letters to Aguirre how pleased they were with his work at the university. Aguirre taught courses called Advanced Research in the Modern History of Western Continental Europe and Advanced Research in Latin American History.

IT IS CLEAR that Aguirre and the Basque government-in-exile collaborated with the State Department during Aguirre's stay in New York. He took a leave of absence from his lecturing position in 1942 and wrote in his letter to Columbia University, "Beside the cultural character of my journey, I shall also fulfill a confidential mission that an agency of the U.S. Government has entrusted to me." In March 1945, he again asked for a leave of absence "on an urgent mission related to France and other countries with the knowledge and special approval of the American authorities" (Totoricagüena 2004). Aguirre's official resignation from his lectureship at Columbia went into effect in June 1946. His letter of resignation stated:

> My duty lies with my Basque people's cause of freedom and with the cause of Iberian freedom …. Only those of us who come to these lands of freedom exiled by tyranny can appreciate the deep human understanding to be found in America and the hope it symbolizes for all …. Someday, perhaps soon, we Basque shall return again to our freed country and once again open the Basque University which General Franco closed in his systematic persecution of our culture.

He then asked for help from Columbia University for pedagogical direction, books, and cultural assistance for a future education system for Euskal Herria. The *lehendakari* returned to Paris in 1946, where he continued

the struggle of the Basque government-in-exile until his
death in 1960. His body was taken to Donibane Lohitzun-
St. Jean-de-Luz in Lapurdi and buried there.

ADDITIONAL BASQUE DELEGATIONS
The United States and Argentine delegations of the
Basque government-in-exile were officially the first and
second in the Americas. Although there is not sufficient
space here to describe all of the other delegations, those
of Argentina and Mexico were especially significant. The
Argentine offices were established with the arrival of
four delegates in November 1938 under the leadership
of Ramón de Aldasoro. They traveled the country to collaborate with the Basque communities, to organize fund-
raisers for the civilian victims of the war, and to meet
with the media. By May 1939, the newspaper *Euzko Deya*
had resumed publication—now from Buenos Aires—and
eventually had contributing correspondents in fifteen
different countries. The Basque delegation in Argentina
also worked to raise money to buy necessary items for
Basque war prisoners in the homeland. Aldasoro labored
with the established Basques to lobby the Argentine
president to accept the Basque refugees into Argentina.
The publishing house of Ekin was established in 1942,
which would eventually publish more than one hundred
and fifty different titles regarding Basque studies. The
American Institute of Basque Studies was founded in
1943, and their journal, *Bulletin of the American Institute of Basque Studies*, commenced publication in 1950.
After the visit of *Lehendakari* Aguirre, ten new Basque
centers were established in Argentina.

PRESIDENT Lázaro Cárdenas of Mexico declared his
support for the Spanish Republic immediately after
the Spanish military rebellion and even sent military aid
to the Republican forces during the war. Mexico also

Representatives of 50 countries met in San Francisco, California in 1945 for the United National Conference on International Organization in order to write the United Nations Charter. The Charter was ratified later that year and subsequently delegates selected midtown Manhattan in New York City for the permanent headquarters' physical location.

received an estimated twenty thousand Republican refugees, including children and orphans who were evacuated from the Pyrenees war zones to Morelia. The Basque delegation was established in January 1939, with Francisco de Belausteguigoitia and later Telesforo de Monzón, and was active with periodical publications and spreading information regarding current events in Euskal Herria and in other Basque communities around the world. Basques created the Commission of Basque Culture in 1942, and several Basque political parties had their own separate representation in the capital city. In 1946, the Spanish Republican Cortes, the legislative branch in exile, met in session in Mexico City. There were also South American Basque delegations in Chile, Colombia, Cuba, the Dominican Republic, Panama, Uruguay, and Venezuela.

THE UNITED NATIONS

JESÚS DE GALÍNDEZ was a Spanish Civil War exile who was caught and imprisoned in a French concentration camp, from which he later escaped. He later lived in the Dominican Republic as a delegate of the Basque government-in-exile during the dictatorship of Rafael Trujillo. His experiences in the Dominican Republic with the Trujillo régime led to his interest in the Dominican government, and his PhD dissertation investigated the corruption of that regime. He was requested by *Lehendakari* Aguirre to move to the United States in order to serve in the Basque delegation in New York City, and when he arrived in 1949, he was appointed as the Basque government observer to the United Nations. During this time, he also taught courses at Columbia University, where he was simultaneously a PhD student.

In Baiona in 1945, the Basque Consultative Council gathered political and labor leaders to pledge their support for the ongoing clandestine efforts against Franco, to coordinate a strategy for the resistance, and to keep the government-in-exile informed about movements in the Basque Country. In the same year, representatives of fifty countries had met in San Francisco at the United Nations Conference on International Organization to draw up the United Nations Charter. It was signed on June 26, 1945, and the United Nations officially came into existence on October 24, 1945, when the charter was ratified by a majority of the participants. The Basque government lobbied for and was successful in assuring the United Nations' refusal of Spain as a member. In 1945, the PNV-led government had created the Organización de Servicios, the Organization of Services, which worked as an information network to direct reports to the United States government. Anton de Irala worked for the Basque delegation in New York (and also at Columbia University) and for the United States State Department, attempting to influence United States government support for the Republican government.

However, in November 1950, the United Nations lifted the diplomatic embargo it had adopted in 1946 against Spain as a punishment to the Franco regime and its Fascist leanings during World War II, and in 1951, Ambassador José Felix de Lequerica y Erquiza, originally from Bilbao and now working for the Spanish government, presented his credentials to President Harry S. Truman. Jesús de Galíndez and *Lehendakari* Aguirre presented a case to the United Nations Educational, Scientific, and Cultural Organization (UNESCO) in 1952, protesting Franco's request for admission to the UN. They noted the closure of the Basque University created by the Basque government in 1936 under the terms of the Statutes of Autonomy of 1936; the occupation of libraries and social and cultural associations by the

The Basque government-in-exile was faced with the immediate crisis of placing refugee children rescued from the Spanish Civil War in safe homes. The Basque government's publication, *Eusko Deya*, here publishes a call from the Basque Children's Committee in London asking Basques in Argentina to take in forty-six children waiting in London who had been evacuated from Bilbao.

Guardia Civil military police; the mass burnings of books published in Euskara; the elimination of the use of Euskara in all schools, whether public or private, and even in the rural areas, where most families did not speak anything but Euskara; the prohibition of the use of Euskara in all public gatherings, in all publications, and on the radio; the suppression of Basque cultural societies, including the Society for Basque Studies, Eusko Ikaskuntza, and of the Academy for the Basque Language; the prohibition of the use of Euskara in all religious publications and in the celebration of all masses and other religious ceremonies; a decree requiring the translation into Spanish of all Basque names in civil registries and of all other official documents; the prohibition of the use of all Basque proper names in baptismal and other official documents; and a directive ordering the removal of all inscriptions in Euskara from tombstones and all funerary markers (Clark 1979, 137).

However, it was the beginning of the Cold War, and the United States was no longer listening to the Basques. Spain had more to offer in the way of a fight against Communism, and the Basque lobby was losing effectiveness against the worldwide Catholic Church and the advisors in the U.S. State Department, who favored Spain's staunch and sure anticommunism, regardless of its being a dictatorship. The negotiations for a military and economic agreement between Spain and the United States began in 1952, and was it signed and adopted in 1953 under the Eisenhower administration.

GALÍNDEZ CONTINUED as a lobbyist at the United Nations and as a PhD student preparing to submit and defend his dissertation at Columbia University in 1956. Several Basques interviewed in New York remember that he often mentioned that he received death-threat notes because of his involvement and study of the repressive Trujillo government of the Dominican Republic. In March 1956, after finishing his university lecture for a night course that he taught, he walked through the campus grounds, descended the stairs of the street entrance to the New York subway—and then was never seen again, alive or dead.

Over the decades, several conspiracy theories have been advanced by various groups asserting that he knew too much about the Trujillo government and that, before he could publish his dissertation, mercenaries of the Dominican Republic kidnapped and murdered him. Others believe Galíndez knew too much about the United States government's involvement with and aid to Trujillo, as well as U.S. espionage details he had learned from the Organization of Basque Intelligence, and that the United States government had him kidnapped and killed. Others even speculate that Galíndez was a spy for the United States government working to gather information on the Basques. To this day, the case has not been solved.

IT IS EVIDENT, however, that after Galíndez vanished, the institutional involvement of the Centro Vasco-Americano with the New York delegation diminished drastically. There are many other intervening variables, however, such as the death of activist Valentín Aguirre in 1953, the Catholic Church's support for the Franco government, the United States government's support for Franco, *Lehendakari* Aguirre's move back to Paris, and a later generation of leadership in the Centro Vasco.

By 1948, Aguirre had returned to Paris, and he participated at The Hague Congress, where European leaders discussed the idea of a united and federated Europe, with Aguirre promoting his idea of a European union of nationalities, or of peoples. The Basque government also promoted the massive general strikes in the Basque

Country of 1947 and of 1951. The offices of the Basque government in Paris were then confiscated and given to the Spanish in June 1951. In 1954, Francois Mitterand, then the minister of the interior, banned Radio Euskadi from the airwaves. However, the worst blow came when Spain was admitted to the United Nations in 1955 and José Felix Lequerica was appointed as Madrid's permanent representative. The Basque nationalist leaders had hoped to work alongside the Western democracies to overthrow Franco's regime and to return the autonomous Basque government-in-exile to its homeland. The Basque government-in-exile wanted to aid the Allies in any way possible in order to win their favor and help in evicting Franco and reinstalling a democratic, representative form of government. To appease the United States, they even expelled representatives of the Communist Party from the coalition of the Basque government-in-exile. Antonio Dupla claims that the Basque government-in-exile expelled Communists from its coalition government in May 1948 as a result of Nelson Rockefeller's suggestion to the Spanish Republicans that they should flee from any political contact with the Communist Party (Dupla 1992, 137).

CYRUS ERNESTO Zirakzadeh (1991, 147–48) points out that after 1947, the Basque government generally even avoided supporting labor union mobilizations. However, self-restraint by the Basques in Paris, London, Buenos Aires, Mexico, and New York did not result in their vindication or in convincing the Western powers that Franco had to be overthrown. Instead, the United States eventually deemed the Franco regime a reliable ally in the fight against Communism—and even worse for the Republicans—the United States formally recognized Franco's government in Spain and began giving it economic aid.

THE BASQUE GOVERNMENT LOOKS AHEAD

In 1956, on the twentieth anniversary of the formation of the Statutes of Autonomy, the PNV and the Basque government-in-exile sponsored the First World Basque Congress, bringing together in Paris nearly four hundred scholars, political and economic specialists, and activists from all over the world in order to discuss politics, economics, language, and projects for preserving Basque culture. They formed the Confederation of Basque Entities in America, which was to link all of the Basque centers in the Western Hemisphere, and chose Caracas for the headquarters.

AFTER THE death of Aguirre in 1960, and under leadership of Jesús María Leizaola, the Basque government-in-exile continued the same Christian Democratic, pro-European, and international policies. Many Basques attended the 1962 European Movement Congress in Munich and favored the Basque Country, and Spain also, joining the Council of Europe and the European Economic Community. The Basque government-in-exile, now at a different location in Paris, supported homeland workers' strikes, issued manifestations against Franco, and participated in the clandestine distribution of propaganda and information about activities inside Spain and about other Basques in exile. However, Leizaola was opposed to the formation of ETA and the use of violence in any attempt to achieve change in Spain. Leizaola returned to the Basque Country after the death of Franco and during the transition to democracy to witness the first elections for the Autonomous Basque Community and separate elections for the Foral Community of Nafarroa in the early 1980s.

Although the Basque government-in-exile was unsuccessful in many of its international political endeavors, nevertheless, historians Javier Tusell and Alicia Alted

Approximately thirty thousand Basque refugee children were evacuated from the southern provinces during the Spanish Civil War. They were usually received first in Iparralde before being moved to other camps in other countries. Here, children do their morning exercises at the Citadelle in Donibane Garazi, St. Jean Pied du Port. *Photograph as published in Gregorio Arrien,* La generación del exilio: Génesis de las escuelas vascas y las colonias escolares (1932-1940) *(Bilbao: Gurelan, 1983).*

---

argue that "the post-1977 negotiations for the Statutes of Autonomy for Catalonia, the Basque Country, and Galicia reflected the historical legitimacy these statutes had acquired during the Republican period—a legitimacy that was preserved throughout the Franco period by the exiled officials of these regions" and thus by the activities of the Basque government-in-exile (Tusell and Alted 1991, 160).

Lesson fourteen

BIBLIOGRAPHY

Aguirre, José Antonio. *Veinte años de gestión del gobierno vasco (1936–1956)*. Durango: Leopoldo Zugaza.

Anasagasti, Iñaki, and Koldo San Sebastián. *Los años oscuros: El gobierno vasco—el exilio (1937–1941)*. Donostia–San Sebastián: Editorial Txertoa.

Clark, Robert P. *The Basques: The Franco Years and Beyond*. Reno: University of Nevada Press, 1979.

Dupla, Antonio. 1992. *Presencia vasca en América, 1492–1992: Una mirada crítica*. Donostia–San Sebastián: Tercera Prensa—Hirugarren Prentsa, S.L.

Palacios Fernández, Emilio, ed. *Memoria del exilio vasco: Cultura, pensamiento, y literatura de loa escritores transterrados en 1939*. Madrid: Editorial Biblioteca Nueva, S.L.

San Sebastián, Koldo. 1998. *El exilio vasco en América: 1936–1946. Acción del gobierno*. Donostia–San Sebastián: Editorial Txertoa.

———. 1991. *The Basque Archives: Vascos en Estados Unidos (1939–1943)*. Donostia–San Sebastián: Editorial Txertoa.

———, and Peru Ajuria. 1989. *El exilio vasco en Venezuela*. Vitoria-Gasteiz: Servicio Central de Publicaciones Gobierno Vasco.

Totoricagüena, Gloria. 2004. *The Basques of New York: A Cosmopolitan Experience*. 2d ed. Basque Migration and Diaspora Studies Series, no. 2. Reno: Center for Basque Studies, University of Nevada, Reno.

Tusell, Javier, and Alicia Alted. "The Government of the Spanish Republic in Exile: (1939–1977)." In *Governments-in-Exile in Contemporary World Politics*, ed. Yossi Shain. London: Routledge. 1991.

Zirakzadeh, Cyrus Ernesto. 1991. *A Rebellious People: Basques, Protests, and Politics*. Reno: University of Nevada Press.

REQUIRED READING
José Antonio de Aguirre, *Escape via Berlin: Eluding Franco in Hitler's Europe* (Reno: University of Nevada Press, 1991).
Robert P. Clark, *The Basques: The Franco Years and Beyond* (Reno: University of Nevada Press, 1979), chapter 4, pp 79–106
Gloria Totoricagüena, *New York Basques: A Cosmopolitan Experience* (Serie Urazandi. Vitoria-Gasteiz: Gobierno Vasco, 2003), chapter 7.
Javier Tusell and Alicia Alted. "The Government of the Spanish Republic in Exile: (1939–1977)," in *Governments-in-Exile in Contemporary World Politics*, ed. Yossi Shain (London: Routledge, 1991), pp 145–65.

WRITTEN LESSON FOR SUBMISSION
Compare the French and United States positions toward the Basque resistance and their requests for political influence to bring an end to the Franco government. In what ways did United States politics of the 1940s and 1950s affect Spain's future? In what ways did this latest wave of political immigration affect the already existing Basque communities?

"Gernika generation"
Civil War's refugee children.

THE HISTORY OF the evacuation of the Basque children from the war-torn northern provinces during the Spanish Civil War is a story of the desperation of parents to transport their children to safety. It is also an example of how innocent victims are used in political debates by one group or another to justify their peace and wartime foreign-policy actions. When Europe was recovering from World War I and tensions were building on the eve of World War II, Basque refugee children became symbols of the elected Spanish Republican government for European leftist parties favoring democratic transitions in state politics and for those who favored a separation of church and state and the removal of Catholic control over politics in Catholic Europe. Conversely, Franco's depiction of the Basques as "Communists" and "Bolsheviks" intensified the rejection by conservatives around the world of assistance to the refugee colonies.

The military uprising against the Republican government began July 17, 1936, with Spanish forces in Morocco, and by July 18 had ignited in Spain itself. Although the European democracies had signed a non-intervention pact and did not assist the elected Republican government, troops from Italy and Germany, and Moroccan's foreign legionnaires fought on the side of the Spanish military coup and aided the Falangist forces during the Civil War. Only Mexico provided immediate aid to the Republic, with shipments of food and war equipment. Within weeks after the initial military rebellion, nearly eight thousand Gipuzkoans had abandoned their *baserris*, shops, and small businesses and the city of Donostia–San Sebastián to seek refuge in Iparralde. By the end of the summer of 1936, the Spanish military rebels had closed the Pyrenees border with France, stopping the possibility of Basques fleeing to safety in the northern Basque Country. Families that had begun a walking trek toward the mountains and the border to cross into France were now forced to reverse their direction and turn toward Bizkaia, and particularly Bilbao, which were still under the control of the Republicans and Basque nationalists. Dorothy Legarreta reports that of the prewar eighty thousand inhabitants of –San Sebastián, there were fewer than twelve thousand people remaining when the insurgent military General Mola arrived with regiments from Nafarroa (Legarreta 1984, 15).

ADMINISTERING THE EVACUATIONS

THE NEW Basque government, established with the Statutes of Autonomy in October 1, 1936, went to work immediately to construct networks of information for medical aid and support for fleeing exiles. The fledgling Department for Social Assistance organized humanitarian efforts to feed, clothe, and shelter tens of thousands of homeless war refugees, and within the first months of its existence, the Basque government had to react to the arrival of over one hundred thousand displaced persons in Bilbao alone. Soon thereafter, Bizkaia had an extra two hundred thousand homeless Basques from the other provinces. Schools were converted to military barracks and hospitals, and public buildings and private residences accommodated the onslaught of refugees. City officials also attempted to help the Basque government with record keeping to document the names of the living and the dead and to register the whereabouts of the members of divided families. Agricultural production declined as a result of the lack of labor to prepare and harvest gardens and orchards and from insufficient care of animal herds. After the crisis of food rationing

Basque war exiles included thousands of children who traveled without parents, and although attempts were made to keep siblings together, sometimes families were separated out of necessity. They were often accompanied by Basque priests and teachers who attempted to maintain the Basque language, music, song, and dance. The Mas-Eloi Limoges boarding school was home to Basque children for several years.

Photograph as published in Gregorio Arrien, La generación del exilio: Génesis de las escuelas vascas y las colonias escolares (1932-1940) *(Bilbao: Gurelan, 1983).*

---

began in the Basque provinces, Mexico sent fifty million pounds of garbanzo beans, which would eventually sustain the lives of this starving population for months during the Franco blockade of Bilbao and in the times of the worst sieges. The French trade unions also organized a food drive and delivered several thousand tons of food to Republican Spain.

In France, the Committee to Aid the Children of Spain was formed in November 1936 by the major trade unions, teachers' unions, production workers associations, and the French League for the Defense of the Rights of Man (Legarreta 1984, 35). More than five thousand French families volunteered to sponsor and care for evacuee children, and by April 1937, twenty "colonies" had been created to receive the homeless Basque children. The Soviet Union also signed the nonintervention pact, but remained sympathetic to the -Republicans. Soviet trade unions and educational and agricultural associations organized rallies in favor of the Spanish Republic, and fund drives raised millions of dollars for humanitarian aid. In several countries, "Communist-assisted Popular Fronts also sent in food, clothing, and medical supplies estimated to total as much as fifty million dollars" (Legarreta 1985, 191).

THE AERIAL bombardments of Durango and Gernika in the spring of 1937 were the first examples of the intentional military targeting of civilians in the history of modern warfare. The German forces' bombing of Durango on March 31 and of Gernika on April 26, 1937—and the subsequent eyewitness accounts published by war correspondents in international newspapers—shocked the world. Although Franco denied the bombing and then even attempted to argue that the Basques had done it to themselves, eyewitness accounts in the international press maintained the truth. Gernika had no military or strategic significance, but incendiary bombs had been used to set fire to the town and to cause further destruction in addition to that of explosive bombs. Civilians, including children, running from the devastation toward the forested mountains, had been machine-gunned. In England, the National Joint Committee for Spanish Relief raised funds for humanitarian aid, and word circulated in the Basque government of the possibility of an evacuation from the Basque Country for children and the elderly. In France, the positive response and aid came not from the French government, but from unions and associations of the political Left. As early as January 1937, the Spanish Republican government representatives in Paris had been informed of the possibility of French colonies prepared to receive thousands of Basque children, and now the Basque government swung into action.

IN BILBAO, refugees lived in train tunnels and in the hallways and foyers of public buildings and of residential apartment dwellings. *Bilbainos* received thousands more Basques into their own homes and living-room floors. Food was scarce because of the Spanish military blockade of ships delivering goods to the Basque coast. The war also interrupted the agricultural cycle of planting and harvesting, and food rationing was strictly enforced.

In the United States, press coverage of events in Spain included headlines from the *New York Herald Tribune*, "Women Slain in Street as German-Made Planes of Rebels Strafe Bilbao"; the *New York Post*, "Bilbao gets a Message from the Fascists"; the *New York Times*; "Ship Takes Aboard 4,000 Bilbao Girls"; and from the *New York Evening Journal*, "Basque Children to Come Here." A large number of Basques in New York were from Bizkaia, and the news of the Franco-ordered bombings of civilians in their hometowns and places they knew, such as Durango, Mungia, Gernika, and Bilbao, was overwhelming. In April 1937, the various Basque societies and organizations in New York that were related to Spain organized a joint dance to raise money for the hospitals of the Spanish Republican government in Spain and for its fight against the Falangist forces of Franco.

THE MEMBERSHIP of the New York Basque Center, Centro Vasco-Americano, and its president, Florencio Laucirica, agreed to support a June 1937 petition from the American Board of Guardians for Basque Refugee Children asking for its moral support and collaboration in their plans to rescue 500 Basque children from war in Bizkaia and to bring them to the United States. An "Extraordinary General Meeting" was called for the entire membership of the New York Basque society, and a commission of twenty-seven members headed the organization and collaboration plans. They also asked for the specific rules and regulations for Basque families who might wish to adopt any of these children. Publicity flyers included information with newspaper articles titled "500 Little Basque Refugees Coming to the U.S.A.," "Food and Peace for Little War Victims," "Liner Being Chartered to Bring Basque Children," and "Washington May Admit 500 Basque Children on Visitors' Visas Granting Six-Month Stays." The *New York Evening Journal* reported on May 21, 1937, that the American Board of Guardians for Basque Refugee Children, headquartered in New York, had chartered the French liner *Sinaia* to hasten the evacuation of war-demolished Bilbao and the transport of 500 Basque children to the United States. Board members included Dr. Frank Bohn; Dean Virginia Gildersleeve of Barnard College; Professor James T. Shotwell of Columbia University; Mary E. Woolley, president emeritus of Mount Holyoke College; Representative Carolyn O'Day of New York. Journalist Dorothy Thompson and scientist Albert Einstein also were leaders, and Eleanor Roosevelt accepted the position of honorary president. The original plan was to have the children depart Bilbao and disembark at Donibane Lohitzun, or St. Jean-de-Luz, in the northern Basque Country, then to take them by train north to Paris, to board the *President*

Harding at Le Havre, with the expected arrival in New York City on June 19, 1937. The older children were to be placed in private homes, and the younger children were to stay together under the tutelage of the Basque priests and teachers who would accompany them to a large nursery home to be established in New York City. Another United States group, the Committee for German-American Relief for Spain, was established at the same time in New York "to redeem the honor of Germany and the humanitarian tradition of the German people, decimated by Hitler's aviators in their massacre of the Catholic civilians of Guernica," stated Dr. Jacob Auslander, chairman of the committee.

WHEN TWENTY-SEVEN hundred New York families immediately responded offering their homes and the necessary money to care for and possibly adopt the Basque children, the American Board of Guardians asked permission to bring 2,000 children instead of the 500 previously agreed upon refugees. However, the leadership of the Catholic Church, and specifically Cardinal O'Connell of Boston, expressed opposition to allowing the Basque children in to the United States. The Basques had been branded as Communists and anti-Catholic by the Franco regime. Soon after, Eleanor Roosevelt stated in a press conference that perhaps it was not such a good idea to move the children so far away from their homeland to the United States, and by June 25, 1937, the U.S. State Department systematically denied all visa requests for the Basque refugees and orphans (Totoricagüena 2003).

Following the bombing of Gernika, President Aguirre and the Basque government's ministers pleaded their requests to the European capitals for urgent aid. As Franco's forces surrounded Bilbao, Aguirre's government initiated a plan to evacuate the entire civilian

Paul Oribe learned English as a Spanish Civil War child evacuee in England. He later moved to Australia as an adult with his wife, Carmen "Mentxu" Belon, also a war refugee who had been sent to England. Together, they worked to educate Australians about the suffering of Basques at the hands of the Franco dictatorship, and they lobbied Australian members of parliament in attempts to influence their foreign policy decisions toward Spain. Here, Oribe speaks to the Basque center membership of the Gure Txoko of Melbourne.
Photograph courtesy of Javier Amorebieta Zuñega.

population and relocate them to established Basque families spread throughout France. Between May and June 1937, all categories of ships were used to evacuate people from the ports of Bilbao in the most orderly fashion possible, and Legarreta reports than in one week alone, thirteen thousand refugees fled the city by sea (Legarreta 1984, 46). In Bilbao's center, the Hotel Carlton was established as an evacuation registration point for parents who now desperately sought any kind of safety for their children. Children from ages five to twelve years old were accepted for placement in France with the families of French Popular Front and the Committee to Aid the Children of Spain. Children were given registration numbers in order to track them throughout their movements, had medical exams and vaccinations, and were placed with French families with which they would live for the duration of the war, and others were transferred further to Belgium or England. The families had been selected and approved by the French unions. Bilbao newspapers reported that nearly two thousand children had been registered by their parents within the first few days. Groups of children were sent with Basque priests, doctors, and teachers who had volunteered to accompany them. Soon, Belgium, the Soviet Union, Mexico, Switzerland, and Denmark also pledged to became hosting countries, and Sweden, Holland, Canada, Uruguay, Czechoslovakia, and even Egypt offered to sponsor Basque colonies in France and Catalonia.

BILBAO FELL on June 19, 1937, and approximately one hundred thousand people began another race to safety, this time by land to the west of the Bizkaian coast, to Santander. Although thousands more Basques were evacuated from Santander, it, too, fell, on August 26, and the Basque Ministry of Evacuation moved farther west, to Gijón, in the province of Asturias. In all, approximately one hundred and twenty thousand citizens were registered as evacuees through Basque government channels: 26,000 from Bilbao, 30,974 from Santander, and 62,199 from Asturias (Legarreta 1984, 50). French and British nongovernmental organizations, labor unions, and the British Quakers established centers for hundreds of thousands of exiles now moving toward Catalonia, and particularly to Barcelona, and they installed special dining rooms where starving children could receive one meal per day.

COMMUNITY REACTIONS TO THE PRESENCE OF THE BASQUE CHILDREN

THE PRESENCE of the over twenty thousand unaccompanied Basque children in England, France, Belgium, and the Soviet Union became a political factor in several of the communities and tested the nonintervention and neutrality policies of several nations on the eve of World War II. Political party affiliation and religious practices were factors in the registration and in the placement of the Basque refugees. The overwhelming majority of the Basque children came from fervent Catholic families, but individuals were to be placed with families that were often anitclerical. Later, Catholic relief agencies also sponsored assistance for the Basques in France and Belgium. Belgian trade unions and workers' associations collaborated with Belgian Catholic organizations when the Belgian Popular Front agreed to sponsor 2,000 of the young evacuees, and the Belgian Catholic groups another 1,200 exiles. Those who were sent to Belgium lived mostly in adoptive homes or in Catholic boarding schools. Archbishop Jozef-Ernest Van Roey was instrumental in promoting the humanitarian efforts of the Catholics in Belgium and also in ensuring their safe repatriation after the Civil War.

Civil War food shortages resulted when farms were destroyed, abandoned, or captured by the enemy, forcing Basque refugees to plead for rations organized and distributed by the newly autonomous Basque government. In Gipuzkoa, which was invaded first by Spanish nationalist rebel forces from Nafarroa, after the fall of Donostia-San Sebastián, families fled toward the border, which was promptly sealed off, and then to Bilbao. Hundreds of thousands of refugees sought shelter in public buildings, train stations, and even train tunnels.
Photograph as published by DEIA.

IN FRANCE, over five hundred colonies and refugee houses were established for Basques, and more than five thousand families with union ties were selected to adopt children temporarily. However, the reception began to cool as thousands more refugees made their way north. The French press reported the Basques as "Reds," "Red Separatists," and "Communists" and began to complain about the costs of helping the Basques. French Catholics attempted to match the Vatican's description of Franco as the savior of the Catholic Church in Spain—from the communist, anticlerical Basques—with the daily examples they witnessed of the devoutly Catholic Basque exiles.

F RANCO'S BLOCKADE and the starving of the Basques had caused an uproar in Great Britain, and war correspondents' reports from the Basque provinces had educated the British about the true situation of the refugees and children fleeing Bilbao. Approximately four thousand Basque children found asylum in 100 different colonies in England, Scotland, and Wales, traveling on ships protected by the Royal Navy. However, in Britain, as in France, the existence of the Basque refugees reminded citizens of their government's nonintervention policy, and many also questioned the Catholic Church's support for Franco.

In Denmark, as well, the 102 asylum seekers from Asturias and Santander were protested by the German ambassador, who tried to convince the Danish parliament to send them back to Spain, although they had arrived only one week prior. The 1938 parliamentary debate included Conservative Party members referring to the children as the "enemies of society." Conservative Party leaders led town councils in voting to expel the children, and they were all removed to a remote island accessible only by ferry. They were then moved again out of Denmark and to the Basque colonies in France.

The historically neutral Switzerland also gave guardianship to 245 Basque children with Catholic and Socialist sponsorship, but no political conflict arose from their stay, and they were repatriated without problems after the Spanish Civil War had completely ended. The two thousand five hundred Basque children arriving in

Odessa in the Soviet Union in June 1937 were treated like "princes and princesses" until the Nazi invasion in 1941. They were evacuated again to safer locations, but were caught in another war, World War II.

In Mexico, the leftist president, Lázaro Cárdenas, had immediately declared support for the Republic. A group of elite Mexican women cooperated with the trade unionists and members of the Popular Front to prepare the reception of five hundred child refugees, mostly from Catalonia, Valencia, and Madrid, although they were referred to as Basque. "Los Niños de Morelia," as they were known, were housed in a government-operated school in Michoacan that soon attracted criticism regarding the government's expenditures and the anti-Republican views of other Mexicans. In 1942, the new president of Mexico, Manuel Avila Camacho, ended the government subsidy for the facilities, and the war refugees were forced to find their own accommodations. The Spanish government-in-exile's delegates living in Mexico attempted to find the children housing in hostels, and others lived day to day on the streets of Mexico City. Very few were ever repatriated to Spain.

REPATRIATION to the Basque Country was problematic in many of the individual cases. Some of the children were now orphans and had no family to which they could be returned. In other cases, children were in Mexico or Belgium while their mothers and fathers had fled to Iparralde, causing added confusion and difficulty to the rejoining efforts. Animosity toward the Basques and their supposed Communist and anti-Catholic ties resulted in English groups calling for their removal from Britain before the Civil War had ceased, and by the end of 1937, a few hundred Basque children from the Catholic colonies in Britain had been sent back to the Basque Country. At the other extreme, of the 2,500 children cared for in the Soviet Union, only 200 had been rejoined with their families by 1945, and in 1956, when the majority returned to the Basque Country after almost twenty years, they often found it impossible to fit in. They had forgotten Euskara and Spanish, had been educated in Russian with Soviet values, and many did not recognize their family members or feel like they belonged in Basque society. Hundreds returned to the Soviet Union to live permanently.

THE DECISION to send one's own children away into exile (the ultimate unknown) for their own physical, psychological, emotional, and spiritual safety marked both the parents and the children permanently. This incredibly heart-wrenching decision made by parents was an enormous gamble. In some cases, the children were never returned, several died on the voyages, and others returned after years of absence failing to recognize their families, language, or way of life. The research of Gregorio Arrien and of Dorothy Legarreta have chronicled the impressive efforts of the Basque government and the heroic actions of teachers and clerics who volunteered to accompany and safeguard the children to exile. Their dedication and devotion to their students and to the effort to maintain the students' Euskara and knowledge of the Basque Country and culture are indeed remarkable.

Lesson fifteen

BIBLIOGRAPHY

Alonso Carballés, Jesús J. 1998. *1937 Los niños vascos evacuados a Francia y Bélgica: Historia y memoria de un éxodo infantil, 1936–1940.* Bilbao: Asociación de Niños Evacuados.

Arrien, Gregorio.1991. *Niños vascos evacuados a Gran
Bretaña, 1937–1940*. Bilbao: Asociación de Niños
Evacuados.

———. 1983. *La Generación del exilio: Génesis de las
escuelas vascas y las colonias escolares, 1932–1940*.
Bilbao: ONURA

Legarreta, Dorothy. 1985. "Basque Refugee Children
as Expatriates: Political Catalysts in Europe and
America." In *Basque Politics: A Case Study in Ethnic
Nationalism*, ed. William A. Douglass. Basque Studies
Program Occasional Papers, series 2. Reno: Associ-
ated Faculty Press and Basque Studies Program.

———. 1984. *The Guernica Generation: Basque Refugee
Children of the Spanish Civil War*. Reno: University of
Nevada Press.

Totoricagüena, Gloria. 2004. *The Basques of New York:
A Cosmopolitan Experience*. 2d ed. Basque Migration
and Diaspora Studies Series, no. 2. Reno: Center for
Basque Studies, University of Nevada, Reno.

REQUIRED READING

Dorothy Legarreta, *The Guernica Generation: Basque
Refugee Children of the Spanish Civil War* (Reno: University of Nevada Press, 1984), chapters 1, 7, and 8, pp
8–50, 201–40, and 241–98.

Dorothy Legarreta, "Basque Refugee Children as Expatri-
ates: Political Catalysts in Europe and America." In
Basque Politics: A Case Study in Ethnic Nationalism,
ed. by William A. Douglass, Basque Studies Program
Occasional Papers, series 2 (Reno: Associated Faculty
Press and Basque Studies Program, 1985), pp 175–99.

WRITTEN LESSON FOR SUBMISSION

Compare the reception of the Basque refugees in the
various countries and describe why the politics of the

era were so influential in the warm or cool acceptance of the young Basque exiles. Then, imagine you are a parent in this situation and you have the choice of keeping your young children with you in danger and in harm's way or sending them into unknown exile. In your country, there is a real expectation of lack of shelter, food, and medical supplies and the real possibility of political violence toward you and your family. Your hometown is destroyed, and your family is separated. If you send your children away, you do not know with whom they will stay, you cannot even choose to which country they will be sent, and you cannot go with them. Will they be safe with complete strangers? They may forget you, and they most likely will resent you. They probably will not speak your language upon their return and likely will not have been educated or taken to church to worship in the way you choose. Will you ever see them again? What would you do if you were in the situation of these hundreds of thousands of Basques? Explain why you chose the option you did.

16 · "The opposite end of the Earth"
Contemporary Basque migration to Australia

IN THE HISTORY of Basque migration, the most significant push factors influencing emigration from Euskal
Herria have included economic hardship and political
oppression. The magnetism of growing economies and
democracies in Argentina and Uruguay first, then in
the United States, Australia, and Belgium, also pulled
Basques to those host societies in search of opportunity
and political freedom. As we have seen, in the 1900s,
Basque emigration to the Río de la Plata region was
reduced to a trickle and was replaced with emigration to
oil-rich Venezuela and to the English-speaking countries
and booming economies of the United States and Australia. Since World War II, millions of immigrants from
all regions of the world have made Australia their new
home.

Australia, like other host societies of Basque diaspora communities, is an immigrant or settler society.
Although it pursued a "White Australia Policy" for
immigration until 1976, Basques tended to be unaffected
by the country's racist policies because of their European
origins. From the nineteenth century on, they were welcomed and even sought after as workers for construction,
interior clearing, and hydro projects and for the sugar
industry in North Queensland.

Although for three centuries the Spanish empire laid
claim to the Australian continent, Australia del Espíritu
Santo, the Spanish never bothered to colonize the territory. In 1790, the British began to arrive after a settlement had been reached with Madrid to drop its claims
to controlling the South Pacific. William A. Douglass
has tracked possibly the earliest legally recorded Basque
immigrants to Australia, five Basques from Iparralde

who entered between 1855 and 1861. Two of these listed their occupation as miners and might possibly have departed the California Gold Rush for the gold strikes in Australia, as did many others. A Nafarroan arrived to Melbourne in 1863, and thereafter, several Bizkaian Basques began arriving who listed other locations, such as Peru, Argentina, Java, and St. Thomas, as their previous departure points, not Euskal Herria. There were Basque-owned sugarcane properties in North Queensland in northeast Australia by the early 1900s, and between 1907 and 1933, 102 Basques from Spain entered Australia and the majority (88 percent Bizkaian) traveled to North Queensland (Douglass, unpublished manuscript).

RESTRICTIVE immigration policies of the 1920s and 1930s in South American countries and in the United States produced a situation whereby many Basque emigrants were unable to obtain entrance visas for their initially preferred destinations. Australia served as an exciting second-best option. Its own restrictive immigration politics resulted in the "White Australia Policy" legislation of 1901 and also in policies promoting the immigration of European labor for sugarcane cutting. In North Queensland, government-sponsored projects included free passage for European workers and cheaply and easily available land contracts for European immigrants. Entry to Australia was quite uncomplicated if the emigrant was European and had a personal sponsor who would claim responsibility for the newcomer. One Basque couple in the Ingham area, Tomás and Teresa Urigüen Mendiolea, are documented to have sponsored hundreds of Basque men, advancing them travel costs and giving them help securing lodging, medical care, and employment (Mendiolea Larrazabal interview 2000). Similar to Basque immigrants in the United

SYDNEYKO

BASQUE CLUB "GURE TXOKO"

EUZKADI

EUZKADI'GATIK

ALKARTUTA

SYDNEY

GURE TXOKO

Basque immigrants in the Sydney, Australia, area
founded the Sydney'ko Gure Txoko, Our Place in Sydney,
on the feast day of Saint Ignatius, July 31, in 1966. The
eusko etxea is located in the Darlinghurst area of downtown Sydney and includes a small *fronton*, a separate
apartment for a caretaker, a members' dining area and
kitchen, and an upstairs meeting room and library. Total
membership has averaged under 100 individuals.
*Photograph courtesy of Carlos Orue and the Sydney'ko
Gure Txoko.*

States at this time, Basques in this Anglo host society
were disadvantaged for socioeconomic mobility by their
limited English communications and language skills and
by the fact that the type of person migrating for manual
cane-cutting labor was generally undereducated. These

Basques relied on ethnic networks for employment, housing, medical care, socializing, and education.

After World War II, Australia experienced simultaneously an economic boom and a labor shortage, and its remedy was to attempt to increase the country's population growth by passing liberal immigration policies. The country again embarked upon a policy intended to increase white European immigration, which included allowing Basque sugarcane farmers to travel to Spain in order to select workers who would be given permission to immigrate. In 1958, the Sugar Growers' Association of North Queensland sent a representative, a Basque immigrant from Kortezubi, Bizkaia, Alberto Urberuaga Ortuzar, to Spain to recruit emigrants. He was responsible for three separate groups of Basques departing, mostly from Bizkaia and Nafarroa, to work in the sugarcane fields with three-year contracts. Over the subsequent seven years, over five thousand Spanish citizens entered Australia, approximately half of whom were Basque (Douglass interview 2004).

AUSTRALIAN policies encouraged recruiting entire families to come as units with the hopes that they were more likely to stay and populate the country. Basque women were also specifically recruited to come to Australia and work in domestic employment in order to balance the sexes and to marry and create families that would stay on the continent. Douglass cites an immigration report from 1959 that describes the departure of the ship *Monte Udala* from Bilbao on December 19 with fifty-five married couples, seventy-seven children, and another 214 single or unaccompanied males. This was one of the groups recruited by Urberuaga that finally arrived in Australia in late January.

Basque migration to Australia again highlights the importance of chain migration and the networks of

family and village information in the movement from
homeland areas to specific regions of Australia. From
the earliest noted Basques arriving in the second half
of the nineteenth century to those traveling to the cane
fields one hundred years later, brothers sent for siblings,
uncles sent for nephews, and departed villagers aided
other villagers' transport and employment.

NOT ALL immigrants have been as welcome. Australia
is a relatively new country, and a few public figures many of Anglo descent have demonstrated an
overt prejudice toward Asians, Latin Americans, the few
Africans, and against darker-complexioned European
immigrants. The politically and economically dominant
Anglos continue to speak of Italians and Greeks with
prejudice, as well. During World War II, thousands of
males with Italian ancestry were interned in war camps
in North Queensland. However, J. J. Smolicz's research
has documented recent social changes in Australia that
have resulted in a push for a multicultural society and
appreciation for diversity.

The Irish and British dominance in Australian contemporary history began to diminish in the 1970s. In 1972,
Don Chipp, a minister in the ruling Liberal government,
suggested that Australia should become a multiethnic
society that could take in "ideas, cultures, and even people from overseas." However, Arthur Calwell of the Labor
party replied that no red-blooded Australian wanted to
see a "chocolate-colored" country (Button 1992, 57). In
1992, Prime Minister Paul Keating spoke of an Australia
freed from its ties to England and rooting itself in Asia,
rather than looking to Europe for a sense of its identity
and economic future. Australia's time as a "cultural
derivative of Britain" was finished, according to Keating.
My own fieldwork in Australia with 102 anonymous written questionnaires and 98 personal interviews with

Basques in the areas of Sydney, Melbourne, Townsville, Ingham, Ayr, and Trebonne conducted between 1995 and 2003 showed that higher numbers of Basques in Australia identified themselves as preferring the Labor Party and its platform and fewer were partial to the Liberals. However, many citizens disagreed with Keating's policy orientation and were angry with the idea of a policy shift.

In the personal interviews I conducted in Australia, Basque interviewees said they do not generally experience overt discrimination, but they also said that in Australia, they are often mistaken by others as being Italian or Greek. They also consistently mentioned that the overwhelming majority of non-Basques in their communities do not know what "Basque" is, nor do they know anything about the culture or history of the Basque Country.

BECAUSE THE Australian-Basques have almost no social recognition in society and the numbers of people of Basque descent are relatively low, many members of the community think there is no future for Basque identity maintenance on the continent. As in most other Basque organizations around the world, the worry is that the younger generations do not interest themselves in their Basqueness, do not participate in Basque center activities, intermarry with other ethnic groups, and care nothing for the preservation of the Basque language and Basque culture. Basques continue to define Basqueness strongly, using ancestry as a category marker.

Language has historically been used as one of the strongest markers of Basque ethnicity, and as we have discussed, is significant in the definition of Basqueness. In Australia, however, only 36 percent of the respondents agreed that a person should actually speak Euskara to be considered a Basque. This may be a result

Table 16-1

Which political party do you usually associate yourself with in Australia?

47% Labor
13% Liberal
10% Country
 5% Other
25% I do not participate in Australian politics

Total respondents: 200

Australian Political Party Preference by Basques
Despite its name, the Liberal Party is the major conservative party in Australia. The rural-based Country party has changed its name several times and is now known as The Nationals. Labor believes in a strong role for national government and according to its official platform document, "Labor's commitment to a strong economy is therefore matched by its commitment to justice, fairness and equity for all."

of Basque-speaking parents who have children who are English-only speakers. Although they have lost their language skills, they still want to be included in the category "Basque." When comparing Australian Basques to Basques in other countries, we see a similar trend.

NEVERTHELESS, Australian Basques' definition of Basqueness including language is higher than any of the other countries for which we have data, and so is their Basque language ability.

Only 8 percent of Australian respondents report knowing no Basque language at all. The significant data here show that while in Australia 37 percent know either no Euskara or only a few words, 53 percent of those who do

The North Queensland Basque migration began in the early 1900s, but in 1958, the Australian government sent an immigrant from Kortezubi, Bizkaia, Alberto Urberuaga Ortuzar, to the Basque Country to recruit Basques for sugercane-cutting jobs. As a result of three trips, hundreds of Basques, mostly single young men, but also complete families, had departed to Australia with three-year work contracts to work in the sugar industry. Many stayed after their contracts expired and found work in different areas, and others returned to the Basque Country. Photo 1932.
Courtesy of the Basque Library, University of Nevada, Reno.

know the language do not use their Euskara at all, or, use it only for a few special phrases. The relatively low percentage of those who know Basque, but do not use it points to probable long term language death.

BASQUES IN these three main regions do, however, focus on other cultural traditions and behaviors. Regardless of age, 84 percent of Australian Basque respondents agreed overwhelmingly that "singing traditional songs in Basque" is of "some," "great," or "very great importance" and that maintaining Basque cuisine is also essential to maintaining a Basque ethnic identity.

In Australia, 90 percent reported that they keep themselves informed regarding homeland current events and with information about the Basque Country. Although issues through personal contacts at least once a year and also by regularly reading newspapers or journals from or Australia's respondents demonstrated a low level of frequent reading, it is important to note that Australian cable television transmits one hour of Spanish broadcast news daily on the Special Broadcasting Services, SBS, which includes stories from the Basque provinces. Interviews revealed that rather than trying to find printed information about the Basque Country, one could just turn on the television for daily news and watch or record the program. Although most believe the news to be biased in favor of Madrid and anti-Basque, they watch the reports anyway to maintain an awareness of current events. When asked about readership of newspapers or journals from or about Euskal Herria, 34 percent of Basque respondents in Australia reported this as an "at least once monthly" activity.

NORTH QUEENSLAND, SYDNEY, AND MELBOURNE
Basques in the North Queensland area are grouped on the South Pacific coast of the Great Barrier Reef, mainly

Table 16-2

"A person must have Basque ancestors to be Basque"

	"Agree" or "Strongly Agree"	"No Opinion"	"Disagree" or "Strongly Disagree"
Australian Basques	73%	4%	23%

Total respondents: 200

The primordial definition of ethnicity is manifest here in the Australian respondents' opinions of the importance of ancestry, a biological factor, for determining whether or not one is Basque. This is different from a civic approach which defines as Basque all those who live and work in the Basque Country, or those who work to promote Basque culture.

near Townsville, Ayr, Home Hill, Trebonne, and Ingham, and were originally involved in the traditional, premechanized sugarcane industry of the early 1900s and later in civil-engineering projects, construction, and farming. During the 1950s, Basque sugarcane farmers worked to recruit additional Basques to come and work in their fields. Because of their successes, letters from industry officials to the office of immigration asked the Australian bureaucrats to consider making arrangements for free passage "for attaining Spaniards of the right type." In 1958, two Australian immigration agents traveled to the north of Spain with Alberto Urberuaga and recruited 159 workers to depart for Australia and to labor in the sugarcane fields, and in 1959, another 169 males

The Queensland sugarcane farm of the Menchaca family was instrumental in giving employment to hundreds of Basques over the years in the early 1900s. The Menchacas sponsored individuals mainly from the Lekeitio area of Bizkaia, and once they had arrived, the Menchacas cared for them by finding employment and housing. Photo circa 1920.
Courtesy of the Basque Library, University of Nevada, Reno.

---

embarked for North Queensland. In total, between 1958 and 1960, 387 individuals left their residences in the Basque Country and emigrated to Australia (interview with Alberto Urberuaga Ortuzar). In the mid-1960s, Johnny Mendiolea (son of Tomás and Teresa Urigüen Mendiolea) reported signing migration papers assisting about one hundred and twenty Basque immigrants into their area. He estimated that about one thousand

Table 16-3

"To be considered a Basque, a person must speak the Basque language"

	"Strongly Agree" or "Agree"	"No Opinion"	"Strongly Disagree" or "Disagree"	Respondents who do "speak Basque fluently" or "with some difficulty"
Belgium	13%	4%	83%	42%
Peru	8%	8%	83%	23%
Uruguay	12%	6%	83%	2%
United States	15%	9%	76%	46%
Argentina	24%	8%	68%	16%
Australia	36%	13%	52%	56%

Total respondents: 832. Totals above and below 100% result from rounding.

Practicing a foreign language in the diaspora is much more difficult than preserving dance, music, or cuisine. Here we see that the majority of Basque respondents in every country disagree that speaking Euskara is necessary for being considered a Basque. The far right column shows that—except for Australia—most of these Basques do not themselves speak their ancestral language.

individuals had moved from Spain to the area near Trebonne between World War II and 1967, and about 85 percent were Basques (Foley 1967, 17).

Cane cutting was a seasonal occupation, and many of the Basque laborers found additional employment in building construction in Melbourne or in Sydney during the off-season. Others traveled the migrant farm labor circuit, harvesting vegetables and fruit or tobacco in the appropriate seasons. Several Basque "teams" would cut sugarcane and then would move to the northern Atherton tableland to cut tobacco. With the mechanization of the sugarcane harvest in the mid--1960s, most cane cutters were put out of work and forced to search for other permanent employment in various government-funded infrastructure projects or in the private sector. Numerous Basques returned to the Basque Country, and others searched for new employment in other areas of Australia.

THE TREBONNE Hotel, the town's only hotel, which was owned by Italians, constructed a *fronton*, or handball court, to thank their Basque clientele, and the court was inaugurated and blessed in 1959 by the Basque priest Tomás Ormazabal. Residents of Trebonne remember meeting every Sunday for weightlifting (*harrijatsozaile*) and weight pulling (*probak*), with thirty or forty Basques also playing handball(*pelota*). Barbecues were also common entertainment. Basque families had first settled there in the 1940s. In 2000, the *fronton* was listed on the official Queensland Heritage Register for special and historic buildings.

Compared with the Basques in South and Central American countries, Basques in Australia are better off financially and have more opportunities for assistance and grant allocations for cultural maintenance from their central government in Canberra. Instead

Table 16-4

Language knowledge, Usage, and Literacy by Host Country

	"I know only a few words" or "none"	"I only use Basque for special phrases" or "none"	"I can write a few words in Basque" or "none"
Uruguay	94%	98%	95%
Argentina	69%	84%	68%
Peru	54%	85%	54%
United States	41%	67%	58%
Belgium	38%	71%	46%
Australia	37%	53%	56%

Total respondents: 832

The difference between columns one and two is especially important to analyzing the percentages of individuals that know but do not use their Basque language skills. Though 37% of Basque-Australians report knowing very little or no Euskara, 53% report not using it but for a few phrases. This suggests that sixteen percent of those who do know some Euskara are not using it. The same pattern exists in each of the six countries' Basque communities.

of receiving grant money, however, they need experts
such as Basque language teachers, artists, dance and
instrumental music instructors, and athletes from the
Basque Country to go to their communities and infuse
them with information and culture. For example,
Basques from Townsville have stated several times that
what they would most prefer is to have a person that
is a musician/dancer who could teach them the necessary skills to form a dance group or a musician to give
accordion lessons. They would like to select several
young Basques from Australian society and send them to
Euskal Herria on scholarships with the expectation that
they would then return and perpetuate their knowledge
in their Australian communities. Once a small group of
dancers could be established, leaders believe that additional younger people would become interested and stay
involved. Having Basque music for their ethnic events
would produce a more enjoyable atmosphere for everyone, and parents would bring their children, beginning
the first phase in a generational cycle of participation.

WHILE THE Sydney Basques and the Melbourne
Basques have separately been formally organized
for more than thirty-five years, Basques in the Townsville
area had never formed an official Basque association or
organization until 2003. A large number of those interested are emigrants from Bizkaia or are members of
the first generation born in Australia. However, this is
similar to the situation in Sydney and Melbourne, where
most emigrants are from Bizkaia and Gipuzkoa or members of the first Born-born generation.

The Sydney'ko Gure Txoko *euskal etxea*, or Basque
center, celebrated its thirty-seventh anniversary in 2003.
Originally founded by twenty-six families, many of which
eventually returned to the Basque Country, it is the
only official Basque organization in Australia that has

Basques in Melbourne, Australia, created networks of information for employment, housing, and social functions. During the 1960s, Basque immigrants formed their own Basque soccer team and competed against other nonprofessional squads in municipal leagues. *Photograph courtesy of Javier Amorebieta Zuñega.*

---

maintained itself since its inception. Although the Basques in Melbourne also initiated their own Gure Txoko at approximately the same time, (it is merely a coincidence that they have the same name, because they seem to not have had any communications), and some say that they were having informal gatherings before 1966, there were years when the association was defunct.

THE SYDNEY Basques have a physical meeting place in the Darlinghurst section of the city, which includes a limited kitchen and bar, eating space for eighty to ninety, an upstairs office and modest library, and a connected manager's apartment for the family

that cares for and operates the Gure Txoko. There is also
a small outdoor *fronton* that is not used, but could be
cleaned and outfitted for players if there were any interest. The Basques of Sydney and Melbourne annually
celebrate Aberri Eguna, or the Day of the Homeland, on
Easter Sunday or the following Sunday. They also com-
memorate the Basque patron saint, Saint Ignatius of
Loyola, on July 31, and the membership organizes various informal dinners throughout the year.

BASQUE ETHNIC solidarity in the three communi-ties
has served a significant psychological purpose. In
analyzing the comparative adaptation of immigrants
to Australia and their emotional and psychological
health, researchers William A. Scott, Ruth Scott, and
John Stumph determined that most immigrants tend
to regard their new circumstances as an improvement
over those that they left, except in the areas of the type
of their employment and their friendships, and that
those who settle in rural areas tend to be more satisfied
with their jobs and are better assimilated. Men are more
likely than women to profess emotional well-being and
high self-esteem (Scott, Scott, and Stumph 1989, 168–69).
Once in the host country, men tend to work outside the
home, learning the host-country's language, customs,
expectations, and so on and how to "move" in the new
society. Interviews with Basques supported this research,
with males more likely to talk about their varied employment, meeting new friends at work, and learning the
host-society language and customs, while many women
discussed the loneliness and difficulties experienced
while working at home without significant adult companionship, without establishing friendships, and lacking English communication skills. Many women narrated emotions of tremendous loneliness, isolation, and
depression and a lack of both self-esteem and a sense of

self-worth from the inability to express themselves. They had been "robbed of their youth, of their own dreams, and careers." Hence the salience of the Basque organizations as an outlet for these women to communicate through their ethnicity. Social circles for ethnic identity provide empowerment and recognition, and they certainly have for these Basque women. Ethnic and community solidarity gives one a history, a collective feeling of belonging, support from the "family" of other ethnics, and self-worth.

Those who emigrated from rural areas in Euskal Herria to urban regions experienced that change as an additional rupture in their understanding of their surroundings. The move from the category of *baserritarrak*, or rural, to *kaletarrak*, or urban, was very difficult for many Basque immigrants. Those migrating to Melbourne or Sydney entered urban settings of hundreds of thousands or millions of residents—quite a shift from agricultural and fishing cultures of small villages and farmsteads. The demands of city life, compounded by geographical, language, and cultural change could be overwhelming. The transition from traditional to modern was and is not a simple or a linear one.

TODAY, HOWEVER, perhaps as a result of the numbers of immigrants who have made that transition with their children, the Sydney and Melbourne organizations report losing numbers of participants. However, there is a new organization in Queensland. Currently, there are several prominent families interested in actively maintaining Basque culture and are in the process of deciding the best manner in which to organize themselves and a few activities to spark the interest of other Basques in the area. In August 2003, several Basque activists met and formally established a Basque organization for North Queensland. Their paid

Basques in Melbourne, Australia, formed the Gure Txoko, or Our Place, a Basque center, in 1964 as an association that would work to maintain the Basque language,
culture, and traditions. The private club was inaugurated
on Aberri Eguna, Day of the Homeland, on March 29,
1964, with a celebration of dancing, music, and food. *Txistulari* Javier Amorebieta Zuñega, originally of Gernika,
is seen here at center.
Photograph courtesy of Javier Amorebieta Zuñega.

membership reached 150 individuals in the first month.
There are an estimated two hundred to two hundred and
fifty people in the area who state they would be interested in regularly attending Basque cultural activities
and special events. Until they formally organized and
asked to be legally recognized by the Basque government
of the Basque Autonomous Community, they could not
apply or receive any financial aid or human-capital aid
from the Basque government and continued to use their
own private resources to promote Basque culture. The
group finished this process in July 2004. The Basque

Club of North Queensland, Australia, Incorporated now has joined the over one hundred and eighty Basque communities of the world (one hundred and sixty of which are officially registered and recognized by the Basque Government in 2004) on the path to transnational interaction.

POLITICS

IN AUSTRALIA, Basques are still a relatively unknown ethnic group and have only rarely attempted to influence policy collectively at the central government level or at the community level where they are geographically concentrated. Basque emigration to Australia was much more economically than politically induced, although there are several Basques in Sydney, Melbourne, and North Queensland who describe themselves as political exiles fleeing Franco's repression. Escaping the hardships of the Franco regime, for some, meant traveling "to the opposite end of the Earth." Because of the relatively small enclaves and the long distances between them, there has been very little communication between the three Basque clusters. These Basques' political involvement and their knowledge of and contacts with other Basques in the diaspora are minimal. Although the South American and the U.S. Basques have interacted considerably while also coping with the long distances dividing them, except for contacts with homeland Basques, those in Australia have been relatively isolated from each other and from other Basque populations in different countries. Even so, there is still evidence of individual political involvement with the homeland and a desire to influence Australia's foreign policies con-cerning the Basque Country. However, unlike the Basque diapora communities in South America, the United States, France, England, and Belgium, which all

developed relations with the Basque government-in-exile
from the 1930s through the 1950s, and mobilized anti-
Franco support in the Basque centers and lobbied their
host-country governments to support the Basque cause,
there were not sufficient numbers of Basques in Australia for a visit from President Aguirre, or for an official
Basque delegation. Though there were no official Basque
government-in-exile connections in Australia, the official government-in-exile bulletin, Euzko Deya, did have
a correspondent, Alejandro Lakebed, who reported on
Basques in Australia, and who attempted to disseminate
information about the homeland to Basques living in
Australia.

CERTAIN BASQUE individuals did take action and
there were a few attempts to collect donations in
North Queensland for the Basque government-in-exile.
Urberuaga states they were quite unsuccessful. Others
attempted to influence the Australian government. During the 1960s and early 1970s, according to Pablo Oribe,
who lives near Melbourne, attempting to influence
Australia's government in regard to Spanish politics was
"like talking to a rock." There was almost no interest
in or sympathy for the victims of a remote homeland
unknown to most Australians and unimportant in Australian foreign affairs. Worldwide press coverage of ETA
as radicals and Communists was then mistakenly used
by an uninformed public as a blanket description for
all Basques, which hurt the cause for diaspora Basques'
attempts to mobilize support for international pressure
for democratic change in Spain.

Once again, individuals used their personal friendship and kinship networks to send material and financial
aid to family and friends suffering under the Franco
dictatorship in the homeland. Because there were
established Basque centers in Melbourne and Sydney,

which organized various gatherings, Basques in these areas were more likely to share information and to discuss possible collective actions. Those in the North Queensland areas of Ingham, Townsville, and Ayr were fewer in number, more isolated from communications, and acted individually, if at all. Close to one-third of the interviewees in my study remember their parents or themselves contributing to funds for relief to families in the homeland and believe it to have been general non-partisan, humanitarian aid, mostly to relatives.

IT TOOK the international media attention that accompanied the Franco regime's imposition of martial law following the 1968 assassination of Spanish Police Commissioner Melitón Manzanas to bring the true nature of the Franco dictatorship into focus in Australia. As we noted in Lesson 13, Basques in Melbourne organized a general dockworkers' strike to coincide with those in Bilbao, and arranged for buses to take protestors to Canberra in order to demand some sort of Australian parliamentary or governmental reaction to the military tribunal trying the sixteen Basque suspects in Burgos, Spain. Basque community leader Pablo Oribe worked to explain Franco's authoritarianism and the lack of civil rights in the Basque Country in radio interviews. The Basque communities of Sydney and of North Queensland organized a letter-writing campaign demanding that the Australian ambassador to Madrid object to the treatment of the Basque suspects. Basques from the Melbourne community, led by Pablo Oribe, also met with their members of parliament, such as MP Arthur Calwell to educate them about the Franco regime and the abuses of civil and human rights.

A more recent example of individual interest in political nationalism involved a controversial Herri Batasuna Basque leftist political party campaign video advocating the use of all possible means (including violence) to achieve a united Basque state. Released in 1996 for upcoming elections, it resulted in trials and imprisonment for up to seven years in Spain for the entire national directorate of the Herri Batasuna political party. A copy of the video obtained through personal connections was making its way among homes in Melbourne and Sydney and being reproduced to expand its audience throughout Australia. Conversations at the Gure Txoko Basque Center in Sydney indicated outrage that the "supposed democracy" of Spain could imprison the entire directorship of a legal political party for advertising its political ideology. "Nothing has changed since Franco died. State terrorism will create reactionary defensive terrorism," stated one member.

In discussions regarding the instrumental use of violence to achieve a political end, Basques in Australia were almost evenly divided into three opinion groups, and questionnaire data reflected the same. Although this was an anonymous survey, one-third did not agree or disagree with the following statement: "Whether or not I agree with its use, I think political violence has been effective for achieving more autonomy in the Basque Country."

EVEN FOR earlier Basque immigrants who had learned English, current news and accurate information regarding homeland political developments were extremely difficult to obtain, although not impossible. Basques in the rural agricultural areas tended not to be so involved with homeland politics, perhaps as a result of this lack of information. For example, in fifty-four interviews held in the Townsville, Ayr, and Ingham areas, not one person could recall firsthand or from hearing an older Basque recount it whether there had been any organized collective action from their area in

Juan Balanzategi Loyola and Gregoria Arkarazo Urigüen were early Basque pioneers to North Queensland, from Lekeitio and Gernika, respectively. Their successful sugarcane farms made it possible for them to assist and sponsor numerous Basque immigrants, beginning in the 1920s. Juan established the Stone River farm with his brothers Vicente and Fernando and later moved his business to Ingham. Photo 1951.
Photograph courtesy of Jon Balanzategi and Eugenia Oleaga.

---

response to the Spanish Civil War. Basques who immigrated to North Queensland tended to be economic emigrants, as we have noted was the case in general, and more of them entered Australia after the Spanish Civil War had ended, while the political refugees who fled to Australia were more likely to settle in Melbourne or Sydney, and in 2004, these members still exhibited stronger interest in complex homeland politics. Basques from Melbourne and Sydney were and are more politically aware and involved, as is evidenced by their collective mobilization and political actions in the 1970s to the present and in their knowledge and understanding of the various contemporary political factions in the home-land. Numerous Basques in Sydney and Melbourne, and a few in North Queensland, continue to hold double citizenship for Australia and Spain in order to retain voting rights in the Basque Country.

A T THE Second World Congress of Basque Collectivities, held in Vitoria-Gasteiz in October 1999, the majority of the delegates representing Basques from twenty countries were interested in discussions of the ETA cease-fire and the Lizarra-Garazi Agreement, signed on September 12, 1998 by nine political parties as well as by trade unions and social organizations in the Basque provinces with the main purpose of facilitating a peace process and a democratic settlement of the conflicts in the Basque Country. All of the Australian delegates knew the details and history of the circumstances from their own access to news and from discussions with other Basque friends. In several of the other countries with Basque communities, homeland political-party information networks function within the diaspora communities. However, in Australia, there are no formal organizations representing any Basque Country political parties and certain individuals are active only privately. There is no systematic official representation of Basque party politics, and interviewees mentioned frequently that they prefer ethnic cultural activities to political mobilization, which is similar to Basques in other countries.

THE DIASPORA EXPERIENCE IN AUSTRALIA TODAY
Today, the physical disconnectedness that separates Basque immigrants to Australia from Euskal Herria has

Table 16-5
"Whether or not I agree with its use, I think political violence has been effective for achieving more autonomy."

Australia Basques
31% "Disagree" or "Strongly disagree"
37% "No Opinion"
33% "Agree" or "Strongly Agree"

Total respondents: 102. Total in excess of 100% results from rounding.

This is an extremely controversial topic and Basques living in Australia are divided almost equally in their responses. The 37% answering "No Opinion" may actually have an opinion, but because of the topic may not be willing to share it. In personal interviews, participants often ask to turn off the tape recorder when discussing political violence in the Basque Country for fear of the information being used against them.

been replaced by an emotional and intellectual interconnectedness with other Basque men and women. Immigrants understand each other's horrors of political exile, loss of family and friends, and fears of dealing with life in their new country. First-generation and second-generation ethnic Basques born in Australia understand each other's upbringing and how they are different from their non-Basque friends. From constantly spelling and explaining their surnames to interpreting ETA activities to other Australians, Basques of all ages in each of the three regions of Basque settlement agreed, "We have more in common with each other in different countries than we do with other immigrants equivalent to

Basque migrants to North Queensland worked and lived
together as cane gangs of usually six to twelve men. In
general, one would serve additionally as the cook and
would leave the fields a little earlier than the others to
begin preparing food. The remaining men would then
divide his work among themselves.
Photograph courtesy of Alberto Urberuaga Ortuzar.

---

ourselves in this country." Their imagined connection is
through their Basque ethnicity and its experiences.

IN AUSTRALIA, maintaining Basque ethnic identity
is generally viewed positively when it does not conflict with Anglo-Saxon Christian values. There are no
physically differentiating characteristics of Basques that
are identifiable from other white Europeans, preventing
the racial discrimination so prevalent in European settler societies.

The "New Australians'" white, European ethnic
identities are celebrated by the society, although not necessarily the ethnicities of the Aboriginal peoples or

Table 16-6

"I prefer to participate in Basque cultural events and not Basque political events."

	"Strongly Agree" or "Agree"	"No Opinion"	"Strongly Disagree" or "Disagree"
Female	82%	8%	10%
Male	79%	13%	8%
Peru	92%	8%	0
United States	83%	10%	7%
Uruguay	81%	12%	7%
Argentina	81%	10%	9%
Australia	75%	13%	13%
Belgium	58%	8%	33%

Total respondents: 832. Totals above or below 100 percent results from rounding.

Basques in Australia are similar to those in the Americas in that they prefer cultural activities to political ones. However, in Belgium, Basques demonstrate a stronger interest in political participation. Likely, this is a result of their being recent immigrants who maintain stronger links with the Basque Country. They also have access to daily European news that includes the Basque Country, and this likely influences their knowledge about, and therefore their willingness to participate in, political activities affecting Basques.

necessarily the ethnicities of the Aboriginal peoples or those of the many varied Asian communities present. Today's Basques in Sydney, Melbourne, and North Queensland tend to feel as though they have been socially accepted with a semipositive status (if they are known at all) because of their excellent work reputations with non-Basque employers.

Lesson Sixteen

BIBLIOGRAPHY

Button, James. 1992. "Australia: In Search of Itself." *Time Magazine*. May 4.

Chant, Sylvia, ed. 1992. *Gender and Migration in Developing Countries*. London: Bellhaven Press.

Douglass, William A. 2004. Personal interview.

————. 1996. *Azúcar Amargo: Vida y fortuna de los cortadores de caña italianos y vascos en la Australia tropical*. Bilbao: Servicio Editorial Universidad del Pais Vasco.

————. "Basques in the Antipodes." Unpublished manuscript.

Foley, Larry. 1967. "The Basques—Strongmen of the Canefields." *People Magazine* (Australia) (October 18).

Lettler, Willy, and M. A. Leguineche. 1967. "Cortadores de caña en Australia." *La Actualidad Española*, no. 804 (June).

Orúe, Carlos, et al. 1995. *Sydneyko Gure Txoko: 30 Urteurrena*. Newtown, New South Wales: El Faro Printing, 1995.

Scott, William A., Ruth Scott, and John Stumpf. 1989. *Adaptation of Immigrants: Individual Differences and Determinants*. Oxford: Pergamon Press.

Smolicz, J. J. 1997. "Australia: From Migrant Country
to Multicultural Nation." *International Migration
Review* 31, no. 1 (Spring): 171–86.
Totoricagüena, Gloria. 2004. *Identity, Culture, and
Politics in the Basque Diaspora.* Reno: University of
Nevada Press.

REQUIRED READING
William A. Douglass, "Basques in Australia" (2000),
http://euskonews.com, KOSMOpolita, issue 72, 2000/
3/24–31.
————, "The Basques," in *The Australian People: An
Encyclopedia of the Nation, Its People, and Their Origins,* 2d ed., ed. James Jupp (Cambridge: Cambridge
University Press, 2001), pp 181–83.
Larry Foley, "The Basques—Strongmen of the Canefields," *People Magazine* (Australia), October 18,
1967.
J. J. Smolicz, "Australia: From Migrant Country to Multicultural Nation," *International Migration Review* 31,
no. 1 (Spring): 171–86.

WRITTEN LESSON FOR SUBMISSION
Why do you think the Basques in North Queensland
had not formed some sort of Basque ethnic organization
before 2003? Which elements of their Basque population movement, time in history, economic situation,
and so on would affect this lack of a desire for or need
for an association for the maintenance of ethnicity? How
could Basques in Australia best benefit from the current
Australian governmental policy emphasis on multiculturalism? Do you think it is more difficult to maintain
a Basque identity and to preserve Basque culture in
Anglo-dominant Australia, the country farthest away
from Euskal Herria, but a nation that lately has seemed

to embrace multiculturalism, or is it more difficult in the South American countries, which are already Hispanic, recognize the Basques, but have not yet begun to promote the ideas of multiculturalism or of citizens preserving an ethic identity? How has this been affected by the Australian Basques' return to Euskal Herria versus the South American Basques' staying in their new host countries?

17 · Other Ethnic Diasporas
A comparison

ALTHOUGH THERE ARE no official statistics demonstrating so, Basque migration specialists assume
that the majority of Basque families in Euskal Herria
today have at least one relative in a diaspora community
abroad, and it is a part of the cultural folklore that every
Basque has an uncle in the Americas. We have seen that
in the Basque case, the political, economic, and social
factors determining migration are numerous, epoch-specific, and person-specific. In this lesson, we will return to
the general characteristics defining a diaspora examined
in Lesson 1 and use them to compare the Basque diaspora today with other ethnic communities whose members have also left their homelands and maintain their
ethnic identities and ties to their places of origin.

No ethnic group can continue to be exclusively his-
tory-oriented, and each has to create identity from the
present, with ideas of looking to the future. Here I will
introduce a broad summary of issues affecting all ethnic
diasporas today: economic networks, the idealization of
homeland and of return to it, ethnic solidarity, involvement in hostland politics, and the political and economic globalization of diaspora populations.

ECONOMIC NETWORKS
As Cohen notes, one characteristic of diasporas is that
their members often have left the homeland in search
of work, trade, or opportunities in the colonies. Even
when, as he also shows, their departure may have been
forced and traumatic, diasporans have forged ahead and
exploited economic networks with other diasporans.
This is true of both the Basque diaspora and the diasporas of many other homelands such as Mexico, India

and the Philippines. Now, homeland governments in their turn are seeking to take advantage of the economic networks that diasporans have constructed, using their diasporas as a source of investments and business activities to help homeland commercial interests in the host country where the diasporans now live.

Long left dormant, today the Basque Autonomous Government is renewing and recreating the commercial networks described in previous lessons by using Basque diaspora communities to further homeland businesses. They have established trade offices in Argentina, Chile, Mexico, Venezuela, the United States, and Belgium with the intention to capitalize on the positive status of Basques. Just as the Basque Autonomous Government uses institutes, foundations, and delegations to promote economic trade and commerce between host countries and Basque homeland businesses, other ethnic groups are also looking to the possibilities of creating ethnic networks of trade. For example, in 2000, Tehran's press recognized the possible importance of Iranian exile investors, identifying eighty major entrepreneurs, six thousand doctors and three thousand medical students in the United States alone who could be lured into investing in their ancestral homeland.

SCOTLAND'S GOVERNMENT also is seeking to emulate the positive contributions that diaspora populations can make to their homeland's finances. The Scottish government has initiated a program known as Global Connections that encourages business networking between Scots around the planet. In a speech delivered in New York in 2001, Scottish Secretary of State Helen Liddell appealed to members of "'the extended Scottish family'" to champion the country and use their influence to promote it. The hope is that professionals abroad will broker new businesses and help restore the ailing tourist industry. Similar to the Basque journal and weekly Web site called *Euskal Etxeak,* a Web site started by the Scotland Office keeps overseas Scots informed about events in the country and even provides ready-made text for speeches espousing Scotland's virtues. Liddell was concerned that the image of Scotland abroad was too nostalgic and outdated, based on folkloric images of kilts and Highland Games, and she preferred a modern and businesslike campaign.

THE SCHEME is modeled on Ireland's successful relations with its own diaspora. However, Scots abroad lack the kind of diaspora organization that characterizes other ethnic groups, such as the Irish and the Basques. There have been no effective transnational social structure or organizations—similar to the Basque centers or Armenian churches, or even the Irish bar, for example—that linked Scots with Scotland. Most of the two million people who emigrated from the homeland in the nineteenth and twentieth centuries were lowland Scots leaving industrializing towns and cities: economic migrants, rather than refugees from famine. Like the Basques who departed for South America, many Scots were professionals or skilled workers. In an attempt to construct some sort of diaspora consciousness or imagination, a company based in Edinburgh and St. Andrews has established a Web site where Scots around the world can participate and register. One objective of "StAndrews.com" is to create a global census of the Scottish diaspora. The founders believe that there are between forty and ninety million people of Scottish descent in the world, easily outnumbering the five million living in Scotland itself.

The governments of New Zealand and Malaysia also are considering their nationals overseas as valuable economic assets and are both looking at ways of attracting them back to their homelands attempting to make use of those who remain abroad to the advantage of their respective countries. The Malaysian government is attempting to reverse the brain drain by offering to highly skilled expatriate professionals a specific tax incentive to return home. The incentives are aimed at Malaysians with PhD degrees and other higher qualifications. Initiated in 2001, the five-year program is aimed at filling a shortfall of thirty-five thousand skilled workers, especially in technology and engineering. Thousands of trained Malaysians work in Singapore, Britain, the United States, Australia, and elsewhere. Britain alone is home to four thousand medical professionals of Malaysian ancestry. The program offers tax exemption for remittances, savings, and assets brought into the country by members of the Malay diaspora.

THE GOVERNMENT of New Zealand is planning to establish a global network of New Zealanders working in science and technology in order to tap their expertise for the country's development. The minister of science, research, and technology said that expatriates need not return to be able to contribute to the country. Their contacts in the worlds of science, research, and business abroad could still be useful to New Zealand. In California, two entrepreneurs have started a Society of Silicon Valley Kiwis, and they have plans to create a global network of professionals. These New Zealanders are duplicating an academic ethnic network of researchers similar to that of the Real Sociedad Bascongada de los Amigos del País, the Royal Society of the Friends of the Basque Country, which was established in 1765 in Euskal Herria, with branches throughout the Americas and which still functions transnationally today.

A special 2002 government report in India regarding their diaspora of millions concluded with many recommendations to facilitate economic investment by Indians

Basque diasporic identity tends to be based on cultural factors such as language, cuisine, literature, history, music, song, and dance. In Argentina, hundreds of youths participate in their *eusko etxea* folk dance troupes and begin their Basque education with social relations in the dance group. Every year, the Argentine National Basque Week features the performances of Basque dancers. Audiences are treated to an impressive display of hundreds of dancers demonstrating their skill and love for Basque traditional dance.
Photograph by the author.

---

living outside of the country: setting up special economic zones exclusively for nonresident Indians (NRIs) and persons of Indian origin (PIOs), with streamlined advice and consultancy services for NRIs and PIOs; a fast-track mechanism to address grievances from NRI investors; special infrastructure bonds modeled on an Israeli scheme, bonds that could be used to fund hospitals; tax exemptions on foreign donations to health, educational, and related causes; revision of the Foreign Contribution Act of 1976 in order to ease philanthropic donations; and lower corporate taxes and easier arrangements for repatriating profits. There was also a recommendation for a welfare fund to assist repatriated overseas workers. The government committee proposed a standard labor export agreement with countries accepting Indian workers and greater monitoring and supervision of employment contracts for Indians in their new host country. It also suggested compulsory insurance schemes for overseas workers. To support Indian culture abroad, the report proposed an equivalent of the British Council or the Alliance Française to be funded and created in major areas of Indian diaspora communities worldwide.

IDEALIZATION OF THE HOMELAND AND OF RETURN

DIASPORIC populations generally have shared, collective memories and myths about the homeland and a idealization of its history, as Cohen notes. In the Basque case, nationalist Basque history creates a perception of victimization and continuous attempted domination by Castilian Spain. Basques also idealize their homeland as pristine farmsteads sitting atop steep, green hills or placed majestically along a river valley. Jews think of themselves as the "chosen people," and Armenians tell of how Noah's ark came to rest on Mount Ararat, where life was reborn in Armenia. For Basques, their idealized "golden age" includes their defense from invaders, including the Romans, Visigoths, Franks, and Moors; political and economic autonomy from Castile; superiority of seamanship; the democratic and collective society ruled by the *fueros*; and a rural lifestyle in which Basque culture and language were maintained. These shared collective memories were also a part of each Basque community abroad, regardless of whether the result of recent or old migrations, whether they are large or small communities, and regardless of host country. This is not surprising, because it is the same nationalist history that was promulgated in the homeland. Regardless of its veracity or authenticity as judged by different historians, what is important is that it is accepted and believed as the truth by the diaspora Basques themselves. This foments ethnicity maintenance and diaspora consciousness. These particular Basques feel they have a responsibility to their ancestors and to the "maintenance, restoration, safety, and prosperity" (Cohen 1997, 26)of Euskal Herria, their beloved homeland.

MANY MIGRANTS left the Basque Country believing they would return after making their fortunes, but these were individualized plans, and there was no collective return movement for Basques to their homeland until the wave of Spanish Civil War exiles. Previous emigrants had arguably chosen to leave, albeit pushed by economic hardship and war reparations, and they had moved as individuals or families. The Civil War exiles were thousands upon thousands who moved at once—traumatically and involuntarily. Their return depended upon the elimination of Franco and also became a myth as the decades wore on. Today, there is no evidence of a contemporary effort at collective, permanent return to the Basque Country by these exiles. The majority of refugees who returned—a low number—did so after Franco's death in 1975 and on into the early 1990s. Nevertheless, although it may not come to a physical fruition, numerous Basques continue to speak of the day when they will go back to Euskal Herria, even if for the majority it is not feasible to return because of family or economic reasons. For most, there is no desire to retire to the Basque provinces, because they live successful and enriched lives in their host countries.

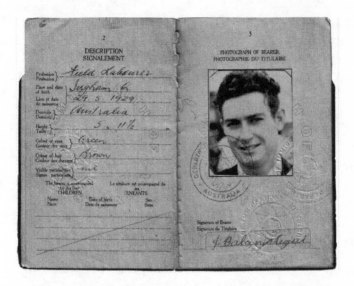

Jon Balanzategi Arkarazo was born in Ingham, Australia, in 1929. He made his first trip to the Basque Country in 1951, when he met and later married Eugenia Oleaga in Gernika. They moved to Ingham, working in the sugar industry, and lived there with their daughter, Igone, for years before returning to the Basque Country in 1970. *Photograph courtesy of Jon Balanzategi and Eugenia Oleaga.*

IN OTHER diaspora communities, such as the Iranian, a return is still neither safe nor feasible. It is estimated that as many as two million Iranians, most of them professionals, either left or chose not to return from study abroad after the 1979 Iranian revolution. Government officials have discussed how they might encourage expatriates to return, since previous attempts to entice exiles back have generally failed. At the same time that the Iranian government renewed appeals for exiles to return, the Iranian parliament stopped a bill to grant amnesty to those who fled after 1979. Many are not willing to take their chances on a return to the country where they might be prosecuted for political reasons.

Cuban exiles also dream of return and of the removal from power of Fidel Castro. Filipinos often immigrate to the United States with the intention of working extremely hard, living frugally, and saving all of their money in order to return to their homeland, but thousands stay. Mexican ethnics in the United States return regularly to their homeland, then come back to the United States. In the days prior to Christmas 2001, officials anticipated that as many as 2.5 million people would return to their ancestral homeland in Mexico for the holidays. To ease the process, Mexican consulates in the United States even distributed guides for families, complete with complaint forms and phone numbers to facilitate the campaign against United States border officials demanding bribes for reentry

A PERMANENT return *is* possible for others, such as those Argentine-Basques who have been repatriated to the Basque Country with homeland government aid during the latest economic crisis in the new millennium. The growing chaos in Argentina saw banks close, protestors take to the streets, and a succession of presidents resign their posts. Argentine Basques, Jews, and Italians took advantage of their dual citizenships to leave the country. Before the economic collapse in Argentina, the Israeli government had already offered generous incentives to Argentine Jews to depart for a "return" to Israel, even though many were second-generation Argentines or later. The package included automatic citizenship and subsidies toward airfare, buying an apartment, and relocation costs. Prime Minister Ariel Sharon was seeking to attract one million new immigrants over the next ten years. Argentina had been targeted, along with South Africa and France, because of its economic conditions. The Jewish Agency sent eighteen emissaries to Argentina to recruit Jews to move to Israel, and it now employs fifty local people there. Nearly fifteen hundred Argentine Jews departed for Israel in 2001, and another six thousand individuals expressed interest by obtaining the necessary paperwork and information.

HOWEVER, a "return" to the homeland need not be a permanent one. Like those of Mexican descent, a large number of Basques have toured and/or regularly visit their homeland, my fieldwork research shows, while others have virtual visits daily on the Internet, reinforcing a transnational diasporic identity. It is often the case that a homeland is unprepared for its returning diasporans, whether it be a physical or a virtual return. Although there are literally thousands of Web sites with information about the Basque Country, the homeland has not yet provided the institutions to receive the thousands of Basque diaspora tourists, students, or persons who want to return permanently to study or live in their original homeland.

ETHNIC SOLIDARITY

The ancestors of today's Basque diaspora tourists likely arrived in a host community with other Basques, co-ethnics who provided a social space where Basques could create a sense of continuity between homeland and host country. This resulted in commercial networks, collective action, mutual assistance programs, schools for Basque children, and associations and societies for the maintenance of the Basque language, culture, and traditions. As Cohen has said, a strong, sustained ethnic group consciousness and a sense of solidarity with members of that group in other countries are defining features that separate diasporas from other migrant groups. Many Basques have exhibited their ethnic group consciousness by preferring each other in trade, labor, and chain migration networks since the 1500s. This time-proven cohesiveness separates diasporas from recent immigrant communities, and although the Basque communities in Belgium and Australia are relatively recent compared with those in South America, Basques in the United States, Cuba, Mexico, El Salvador, the Dominican Republic, Venezuela, Colombia, Peru, Chile, Uruguay, and Argentina continue to maintain their ethnic identity after more than six generations.

As WE HAVE seen, Basques began establishing ethnic organizations for themselves in the 1600s in Peru and Mexico and then throughout Latin America, and later in the 1900s in the new migration destinations of the United States, Canada, Australia, and Belgium. The processes of settling included acquiring a new language, finding employment, changing gender roles, and constructing new social spaces for the maintenance of Basque ethnicity, and these communities soon produced their own *euskal etxeak*, or Basque centers.

Argentine Jews likewise have depended on ethnic organizations to preserve ethnic solidarity. Hebrew is taught and spoken among the Jewish community, and the majority of children have attended Jewish day schools. There were an estimated two hundred thousand mainly middle-class Jews in Argentina before the economic crisis of 2001. Today, a large number of these families are being supported not by the Argentine state, but by Jewish welfare organizations.

Likewise, to meet the same crisis, the Basque Autonomous Government sent 30,000 dollars in 2002 and another 65,000 dollars in 2003 for humanitarian aid to Basques in Argentina, while Euzkaldunak, Inc., of Boise,

Idaho, also pledged several thousand dollars in solidarity, using personal networks and contacts with the federation of Basque centers in Argentina, Federación de Entidades Vasco Argentinas (FEVA) to make the necessary
connections. Separately, in October 2003, the government of the Foral Community of Nafarroa also pledged
to help those of Nafarroan descent in the five Nafarroan
centers in Argentina.

In the Indian communities abroad, January 9—the day
Mahatma Gandhi returned to India after twenty years in
South Africa—is celebrated as Indian Diaspora Day, with
festivals of solidarity for Indians not living in India. In
2002, Prime Minister Atal Behari Vajpayee also declared
that each year on January 9, ten nonresident Indians
would be given awards for their outstanding contributions to Indian culture, society, science, or the arts.
Although Indians living abroad are not allowed Indian
citizenship, persons of Indian origin qualify for a special identity card. The Global Organization of People of
Indian Origin (GOPIO) is working to lobby Indian politicians to continue with the positive changes they have
instigated since 2000, which have resulted in positive
solidarity among Indians worldwide.

THE HISTORY and experiences as immigrants that
diasporans share contribute to their sense of
empathy and solidarity with other co-ethnics abroad.
In the Basque diaspora, this is especially true among
the women, and more intensely so for the women who
migrated to English-speaking host countries, who
encountered the added difficulties of language and communication, as we have seen. This fellowship is now
transcending the single Basque community-to-homeland
bilateral relationship and is recently incorporating dias-
pora-to-diaspora relations, as well as multilocal networks
and relationships among the homeland institutions and

Josu Legarreta Bilbao has led the Office of Relations with the Basque Communities to its enormously successful worldwide diaspora programs. The substantial growth in the numbers of Basque organizations abroad and their participating members are a direct result of his determination and influence.
Photo courtesy of Euskal Etxeak.

the approximately one hundred and eighty communities abroad. For example, Basques participating in the Euskal Etxea of Lima, Peru, reported feeling a similar connection to Basques in Belgium, in Argentina, or in the homeland. The scale of their ethnic identity changes from local—during community celebrations, festivals, or dinners at their Basque center—to global when they click on the Euskal Irrati Telebista, Basque Radio and Television (EITB) Web site to read news about other Basques around the world on Canal Vasco. Technology transforms Basque identity from an intimate identity with family, home decoration, foods, and family ethnic traditions to public manifestations of Basqueness at world congresses, on Web sites, and in international spheres. These opportunities facilitate ethnic experiences at the click of the mouse. We will explore this phenomenon further in a subsequent lesson.

H OWEVER, TECHNOLOGY is not the *cause* of Basque transnational communications, it only simplifies and facilitates access to them. Regardless of geography and the time of migration, Basque women have been instrumental in constructing and maintaining the transnational networks of social interaction—with or without technology. My qualitative and quantitative data for Basques in eight countries demonstrated that in nine out of ten Basque households, females (even if they were non-Basques married to Basques) were the communicators and sharers of familial information and greetings. They serve as the social agents who maintain nearly all family records and communications between the diasporas and the homeland branches of relatives.

INVOLVEMENT IN HOSTLAND AND HOMELAND POLITICS

Cohen notes that it is characteristic of diasporas that immigrants to a new area experience some sort of a troubled relationship with or have their political loyalty questioned by their host society. However, as we have noted before, unlike most diasporas, the Basque diaspora has not had to endure such relationships. Basques are generally white-skinned Catholics who migrated to white, Christian-dominated societies, many of them Spanish-speaking, and they have not experienced mass overt discrimination based on their origin.

BASQUES HAVE not made political demands on any of their host-country governments for any special group rights or group benefits that would call attention to themselves, even if programs were available. For example, in Australia in the 1990s, government funding was available for after-school ethnic-language programs for youths to maintain their maternal language. In Sydney, more than thirty languages were being taught at different points in the city on any given Monday through Friday. However, the Basques did not apply for any of the public funding and instead organized their own language classes at private residences and at the Basque cultural centers. However, as we have seen, Basques *have* mobilized politically to influence their host governments to help their kin in Euskal Herria. In Argentina, in 1940, Basques lobbied their national government to open the doors immediately and allow several thousand Basque political exiles and refugees from the Franco dictatorship to enter Argentina. The government passed the special legislation, and once the Basques began to arrive, other established Basque families—from the first to the sixth generation in Argentina—took over the provision of

Euskal Irrati Telebista, Basque Radio and Television
is utilizing satellite telecommunications to transmit
live audio and visual programming over the Internet
to Basques in diaspora communities. ETB-Sat, Basque
television transmitted by satellite to cable companies in
various countries, allows audiences abroad to watch the
same television programming as seen in the homeland.
Photo courtesy of Euskal Etxeak.

accommodations, employment searches, and medical
care.

Basques from Venezuela sent radio broadcasts into
Iparralde during the Franco dictatorship when Euskara
was outlawed and any political dissent was crushed, as
we have noted before. In a similar manner, but using
advances in technology, today, other exiles, such as the
Iranians, broadcast dissident satellite television into
their homelands with the consent or tolerance of their
host governments. Although it is illegal to own a satellite dish in Iran, by some counts there are two million

homes in the country able to receive the broadcasts. NITV, for example, is run from West Hollywood in Los Angeles. It shows old movies and music shows from before the revolution that are currently banned inside Iran. The station gets much of its funding from donations by the Iranian diaspora. KRSI Radio also broadcasts on short wave from Beverly Hills into Iran, drawing big audiences for its phone-in programs. The authorities in Iran are aware of the broadcasts, but recognize the tremendous practical difficulties of hunting down every hidden satellite dish and are unable to stop the flow of diaspora-homeland communications.

DIASPORA INVOLVEMENT in politics can cause diplomatic problems, however. To that extent, Cohen's claim can be predictive for many diasporas other than the Basques'. France's 2001 decision to recognize the Armenian "genocide" by Turkey represented a major success for the French-Armenian diaspora lobby, but threatened to disrupt relations between Turkey and France, as well as to interfere with negotiations for Turkey's European Union membership. France has the largest Armenian community in Europe, estimated at between five hundred thousand and seven hundred thousand, and there are an estimated one million Armenians in the USA and four hundred thousand in Canada. Armenians first arrived in France as merchants in the seventeenth century, and then thousands fled the violence of 1915. This diaspora campaign involved many Armenian exile organizations, including the Defense Committee for the Armenian Cause. France joined the countries officially recognizing "the Armenian genocide of 1915" and the vote in the lower house of the French assembly was unanimous. Middle Eastern specialists, together with Armenian nationalists, allege that between 1915 and 1923, some 1.5 million Armenians died by a

---

combination of violence, starvation, disease, and deportation from eastern Turkey to modern-day Syria and Iraq. Although the declaration did not refer to Turkey by name, the Turkish government was furious at the implication that there had been a policy of extermination of Armenians in the last years of the Ottoman Empire. Turkey states that there were fewer deaths and that there were multiple causes, including the Russian occupation and internal fighting. It points out that Armenians also carried out massacres.

A SIGNIFICANT campaign of economic and diplomatic reprisals quickly followed the French vote. The Turkish prime minister stated that "lasting damage" had been done to relations between the two countries. The Turks cancelled a deal worth 176 million U.S. dollars for French satellite technology and barred French firms from bidding for defense contracts. When the bill passed into law on January 30, they cancelled a 250-million-dollar contract for France to upgrade Turkey's military planes. In Turkey, demonstrations clogged the streets with French flags burning, and soon French wines and foods disappeared from menus. The Turkish press criticized the government for being slow to react and ineffective in combating the Armenian diaspora's lobbying. Some politicians demanded the end of flights to Armenia and sanctions against the country.

Armenia and Turkey have no diplomatic relations, but behind the scenes there are moves to restore relations, interestingly, often using diaspora Armenian-Americans as the informal go-betweens. Armenian-Americans have been busy themselves, lobbying the Maryland state assembly to pass a vote on the genocide and to include it in school history textbooks. Armenian media reported that one hundred thousand postcards from members of the Armenian diaspora were sent to President George

W. Bush in his first month of office. Some members of the Turkish, Azeri, and Jewish communities in the state oppose the Armenian lobby, but it receives the support of some Greek-Americans.

THE GLOBALIZATION OF DIASPORA POPULATIONS
Cohen notes that the existence of a return movement is one of the defining characteristics of a diaspora. However, the processes of globalization have increasingly subverted the boundaries separating the diaspora from the homeland and have increased both the real and the virtual presence of each within the other. Diasporas shatter the concept that citizenship equates to loyalty and belonging to only one state, and they replace simple notions of single national identity with multiple layers of orientation and participation in ethnicity and cultural identities that do not derive from a single territory. Diasporans' participation in homeland elections and political policy making, their participation in world congresses, and their exercise of dual citizenships are manifestations of these processes at work.

Basques who maintain Spanish citizenship have the right to vote in all Spanish national, regional, and local elections, and in the 2001 elections, nearly thirty-three thousand Basques abroad registered, although only about twelve thousand actually voted. In the same year, in expectation of a close election in Australia, the nation's main political parties campaigned for votes among Australian expatriates in Great Britain. Campaigners agreed that it was difficult to track down Australian voters, there being no register and no particular areas of settlement in Britain. They had to make do with garnering support at cultural and sporting events likely to be attended by Australian voters. The most important polling booth of the entire 2001 Australian

elections was actually the Australian High Commission in London, where it was anticipated that eighteen
thousand votes would be cast by Australians living in
England, and another six thousand votes were sent to
London by post. In the last general election for Australia,
twenty-one thousand diasporans living in Britain voted
from abroad. There are an estimated eight hundred and
thirty thousand Australians living abroad, and in 1998,
only sixty-five thousand cast a vote.

IN 2002, BASQUE communities in the United States
and Argentina demonstrated their ethnic consciousness regarding homeland politics by successfully lobbying and passing in their respective state and provincial
legislatures resolutions asking their central governments
to help promote an end to all Spanish and Basque violence, mandatory all-party talks, and the Basque right
to self-determination. The Spanish government was not
impressed, however, and it is not likely a coincidence
that on a Wednesday morning in September 2002,
United States government officials were negotiating in
Madrid for the use of military bases in their war against
Iraq and that by Thursday afternoon, Idaho Senator Larry
E. Craig's staff visit to the Basque Country was cancelled.
Diaspora groups are more likely to obtain measures of
cultural support for their homelands, but controversies
that may affect economic and military might are usually
dodged by the host-country governments.

In addition to participating in homeland national
politics, numerous ethnic diasporas have organized
international congresses for political and economic
policy analysis and even for policy making for relations
between the homeland and the diasporic communities
abroad. The Basque Autonomous Government organizes
a Basque World Congress, held every four years (1995
was the first gathering) to help create and evaluate pro-

Delegates representing Basque communities around the world meet every four years for the World Congress of Basque Collectivities. Although they do not have the power to vote in the Basque Country homeland parliament, they do collaborate with the executive branch to create diaspora programs in the Four Year Plan of Institutional Action.
Photo courtesy of Basque Government Press Agency.

grams regarding Basques abroad. In the last decade, there has been a proliferation of such diaspora congresses meeting in their homelands to discuss dual citizenship and diaspora political and economic policies and projects. Armenians, Russians, Rwandans, Azeris, Somalis, Hungarians, and Bulgarians have all organized to work with their homeland governments to debate political rights, and several countries, such as Croatia, even have an elected seat in the homeland parliament filled by a person elected from and to represent the diaspora.

In Romania, the government is considering establishing an upper council of representation for Romanians outside the country, thought to number ten million. The council would be filled by an election held at the same time as parliamentary elections. President Emil Constantinescu argued that such a council would help lift Romania's international image and at the same time preserve the country's language, traditions, and culture.

The congress of the World Federation of Hungarians, held in Budapest in 1999, ended with a call to create a status of foreign-resident Hungarian citizenship with a right to travel to Hungary, but not to vote in elections. In the first six months of 2000, over twenty-six hundred people from abroad were granted Hungarian citizenship, over half of them from Romania and others from Yugoslavia and Slovakia. The idea was modeled on forms of British overseas citizenship. The congress also pushed for Hungarians beyond the borders to be represented in a second chamber of the Hungarian parliament, and the new representation would be founded on the principle that the Hungarian state is for all Hungarians in the world. Other suggestions at the congress included a greater role for Hungarian Duna Television and a network of Hungarian universities in Romania and Slovakia, where there are substantial Hungarian communities. The congress also discussed creating a diaspora council to be a permanent consultative body to the government.

APPROXIMATELY three hundred expatriate Rwandans convened in Rwanda in the last week of December 2001 to discuss how the diaspora could assist the country's economic and political development. The five-day convention was the first such congress of their diaspora, and the meetings discussed globalization, economic development, the diaspora and national development, the constitution and governance, and technology and human resources. The delegates were told by President Paul Kagame that they had a "crucial role" to play in Rwanda's development from abroad.

IN 2001, THE Russian president, Vladimir Putin, addressed the Congress of Compatriots held in Moscow, stating that the government had not done enough for Russians abroad. Putin stated that Russia is interested in much closer ties with its diaspora, estimated at twenty-five million people. He announced that the government would allocate 105 million rubles (approximately 3.5 million U.S. dollars) for diaspora activities and interests. He added that Russia should support Russian-language media and schools and do more to disseminate access to the Internet and other electronic means of communication. The Congress of Compatriots assembled 600 representatives of Russian-speaking communities from forty-three countries, with the largest delegations coming from the Baltic states. It lasted two days and was the first such convention for six years. Earlier planned congresses were cancelled because they clashed with national elections. Among the matters discussed were the formation of a permanent international organization to protect the rights of the Russian diaspora and how to facilitate issuing visas and applications for naturalization.

The first ever congress of the Azeri diaspora was held in the Azerbaijan capital city, Baku, in 2001, with attendance of diasporans from over thirty-five countries. The Azeri president, Heydar Aliyev, stated that the event would "reinforce the solidarity between compatriots and create a platform for cooperation between the Azeris of the world to reinforce the international authority of their country." He also invited the congress to work to enhance Azerbaijan's image and prestige abroad. There are thought to be several million Azeris abroad,

BASQUE NEWS

No. 65 - 2003

The Lehendakari submits his proposal for a new form of relationship with the State

Ibarretxe: "It's not a break-up that we want but co-existence"

President Juan José Ibarretxe presents his plan for a new political structure between Euskadi and Spain to the Basque Parliament in Vitoria-Gasteiz.

---

outnumbering the 7.5 million resident in the state itself. Azeri World Solidarity Day is December 31 and is a national holiday in the homeland. President Aliyev addressed Azeris by radio, stating:

> The basis of the unity and solidarity of world Azeris, which is a pressing task of the historical self-determination of our people, is formed by ideas of Azerbaijanism and Azerbaijani statehood. The idea of Azerbaijanism provides above all for the development of realization of Azeris' national dignity, their national-spiritual

values, language, culture, rites and traditions, which have stood the test of time, and the creation of Azeris' unity with their historical homeland and between themselves on the basis of this idea. At the same time, the independent Azerbaijani state is a powerful factor in the solidarity of world Azeris, a reliable point of rest for their organization and membership of the international community as an influential force. The Azerbaijani state is a protector of the human rights and legal interests of world Azerbaijanis.

H E NOTED that the congress was a stage in "the process ... of uniting world Azeris around the true idea of national self-consciousness and the nationwide idea—Azerbaijanism, independent statehood and national-spiritual values."

The Bulgarian prime minister, Ivan Kostov, organized the first meeting of Bulgarian expatriates aimed at enlisting their aid in lobbying for European Union membership. The Bulgarian Easter Initiative, as the meeting was named, established an Internet communication system, and Bulgaria's ambassadors were instructed to work with members of the diaspora communities to enhance the country's international image. As the processes of globalization advance, prior fears of conflict between a person's loyalty to one or another territory are beginning to be replaced with an understanding of the opportunities to allow for multiple identities and multiple citizenships. Nearing the end of 2004, there were approximately 100 countries that allowed dual and multiple citizenships. Diaspora populations have led the way in obtaining and maintaining their homeland citizenships in addition to their new host country citizenship, and in general, they experience no conflict whatsoever. In the Basque case, because there is no separate Basque state, dual citizenship laws and procedures are left up to the state central governments in Paris and Madrid. For other ethnic groups, dual and multiple citizenship policies are monitored closely, but seemingly without great problems to date.

THE HIGH Level Committee on the Indian Diaspora, set up by the Indian Foreign Ministry in September 2000, presented its nine-hundred-page final report to Prime Minister Vajpayee in 2002. It is estimated that the Indian diaspora numbers twenty million people and is worth 300 billion dollars in annual income, an amount comparable to India's total gross domestic product (GDP). There are Indians in fifty-three countries in the world, and ten of those countries have more than half a million people of Indian origin. The commission recommended dual citizenship for residents of selected countries within the provisions of the Indian Citizenship Act. The proposed legal framework for dual citizenship was based on the United Kingdom's model. The provision would initially apply only to Indians who are residents of Europe the United States, Canada, Australia, New Zealand, and Singapore because, supposedly, these countries, in which seven million Indians reside, are already familiar with the concept of dual citizenship. But Indians in other countries—such as Mauritius, Sri Lanka, and Malaysia—would be eligible only for a person of Indian origin (PIO) identity card, which carries fewer privileges. Dual citizenship as recommended would not involve voting rights, and citizens of another country could not vote or stand for office in Indian elections. The new status would grant only economic rights to these Indians living outside India.

In 2001, the senate of the Philippines introduced legislation giving six million overseas Filipinos the right to vote in national elections and allowing naturalized citizens of other countries to recover their Filipino citizenship. The legislation allows Filipino citizens overseas to vote in elections and on referendums of national issues. Filipino diasporans living elsewhere are also allowed to run for elected office, as long as they do not already hold an office in another country. Members of the armed forces of other countries are not eligible for Filipino citizenship. As with Basques voting from abroad, absentee ballots can be cast only by those who have properly registered with the homeland government.

The lower house of the Polish parliament passed a new citizenship law in 2000 allowing Poles who were displaced or who fled during the period of Communist rule to apply for the restoration of their rights. People eligible for restored citizenship include soldiers who joined the Allied armies after World War II and anyone leaving between 1939 and June 1989. The new law is in accord with the European Citizenship Convention

THE NUMBER of countries granting dual citizenship is increasing, but there is still opposition to the idea, as well. A law passed in 1999 giving Koreans overseas the status of Korean citizenship was declared unconstitutional by the country's constitutional court in 2001. The main flaw in the legislation was its definition of who was eligible. Under the rules, Koreans in the United States and other affluent countries qualified, but not the 2.6 million ethnic Koreans in China, Russia, and Japan. There are many ethnic Koreans from China now living illegally in Korea who had not benefited under the regulations. In 1999, the government omitted these people for fear of offending the Chinese and Russian governments by being seen to claim some of those citizens. Under the new ruling, the court required the government to come forward with revisions eliminating any discrimination against Koreans living in different countries.

INDONESIAN citizenship laws also contain citizenship discrimination against nationals who marry foreigners. According to the *Jakarta Post*, the child of an Indonesian woman married to a foreign man cannot become Indonesian and will have the father's citizenship. But if a foreign woman marries an Indonesian man, she and their children are eligible for citizenship. This discrimination based on the sex of the father has not yet been changed.

Another example from Argentina points to a possible future issue regarding people abandoning countries and moving to their second (or third) country during times of political and economic hardship. Nearly half of Argentina's 36 million people are of Italian heritage, and an estimated quarter of a million Argentines have Italian citizenship. The Italian government responded to the recent economic crisis by organizing temporary repatriations and speeding up the process of applying for passports and visas. In the first few days after rioting began on the streets of Buenos Aires, thirteen thousand people applied for Italian citizenship. If those of Basque, Italian, and Jewish descent were escaping the country with their assets, others were likely doing the same, leaving the economy in a worse position.

INDEED, THE mobility of assets is a principal feature of the globalization of diasporan relations. Diasporans frequently have not just sought, but found the possibility of leading fuller, richer lives in their host countries, as Cohen notes—fuller lives emotionally, socially, and politically perhaps, but also and primarily economically. One aspect of their success in doing so is the ability of diasporans to send money back to the homeland. Unfortunately. there are no sufficiently scientific studies that

Political propaganda regarding the "Plan Ibarretxe" to create a new political relationship of free association with Spain was sent to Basques abroad; including this informational pamphlet, which states, "Ultimately the decision is yours. Inform yourself, it's your right. A New Political Statute of Euskadi."

convincingly tally the annual amounts for Basque remittances to their homeland, no studies that demonstrate the monetary value for village public improvements funded by Basque fellow villagers abroad, no studies that sum the value of money sent home to the families of emigrants. It is a significant and fundamental topic for a future PhD thesis. The figures for the monetary remittances being sent home by those in other ethnic groups who have emigrated, however, are staggering. A 1999 United Nations report indicated that Cuba received 725 million dollars from diasporans abroad in that one year alone. There are nearly one million Haitians and Haitian-Americans in the United States, and in 2000, they remitted 699 million dollars to the Caribbean country. There are approximately seven million Filipino workers overseas, and they remit to their homeland nearly eight billion dollars a year.

SOON AFTER his inauguration as President of Mexico, Vicente Fox confirmed his election commitments to govern on behalf of "118 million Mexicans" in both Mexico and the United States. During the election campaign, the former businessman had spoken of his intention to reach out to the long-neglected Mexican-origin communities north of the border. They remit between five and eight billion dollars a year to Mexico—the country's third-highest source of income after oil and tourism. The newspaper La Jornada reported that Mexican emigrants had remitted 28 billion dollars in the six years after North American Free Trade Agreement came into effect, which is equivalent to 83 percent of United States investment in that period. The newspaper further said that 80 percent of these funds go to subsistence for families, and only 1.7 percent in investment. Fox referred to the Mexicans abroad as "our beloved migrants, our heroic migrants." He said that "my goal is to build a

relationship of equals, of neighbors, of friends and partners and, in the process, I want us to view one another
as investors in a joint venture with a shared future." He
also stated that the government would make it easier for
emigrants to remit money home. Mexico is pursuing a
strategy known as the *padrino*, or godfather, scheme. A
padrino, who will be specifically identified for the purpose and encouraged, will invest in a specific community
project. The federal government has identified ninety of
the poorest municipalities that have suffered from emigration to be targeted under the development program.
It will also offer three-for-one matching funds for each
dollar invested from diaspora Mexicans.

DATA FROM the Inter-American Development Bank
(IDB) show that total remittances to Latin America
are near 23 billion dollars annually. This figure has
exceeded all other forms of foreign aid to the region
and is approximately equivalent to a third of the total
foreign investment. At a projected growth rate of 7 to
10 percent annually, the IDB calculates that remittances
will be worth more than 70 billion dollars in 2012. A
report issued by the Inter-American Development Bank
emphasized the significance of remittances for regional
development and pressed for further reductions in the
cost of transferring money. The report, based on a study
by Bendixen and Associates, stated that it costs 3 billion
dollars to remit 23 billion dollars, and this was money
the region could not afford to lose. In some countries,
remittances are equivalent to 10 to 20 percent of the
GDP. Among the major recipients, only Brazil is not
heavily dependent on them. It received 2.6 billion dollars
in 2001, far less than Mexico's 9.273 billion. Other major
recipients were El Salvador, Ecuador, and the Dominican
Republic (1.807 billion dollars).

Remittances from early Basque migrants assisted in paying for baserri additions or remodeling, new farming implements, and the general expenses of farmsteads housing extended families. Several homes in the Basque Country are named after the host society of the departed migrant, such as Argentina, California, and La Plata.

Photograph by Eulalia Abaitua Allende Salazar. Courtesy of the Basque Archaeological, Ethnographic, and Historical Museum, Bilbao.

The average amount of money sent home by each individual is 200 dollars seven or eight times a year. This represents more than 100 million separate transactions, 40 percent of which were via private companies such as Western Union or MoneyGram. The report also found that younger and poorer migrants sent home the most money to their families and that 70 percent of Latin American families resident in the United States remitted funds.

Clearly, we have numerous examples here of diaspora populations' involvement in international finance and economics, as well as in international politics. It would be a mistake to see the role of ethnic groups on the international scene simply as folkloric peoples maintaining their ancestral cultures through their languages and symbolic festivals. To fail to recognize their influence in a globalized world of transnational politics and economies would be a gross error for the student of diaspora studies.

Lesson seventeen

BIBLIOGRAPHY

Basch, Linda, Nina Glick Schiller, and Cristina Szanton Blanc. 1994. *Nations Unbound: Transnational Projects, Postcolonial Predicaments, and Deterritorialized Nation-States*. Amsterdam: Gordon and Breach Science Publishers.

Boyd, Monica. 1989. "Family and Personal Networks in International Migration: Recent Developments and New Agendas." *International Migration Review* 23: no. 3 638–70.

Cohen, Robin. 1997. *Global Diasporas: An Introduction*. London: University College London Press.

Cohen, Robin. 1997. "Diasporas, the Nation-State, and Globalization." In *Global History and Migrations*, ed. Wang Gungwu. Boulder, Colo.: Westview Press.

————. 1996. "Diaspora and the Nation-State: From Victims to Challengers." *International Affairs* 72: 507–20.

————.1994. *Frontiers of Identity: The British and the Rest*. London: Longman.

————, ed. 1995. *The Cambridge Survey of World Migration*. Cambridge: Cambridge University Press.

————, and Zig Layton-Henry, eds. 1997. *The Politics of Migration*. Cheltenham, England: Edward Elgar.

Castles, Stephen, and Mark J. Miller. 1993. *The Age of Migration: International Population Movements in the Modern World*. London: Macmillan.

Shain, Yossi, and Juan J. Linz. 1995. *Between States: Interim Governments and Democratic Transitions*. New York: Cambridge University Press.

Sheffer, Gabriel. 1996. "Whither the Study of Ethnic Diasporas? Some Theoretical, Definitional, Analytical, and Comparative Considerations." In *The Networks of Diaspora*, ed. Georges Prévélakis. Paris: Cyprus Research Center KYKEM.

————. 1994. "Ethno-National Diasporas and Security." *Survival* 36, no. 1 (Spring): 607–79.

————. 2003 *Diaspora Politics: At Home Abroad*. Cambridge: Cambridge University Press.

————, ed. 1986. *Modern Diasporas in International Politics*. London: Croom Helm.

Totoricagüena, Gloria. 2004. *Identity, Culture, and Politics in the Basque Diaspora*. Reno: University of Nevada Press.

————. 2003. Keynote address delivered to the Third World Congress of Basque Collectivities. Vitoria-Gasteiz, July 14.

TRACES. An electronic bulletin established by the Transnational Communities Project. Oxford University.
Oxford, England.

REQUIRED READING

Sylvia Chant, ed. *Gender and Migration in Developing
Countries* (London: Bellhaven Press, 1992).

Robin Cohen, *Global Diasporas* (Seattle: University of
Washington Press, 1997), pp 180–96.

Gabriel Sheffer, "The Emergence of Ethno-National
Diasporas," in *Migration, Diasporas, and Transnationalism*, ed. Steven Vertovec and Robin Cohen
(Cheltenham, England: Edward Elgar, 1999), pp
396–419.

Gloria Totoricagüena, "Basques Around the World:
Generic Immigrants or Diaspora?" http://
euskonews.com, issue 72, 2000/3/24-31.

Gloria Totoricagüena, keynote Address delivered to the
Third World Congress of Basque Collectivities. Vitoria-Gasteiz, July 14, 2003.

WRITTEN LESSON FOR SUBMISSION

Compare the definitions of "diaspora" in our readings
by Sheffer and Cohen. Give examples from this and previous lessons and readings to explain how each does or
does not apply to the Basques. Based on what you have
learned so far, and your personal experiences, do you
agree or disagree with Sheffer and the argument from
the "synthetic" approach that the origins of modern ethnicity and "incipient" or commencing diasporas lie in
an inseparable combination of primordial, instrumental,
and environmental factors?

18 · Globalization
Basque transnational identity. The Internet

A S THE PHENOMENA of globalization that we examined at the end of the last lesson show, the relations
between diasporas and their homeland are changing.
However, in diaspora communities such as the Basques',
the basic elements that constitute globalization are not
new at all. As a result, both the Basque diaspora and
the Basque homeland find themselves in a position of
privilege in dealing with a worldwide phenomenon that
everyone, everywhere must confront.

"Globalization" refers to the social, political, and economic interconnectedness of the world and its people
and to the development of networks of interaction and
exchange between governments, people, and institutions. David Held and his associates define globalization as "a process (or set of processes) which embodies
a transformation in the spatial organization of social
relations and transactions—assessed in terms of their
extensity, intensity, velocity and impact—generating
transcontinental or interregional flows and networks
of activity, interaction and the exercise of power" (Held
et al. 1999, 16). Basques have linked themselves simultaneously to networks of relationships and meaning
from both the host country and the home country since
the era of marine trade and Spanish colonialism. As
Benedict Anderson says, "Communities are to be distinguished, not by their falsity/genuineness, but by the
style in which they are imagined" (Anderson 1991, 6).
The dispersed Basque transnational communities always
have imagined themselves in terms that bridge the gap
between local and national identities. Globalization has
simply enhanced the abilities of the diaspora to continue
growing in numbers and to intensify its ethnic identity.

The effect of globalization on the style in which Basques are imagining their communities involves qualitative shifts that alter the nature of communities and the outlook of individuals toward themselves, their societies, and their world. As a result, these developments are difficult to demonstrate with quantitative evidence, case by case In the many countries where I have conducted fieldwork, however, interviewees' statements regarding their feelings of connectedness and identification with Basques around the world give an indication of the growing "extensity" and "impact" of globalization processes in the Basque diaspora. The flow of e-mail and the exchanges of information by newsletters and bulletins and travel of Basques from one community to visit another have mushroomed. At the 2000 Jaialdi International Basque Festival in Boise, Idaho, attending Basques included those from Canada, Mexico, Peru, Argentina, Uruguay, Australia, and hundreds from the Basque Country.

TODAY'S PATTERNS of globalization manifest a distinctive historical form that is a product of a unique conjuncture of social, political, economic, and technological forces, and it is important to note that particular forms of globalization may differ between historical eras. In their research of discrete historical epochs of globalization, Held and his team argue that contemporary global infrastructures of culture and communication have contributed to "the development and entrenchment of diasporic cultures and communities" (Held et al., 370). Stanley Brunn (1996, 259–72) stresses the effects of modern technological progress as a major factor in the proliferation of diasporas. However, although the resurgence in ethnic identity and globalization are correlated, there is not strong evidence to argue that globalization causes the creation or growth of diasporas themselves or of diaspora consciousness. They are related but there is no causation; it just so happens that they exist at the same time.

Instead, globalization facilitates preexisting transnationalism, as we noted in the last lesson. It does so in the Basque diaspora by aiding the creation and maintenance of communications among Basque collectivities abroad and with the homeland. A swelling in interest in Basque identity maintenance is not a defensive reaction to globalization, but an unplanned embrace of the tools and results of globalization. A renewed interest in some Basque communities resulted in their reestablishing diaspora organizations, while others have created associations for the first time, but there is no reason to suggest a direct precipitating effect. Many of the new organizations in Uruguay and Argentina, for example, were founded prior to the availability of Internet access in their countries and in towns that would not be considered transnational, cosmopolitan, globalized communities.

WHAT SEPARATES today's Basque transnational networks from those that stretch from the fifteenth to the nineteenth and twentieth centuries are the speed and pervasiveness of today's world intercommunications and how they have affected the process of globalization. Basques now manifest their transnational networks and identity on a world scale that globalization facilitates.

As we saw in the preceding lesson and will examine in more detail below, one of the most salient characteristics if globalization is the rise of transnationalism. Alejandro Portes argues that "the main impulse for the rise in grass-roots transnationalism is found in the confluence between new communications and transportation technologies" (Portes 1999, 467). However, Manuel Castells (1996), cautious of predicting, argues that the new

The Belgium Basque community had plans to renovate
this building and reestablish their organization in 1997.
However, disagreements between members and lack of
participation by others led to the demise of the Belgian
eusko etxea. Although there are hundreds of Basques
employed in European Union posts and in the Basque
delegation offices in Brussels, in 2004, no Belgian
Basque diasporic organizations existed.
Photograph by the author.

technologies that are at the heart of today's transnational networks do not create, new social patterns, but instead reinforce them. Global telecommunications and the Internet are only instruments and tools for communication, which can be used by Basques around the world in numerous ways. New technologies, especially telecommunications technologies, foment transnational ties with increasing speed, and despite great distances and eras of immigration, transnational ties in the Basque communities have been intensified with the globalization of communications.

BY MEANS of faster, cheaper, and easier communications and travel, globalization also has promoted the deterritorialization of identity. Globalization is aterritorial because it involves a complex deterritorialization and reterritorialization of political and economic power (Held et al., 28) and, for Basques abroad, a shift in their evolving paradigm of ethnic identity. The era of globalization "creates communities not of place, but of interest," making it more likely that people loosen their affiliation and allegiances to nation-states (Cohen 1996, 517). The technological age implies that physical location is no longer required for the practice of community. The globalization of telecommunications eases the "interlacing of social events and social relations 'at distance' with local contextualities" (Giddens 1991, 21). Distance has ceased to be a barrier to interaction and communication, and various groups and individuals will make decisions on the basis of their own networks of communication and information. The political significance of diasporas will continue to grow because of the factors of globalization of the economy and international relations (Claval 1996, 444). They influence their homelands and host countries and contribute increasingly to the transnational networks of the world, which have yet to be studied. However, Basques will not likely be practicing or celebrating their culture exclusively via electronic screens soon. The local scale of places where they live, the Basque centers, and the people with whom they socialize are all integral parts of their ethnic identity.

THUS, WHILE A homogenized global culture is emerging, the proliferation and resurgence in local identities, mixed with the overarching global culture, simultaneously produces different combinations. The previously negative connotation of not fitting in here or there is now likely to be perceived differently as belonging here *and* there. Basque identity is not hierarchical, but multilocal, with sentimental ties to villages, regions, nations, and states—all plural. Locations are linked by the flows and returns of people, resources, and remittances, by New World and Old World lifestyles, and by the economic and political relations between the Basque Country and the host countries, the "migration dialectic." The globalization of economic relations and telecommunications has shifted the focus away from territorially based forms of political organization and identity to nonterritorial, nonstate, and suprastate levels. The Basque diasporic consciousness provides an example of this suprastate identity. The "area" in area studies thus must now be extended to the transnational, nonphysical territories of in which the diasporas and their homelands are divided and reunited in both new and old ways.

TRANSNATIONAL IDENTITIES AND ETHNICITY

AMONG THE most salient changes wrought (or accelerated) by the processes of globalization are the rise in awareness of transnational identities that unite people across previously established borders and the simultaneous empowerment of modes of differentiation, including ethnicity, that distinguish people from each other.

Basque transnationalism and ethnic networks have existed for centuries, as depicted in this map created by Manuel de Ynchausti in 1948. Ynchausti used this map to educate audiences about Basque history and Basques' participation in the development of global commerce. *Photograph courtesy of Basque Government Urazandi Collection.*

"Transnationalism" broadly refers to the possession of multiple ties, cultural references, and interactions that link people or institutions across the borders of states. Transnationalism is also described as "the formation of social, political, and economic relationships among migrants that span several societies" by people whose "networks, activities and patterns of life encompass both their host and home societies (Basch, Glick Schiller, Szanton Blanc 1992, 1). When differentiating "diaspora" populations from "immigrant" groups, we specifically look for these maintained networks of exchange and also for ethnic consciousness that spans temporal and spatial constraints.

"Transnationalism" is also defined by Nina Glick Schiller as "the formation of social, political and economic relationships among migrants that span several societies" and between people whose "networks, activities and patterns of life encompass both their host and home societies (Basch, Glick Schiller, Szanton Blanc 1992, 1). This definition seems to fit self-defining Basques who participate in Basque organizations. Many exhibit an unconscious multidimensional identity, not merely a hybrid two-dimensional one. They embody Basque identity, host-country identity, and a diaspora identity, all at the same time.

THE PROCESSES of the current form of globalization facilitate a transnational ethnic identity in the Basque diaspora by aiding the creation and maintenance of communications among Basque collectivities and Euskal Herria. Diaspora identity bridges this gap between local and global identities. However, although globalization and diasporization are separate phenomena with no necessarily direct causal connections, the latest processes of globalization facilitate both the maintenance of Basque ethnic identity and the "extensity" of the diaspora.

"Identity" has been seen as a person's source of meaning and experience, and "ethnicity" as a founding structure of meaning, social differentiation, and social recognition. Ethnic identity is a process of construction, building meaning into what I believe I am—and what I want to be—based on cultural attributes or characteristics. As conceptions of identity and ethnicity evolve in a global setting, the nature of ethnic identity is evolving, as well.

Identity is a source of meaning, understanding, and values for how I perceive input from the world and for the output that I give to the world. However, "the world" changes, and one's identity also changes and evolves over time. In the modern era, identity became strongly linked with national identity. With globalization, identity can become transnational, and the concept of transnational identity matches well with diaspora consciousness. Transnational identity has been aptly defined as:

> the ability to add identities rather than being forced to substitute one for another; multiple identities and "cross-pressures" to enhance rather than inhibit one's options; to anchor one's uniqueness in the complex constellation of communities to which one chooses to make a commitment; the opportunity to be different people in different settings—these implications of communities in the unbundled world appear to be mutually reinforcing elements of a broad syndrome which fits our current self-image as autonomous individuals and stands in marked contrast to older notions of rank, status, and duty within an overarching community which claims all our loyalties ... each individual is, in effect, a community of the communities individually accepted or chosen. (Elkins 1997, 150)

THE TRANSNATIONAL individual does not have to replace one identity with another upon their moving to a new physical location or upon moving into a new phase of life. One can add identities to the original foundation.

As a result, the concept of ethnicity changes, as well. Ethnicity need not be hierarchical—need not be a matter of being "more" or "less" Basque. One can be Basque in this way or that way, and there are myriad avenues in which to manifest one's interests in the Basque Country and its language, people, history, art, sculpture, cuisine, politics, and so on.

A TRANSNATIONAL identity has numerous layers and need not be threatening to existing political power structures, which often question a citizen's loyalties. Adding layers to one's personal identity does not diminish that identity, but supplements it Someone who learns to speak Basque does not forget how to speak Spanish, or English, or whatever their first language might be. They simply add another form of communication. Hundreds of Basque interviewees who narrated their feelings of having multiple identities, "just as much Peruvian as Basque and vice versa," fit the definition of transnationalism given by Mike Featherstone:

> the capacity to shift the frame, and move between varying range of foci, the capacity to handle a range of symbolic material out of which various identities can be formed and reformed in different situations, which is relevant in the contemporary global situation .... There has been an extension of cultural repertoires and an enhancement in the resourcefulness of groups to create new symbolic modes of affiliation and belonging (Featherstone 1995, 110)

The effects of globalization on transnationalism and diasporas thus "disrupt the spatial-temporal units of analysis" (Lavie and Swedenburg 1996, 14). Basques are physically connected to the host countries where they currently live and are quite patriotic and proud of their civic identities and at the same time are still emotionally and psychologically connected to their ancestral homelands. This is a transnational identity. When at home in the diaspora setting, say the United States, they are thinking about the Basque Country, and when they are in the Basque Country, they are thinking about their home in the United States.

To cite one good example of transnationalism, in
May 2001, Basques gathered at the Laurak Bat Center
in Buenos Aires to watch Basque parliamentary elections results live on Euskal Telebista (Basque Television) cable, the public television funded by the Basque
government, while others participated in live Internet
chat rooms. The Euskal Telebista transmissions provide
constant and consistent positive images of the homeland
provinces, prompting currently uninvolved Basques
to return to their roots and connect with the positive
social identity and communal belonging of the Basque
centers. And although the Basque government's funding of computers and Internet hookups for each Basque
center found some organizations unprepared and unac-
quainted with the technology, since 1996, the centers
have "caught the wave" and are intercommunicating
via the Internet. The frequency of such communications
and contacts among the diaspora communities and
between the diaspora and the Basque Country, will continue to increase. Political scientists suggest the world
is witnessing a slow emergence of interstate societies
and the worldwide Basque diaspora is one such community. Basques are transnational actors as they go back
and forth between societies, and the societies that they
traverse are also becoming more transnational from the
effects of globalization. Their members tend to move
between the local and the global with ease.

PERHAPS, therefore, diaspora populations are better
prepared for the future trends of globalization and
transnational consciousness. They do not need to
react to globalization because they already possess
transnational identities and live in a globalized world.
The Basque Autonomous Government and the Foral
Government of Nafarroa may also be better prepared for
the future as the conceptualization of political units and

Capitalizing on the prestige of the Basques in Chile,
Basque President Juan José Ibarretxe met with business
leaders of the Chilean Center for Public Studies.
Photo courtesy of Euskal Etxeak.

---

administration evolve in Europe. Their understanding
of nonstate actors' roles in global politics is from experience and is not hypothetical. Their relationships with
diaspora constituents may prove to be equally important
as those that they have with their own homeland residents.

THE INTERNET AND GLOBAL TELECOMMUNICATIONS: HTTP://WWW.IDENTITY.ORG

USING PRINT media as an example of communications, Ernest Gellner and Benedict Anderson regard
that communications medium as a crucial factor in the
construction of nations, because it interconnects people
over space and time. The possibility of a people existing
as a nation, they argue, depends on the book and the

---

newspaper and a literate public able to read the publications and imagine themselves as a unified community.

In that spirit, In 1989, the first issue of the journal Euskal Etxeak was published by the Basque government for the diaspora Basque centers with the aim of presenting contemporary Basque reality. It's free subscription in Spanish and English continues with tremendous popularity and has provided a common forum in which the diaspora collectivities enhance their awareness and knowledge of one another's activities.

Today, however, as we have seen, the Internet subverts older notions of national identity and fosters the construction and manipulation of a virtual identity that breaks free from traditional paradigms of territoriality, ancestry, and language and enables a construct of identity based on the actor's own definition. Internet access will likely provide the most significant catalyst for exponential increases in intradiasporic communications. The exploitation of telecommunications introduces expanded dimensions for the creation and re-creation of ethnicity and carries the potential to unite virtually what is impossible to unite physically.

As Robin Cohen puts it, "Transnational bonds no longer have to be cemented by migration or by exclusive territorial claims. In the age of cyberspace, a diaspora can, to some degree, be held together or re-created through the mind, through cultural artifacts and through a shared imagination" (Cohen 1996, 516), via an electronic screen.

INTERNET LINKS established in 1995 among the majority of the Basque diaspora's centers have produced an explosion of personal communications, usually among the younger Basques, who understand how to use electronic mail. They share information, send invitations, take Basque language lessons, and visit Basque Web sites. They also become communicators who relay messages and information for the many members of the Basque centers who still have not mastered contemporary telecommunications technologies. Since the Basque government financed the "wiring" of the diaspora centers, transnational connections have proliferated via lists, chat rooms, and thousands of Web sites that give Basque Net surfers myriad choices of information and entertainment respecting Basque themes. Inquiries that otherwise might be disregarded because of the difficulties they might cause are now made and answered simply with several clicks of a mouse. Basques from the United States interested in investing in real estate in Argentina have used Basque center e-mail and connections to get information. Basques from Belgium desiring to practice their English have made institutional and personal contacts through the centers in the United States, Canada, and Australia. Basque researchers and journalists find opportunities to make connections and arrange fieldwork while benefiting from access to institutional networks. While the previously established communications between Basque centers tended to be institutional and instrumental for the institution, Internet communications have the ability to encourage personal—and personally instrumental—interactions.

DIASPORA POPULATIONS are accustomed to experiencing psychological and emotional ties without the benefits of physical contact. However, the Internet does not give a public or social identity, and is therefore not perceived as a threat to the Basque centers or cultural organizations. Because technology is available only to those with the requisite knowledge and financial ability, it is currently used at the Basque centers by a few skilled members and at home by those who can afford the computer and Internet access.

The availability of cutting-edge technology in telecommunications facilitates people connecting with each other in ways that are new to the imagination. Diaspora populations are holding teleconferences across the oceans.
Photo courtesy of Euskal Etxeak.

TELEVISION is much more accessible and effective for information transfer and entertainment. Basque public television and radio, Euskal Irrati Telebista (EITB), now broadcasts one television channel and two radio stations via satellite and cable to Europe, South America, and the east coast of North America, and their Web site includes Canal Vasco with news about Basques in the diaspora. However, while most other homelands are keen to provide news for their communities abroad and for academics around the world, there is a problem for international academics and the English-speaking Basque diaspora because there are very few English-language news sources from or about the Basque Country.

Currently, the daily newspapers *Gara* and *Berria* have English editions on the Internet, and EITB has English-language short news updates about the diaspora activities.

Media policy experts in the Basque Country hope that the consistent homeland transmission from EITB will show a different perspective on current events in the Basque society and will educate and update those who watch. It has been a very popular idea among the Basques in these diaspora countries to be able to receive current news broadcasts, films, game shows, sporting events, and cultural entertainment in Basque and in Spanish. EITB also broadcasts documentaries and reports regarding the diaspora population to the homeland audience. This promotes a more realistic and less symbolic or nostalgic knowledge of each other. The influence of the media and the globalization of telecommunications are being used to achieve positive results for Basque ethnic identity as Basques are becoming more and more interconnected with each other around the globe. The imagined community is expanding into a virtual reality: a transnational and cosmopolitan Basque identity, a traditional and simultaneously contemporary manifestation of Basqueness.

DIASPORAS TEND to live at the intersection of history and the future, therefore one's identity must provide for both. Basques are both traditional and postmodern. Because ethnic identity is a social construction, new circumstances require new concepts, with each generation reconstructing its own existence. Today, the globalization of communications results in diaspora communities that can formulate their own projection of Basque culture not just to their immediate association members, but also to the wider world. Basque centers can use the tools of technology and interconnectivity to advocate and foster Basque studies, language, political awareness, cuisine, sport, art, music, and tourism, reinforcing a feeling of solidarity Basques everywhere. Institutional relationships that in the past have been only bidirectional between the Basque Country and one diaspora community or federation, and vice-versa, are expanding so that Basque communities are interacting among themselves to solve common problems.

ON THE OTHER hand, Basque political scientist Gurutz Jáuregui Bereciartu (1986; interview 1998) argues that the upsurge in ethnonationalism and return to ethnicity by Basques in Euskal Herria and around the world is actually a protest against the depersonalized, postmodern, technocratic world. It could be that those who fear the future and the globalized social trends they are witnessing are turning to the past for comfort and identity, recognition, and self-actualization. Likewise, Manuel Castells points to the resurgence of nationalism and ethnic identities as the products of the conflicting trends of globalization, as the information technology revolution and the restructuring of capitalism create a network society while expressions of collective identity challenge modernization in favor of local and communal identities and cultural distinctiveness (1997, 1). He argues that many are choosing to move from the unknown future to the known and understood traditional past. However, neither of these theories quite explains the consistent and persistent maintenance of Basque ethnicity of over five centuries of emigration prior to this particular phase of globalization and modernization. I repeat, Basque transnationalism is not new, although the methods of maintaining these networks and identities are influenced by the globalization of communications.

Speedy, inexpensive, and accessible global communications also give added value to global media and the Internet (Van Hear 1998, 251)because they allow mass media to be replaced by targeted media with specific audiences. In particular, these technologies allow ethnic groups to create and maintain ties to their homeland government, institutions, and populations. They also allow homelands to project information and policies out to their diasporas. As Internet access and computer hardware become more affordable and available, additional people in different geographical locations interact, like the Basques around the globe, educating each other, sharing their values, their opinions, and their conception of their ethnicity. Many diaspora organizations receive almost weekly e-mail requests for information regarding genealogical searches, tourism, or au pair or student exchange possibilities. Although former job qualifications for Basque organization employees tended to deal with bartending and cooking requisites, currently sought skills focus on computer communications.

HOWEVER, COMPUTER and global telecommunications access and capabilities are not being used to potential in the Basque centers of any diaspora countries. Although no precise data exists regarding Basque diaspora Internet use today, in 1998, less than 4 percent of the Basque homeland population used the Internet (Alonso 1998). Few seem to appreciate or exploit the potential of the Internet to create Basque culture and reinforce its presence in the outside world. There is no evidence that the Internet is causing people who heretofore did not identify themselves ethnically as Basque to do so, but rather interview evidence demonstrates that access to Internet information enhances the interests of those already curious about their ethnic ancestry and history, and e-mail communications foment information exchange and the creation of ethnic networks.

The Internet allows virtual interaction between people interested in Basque culture, history, society, politics and economics. It provides another avenue for manifesting one's existing identity. Individuals may not have friends in the local Basque organizations or may choose not to attend activities for whatever reasons, but can establish and/or maintain ties to their homeland. Basque Internet surfers are still interacting with Basque society. However, they are using a different medium, and the language of these communications is not likely to be Euskara. Chat rooms often have Basques from the United States, Belgium, Australia, Argentina, and the homeland all communicating, but using English as the means of communication.

THE INTERNET will most affect Basques who are widely dispersed and isolated from other Basques. It will aid those who do not get what they want or need to fulfill their self-identity as Basques from their local Basque organization. They can now search for that information or those experiences on the Internet, in effect downloading identity. The Internet thus functions for Basques—and in similar ways for other ethnic diasporas—as http://www.identity.org. Basque cybernauts can receive mutual support from others interested in Basque themes. At sites such as Buber's Basque Page, http://www.buber.net, and Eusko Ikaskuntza-Basque Studies Society's diaspora initiative, http://www.euskosare.com, people can exchange ideas and hypotheses about Basque topics and feel acknowledged, important, recognized and a part of a community. Virtual communities have the potential to be as fundamental in identity building and in the process of socialization as physical, geographical communities. Although they will not replace existing

Nearly all communications among the Basque
communities and between the diaspora and the Basque
Government are virtual and facilitated by Internet tools.
Diaspora specialists working in the Basque Government
include Asier Abaunza Robles (seated), Iera Azkarate de
la Cruz (center), and Urko Apaolaza Avila.
Photo courtesy of Euskal Etxeak.

---

ethnic communities, these technologies will likely better
enable and enhance the ability of existing dispersed ethnic communities to communicate with each other and
with their homelands (Elkins 1997). They facilitate new
developments in individual ethnic identity. Individuals
now have control over the content of their ethnicity and
ethnic identity, as opposed to what is available at the
local Basque center or a few times a year at the center's
organized events. Each person can click his or her way to
individual ethnic options by "selecting" or "undoing"
according to particular interests.

DIASPORA IDENTITY IN A GLOBALIZED SOCIETY

WHEN INDIVIDUALS become inhabitants or subjects of an *ethnic* social space, instead of just a physical territory, that transnational identity nevertheless entail rights, responsibilities, and obligations, just as citizenship in a traditional nation-state did and does. Members of a diaspora enjoy rights in their own community and in some cases in their homeland and the material, social and psychological benefits of belonging to a group that gives a sense of self-worth, uniqueness, and group protection at the same time. This is extremely important to create for teenagers in Basque communities who are struggling to shape their personalities and identities. But members of a diaspora also have responsibilities and obligations to the group, to both ancestors and descendants. Diasporic identification connects people to their common past, their present, and their collective future. Transnational groups often try to instill feelings of loyalty or sense of duty and responsibility to the greater ethnic community.

Diaspora communities have created their own self-consciousness as a collectivity and have fashioned a group identity out of their shared experiences of exile, immigration, and life in their new host societies. They also react and evolve, transforming and mutating according to outside influences. Cohen suggests that "diasporas can be constituted by acts of the imagination" (Cohen 1996, 516). A diaspora can be held together and recreated through a shared experience of ethnogenesis—a process whereby immigrants practice a transfigured cultural identity by creating a sort of hybrid culture or synthesis from the ancestral culture of the Basque Country with that of the new environment. This provides a link from the homeland to the new country for recent emigrants and ties from the new society to the homeland for the latter generations.

Ethnicity and ethnic identity are not merely behavioral, but also incorporate deeper, more profound attitudes, feelings, and psychological outlooks. Milton Esman concludes that ethnic solidarities become internationally significant by way of transnational economic and political networks (Esman 1995, 114). However, what is "significant" for Basques, although not necessarily to the international economic system, is the consistent commitment to maintain ties—sentimental political, religious, and kinship, as well as economic—with the homeland. As a result, identity and ethnicity increasingly seem to be performed outside existing economic, political, and cultural institutions. As a result, as well, the role of "unofficial ambassador" may be quite influential in the future. However, diaspora communities do not operate as monolithic blocs of ethnic or political consciousness, and personal conflicts and individual agendas interfere with economic and political ties between and among the diaspora and homeland populations, disrupting projects that require cooperation.

TODAY, BASQUE communities are creating and consuming identity in a very different fashion than they have in the past, and at an accelerated rate. They are using the new telecommunications networks to increase the frequency and intensity of their relations with each other and with the Basque Autonomous Government. They forward each other's newsletters, and they have created Basque Web pages with calendars of events, language courses, and information regarding Basque history, anthropology, and literature. They also use e-mail for institutional and personal communications and networking with fellow Basques. "Each diaspora has its 'professional' custodians of traditions, customs, and values of the community. They have and do include scribes,

---

rabbis, teachers, intellectuals, and now, perhaps, web-masters" (Totoricagüena 2000).

Lesson eighteen

BIBLIOGRAPHY

Anderson, Benedict. 1991. *Imagined Communities: Reflections on the Origin and Spread of Nationalism.* London: Verso.

Basch, Linda, Nina Glick Schiller, and Cristina Szanton Blanc. 1992. *Nations Unbound: Transnational Projects, Postcolonial Predicaments, and Deterritorialized Nation-States.* Amsterdam: Gordon and Breach Science Publishers.

Brunn, Stanley D. 1996. "The Internationalization of Diasporas in a Shrinking World." In *The Networks of Diaspora,* ed. Georges Prévélakis. Nicosia: Cyprus Research Center KYKEM.

Castells, Manuel. 1997. *The Power of Identity. The Information Age: Economy, Society, and Culture.* Vol. 2. Oxford: Blackwell.

———. 1996. *The Rise of the Network Society. The Information Age: Economy, Society, Culture.* Vol. 1. Oxford: Blackwell.

Claval, Paul. 1996. "Diasporas and Politics: An Overview." In *The Networks of Diaspora,* ed. Georges Prévélakis. Nicosia: Cyprus Research Center KYKEM.

Cohen, Robin. 1997. *Global Diasporas: An Introduction.* London: University College London Press.

———. 1996. "Diaspora and the Nation-State: From Victims to Challengers." *International Affairs* 72, no. 3 (July): 507–20.

Elkins, David J. 1997. "Globalization, Telecommunication, and Virtual Ethnic Communities." *International Political Science Review* 18, no. 2: 139–52.

Esman, Milton J. 1986. "Diasporas and International Relations." In *Modern Diasporas in International Politics*, ed. Gabriel Sheffer. London: Croom Helm.

Featherstone, Mike. 1995. *Undoing Culture: Globalization, Postmodernism, and Identity*. London: Sage.

Gellner, Ernest. 1983. *Nations and Nationalism*. Ithaca: Cornell University Press.

Giddens, Anthony. 1991. *Modernity and Self-Identity*. Cambridge: Polity.

Held, David, et al. 1999. *Global Transformations: Politics, Economics, and Culture*. Stanford: Stanford University Press.

Jáuregui Bereciartu, Gurutz. 1986. *Contra el estado-nación: En torno al hecho y la cuestión nacional*. Madrid: Siglo XXI de España Editores.

Lavie, Smadar, and Ted Swedenburg, eds. 1996. *Displacement, Diaspora, and Geographies of Identity*. Durham, N.C.: Duke University Press.

Portes, Alejandro. 1999. "Conclusion: Towards a New World: The Origins and Effects of Transnational Activities." *Ethnic and Racial Studies* 22, no. 2 (March): 463–77.

Sheffer, Gabriel. 1996. "Wither the Study of Ethnic Diasporas? Some Theoretical, Definitional, Analytical, and Comparative Considerations." In *The Network of Diasporas*, ed. Georges Prévélakis. Paris: Cyprus Research Center KYKEM.

Totoricagüena, Gloria. 2004. *Identity, Culture, and Politics in the Basque Diaspora*. Reno: University of Nevada Press.

———. 2000. "Downloading Identity in the Basque Diaspora: Utilizing the Internet to Create and Maintain

Ethnic Identity." *Nevada Historical Society Quarterly* 43, no. 2 (Summer): 140–54.

Van Hear, Nicolas 1998. *New Diasporas: The Mass Exodus, Dispersal, and Regrouping of Migrant Communities*. London: UCL Press.

Vertovec, Steven. 1999. "Conceiving and Researching Transnationalism." *Ethnic and Racial Studies* 22, no. 2 (March): 447–62.

Waters, Mary C. 1990. *Ethnic Options: Choosing Identities in America*. Berkeley: University of California Press.

REQUIRED READING

Andoni Alonso, and Iñaki Arzoz, "Basque Identity on the Internet," in *Basque Cultural Studies*, ed. William A. Douglass et al. (Reno: Basque Studies Program, 1999), pp 295–312.

David J. Elkins, "Globalization, Telecommunication, and Virtual Ethnic Communities," *International Political Science Review* 18, no. 2 (1997): 139–52.

Gloria Totoricagüena. "Downloading Identity in the Basque Diaspora: Utilizing the Internet to Create and Maintain Ethnic Identity," *Nevada Historical Society Quarterly* 43, no. 2 (Summer 2000): 140–54.

Steven Vertovec, "Conceiving and Researching Transnationalism," *Ethnic and Racial Studies* 22, no. 2 (March 1999): 447–62.

WRITTEN LESSON FOR SUBMISSION

Explain which aspects of globalization and transnationalism you think most affect diaspora populations and why. Explain in what ways they could influence Basque ethnic identity maintenance. Do you think global telecommunications will drastically change the maintenance of Basque ethnic identity in the communities outside of

Euskal Herria? Why or why not? How could they be used by Basque diaspora institutions for Basque causes? How could the Internet be used by individuals interested in Basque topics? How could it be used by homeland institutions and individuals?

Traditional identity in the diaspora
Modern identity in the homeland

THIS PUBLICATION'S topics of nationalism, ethnic identity, and ethnicity maintenance are not generally those to be trotted out on special occasions such as performances of Basque music or dance or for Boise's Jaialdi festival. You are what you do every day, and the construction of Basque transnational and ethnic identity is as much a matter of the small things that make up everyday life as they are of grand political and ethnic allegiances. A person's home has vast social significance, for example, because it is generally where one's primary emotional connections are formed and where self-identity is created and nurtured. And although the idea that home and personal ethnic decoration reinforce ethnonationalist sentiment generally has been ignored, heretofore overlooked as female triviality and therefore not worthy of serious academic research, in fieldwork with Basques from around the world, I have found that both of these forms of expression often recreate ethnic identity through the use of intimate objects, thereby psychologically reinforcing ethnicity and ethnic socialization for the individual and for their family. In addition, they also demonstrate one's Basqueness to home visitors and to the public.

Psychologists refer to this sort of behavior as symbolic self-completion. We travel through our lives constructing and reconstructing our self-definitions and answering the questions "Who am I?" and "Who do I want to be?" Specialists hypothesize that some individuals exhibit an incompleteness that they attempt to fill with symbolic representations of what they lack. The incomplete individual implements symbols "to build and retain the

completeness of the self-definition" (Wicklund and Gollwitzer 1982, 9).

In the diasporic communities, for Basques who feel
that they lack some sort of *real* Basqueness or that they
are less Basque than others in their ethnic community,
this use of symbols takes on urgency, prominence, and
consequence. Some believe they must change their
names to a Basque given name or surname, others
believe their Basque language skills must be improved,
while others believe they must make a trek to the Basque
Country in order to be truly Basque. "Half Basque,"
"part Basque," and "doesn't speak Basque" are phrases
often used to describe others and in certain cases to create hierarchies of Basqueness. These attitudes tend to be
detrimental to other Basque ethnics attempting to maintain an identity and might even encourage a sense of
incompleteness that previously was nonexistent. "Maintaining ethnic identity should not be a competition,"
one Basque diasporan has commented.

HOWEVER, the theory of symbolic self-completion
through material items also seems to explain the
less problematic behavior of many of the hundreds of
thousands of Basques who wear ethnic jewelry; wear T-
shirts, belt buckles, and scarves with Basque themes; tat-
too themselves with Basque symbols such as the Tree of
Gernika, a *lauburu* (Basque cross), or an *ikurriña* (the
1894 Basque Country flag); and/or hang Basque posters in their bedrooms and Basque flags from their car
mirrors. The resurgence in the use of Basque names
for children is also prevalent and marks an obvious and
public ethnic boundary for that person for the rest of
his or her life. It is another constant reminder—especially in English-speaking societies, every time it is
spelled, explained, and its pronunciation corrected—
that one is Basque. Such symbolic representations and

objectifications merely compensate for the lack of tangible and physical proximity to homeland culture, cuisine, language, family, and traditions.

We will examine some of these everyday methods of representing Basque national, transnational, and ethnic identity, along with the traditional content of diasporic identity. In addition to everyday examples demonstrating how Basques understand and manifest their identity in private spaces, we will look at the National Monument to the Basque Sheepherder as an example of how Basques in the United States wanted themselves represented in public spheres.

ETHNIC HOME DECORATION

A home provides the setting for modern intimacy and moral community. The specific types of objects that are selected for display transmit and intensify values and expectations, and many Basque women use their homes and home decoration as a means to create and express their identities. Residence decoration tends to be the domain of the female head of household, and in many of these cases, non-Basque women who married Basques also tend to use ethnic symbolic objects in home decoration. Photographs of family and ancestors, family farmhouses and villages, punctuate the importance of descent and connection to the Basque Country. Mementos from tourist gift shops are, likewise, placed in areas of importance and displayed with care.

CARVED WOODEN busts of *amumas* (grandmothers) and *aitxitxes* (grandfathers), Tree of Gernika artistic representations, coats of arms of the seven provinces of Euskal Herria, pictures of *txistulariak* (Basque flute players), and *ikurriñak* in my fieldwork, Basque flags were everywhere) greet visitors to thousands of Basque homes in the diaspora. The ubiquity of these day-to-day

The National Monument to the Basque Sheepherder in Reno, Nevada. Sculptor Nestor Basterrechea is standing at center at the dedication on August 27, 1989. This was an international project of the Society of Basque Studies in America, led by José Ramon Cengotitabengoa of Chicago.
Courtesy of the Basque Library, University of Nevada, Reno.

reminders of one's ancestors and one's ethnic identity is an example of what social psychologist Michael Billig calls "banal nationalism" (Billig 1995). Ordinary every-day habits, language, food, and the display of cultural artifacts, to cite but a few examples, serve as a constant evocation to these families of their Basque heritage. I have conducted personal interviews with Basques in their private residences in numerous countries, and the majority used ethnic cultural decoration in tablecloths, kitchen towels, kitchen serving pieces and utensils, cof-fee-table books, and almost always in wall art. Although I was consciously looking for such material and noticed it quite easily, the Basques welcoming me into their homes specifically and affectionately pointed out their objects.

BASQUES IN the diaspora use the *ikurriña*'s red, green, and white colors for myriad choices, from linens for dressing tables to the painting of the house's exterior and the colors of flowers to plant in the garden. Several women mentioned (without being prompted) that they will not plant red-blooming and yellow-blooming flow-ers together because they are the colors of the Spanish flag. Whether in clothing, jewelry, or house decoration, because they use quantities of green and red, many stated that they seldom buy anything yellow, just to ensure they never mistakenly put the two together. One man upon receiving two different yellow shirts as a birth-day gift remarked that he would have to make sure he wore nothing red when he dressed in either of the shirts. He said he had never in his life bought a yellow shirt, specifically because the Spanish flag has yellow. Every-thing from the choices of wedding and funeral flowers to furniture fabric and stoneware glaze seemed to be at least subconsciously affected by whether or not the choice might promote a Basque awareness. A few diaspora cou-ples even used Basque ethnic clothing for wedding ceremonies, and others dressed children in traditional *baserritarra* farmstead clothing for their baptisms. What remains conscious is the deliberate separation of red from yellow, the two colors that, when combined, seem to trigger a negative response, especially from emigrants and first-generation Basques living away from Euskal Herria.

OUR HOMES are the most significant element in our socialization process as youths. This space is where the most important social processes take place. It is where we conceive of ourselves and our families as "insiders" and others as "outsiders." The decoration of the home helps build that definition of "insider," and in the case of diaspora Basques, the "insiders" are not only the family members, but symbolic family members as depicted by symbols from the Basque Country. Basque transnational teenagers living in the diaspora often have bedroom walls full of posters from the homeland. Internationally renowned cyclists such as Miguel Indurain, Abraham Olano, and Joseba Beloki join golfer José Mari "Txema" Olazabal and numerous Basque mountaineers on wall posters. Maps of the seven provinces and aerial photos of the *concha* beach in Donosti-San Sebastián and the Old Part of Bilbao often accompany posters of the Bilbao Guggenheim Museum. Kukuxumusu-brand T-shirts, watches, blankets, sunglasses, computer mouse pads, and headphones are also popular, usually with traditional Basque themes. Lapel pins and embroidered patches for clothing, hats, notebooks, school bags, and luggage promote various issues of the Basque Country, from Amnistia, or amnesty for Basque political prisoners, to protests over the construction of a nuclear power plant in Lemoniz, Bizkaia. Others advertise a province or one of the Basque soccer teams. They are from the Basque Country, and that is what matters.

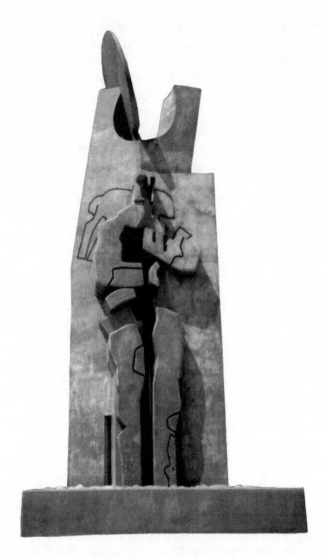

Nestor Basterretxea's *Bakardade* (Solitude) was selected by the Society of Basque Studies in America as the work to become the National Monument to the Basque Sheepherder in Reno, Nevada.

WHAT MEANINGS come from the study of our domestic spaces? What do children learn from the use of certain spaces in the home for decoration? Why *do* we cover our home's interior walls? Perhaps we do so because we cannot open the window and see the neighbors' *baserriak*, or farmhouses, nor can we hear the upstairs residents speaking in Euskara or walk down to the neighborhood *fronton* and see children playing *pelota*, Basque handball. We have to create this artificial, representative, and symbolic environment in our homes because it does not exist on the outside. Many Basques in the Basque Country often decorate their own homes with ultramodern representations, international art, and the indigenous art of other cultures, actually doing the same thing as diaspora Basques—filling their homes with symbols of what they desire, but do not possess. Either way, the socialization process of those resident in the home is affected by surrounding themselves with

---

Basterretxea's dedication reads:

A figure
As if sculpted by the wind itself,
A man solitary and strong,
Held straight by his own will,
Patient laborer
Facing onto the uncertain horizon of adventure.
Endless stretches of silences of moon
And stars,
Through mountain trails:
This monument is eternal homage and memorial
To the Basque sheepherder.

Photograph by the author.

objects that represent concepts of importance, in the case of these diaspora Basques, symbols of the homeland.

PERSONAL EXPRESSION AND ETHNICITY

PERSONAL ORNAMENTS and jewelry have often been used as expressions of group identity with intense symbolic significance. In India, for example, there are rigid laws of caste that restrict the wearing of gold to people of certain groups only. Within Basque communities, gold religious necklaces and medals for baptisms or first Holy Communions are customary, and although some of the younger interviewees stated they do not wear their medals regularly to host-country social functions, they almost always wear them to similar Basque occasions. These gold necklace medals are usually a gift from a godparent or grandparent from the homeland or are ordered when a Basque friend travels to the Basque Country. In several Basque communities, there have been recognized informal jewelry buyers and transporters, women whose trips home to Euskal Herria were found out and who were then asked to select and transport gold medals back to new parents. One woman in Boise, Idaho, estimates that on her fifteen trips to the Basque Country, she has been asked by relatives and friends to select and carry back to the United States nearly two hundred gold medals for baptisms, confirmations, and other gifts. Men typically wear them inside their clothing, and women are more likely to display them outside of their apparel.

Lauburu, the Basque four-headed cross, emblem rings, earrings, and necklaces are also popular with males and females, as are T-shirts, baseball caps, belt buckles, and car bumper stickers with Basque themes. Several Basque males in Australia and the United States even have permanently tattooed *lauburus* on their arms, and a few women have *lauburus* or Basque flags on their ankles. In the United States, it is common to see people wearing jackets, baseball hats, T-shirts, and sweatshirts advertising a university allegiance or loyalty to a professional sports team, and many feel compellingly deep-seated ties to these institutions. Ethnics behave in similar ways and wear their cultural identities on their persons.

B ESIDES PUBLIC displays of Basqueness, there are also those closer to the heart, such as that of Juan Miguel Salaberry, an elderly gentleman from Rosario, Uruguay. For decades, Juan Miguel has worn his grandfather's *txapela*, or beret, every day, and in his wallet has carried a small tattered paper *ikurriña*. He says together they keep him safe. His emotional and psychological connection to his grandfather is manifest in his remembering his grandfather as a Basque, and he now has shifted that love to Basque culture and his own Basque identity, represented by the beret and *ikurriña*. Similarly, after migrating to Melbourne, Nekane Candino legally changed her given name from the Spanish "Rosarito" (Basque given names were not permitted in the four Spanish provinces during the Franco years) to the Basque "Nekane." This was self-actualizing for her because, as she described herself, "Being Basque is primordial. There are thousands of years of Basqueness in me. I am not Nekane who also happens to be Basque. I am Basque and that shapes how I manifest myself as Nekane." These insignificant daily demonstrations of Basqueness may be "banal," "symbolic," or "leisure-time ethnicity" to some academics, but for Juan Miguel and Nekane, as well as thousands more like them in the diaspora, maintaining Basque identity is not only a rational matter, but also one of great instinct, emotion, and spirit.

In the United States, Canada, and Australia, where the custom is for a woman to change her surname to her husband's surname after marrying, numerous Basque women do not follow this originally British tradition. They maintain their own Basque surnames. However, Basque women who have married Basque men have mentioned that as long as they have a Basque surname, they are content and have indeed changed their surnames to their husband's. There are even examples of diaspora and homeland Basque brides and grooms taking neither surname and completely changing their surnames to those of an ancestor with a "more Basque" name. We see that questions of authenticity and legitimacy are still very much a part of diasporic identity, and that one's ethnic credentials seem to be strengthened—for some people—based on the old Sabino Arana idea that to be Basque, one would need eight Basque surnames in one's heritage.

HOWEVER, ETHNIC identity is increasingly voluntary in the diaspora communities to which Basques have migrated. Because Basques are not distinguishable by, for example, skin color, unique garments, or diet within these European settler countries, and because their ethnicity is not pushed on them by the surrounding society, which does not tend to categorize and separate them as Basques, maintaining Basqueness becomes a choice. The social and political costs and consequences of being Basque are quite different from other nonwhite and/or non-Christian ethnic groups. It is a "community without cost" (Waters 1990, 149). Basques are marking their own group-identity boundaries, rather than being marked by other outside groups, and the importance of naming provides a clear example of this phenomenon.

Just as Nekane needed a Basque name to fulfill her identity, young parents of all generations are increas-

The development of diaspora Basque institutions has evolved. They now serve educational and promotional ends with a homeland focus. The Basque Museum and Cultural Center in Boise, Idaho, provides language classes and seminars on Basque history, cooking, dance, and genealogy. Its gift shop is as popular with the general public as it is with latter generation Basques.
Photograph by the author.

---

ingly giving Basque first names to their children. There are numerous Mirens, Amaias, Nekanes, Idoias, and Maites, as well as Aitors, Kepas, Josus, Mikels, Xabiers, and Iñakis. In Australia, Canada, and the United States, special care must be given to how English-speaking people will pronounce (or mispronounce) a name and the psychological impact that a unique name has on a child. As adults, interviewees stated that they were proud of their given and surnames, although as children, a few hated them because of endless childhood teasing and the constant spelling and correction of pronunciation.

Because a person's name carries significant weight in the formation of individual identity, this serves as yet another constant demonstration and reminder of ethnic identity.

ALTHOUGH there are respondents during my years of fieldwork whose Basque ethnicity has favored them for employment, in the greater part of these Basques' daily lives, their ethnicity does not matter (housing, schooling, social integration, etc.). They tend to take for granted that when it does matter, it is indeed largely an issue of personal choice for positive status or for enjoyment. It may be that for each Basque person abroad, the maintenance of ethnic identity is voluntary, costless, and a matter of personal preference. However, it is made ever so much easier because he or she likely lives in a society dominated by Christians of European descent, as we have noted before. The selective aspects of voluntary ethnicity are what make it so positive for many Basque individuals, because they do not experience the racism connected to their ethnicity that Asians, Middle Easterners, or Africans do in these same countries.

TRADITIONAL IDENTITY IN THE DIASPORA AND MODERN IDENTITY IN THE HOMELAND

Basque private homes and public community activities tend to use more traditional than contemporary representations of Basque culture, and displayed objects are usually those that are based in history. Homeland Basques who travel to the diaspora communities are likely to say that these communities are "folkloric," in a pejorative way. When diaspora Basques travel to Euskal Herria, they are often surprised at the modernity, and to them, contemporary Basqueness seems to be somehow "less Basque." Let us examine the best case study we have for United States Basques that exemplifies this anomaly.

In *Solitude: Art and Symbolism in the National Basque Monument*, Carmelo Urza points out many examples of historic Old World culture that are promulgated by diaspora Basques, although not necessarily by Basques in the homeland any more. Basques in the diaspora are practicing historic ethnicity and an adapted version of their cultural traditions. Many are surprised to visit the homeland and not see any known "Basque" ethnic dress or not find what they believe to be "Basque" ethnic foods—or to find out the foods are not Basque at all, but Spanish in general, such as tortillas, paella, chorizos, and so on. Homeland Basques laugh when they visit the San Francisco or Chino Basque festival and see people wearing *txapelas*, because these men's berets typically were worn before the 1970s and now perhaps are donned only by the elderly and by farmers.

BASQUE SCULPTOR Nestor Basterrechea's work *Bakardade—Solitude* was selected for the National Monument to the Basque Sheepherder in Reno, Nevada, after years of competitions and private fund-raising. As Urza states, "No part of the monument was as controversial and hotly debated as its artistic concept." The symbol of the sheepherder was agreed upon to memorialize the thousands of Basques who had made their lives in the United States as sheepherders, and it represented those who followed, as well. However, the form of expression chosen to depict the sheepherder was debated widely. Should the monument be abstract (modern), or should it be more accessible to the typical viewer, with representational or figurative (traditional) art? Ironically, the U.S. artists who submitted proposals each sent representational ideas, and the homeland Basque artists each offered abstract designs. Many diaspora Basques who were asked to donate funds wanted a traditional, representative sheepherder, complete with a sheep dog at his feet, a sculpture that an audience would look at and know immediately what it was. Others wanted an abstract work depicting modern Basque artists' conceptions. Basterrechea was actually able to design his work to please both without compromising his own artistic integrity. The homeland modern artist was able to please the diaspora traditional Basques.

Solitude is a massive bronze that communicates to Basques and non-Basques the loneliness and social separation of the herder on the range of the American West. It is placed along the nature walks of Rancho San Rafael Park in northwest Reno and has now gained acceptance by most Basques after they have received instruction in its meaning and are pointed out the shape of the sheepherder carrying a lamb across his shoulders. Visiting Basques and recent immigrants from Euskal Herria are more likely to accept the work immediately than are older immigrants or later-generation Basques living in the United States who have surrounded themselves with representational art in their homes and, unless they have traveled to the Basque Country, hold traditional ideas about the homeland based upon information from their parents and grandparents. The "generation gap" in the Basque diaspora thus is quite real. It is between generations of immigrants and also between different age cohorts.

ETHNIC IDENTITIES are created not just through time and subsequent generations, but through space as immigrants carry culture from one place to another. As we have noted, there is also a "geography gap" of cultural differences between the Basque traditional culture practiced in these diaspora communities and the contemporary Basque culture practiced in the Basque Country. It is not necessarily a situation of Basque culture mixing with Mexican culture, or Basque culture mixing with U.S. culture, although this is also a factor of difference. The situations are such that often the communities are stuck in a time warp of the last wave of emigrants and that particular time period's homeland culture and ideology. For example, because the last significant waves of Basques to Buenos Aires or Caracas were political refugees in the 1940s and 1950s, the culture they practice tends to be more political and more nationalist than, say, the Basques of the interior of Chile or Uruguay, where Basques settled as economic migrants at the end of the 1800s and early 1900s. In communities where there has been much travel back and forth and where networks are strong, there is a more contemporary understanding of homeland culture, and those Basques are not shocked when they visit their relatives' ultramodern apartments, call them on their cell phones, and enjoy a rock concert together at the fiestas.

Lesson nineteen

BIBLIOGRAPHY

Billig, Michael. 1995. *Banal Nationalism*. Thousand Oaks, Calif.: Sage.

Cieraad, Irene, ed. 1999. *At Home: An Anthropology of Domestic Space*. Syracuse: Syracuse University Press.

Levitt, Peggy, and Mary C. Waters, eds. 2002. *The Changing Face of Home: The Transnational Lives of the Second Generation*. New York: Russell Sage Foundation.

Totoricagüena, Gloria. 2004. *Identity, Culture, and Politics: Comparing the Basque Diaspora*. Reno: University of Nevada Press.

Totoricagüena, Gloria. 2003. "Interconnected Disconnectedness: How Diaspora Basque Women Maintain Ethnic Identity." In *Amatxi, Amuma, Amona: Writings in Honor of Basque Women*, ed. Linda White and Cameron Watson. Reno: Center for Basque Studies, University of Nevada, Reno.

Urza, Carmelo. 1993. *Solitude: Art and Symbolism in the National Basque Monument*. Reno: University of Nevada Press. Waters, Mary C. 1990. *Ethnic Options: Choosing Identities in America*. Berkeley: University of California Press. 1990.

Wicklund, Robert A., and Peter M. Gollwitzer. 1982. *Symbolic Self-Completion*. Hillsdale, N.J.: Lawrence Erlbaum Associates.

REQUIRED READING

Gloria Totoricagüena, "Interconnected Disconnectedness: How Diaspora Basque Women Maintain Ethnic Identity," in *Amatxi, Amuma, Amona: Writings in Honor of Basque Women*, ed. Linda White and Cameron Watson (Reno: Center for Basque Studies, University of Nevada, Reno, 2003).

Carmelo Urza. *Solitude: Art and Symbolism in the National Basque Monument* (Reno: University of Nevada Press, 1993), pp 18–28, 71–89.

Mary C. Waters, *Ethnic Options: Choosing Identities in America* (Berkeley: University of California Press, 1990), chapter 7, pp 147–68.

Robert A. Wicklund and Peter M. Gollwitzer, *Symbolic Self-Completion* (Hillsdale, N.J.: Lawrence Erlbaum Associates, 1982).

WRITTEN LESSON FOR SUBMISSION

Do you see anything wrong with Basque diaspora cultures maintaining a constructed mythological, idealized, historical, 1940-ish culture of Euskal Herria? Is it preferable that diasporas follow their contemporary homelands? If they do not, what makes them Basque—what culture are they maintaining if it no longer mirrors that of the seven provinces? Do you practice ethnic home or personal decoration? If so, in what ways? If not, why not?

20 · Gender and ethnicity
Basque communities abroad

G EOGRAPHICALLY disconnected from each other and from their homeland, Basque women in the diaspora have endeavored to perpetuate ethnic identities for themselves and their families. Curiously, their struggles and the ensuing results are similar throughout the disparate settings to which they have emigrated. Women are both maintainers and modifiers of social processes, and the role of women as reproducers of ethnic ideologies is often related to women being perceived as the "cultural carriers" of that ethnic group.

WOMEN IN MIGRATION STUDIES
What are the personal decisions and motivations involved in international migration? Because in family migration married couples tend to move to where the husband has the greatest opportunity for employment, there often remains great difficulty in disassociating men's and women's individual motivations and aspirations for migration (Chant 1992). For many women, however, one's homeland conditions *as a female* have had much to do with the decision to migrate, especially for single women. In the Basque diaspora, both women and men escaped political, economic, and social oppression in their search for a better life. However, women also migrated to escape the various forms of oppression that are unique to their gender status. In my years of fieldwork with more than five hundred Basque women, many Basque diaspora female interviewees stated that they had helped convince their husbands, brothers, and fathers to migrate for economic and political reasons and even because of religious oppression in the Spanish Catholic Church. Furthermore, because many Basque

women experienced a gain in economic and social status in their new host countries, they were not as motivated as their male counterparts to try to return to Euskal Herria. For economic as well as family reasons, two-thirds of the females responded that they now maintain their own lives in their host countries and plan to return to the Basque Country only to visit. Thus, for the typical female of the Basque diaspora, family obligation in the Basque Country has been transformed into and obligation to the diaspora family—giving birth to and raising children and grandchildren—and she is now accustomed to the host-country pace and lifestyle.

WHILE SOME Basques welcomed migration, a change in personal status might also be negative for a woman who was accustomed to the respect for motherhood and homemaking customary in the Basque Country, which have lower status in the United States or Australia. They might also compare themselves less favorably with other immigrants in these host societies. Although much of the literature on the diaspora in South American communities emphasizes the importance of Basques in the elite social, economic, and political structures, the views expressed in personal interviews with women paint a different picture. Barely one-fifth of the total respondents agreed that "persons of Basque heritage have a higher socioeconomic status than other immigrants in (the host country)." In Australia, where Basque ethnicity is unfamiliar and unknown, only 7 percent of the respondents agreed, while the highest percentage in agreement with the statement (31 percent) came from the United States, where white European immigrants are generally granted higher status than people of Latino, Asian, or African origin. Basque women tend not to perceive themselves as having a higher socioeconomic status than other immigrants.

The Women's Club of the San Francisco Basque Cultural Center organizes activities for Basque language mainte- nance for children, along with special events throughout the year such as skiing trips, Halloween parties, and Christmas celebrations.
Photograph courtesy of the San Francisco Basque Cul- tural Center.

IN ADDITION, Basque women have had to renegotiate their gender roles after emigrating. The Basque matriarchal social structure, related to the centuries of male emigration, with fathers absent for ten to fifteen years generally, and to the marine economy of men absent for months at a time, has often resulted in female leadership in financial, medical, family, and household decisions. Basque women departed a homeland where they exercised equal power and demanded and received respect and admiration from each other and from men. For many women, the changes in the new host society could be destructive. The self-esteem realized as an agribusiness partner in the family farming or fisheries industry, as a salary earner and financial contributor, as a participant in the community, and as someone who understands one's own society are significant psychological markers of identity. After migration, women have often lost their status as equal partners in a marriage and as head of household.

Emigrant Basque women in all settings—but especially where they had to learn another language—found themselves increasingly dependent on their children for communicating in a "foreign" language and for dealing with school experiences and an outside culture with which they were not as familiar because they worked at home. The children eventually go to school and learn the host-country language and how the host society functions, then they are placed in the role of translator and teacher, eventually even taking on the mother's role. Because of a lack of ability to communicate in the host language, the mother is forced into the role of a dependent child. She relies on her children to accompany her and to translate for her at doctor appointments, the bank, school functions, and so on. This loss of self-esteem and self-assurance equated to a loss of identity for many women.

BASQUE WOMEN'S stated feelings of extreme loneliness, depression, and isolation are critical issues in the process of settling and adjusting. For one hundred and fifty years, the Basque cultural centers have served as social spaces for the reconstitution of Basque homeland gender roles, with women once again assuming their places of power and prestige. Basque centers often served as institutions where they could express themselves, understand the conversations, and recognize the cultural contexts of activities. Later-generation Basque women have not necessarily needed the centers for this

Table 20-1

Maintaining Catholicism Is of "Great" of "Very Great" Importance by Age Category

18–30 years	36%
31–45 years	54%
46–60 years	62%
61–75 years	71%
76–90 years	76%

> Combined results of 400 female responses from Argentina, Australia, Belgium, Peru, United States, and Uruguay (Totoricagüena 2003a, 104).

The percentage figures correspond to those agreeing with the importance of maintaining Catholicism in Basque families. Traditional Basque nationalism focused on ancestry, language, and religion as the pillars of Basqueness, and it seems that the older the person, the more likely one maintains this ideology. The younger the Basque woman is the less likely she thinks continuing Catholic beliefs to be of such importance. This influence could change the future Basque community activities.

particular function, but have understood the important role played for their mothers.

LATER-GENERATION females, and especially teenaged girls, also have reinforced this pattern through their lasting friendships with other Basque girls. Teens who participated in the dancing groups, choirs, and sporting events, for example, reaffirmed what their parents often hope for—they believe their "Basque center friends are friends for life." However, with time and improvement in language skills, women in all age categories responded that they were comfortable with host-country friends, and only 16 percent of the women eighteen to thirty-years old and 21 percent of the women seventy-six to ninety years old women felt more comfortable with their Basque friends.

Women have been essentially omitted from early studies of Basque migration, and when considered at all have been perceived as accessories to the men who migrated, nonthinking, non-emotional appendages with no choices, comparable to the valuable things packed in traveling trunks. They have been treated more as migrants' wives, daughters, and mothers than as migrants themselves, relegated to secondary roles in international migration. In some instances, however, such as in the United States, female migrants outnumber male migrants. Because women are intimately involved with men, any changes in their status obviously affects their male companions and vice versa. It is erroneous, therefore, to perceive women migrants as nonworking and passive dependents.

BASQUE WOMEN who migrated to Mexico, Chile, Argentina, and Uruguay entered host societies where, as we have seen, Basques were historically recognized and highly regarded with a positive general social status. Those in the United States were usually categorized as Spanish or French, whereas in Australia, Basque women, like Basque men, were and still are commonly mistaken for Italian or Greek. For women and men alike, an additional shock in migration resulted from exchanging the farm or fishing-village life for city life. Whether in Melbourne or Montevideo, San Francisco or Buenos Aires, numerous Basque women interviewed between 1995 and 2003 stated that the demands of city life, in addition to the effects of geographical and cultural change, could be overwhelming, and the transition from traditional to modern was, and is, an ongoing difficult process.

THE COSTS of migration are both personal and emotional, and Basque women have suffered the stress that accompanies surviving in a transnational double world, a stress that forces migrants to adapt rapidly and frequently to considerable changes in habits and expectations (Basch, Glick Schiller, Szanton Blanc 1994, 242). A Basque woman also experiences a lack of belonging and of acceptance in both the homeland and the host country, which was often mentioned as especially frustrating. In Venezuela, she is "the Basque woman," yet when visiting in Euskal Herria, she is "the Venezuelan." "En el limbo," or living in limbo, was a phrase repeated often in each Spanish-speaking country, usually by emigrants themselves, but also by the first generation born in the host country. These women did not feel completely connected to only one place—their homeland or their host country—in other words, to no one single territory or culture.

Yet they do feel solidly connected to each other because of their shared experiences. Communication among *haizpak*, or sisters, through their ethnic identity provided them with both empowerment and recognition, for it gave them a history, a collective feeling, support from an ethnic "family," and a sense of self-worth. Within this communicative structure, the Basque centers have not only served as havens for ethnic self-statement, but also have provided other models of host-country integration while at the same time preserving Basque culture, the continuity of tradition, and a place of belonging and connectedness.

Physical disconnectedness to Euskal Herria is thus replaced by an emotional and intellectual interconnectedness with other Basque women. Emigrants understand

Photographer Eulalia Abaitua Allende Salazar was born in Bilbao in 1853. She married in 1872, and with the start of the Second Carlist War in Spain in 1873, she and her husband fled to Liverpool, England, where she studied photography. After the end of the war, they returned to Bilbao, where she built a photo studio in the basement of her new home. She is known for her photos, such as this one, of families and everyday life and work. Eulalia Abaitua died at the age of ninety in 1943.

Photograph by Eulalia Abaitua Allende Salazar. Courtesy of the Basque Archaeological, Ethnographic, and Historical Museum, Bilbao.

Table 20-2

To be considered a Basque, a person should speak the Basque language

	"Strongly Agree" or "Agree"	"No Opinion"	"Strongly Disagree" or "Disagree"	Respondents who do "speak Basque fluently" or "with some difficulty"
Belgium	13%	4%	83%	42%
Uruguay	12%	6%	83%	2%
United States	15%	9%	76%	46%
Argentina	24%	8%	68%	16%
Australia	36%	13%	52%	56%
Female	**18%**	**9%**	**73%**	**31%**
Male	**21%**	**8%**	**71%**	**32%**
18-30 yrs old	19%	8%	73%	25%
31-45 yrs old	20%	6%	74%	26%
46-60 yrs old	20%	7%	72%	27%
61-75 yrs old	18%	12%	70%	38%
75-90 yrs old	16%	14%	69%	61%

Totals from 818 respondents from Australia, Argentina, Belgium, United States, Uruguay. Totals above or below 100% result from rounding (Totoricagüena 2004b, 112).

This table (similar to chapter 16) now includes comparisons of attitudes toward language between genders and also among the various age categories. There are no significant differences between male and female responses. Popular conceptions maintain language preservation in the sphere of female domi-

each other's horrors of political exile, loss of family and friends, and fears of dealing with new cultures in their host countries. First-generation and second-generation women born in the host country understand each other's upbringing and how they are different from host-country non-Basque friends. From constantly spelling and explaining their surnames, to describing food preparation, to interpreting ETA activities, women of all ages in the diaspora declared that they believe they have more in common with each other in different countries than they do with other women equivalent to them in their own host countries. A free journal, *Euskal Etxeak* (Basque centers), distributed to Basques in the diaspora by the Autonomous Basque Government of Euskadi, often appeared as an example in conversations when women compared themselves with other Basques in different countries from the articles they had read.

D O WOMEN preserve Basque traditions more than men, and what exactly is the woman's role in the (re)production and development of ethnicity in her family? The expected role of women as producers and reproducers of ethnic practices and traditions is often related to women being perceived as the carriers of cul-ture for that ethnic group. Women are perceived as the main socialization agents of young children—the teachers who

nation; however, the data demonstrate this is not the case with Basques. In the age categories we see that although the elderly participants have a much higher rate of knowledge of Euskara, this does not strongly affect their attitudes regarding whether or not a person has to speak Basque in order to be considered a Basque. Their responses are similar to others of all ages.

A mother and her two daughters show the profile of age.
Photograph by Eulalia Abaitua Allende Salazar. Cour-
tesy of the Basque Archaeological, Ethnographic, and
Historical Museum, Bilbao.

---

transfer cultural traditions to the next generation. In
the case of the emigrant generation, they are often less
assimilated linguistically and socially within the wider
society because they work in the home. However, the
research data of Basque diaspora communities demonstrate no difference between males and females in their
attitudes toward whether mothers or fathers are more
influential in preserving and maintaining Basque ethnic traditions. Asked to react to the statement "Mothers
have been more influential than fathers for teaching

Basque culture to their children," a majority of the 832 anonymous questionnaire responses from Basques in six countries disagreed or had no opinion. Only 36 percent of males and 40 percent of females agreed with this statement. Usually, then, socialization from host-country peers (in school, in the physical surroundings, and by the media, for example) combines with Basque ethnic socialization from home, the Basque centers, and cultural events with other Basque families, encouraged by *both* mothers and fathers.

DEFINITIONS OF BASQUENESS

WHAT definitions of Basqueness do the women of the diaspora communities maintain? Do they maintain a mind set associated with more conservative and exclusive categories of ancestry, language, and religion, or are they more in tune with a contemporary homeland that accepts as a Basque all those who live and work in Euskal Herria and who promote and extend Basque culture? Religious affiliation is generally considered to be one of many key factors in cultivating Basque ethnic group solidarity, and Catholicism has been historically a significant factor in defining Basque identity. From the data, it would appear that religion continues to occupy an important role in defining Basque identity within the diaspora populations with 71 percent of females and 69 percent males agreeing that "continuing Catholic beliefs and traditions in our Basque families" is of "great" or "very great" importance. Not surprisingly, the older the woman, the higher the percentage that believed Catholicism was of "great" or "very great" importance.

In the United States, where many interviewees mentioned experiencing discrimination against Catholics, 80 percent of the females responded that it is of "some,"

Table 20-3

Basque language familiarity, usage, and literacy: females only

	"I know only a few words" or "none at all"	"I use Basque only for special phrases" or "none at all"	"I can write only a few words in Basque" or "none at all"
Uruguay	94%	83%	98%
Argentina	64%	48%	61%
United States	44%	30%	62%
Belgium	40%	30%	40%
Australia	33%	24%	52%

Totals of 400 female respondents from Australia, Argentina, Belgium, United States, Uruguay (Totoricagüena 2003a, 108).

Recent immigration to an area can significantly affect the use of the homeland language as seen here with the opposite case of Basques in Uruguay. Although Argentina also has older immigration, it experienced higher numbers of political exiles fleeing political persecution of Franco. Many of the newer immigrants did speak Basque, which positively affected the existing community's relationship and usage of Euskara. Uruguay did not experience such high numbers of new immigration. Recent immigration to the other countries also shows they are more likely to speak or maintain the language because there are native speakers in the community.

"great," or "very great" importance to maintain the beliefs and traditions. Basques in Belgium were the least likely to think that religion is important to their ethnic identity, with only 33 percent agreeing with the statement, whereas these levels rose to 54 percent of Uruguayans, 66 percent of Argentines, and 67 percent of Australians, respectively. Religion, then, tends to be a more significant factor in Basque center celebrations in the United States, where a Catholic mass is normally a part of the Aberri Eguna, or, Day of the Homeland, numerous festivals, and NABO (North American Basque Organization) conventions. Therefore, because the majority of Basque celebrations are related to Catholicism, in the United States, Basques maintain the religious link to ethnic identity. In the other countries of the diaspora, as in Euskal Herria, the practice of religion has declined, and festivals are celebrated and saints commemorated without significant fanfare for the religious aspects of the festivities. Mass is usually attended by a minority and remains only a small part of generally secular celebrations of dance, art, film, food, and sports that last anywhere from two days to the week-long program of the annual Argentine National Basque Week.

When considering the factor of ancestry in defining Basque identity, again, American women were the most conservative, whereas those residing in Belgium regarded the issue of least importance in their responses. Responding to the statement "A person must have Basque ancestors to be Basque," 97 percent of the women in the United States "agreed" or "strongly agreed," while 60 percent of those in Belgium did so. In each country, at least a majority agreed (Argentina 66 percent, Uruguay 70 percent, Australia 73 percent). Age categories showed a difference only in the youngest group of eighteen-to-thirty-year-olds, who also agreed that the ancestry factor was important (by 62 percent), while the other categories responded by much higher percentages and agreed by between 80 percent and 92 percent. Regardless of age, when comparing generations of emigrants themselves, between 70 percent and 88 percent of emigrants through to the third generation born in the host country believed ancestry to be necessary to defining Basque identity, but only 35 percent of fourth-generation women agreed. The most recent generation, then, seems to be moving closer to homeland definitions of Basqueness. This may be because of their increased contact (both physical and virtual) with Euskal Herria in comparison with their forbears and also perhaps because by the fourth generation, Basques have usually mixed with other ethnic groups, and one's lineage includes additional heritages besides the Basque one.

IN A 1995 survey conducted in all seven homeland provinces by the Basque Autonomous Government's Department of Culture, people responded that the most important conditions necessary for a person to be considered Basque were "to have been born in the Basque Country" (59 percent), "to live and work in the Basque Country" (51 percent), "to speak Euskara" (27 percent), and "to comprehend and defend Basque culture and folklore" (15 percent). Indeed, only 10 percent thought that "to have Basque surnames" was important in defining Basque identity (Aizpurua 1996). The marked difference between diaspora and homeland populations regarding surnames—and therefore ancestry—illustrates the homeland's move toward a more civic and inclusive definition of Basque ethnic identity, compared with the diaspora's more traditional approach to defining Basqueness.

In the diaspora questionnaire responses, 39 percent of females and 43 percent of males did however agree

The fish market of the Ribera-Bilbao.
Photo circa 1880–96. *Photograph by Eulalia Abaitua Allende Salazar. Courtesy of the Basque Archaeological, Ethnographic, and Historical Museum, Bilbao.*

that "persons permanently living in Euskal Herria should be accepted as Basques, whether or not they were born there." Moreover, within the diaspora, a surprising 84 percent of the females and 86 percent of males who had regarded ancestry as necessary in defining ethnic identity also supported the idea of "accepting as Basques those people who feel and identify themselves as Basques." Differences between women by country ranged from 100 percent of Basques in Belgium agreeing with this acceptance to 74 percent in the United States. Personal interviews detected a general reluctance to accept "outsiders," but several interviewees believed that "if the Catalans do it in Catalunya, the Basques should, too." Once more, as with the responses regarding Catholicism, Basque women in Belgium demonstrated a more civic and less biological definition of Basqueness. They are, of course, more recent immigrants, transmitting a more contemporary ideology from their homeland. Furthermore, because of physical proximity, they are able to visit the Basque Country more easily, more economically, and more frequently, and the constant contact would likely affect their opinions.

BASQUE LANGUAGE KNOWLEDGE AND TRANSMISSION
As a factor of Basque ethnic identity within the diaspora populations, Euskara has lost much of its importance. In Euskal Herria itself, already by the mid-1800s, various areas had lost Basque through an increasing state presence that both promoted and forced the use of Spanish and French. Later, during the Franco regime (1939–75), the Basque language was outlawed as a means of communication. Consequently, many emigrants fleeing the Basque Country in search of political exile did not themselves speak Basque. As the table below demonstrates, although diaspora Basques are extremely proud of their unique and complex language, most do not consider it an important factor in their own ethnicity or indeed in categorizing others as Basque. The following table represents questionnaire responses from males and females and also records the percentages of those who do actually speak the language.

ALTHOUGH traditional Basque nationalism historically stressed the importance of the Basque language, and the last influential wave of migration involved

Table 20-4

Total Number per Country of Diaspora Registered Voters in the Basque Autonomous Community, 1999

Argentina	3,699
United States	2,010
Uruguay	1,022
Belgium	977
Australia	Not Available

Figures from Iñaki Aguirre, Basque Autonomous Community General Secretary of Foreign Action.

Since the early 1990s, regulations regarding who is eligible to vote in elections in Spain have been changed by the Spanish central government. Those in the diaspora who qualify must register with the Spanish Embassy or Consulate in their host country, and are then able to vote by mail. Many do not qualify and do not register, or do not think they know enough about the political parties or candidates to cast a fair vote and therefore do not register or participate.

people most likely raised with this ideology, Basques in these diaspora countries no longer consider the language issue of such great importance. Obviously, because so many of them do not speak Euskara, they would not want to eliminate themselves from the category of being Basque. Finally, according to the data, there are no significant differences between male and female abilities or attitudes.

According to this table, then, 31 percent of the total female respondents are able to speak Basque "fluently" or "with some difficulty." The next table further

Basque women used all means and many different kinds of containers in order to carry essential water from the rivers to their homes.
Photograph by Eulalia Abaitua Allende Salazar. Courtesy of the Basque Archaeological, Ethnographic, and Historical Museum, Bilbao.

highlights just how few Basque women of the diaspora are actually able to speak and use Euskara, as well as how many are illiterate in their ancestral language. Respondents were asked to describe their language abilities and use of Basque in five separate categories. Regarding female respondents alone, the table 3 measures language ability, speaking frequencies, and literacy in Basque and combines the responses of those who have "no Basque language at all" with those who can speak, use, and read and write "only a few words or special phrases such as 'Happy Birthday' or 'Congratulations.'"

UNTIL THE early 1990s, the interior population of Uruguay lacked any Basque organizations at all and had to rely on the two Basque centers in Montevideo for collective cultural fulfillment. Without any new migration, the need for and interest in Euskara basically evaporated, as we can see from the data. Today, there are recreational Basque language classes that meet sporadically, but few serious students. That said, there are Euskara programs at Basque centers in Argentina, Uruguay, Australia, and the United States, as well as university language courses and *ikastolak* (Basque language schools) in both Argentina and the United States. Yet while students and parents are to be commended for their tremendous efforts, sociolinguistic studies demonstrate that without a strong social or economic reason for learning and using a language, it is not likely to be maintained. Diaspora Basques can thus use Euskara with each other (if they are both one of the few who know it), but they can equally use their host-country language without feeling any less Basque. When traveling or communicating with relatives in Euskal Herria, for example, those from Argentina and Uruguay can easily use Spanish, and those from Belgium would use French. However, Australian and U.S. Basques must learn a second language to communicate with other Basques in the homeland or in the diaspora, and they tend to take school courses in French or Spanish to become literate in one of their parents' languages. Interviewees often mentioned the academic and economic benefits of learning Spanish or French for future employment, while those in Argentina,

Uruguay, and Belgium were inevitably studying English. Interestingly, in Euskal Herria, those who are not -Basque nationalists make the same argument for learning English rather than Basque. Unfortunately, French-speaking Basques from Belgium and Spanish-speaking Basques from Uruguay are using English, rather than Basque, to communicate with each other.

POLITICAL BEHAVIOR AND ATTITUDES

For many women in the diaspora, Basqueness carries with it a political dimension that is, on the whole, private and not a salient part of institutional practices such as Basque center activities. There are currently more than thirty-two thousand people in the Basque diaspora who retain their Spanish citizenship and therefore their voting rights in the Basque Autonomous Community (Araba, Bizkaia, Gipuzkoa) and a further thirteen thousand Nafarroans abroad with the same rights in the Foral Community of Nafarroa. The figures are not available for Iparralde. Only a minority of these thirty-two thousand people have actually registered to vote with the Basque Autonomous Community's Government.

IN THE following poll, respondents were given nine Basque political parties to choose from as the party that best represents their political opinions, as well as an "other" option, yet in every country, the traditional and conservative Partido Nacionalista Vasco (the PNV or Basque Nationalist Party) emerged as the most popular choice among the diaspora, while the leftist, radical nationalist Herri Batasuna (HB United Homeland/People's Unity, now renamed Batasuna) came in second. More telling than the choice of party was the respondent's willingness to select "I don't know enough about Basque Country politics to answer this question" or "I purposefully stay out of Basque Country politics." There

Table 20-5

Which political party most closely fits your views in the Basque Autonomous Community (B.A.C.)?

	PNV	HB	I don't know enough about B.A.C. politics to choose a party	I stay out of B.A.C. politics
Female	11%	5%	61%	18%
Male	20%	6%	52%	16%

Combined 818 responses from Australia, Argentina, Belgium, United States, Uruguay. Remaining percentages went to other parties not listed in this table.

Regardless of whether or not respondents had registered to vote they were asked about their homeland party affiliation. The PNV, Partido Nacionalista Vasco, is the Basque Nationalist Party which consistently polls the highest numbers of support in the Basque Country, as well as in the diaspora, as a conservative nationalist party. HB, Herri Batasuna, has been illegalized under several different names but reincarnates itself as the leftist nationalist party. The high numbers of respondents willing to admit they do not know enough about homeland parties to associate themselves with a particular ideology, as well as the others who purposefully stay out of homeland politics demonstrates their interest in cultural and not political identity.

were no significant differences between the genders, and there was little difference between age categories, with stronger support from the elderly for the PNV. Regardless of age, 36 percent of the emigrant generation of females supported the PNV, falling to only 5 percent of second-generation women. In each category of gender, generation, or geography, the majority did not participate in homeland politics, with the exception of Basque women in Belgium, who emerged as 78 percent supportive of the PNV and 22 percent of HB/Batasuna. The proximity of Belgium, the accessibility to news from the home country in the daily media, and their more recent migration translating to closer familial ties increases Belgian Basques' interest and participation in politics.

DIASPORA BASQUES tend to prefer cultural, rather than political activities, and most of the Basque centers' statutes declare in writing that they are apolitical institutions. Seventy-nine percent of males and 82 percent of females agreed with the statement that they "prefer to participate in Basque cultural events and not political events." Differences between generations were also very small, with between 76 percent and 84 percent of all generations preferring cultural events. Geographically, Belgium's Basques once again stood out, with only a 58 percent agreement, while the Basques of the other countries agreed by an 80-percent margin. This is best explained by the fact that Brussels is home to the European Union's various branches of administrative government, and Basques there have taken advantage of their freedom of expression in attempting to influence European Union policy toward civil rights for Basques in Spain. Belgian Basque women are also much more likely than their diaspora kin to participate in political movements that have taken place in their host country if the movement directly affects Basques.

The chain migration of Basques resulted from information networks that provided details and explanations of the migration process itself, as well as possible economic opportunities. Teresa Urigüen Mendiolea, seen here with Basque *mus* champions in North Queensland, sponsored hundreds of individuals' transportation costs, facilitating their migration to the Ingham area as sugarcane cutters. The overwhelming majority was from near her hometown of Lekeitio, Bizkaia.
Photograph courtesy of the Jon Balanzategi and Eugenia Oleaga family collection.

This mosaic of Basques in several diaspora communities demonstrates the slight differences between men and women in their definitions of Basqueness and the general similarities among women regardless of geography, age, and generation. That said, frequent exchange and recent migration have meant that the

Belgian community tends to be closer to homeland ideas of what factors constitute being Basque, whereas a certain distance, both temporal and spatial, marks the cultural divide between U.S. Basques and homeland ideas. As we have seen in other ways, as Euskal Herria has moved toward a more civic definition of Basqueness, including those people who live and work in the Basque Country and those who work for the culture and identify themselves as Basque, the diaspora communities have tended to maintain a traditional, conservative approach to Basque ethnonationalist sentiment. The majority of these Basques are not interested in and do not know the details of the political system of Spain's autonomous and foral communities, for example, but are more interested in preserving cultural aspects of their ethnicity, with the important exception of language, an ethnic marker that requires perhaps a greater and more difficult degree of commitment than other expressions of Basque ethnic identity.

Lesson twenty

BIBLIOGRAPHY

Aizpurua, Xabier. 1995. *La continuidad del Euskera*. Vitoria-Gasteiz: Gobierno Vasco, Departamento de Cultura, Servicio Central de Publicaciones del Gobierno Vasco.

Basch, Linda, Nina Glick Schiller, and Cristina Szanton Blanc. *Nations Unbound: Transnational Projects, Postcolonial Predicaments, and Deterritorialized Nation-States*. Amsterdam: Gordon and Breach Science Publishers.

Billig, Michael. 1995.*Banal Nationalism*. Thousand Oaks, Calif.: Sage.

Chant, Sylvia, ed. 1992. *Gender and Migration in Developing Countries*. London: Belhaven Press.

Simon, Rita James, and Caroline B. Brettle, eds. 1986. *International Migration: The Female Experience* Totowa, N.J.: Rowan and Allanheld.

Totoricagüena, Gloria. 2004a. *The Basques of New York: A Cosmopolitan Experience*. 2d ed. Basque Migration and Diaspora Studies Series, no. 2. Reno: Center for Basque Studies, University of Nevada, Reno.

———. 2004b. *Identity, Culture and Politics: Comparing the Basque Diaspora*. Reno: University of Nevada Press.

———. 2003a. "Interconnected Disconnectedness: How Diaspora Basque Women Maintain Ethnic Identity." In *Amatxi, Amuma, Amona: Writings in Honor of Basque Women*, ed. Linda White and Cameron Watson. Reno: Center for Basque Studies, University of Nevada, Reno.

———. 2003b. "NOKA Euskal Emakume artean." *Emakunde*, no. 51 (June).

———. 2002. "Andrak: Women." *Eusko Ikaskuntza Euskonews and Media Electronic Journal*, no. 184. KOSMOpolita Series. Donostia–San Sebastián: Eusko Ikaskuntza. http://www.euskonews.com.

REQUIRED READING

Gloria Totoricagüena, "Interconnected Disconnectedness: How Diaspora Basque Women Maintain Ethnic Identity," in *Amatxi, Amuma, Amona: Writings in Honor of Basque Women*, ed. Linda White and Cameron Watson (Reno: Center for Basque Studies, University of Nevada, Reno, 2003), pp 99–118.

Caroline B. Brettle and Rita James Simon, eds., *International Migration: The Female Experience* (Totowa,

---

N.J.: Rowman and Allanheld, 1986), chapter 1, pp
3–20.

WRITTEN LESSON FOR SUBMISSION
Gender identity is a social construction. Would the
evidence displayed in this lesson argue that the different societies hosting Basque diasporan women have
greatly affected their identities? Or not? To what factors
would you attribute the differences or lack of differences
between men and women and how they have defined
Basqueness and themselves as Basques?

21 · Today's Basque organizations

THE BASQUE diaspora's networks and institutions have evolved and have been transformed following the needs and demands of their members. Initially, upon arrival, immigrants required employment connections and social services. They attempted to learn the host-country language and to understand its social, political, and economic infrastructure. As with other ethnic organizations in other host societies, the original functions of the Basque networks and organizations were to reduce the strain of newcomer status and alleviate cultural adaptation. The Basque centers have provided immigrants and their families with friendship and belonging in a new setting. Throughout the decades, members have been able to find relationships and camaraderie with others who have similar upbringings, values, and histories.

Today, in contrast, as we have seen in a number of cases, the later generations need the reverse of the original Basque center objectives of introduction to the host society. They require the skills to maintain a weakening cultural attachment to their Basque heritage and to maintain ties to the homeland. The focus has changed: from highlighting the future of the immigrant members to retaining the Basque historical past and educating later-generation Basques about their own culture and identity.

We have read that the development of migrant networks and ethnic institutions is studied in terms framed by theories of chain migration, networks, and cultural capital (Boyd 1989, Fawcett 1989, Coleman 1992). Throughout the centuries of migration out of Euskal Herria, Basque ethnic networks have been composed of relationships that link former, current, and future Basque migrants. Nicholas Van Hear dissects ethnic networks and their importance to chain migration and the dissemination of information about means of travel and entry, finding accommodation, employment, and adaptation to new environments. Although the disruption of a Basque migrant's life may have been overwhelming, the "organic development of personal, family, kin, friendship, community and ethnic ties mean the networks are the strongest when they embrace links with the established populations of the countries of destination" (Van Hear 1998, 60). For centuries, Basques have sought each other out in their new countries and have chosen to help, socialize, and do business with each other.

THE ETHNIC networks enhanced immigrants' capacities to adapt to new circumstances, new languages, and new cultures, and the web of Basque centers often provided the fundamental resources for that adaptation. The organizations of the Basque diaspora, and especially those that have a physical meeting space, help fortify inter-Basque networking for friendship, employment, information, and news of the homeland. Whether visiting or studying in another country, recent Basque migrants still tend to visit the community's Basque center out of curiosity, for instant companionship, and for information.

BASQUE ASSOCIATIONISM: A RECAPITULATION
In Central, South, or North America, and through five centuries, Basque collectivities have originated and then developed in similar manners. As we have seen, from the 1612 founding of the Hermandad of Our Lady of Aránzazu (later developed into the Confraternity in Lima and the Confraternity of the Basque Nation in Arequipa, Peru, in 1630 to the 1700s Colegio de los Vizcaínas,

The participation of youths in Basque folk dancing groups encourages ethnic socialization and community building. Many elderly Basques report that their best friends today are from friendships established in their *eusko etxea* dance group decades ago. Because dancing is relatively easy and fun, it is generally the most popular activity for young members of the Basque centers. *Photograph by the author.*

College of the Vizcayans, in Mexico, through the 1800s in Cuba, Chile, Argentina, Uruguay, and later in other countries, some sort of a *socorros mútuos*, mutual aid society for assisting Basques with the costs of medical care, funerals, and repatriation has been present in nearly every country where a critical mass of Basques existed (Totoricagüena 2004b). These societies have provided local community Basques with trusted networks and financial aid for health care, communications with family in the homeland, and when necessary, with death benefits or repatriation costs.

To cite another example, Basques in the Llavallol area near the city of Buenos Aires created the Euskal Echea, or Basque Home, in 1901. Still functioning today, this began as an institution for Basque senior citizens' retirement and simultaneously as a boarding-school facility for orphaned Basque children. Currently, the Euskal Echea is opened to all Argentines, not only those of Basque descent. And as we noted in Lesson 11, the New York Centro Vasco-Americano Sociedad de Beneficiencia y Recreo formed in 1905 and gained its official legal charter in 1913. Its objectives were to provide an insurance fund for Basque members who took ill and missed work, to help defray medical costs, to cover travel charges for those who were forced to return to Euskal Herria but did not have the funds, and to bear the expenses for funeral services for those who died without family. Boise Basques, too, had various men's and separate women's associations for the same purposes. These associations were essential to economic security before the days of labor unions, government pensions, and social security programs.

As we have seen, throughout Argentina, Uruguay, and the United States, Basque-owned hotels and boarding houses and their employees served as surrogate homes and families. Basques could stay short-term while traveling to the city for doctor visits or during the off-season of agricultural production or livestock raising or long-term, as when bachelors sometimes moved permanently to the establishments. In Argentina, the United States, and on a smaller scale in Uruguay and Australia, these Basque "hotels" served as information centers for news from Euskal Herria and for networking for employment. The significance of the facilities emanates from the chain migration to the area, which fomented continued interaction with updated information and attitudes directly from the homeland for inter-Basque-community relations. They also facilitated intra-Basque-community relations within ethnic communities in the host society. One would receive news from the homeland in personal family letters, but also when hearing others speak about their own correspondence from their own families in the towns and villages of the various provinces. As we have seen in communities of the Basque diaspora throughout the world, Basque hotels and later Basque centers served as spaces for gathering and disseminating information–an unofficial ethnic news bureau.

EVENTUALLY, established immigrants who had lived in the communities for years or generations no longer needed temporary room and board or an informal employment agency, and labor unions and government programs provided other safety nets for medical and missed employment costs. Basques now needed to fill emotional and psychological vacuums. They wanted a place to socialize, to communicate with others in their own language, and to practice their Basque traditions and culture. Beginning with the first modern *euskal etxea*, the Euskal Erria formed in Montevideo, Uruguay in 1876, the institutions of the Basque boardinghouses and hotels were replaced with the social and cultural entity known as the Basque center.

Basque immigrants and later generations who initiated and maintained these centers have chosen to emphasize similar elements of Basque identity. They have focused on cuisine, language, instrumental and choral music and dance, sports, and leisure-time activities such as card playing. Religion and politics have usually been separated for individual and not institutional promotion, although many Basque events continue to have a Catholic mass as a component of the festival. Basque diaspora culture has been constructed and reconstructed, blended with the culture of host societies, rediscovered, and reinterpreted while combining the past, present, and expectations for the future in diaspora Basques' self-definition of what counts as Basqueness. Just as homeland Basque culture has developed and changed over the years, so have the diaspora cultures in these transnational communities.

ETHNIC IDENTITIES are created through time by subsequent generations and also through space as immigrants carry and adapt culture from one place to another. The progression of these Basque collectivities includes the self-development of the diasporic community and its cultural organizations while simultaneously interacting with the effects of new Basque immigration. We should understand that the new immigrants' incorporation into the established diaspora community Basque center could pose various problems. The new immigrant might disappoint the elders by not carrying the same values as the older immigrants because the homeland's culture had also evolved during the years spent away from home. Existing members of the Basque centers tend to think that newly arriving immigrants will be just like themselves in background, attitudes, and behavior. This seldom is the case. For example, traumatized Spanish Civil War political exiles to Venezuela in the 1940s found a community of later-generation Basques who were not knowledgeable about or even interested in, the current Franco politics of the homeland.

Recent Basque immigrants to the American West often find segments of the Basque populations that do not speak Basque, do not read homeland newspapers, and have a historical but not contemporary understanding of today's homeland Basque society issues. These new

Basques living abroad began organizing themselves in ethnic institutions as early as 1612, in Lima Peru. Today's *eusko etxeak* work to provide activities that maintain Basque culture and a love for Euskal Herria, its people, and its history, customs, and society. The Euzkaldunak Incorporated, in Boise, Idaho, was formed in 1949, and initial segments of the building were constructed in 1950.
Photograph courtesy of Bryan Day.

---

immigrants might also be disappointed to find a diasporic community almost exclusively focused on the past. Basque center activities tend to promote the rural realities of the 1930s to 1960s and nostalgia for things that were not a part of the recent immigrant's reality in any of the seven provinces. Basque communities that experienced frequent contact with the homeland or continuous chain migration were less likely to experience tense conflict over cultural authenticity or the clash of disparate cultural identities between the established and recent immigrants. For example, Basques in New York, Mexico City, and Buenos Aires had constant contact with people and news from the Basque Country. The consistent updating of their information and imagination regarding the homeland and their frequent encounters with new immigrants of varying religious, political, and social points of view made the changes seem more gradual.

THE END OF continuous Basque immigration has changed the ways that today's Basque centers function. No longer needed to educate immigrants about the host country, today they function as defenders and preservers of homeland cultural identity, as we have seen, educating their members and the general public about the Basque Country. Participation in these centers is now for psychological, emotional, and social fulfillment, rather than for economic need. Daily member-to-member interactions have been replaced by monthly dinners and social gatherings, *mus* card-game tournaments, dances, annual festival celebrations, institutional newsletters and Web sites. Basque organizations that once taught English courses in the United States and found accommodation and employment for recent Basque immigrants now disseminate genealogical information for Basques to research their own heritage. They teach Euskara, rather than English, and collect travel brochures in order to organize tours of Euskal Herria. Basque immigrants initially needed the immediate services the organizations provided for economic and social survival. Later generations however, are optional consumers.

Other Basque diaspora organizations' roles have changed significantly, as well. In Boise, Idaho, there is now a Basque Museum and Cultural Center, demonstrating that the history of the Basques is significant to the point of dedicating the resources to research Basques in Idaho, not Basques in the Basque Country. In Argentina, there are various organizations, such as the Fundación Juan de Garay, devoted to researching and preserving the history of Basques there, not in the homeland. In 2003. the Basque government initiated Urazandi: Basques Across the Seas, a publication series intended to focus on Basques in their diasporic communities and the history of the maintenance of their ethnic identity. Fifteen Basque communities researched their origins and interviewed immigrants (and later generations as well) in order to archive their Basque communities' histories in book publications. At last, the Basque diaspora has its own recognized identity, separate from that of Basques in the Basque Country and not necessarily an extension of it.

TODAY, ONE reason why the needs met by Basque diaspora institutions are less concerned with daily survival functions for the Basque immigrants and their descendants is because the relatively few recent Basque migrants are more likely to be temporary (students or professionals) and have entered their respective host countries with academic or employment contracts and contacts. Because they have no need to join ethnic organizations in order to remind themselves of their Basqueness or to "prove" it, they often have no economic or psychological need for the institutions as they function today. New Basque migrants working in Peru want to learn about and experience Peru, its culture, and its people, not necessarily surround themselves with the same kinds of Basque people and culture that they have just departed. Basque immigrants studying English or working in Great Britain, Australia, Canada, or the

Diasporic representations and symbols are often
nationalistic, as is this Basque dance, which creates the
ikurriña. Basque centers, homes, businesses, cars, and
personal dress often include artistic representations
of homeland symbols, demonstrating the "banal
nationalism" of everyday behavior and actions.
Photograph by the author.

United States want an international experience and to
meet the people and make friends with those from that
country, but not always with other Basques, with whom
they know they will not practice their English. I have
often heard comments from recent Basque immigrants
who do not participate in the Basque center functions
summed up as "I did not leave the Basque Country to
have a Basque Country experience somewhere else. I am
already Basque. I came here to learn about this country,
its language, its culture, and its people. I am going back
to the Basque Country and want to see as much of this
country as I can while I am here. Would an American in

the Old Part of Donostia go to a McDonald's when you have a selection of fifty bars with Basque *pintxos* surrounding you?"

THE END of consistent flows of emigration out of the Basque Country is a result of the positive economic and political changes in Spain and France. The economies of the Basque provinces have progressed, and there are many additional opportunities for youths to find employment in Euskal Herria and in the European Union. The continual democratic waxing and waning in the central government of Spain has also ceased the compulsion for the type of necessary political exile of the Franco era. However, numerous questions remain regarding the extent to which parties controlling politics in Madrid are committed to continued democratic reform. There no longer are significant numbers of new immigrants to any of the over twenty countries with Basque communities with the exception of Belgium, where an estimated two hundred recently transplanted Basque administrative functionaries are living in Brussels, employed by the bureaucracies of the European Union.

Although emigration from the Basque country has slowed dramatically, after the death of Franco in 1975 and the subsequent establishment of democratic forms of central government and autonomous Basque governments in the early 1980s, in the Basque diaspora there has been unprecedented institutional growth. Since 1985, there are more than forty additional Argentine Basque diaspora organizations, some new and some reestablished, twelve in the United States, six in Uruguay, and in 2004 in the North Queensland area of Australia, activists have created a Basque cultural association and, ironically, purchased a twenty-year lease on the former Polish association's social club building. There are new Basque centers in Andorra, Italy, and in Colombia and other new organizations in countries with established Basque populations. The Basque centers around the world are not looking to new migrants to keep their organizations alive. They could instead focus on the estimated 90 percent of the people with Basque heritage already in their communities who do not participate in Basque collective activities and encourage them to join.

MY QUANTITATIVE research on Basque center members demonstrates specific membership trends. There are later generations joining the organizations as first-timers, and there are more children continuing on in the clubs with their parents than there are leaving or not participating. These data point to stability and possibly growth in the numbers of Basques identifying with their ethnicity through the community centers and associations. However, there are also those who lose interest and, for one reason or another, leave the Basque center activities. Anthropologists have argued that ethnicity becomes more important late in life and also when consolidating a new identity, as teenagers do, or when becoming parents, moving, or retiring. In order to maintain their prominence, the centers will need to provide meaningful activities for people in these stages of their lives.

MAINTENANCE OF TRADITIONAL IDENTITY IN THE DIASPORA

For ethnic populations, the study of the combination of ethnicity, identity, and music known as ethnomusicology is central to linking homeland and "here-land." A network of sounds connects the memories of childhood with the present. Ethnic music is a weighty symbolic mode of affiliation for present-day diaspora Basques. As an element of ethnicity maintenance, preservation of

Table 21-1
How often do you eat Basque style food at home?
Response percentages combine those who answered
"everyday," "weekly," and "a few times a month."

Belgium	96%
Peru	93%
Australia	76%
United States	73%
Argentina	56%
Uruguay	33%
Total respondents	832

Basque cultural traditions, such as maintaining ethnic
cuisine, tend to be promoted in center activities and family settings. Difficulties in obtaining specific ingredients,
especially certain types of fish, may add to Uruguay and
Argentina's not preserving this aspect of Basque identity.
More likely it results from those Basque populations
being latter generations when compared to the other
countries, and Basques there have lost these skills over
time.

instrumental and choral music has significance in each
Basque center. Ethnomusicologists argue that perhaps
only the aroma of familiar foods has the power to evoke
memory that music has. In addition, "music makes specific connections with family members, politics, and significant moments for which melodies are the milestone"
(Slobin 1994, 244).

BASQUE ORGANIZATIONS affirm these links through
music by formal and informal performances of
established Basque choirs, by the performances of various genre musicians, by teaching folk songs to children,

and by providing background music at events. The
seemingly mundane piped-in music of Basque center
bars and restaurants, the music of religious masses and
celebrations, and the singing and dancing at festivals
all contribute to the shared memories, experiences, and
connectedness of the diaspora Basques. Although the
choirs of Australia are less formally organized, and the
choir in Belgium was temporarily disbanded while finishing the renovation of a new center in the late 1990s,
very similar types of traditional and nationalist music
have served as the cornerstones of the songs sung at the
majority of Basque festivals, with homages to the Tree of
Gernika, national anthems, nationalistic hymns of fallen
warriors, and mothers' lullabies. The love songs do not
usually refer to people, but to Euskal Herria, and there
are both traditional and contemporary examples.

YOUTHS WHO travel to the Basque Country return
with the latest CDs of Basque folk rock, such as
Oskorri, Ruper Ordorika, Imanol, Txomin Artola and
Amaia Zubiria, Ene Bada, and Benito Lertxundi, who
all sing in Basque. Although many diasporic customers do not understand the language, they do recognize
the melodies, and such performers have become popular enough to travel to Basque festivals in Uruguay,
Argentina, Venezuela, Mexico, and the United States.
Consequently, when first-time travelers to Euskal Herria
participate in the fiestas and the social scene, they recognize the music and can sing along with the homeland
populations. When visiting other diaspora communities'
Basque festival celebrations, they are also "insiders,"
enjoying the same songs. Music often is the main means
of identification of diasporic groups, and Basques are
known for their *txistus*, accordions, guitars, violins, and
tambourines.

Basque youth from Argentina often continue their early friendships into their adult lives. Participation in folkdance troupes is high and an especially encouraged mode of ethnicity manifestation.
Photo courtesy of Euskal Etxeak.

In the diaspora organizations, regardless of age, respondents agreed overwhelmingly (between 89 percent and 96 percent) that "singing traditional songs in Basque" is of "some," "great," or "very great importance." Geographical location did not seriously affect attitudes, with between 84 percent in Australia and 96 percent each in Uruguay and in the United States also agreeing to its importance. Of course, many who sing these songs can't understand a word that they have sung.

ALMOST EVERY Basque organization has initiated a folk-dance group at one time or another. Depending on the country and on the population of Basques in the area, dance-group participants number anywhere from a few children to troupes of sixty young adults. These groups have served the dual purposes of ethnic

socialization for the youths and entertainment at ethnic
functions. Most groups also perform for non-Basque
gatherings and educate the host-country public regarding Basque culture. *Txistularis* and accordionists accompany the dancers and often give their own separate
performances. Conversations with spectators at musical
performances and festivals revealed that because the
txistu is a Basque instrument, it was preferred over accordions, guitars, and pianos—not because they enjoyed
the sound, which can be quite shrill, but because they
equated Basque functions with Basque music played
on Basque instruments. In the new millennium, however, because there are fewer and fewer Basques in the
diaspora who have dedicated themselves to learning
how to play these instruments, dancing exhibitions are
performed to taped or CD music and no longer have the
equivalent energy of a live production.

T HE DANCE groups and choirs have been effective
elements in the ethnic socialization process for
transnational Basques. Dancers and musicians share
their experiences of Basque ethnic identity not as individuals, but collectively as a special community, and
also as a group with other groups. Peer encouragement
helps friends remain as members of the Basque centers
and stimulates their interest not just in the significance
of the dances and of the lyrics of the songs, but in the
past of the Basque Country and its people. Friendships
formed as youths at the Basque center, in the choir or in
the dance group, endure, binding the members together
around more than just the music and its symbolism
and language. It is one way in which the associations
that bind together the larger Basque community are
formed. Basque Centers have found these programs to
be extremely positive for their community image and
outreach to other ethnic groups in their cities, as well as

for their main purpose of providing activities for members and their families.

YOU ARE WHAT YOU EAT

In every case of my research in over eighty different cities with Basque populations, if there is a physical Basque center, no matter the size or location, there is also a kitchen. The association of ethnic identity with ethnic food mentioned above is steadfast. Around the world in 2004, the Basque centers typically had monthly membership dinners and several special-occasion feasts with Basque-style selections ranging from typical peasant home cooking to contemporary Basque nouvelle cuisine. As in the homeland, often it is the men who rule these *txokos*, or private kitchens, barbecue pits, or industrial-size kitchens. However, home cooking tends to remain the domain of the women. In fieldwork results from hundreds of Basques in Argentina, Uruguay, Peru, the United States, Australia, and Belgium, although 91 percent of the total respondents believed that it is of "some," "great," or "very great" importance to "teach and use Basque cuisine and food preparation in our homes," the reality was that a combined average of 63 percent actually prepare Basque style meals in their homes at least "a few times a month."

DIFFERENCES IN responses among Basques in various countries tend to reflect early versus recent migration and are affected by the specific details of Basque organization activities. In Peru, for example, a substantial number of men meet every Thursday at the Basque center to create a Basque-style meal for each other, demonstrating and maintaining cuisine as a significant factor in their own lives and in the activities of the Lima Euskal Etxea. Recent migration to Belgium

Ainara Arozena, from the Aila de Zarautz cooking school in Gipuzkoa, taught Basque cuisine courses for the Venezuela Sukalde Association in 2001.
Photo courtesy of Euskal Etxeak.

---

shows emigrant and first-generation Basques preserving food traditions to an extraordinary degree.

THE EARLIER migration to Argentina and Uruguay means that it is fourth-generation and fifth-generation Basques who are continuing the cooking traditions. If the next category of "a few times a year" is included, Argentina would add another 36 percent and Uruguay another 43 percent. Cross tabulations of generation and cooking frequencies show a steady decline in Basque-style food preparation with later generations. From those born in Euskal Herria to the fourth generation or later born in their host countries, combining the percentages again for eating Basque style food at home "at least a few times a month," the percentages follow a pattern: born in Euskal Herria 89 percent; first generation born in host country, 73 percent, second generation born in the host country, 51 percent; third generation born in the host country, 31 percent; and fourth or later generation born in the host country, 30 percent.

WHAT HAS become the most popular program in the majority of the Argentine Basque centers? Cooking classes. In the United States, Basque cuisine cooking classes—open to the general public and not only to Basque center members—are used as fundraisers for the organizations and are extremely popular. In Mexico, a separate Basque organization, Sukalde, literally, Kitchen, has been formed by the Basque chefs working in the finer hotels of the capital city. Many of the Basque centers in Chile, Uruguay, Argentina, Mexico, Spain, France (outside of the Basque Country), and the United States have restaurants attached that are open to the general public. The Basque government has sponsored diaspora tours by homeland award-winning chefs, and the Basque centers and private restaurants in Mexico, Venezuela, and Chile have hired several of them to infuse the tradition of ethnic cooking. Several centers enjoy annual celebrations of Basque gastronomy, and in Necochea, Argentina, there is an entire week's festival dedicated to Basque cuisine.

ADDITIONAL ACTIVITIES

Basque organizations around the world also foment the continuation of Basque sports and athletic events. The same traditional activities are practiced regardless of country: competitions in wood chopping, weight carrying and weightlifting, team tugs-of-war, *jai alai*, *pelota*, and *pala*. Although the weight carrying, weightlifting, and wood chopping are for exhibitions during festivals, there are regular games of *pelota* and *pala*. International exchanges and tournaments of *pelota* and *pala* players for festivals are common and enthusiastically received

by the Basque audiences. Teaching and practicing
the Basque sports such as *pelota, jai alai,* wood chopping, weight carrying and lifting also was singled out
as of "some" "great" or "very great" importance to the
respondents in my research. From a low of 70 percent in
Belgium to a high of 93 percent each in Peru, the United
States, and Uruguay (where there are public and privately owned *frontons* in addition to those at the Basque
centers), Basques regard ethnic sports as significant to
their identity.

However, the numerous frontons are often devoid of
players. In several countries, there are national players'
associations whose leaderships are extremely wary of
the continuance of these Basque sports. There is much
encouragement from the organizations and from the
crowds, but the physical hardship of handball played by
Basque rules, with no hand protection whatsoever, deters
younger players from learning. Experienced players'
nerve damage, permanent swelling, and hand surgeries
easily convince youngsters to try other athletic entertainment. In the new millennium, the sporting demonstrations at Basque festivals in Australia, Canada, the
United States, Mexico, Chile, Argentina, Uruguay, Brazil,
Barcelona, and the autumn 2003 grand opening of the
new *euskal etxea* in Paris all relied on athletes brought
from the Basque Country to give demonstrations of their
skills. There was a lack of available local talent.

CARD PLAYING, whether for the International *Mus*
Tournament Championship of Basque diaspora
organizations or sitting at the *euskal etxea* bar literally
playing for beans, produces another avenue for the rein-
forcement of ethnic identity and produces more shared
experiences. Twenty years ago, Sunday nights would
find the majority of the Basque centers around the world
filled with *mus, tute,* and *briska* players, but today, the

typical generation gap exists. The grandparent and adolescent generations are present, playing cards, football, or *pelota* or practicing their dancing. The missing generation is that in the parenting years, between the ages of twenty-five and fifty.

The Basque centers provide newsletters that facilitate communications and the distribution of information and occasionally even have short articles in the Basque language, which the majority of the readership cannot understand. These newsletters are more social in nature and record the marriages, births, and deaths of members, remind readers of upcoming ethnic events and fundraisers, and may have special mention of Basque culture, history, or anthropology to educate their readership. Several Basque associations exchange their newsletters among themselves, expanding the ethnic imaginations of their readers. Today, organizations also post their newsletters on the Internet for the local and global audience.

THERE ARE a wide variety of additional ethnic activities carried out through the organizations, from art exhibitions, lectures, and conferences on literature to medical research on Basque physiology. Those interested in a given topic are encouraged to call meetings or seminars and to invite and educate others regarding their interest. However, the most important aspect of the associations may be the informal socialization that takes place between the Basques themselves. Whether sitting at the bar cheering a soccer team, enjoying a wedding celebration, or attending a Basque cinema event, the exchange of information and shared experiences tie these people to each other through their Basque heritage, reinforcing the Basque centers' and the individuals' identities.

Lesson twenty-one

BIBLIOGRAPHY

Boyd, Monica. 1989. "Family and Personal Networks in International Migration: Recent Developments and New Agendas." *International Migration Review* 23: no. 3: 638–70.

Coleman, David. 1993. "The World on the Move? International Migration in 1992." Paper presented at the European Population Conference, U.N. Commission for Europe, U.N. Population Fund, Geneva, Switzerland (March).

Fawcett, James T. 1989. "Networks, Linkages, and Migration Systems." *International Migration Review* 23: no. 3: 671–80.

Slobin, Mark. 1994. "Music in Diaspora: The View from Euro-America." *Diaspora* 3, no.3 (Winter): 243–51.

Totoricagüena, Gloria. 2004a. *The Basques of New York: A Cosmopolitan Experience.* 2d ed. Basque Migration and Diaspora Studies Series, no. 2. Reno: Center for Basque Studies, University of Nevada, Reno.

———. 2004b *Identity, Culture, and Politics: Comparing the Basque Diaspora.* Reno: University of Nevada Press.

———. 2003a. "Interconnected Disconnectedness: How Diaspora Basque Women Maintain Ethnic Identity." In *Amatxi, Amuma, Amona: Writings in Honor of Basque Women,* ed. Linda White and Cameron Watson. Reno: Center for Basque Studies, University of Nevada, Reno.

———. 2003b. "El País Vasco visto desde la diáspora: Análisis de las relaciones institucionales entre el País Vasco y la diáspora vasca." *Eusko Ikaskuntza XV Congreso Internacional Select Papers.* Donostia–San Sebastián: Eusko Ikaskuntza.

Totoricagüena, Gloria. 2002. "Vascos en el Oeste Americano." In *Enciclopedia General Ilustrada del País Vasco*. Entries regarding Basques in the United States. Donostia–San Sebastián: Editorial Auñamendi. http://www.eusko-ikaskuntza.org. Click "Enter," then "Data Bases." Check the box of *Enciclopedia Auñamendi* and then click on that title. Type in a search word.

Van Hear, Nicolas. 1998. *New Diasporas: The Mass Exodus, Dispersal, and Regrouping of Migrant Communities*. London: UCL Press.

REQUIRED READING
Gloria Totoricagüena, "Celebrating Basque Ethnic Identity in Diasporic Festivals: Anatomy of a Basque Community," *Revista Internacional de Estudios Vascos* 45, no. 2 (July–December 2000): 569–98.

WRITTEN LESSON FOR SUBMISSION
In your opinion, should the Basque center festivals attempt to copy the festivals of Euskal Herria, or should they create their own definition and construction of a Basque festival? Are the diaspora festivals more "authentic" or more "legitimate" if they copy those of the Basque Country? Explain your opinion. Often when Basques from Euskal Herria visit the diaspora communities and their events, they comment on the "folkloric" and "very traditional and almost superficial and artificial" aspect of the Basque centers and the festivals and activities. We have seen here that the centers focus on sports, music, dance, cuisine, language, card playing, and so on. What other types of activities could they add? Do you think the centers should lead the members in "trying to be more Basque," or should the centers' directors follow the members' needs and wants for activities?

Should the activities of the centers be strictly Basque (mirroring some activity of the Basque Country)? Or are they Basque by virtue of Basque people participating in them?

22 · Homeland-diaspora relations
The Basque Country and the Basque diaspora

HISTORICALLY, the institutions of Basque diasporic civil society have included commercial and maritime trade networks, mutual aid societies, fraternities, boarding houses, and the *euskal etxeak* and their various subgroups of dancers, choirs, sports teams, *ikastolas*, and restaurants. Each directs the cultural production and reproduction of the Basque diasporic community, which leads to the maintenance of ethnic identity. This construction of civil society at global and local levels is exactly the diaspora condition of fitting in both "here" and "there." Diaspora Basques are a part of the local civil society and have a Chilean, Venezuelan, or Cuban civil identity, but, as we have discussed, simultaneously identify on a global level with an ethnic identity and with Basques in the homeland and around the world. This final analysis will examine the contemporary development of relations between the government of the Basque Autonomous Community, Euskadi, and the Basque diaspora, including the current state of a deterritorialized and increasingly transnational Basque ethnic identity.

There are currently more than one hundred and eighty Basque associations in twenty-two different countries, and nearly one hundred and sixty of those organizations are officially recognized by the Basque Autonomous Government. However, currently, the worldwide Basque diaspora is sedentary, without unified direction, and not mobilized toward any collaborative political or cultural project. There are contested visions of collective identity, and within the *euskal etxeak* there are disagreements about what it means to be Basque. The definition generally follows a conservative Sabino Arana delineation focusing on ancestry. It is quite nostalgic and folkloric, as we have noted in previous lessons, and is centered on cultural traditions, not necessarily on political or religious identity. Most Basques centers in the diaspora maintain the homeland culture of the 1940s and 1950s—the time of the last great immigrations into their communities. However, in the majority of the Basque communities abroad, there is now an emerging cadre of transnational activists whose uncoordinated and even unconscious promotion of a deterritorialized Basque identity and interconnected diasporic population could eventually mobilize these groups toward mutual, collaborative action. In the age of technology, physical location is no longer required for the practice of social community.

WHEN DEALING with Basques abroad, homeland institutions must understand that, as we also have seen, diasporas tend to "disrupt the spatial-temporal units of analysis" (Lavie and Swedenburg 1996, 14). Basques have a dual orientation and are physically connected to the host countries where they live, but emotionally and psychologically connected to Euskal Herria. My fieldwork demonstrates that more than three-quarters of respondents define themselves with a dual, hyphenated identity—Basque-Australian, Belgian-Basque, Mexican-Basque, Basque-American, and so on. The hyphen marks a nonhierarchic union and also marks two completely different categories—ethnic identity and civic identity. Basques are equally comfortable with this transnational identity in different geographic spaces, an identity that does not rely on physical location. In several cases, Basque attitudes abroad have evolved from the nationalism of exiles to multidimensional diasporic transnationalism. The speed and intensity of that evolution have been accelerated by the new technologies of communications and of access to

Homeland-to-diaspora relations include sister-city connections and exchanges between communities in Euskal
Herria and Basque communities abroad. Boise, Idaho,
and Gernika, Bizkaia, are sister cities and have enjoyed
several visits from each other's municipal officials and
volunteer committee members. In 2000, the Basque government's minister of culture, Mari Karmen Garmendi
(standing on the front steps at left) joined representatives of the Gernika city council as well as representatives of Queensland, Australia, Basques for an official
welcome from the mayor of Boise.
Photograph by the author.

information, as discussed in Lesson 18. The new technology opportunities educate diaspora communities and update the traditional rural images of the seven provinces, although, as we know, they also have the effect of shattering a perception on which many diaspora Basques base their identity.

BASQUE INTERNATIONAL RELATIONS

The diaspora-homeland transnational networks—previously commercial, personal, and occasionally institutional—alternated between periods of latency and periods of frenzied activity over the centuries. However, the establishment of homeland autonomy in the 1980s ushered in a period of stabilization for institutional relations. The creation of an official governmental policy for the diaspora was unique, with several policy makers themselves being returnees from political exile.

IN THE early 1980s, the ties between the Basque government and its diaspora were mostly symbolic and cultural. Basque government delegations traveled to various countries, bearing seedlings of the Tree of Gernika, donating series of videos and books about the homeland, and funding the travel of dance groups and sportsmen from Euskal Herria to exhibitions in Australia, Argentina, Uruguay, Chile, Venezuela, Mexico, and the Unites States. In 1982, the Basque Department of Culture hosted delegates from various communities abroad for a congress regarding the future of the diaspora. However, the congress resulted in no confirmed projects or proposals. In 1984, the Service for Relations with the Basque Centers was established in this department, administratively recognizing the importance of what had previously existed as chains of informal transnational networks based on personal relationships. Visits by Basque government officials, including the *lehendakari* in 1988, were received with profound emotion at the Basque centers, emotion equivalent to that evoked by the visits by President José Antonio de Aguirre nearly a half-century earlier. This recognition given to the Basques abroad increased their own pride and interest in the accomplishment of homeland autonomy.

The General Secretariat of Foreign Action was created under the Office of the Presidency in 1990, and the Service for Relations with the Basque Centers was transferred there in order to consolidate foreign relations in one office. Doing so also served to emphasize the expected importance of international affairs. By the end of 1991, there was a clear effort to use community leaders of the Basque diaspora to facilitate meetings between Basque government officials and those in the highest levels of host-country governments. Using these local contacts, the Basque government established political and economic ties with several hostland politicians at the national level and below. President Ardanza was received with the same protocol and prestige as a head of state while in Chile, Mexico, Cuba, Argentina, and Uruguay. He also met with then Vice President Gore and Congressional leaders in the United States as a result of the influence of host-country Basques, according to Andoni Ortuzar, the then general secretary of foreign action.

IN 1990, THE special program Gaztemundu, or World of Youth, was initiated to encourage youths to visit the Basque homeland. It intends to replace and update the idealized and romanticized myth perpetuated by generations of Basques. Another goal of the program is to educate, train, and prepare the future leaders of the Basque diaspora organizations. Sixty diaspora Basques between the ages of twenty and thirty are chosen to participate in the annual Gaztemundu program. Applicants

Basque festivals celebrated in the diaspora often include demonstrations of traditional and rural sports. Exhibitions include weight lifting and carrying, weight pulling, wood chopping, tug-of-war, handball, and rope climbing. At the 2000 Jaialdi International Basque Festival, athletes from Euskal Herria competed against each other in front of crowds that over three days reached thirty thousand people.
Photograph by the author.

are required to create an individual project regarding one of three themes: promoting cultural activities, economic and industrial relations between their host country and Euskadi, or attracting and keeping youths active in the diaspora organizations. The 2003 edition of Gaztemundu focused on dynamic management ideas for leadership of nonprofit organizations and was hugely successful, according to the participants.

THIS PROGRAM is perceived as an effective investment in the future for diaspora-homeland relations. The Basque government is molding the self-selected future leaders of the diaspora's institutions and preparing them to work inside the current framework of relations. The Gaztemundu initiative has been successful not just in achieving its stated goals, but in meeting the peripheral objective of strengthening ties among diaspora communities through these youth conferences. Gaztemundu participants interviewed from one month to six years after attending their conference each stated that they remain in constant contact with at least one person from a different country and exchange ideas for each other's centers.

THE GOVERNMENT of the Foral Community of Nafarroa opened communications with a few Basque centers in the 1990s, mostly as a response to diaspora queries. In 2004, they still had not established a specific office to deal with external relations with Basque communities, but did have one officer in their public-relations and press department who accommodated requests for information, especially about tourism, through the Basque centers. There are specific Casas Navarras, or Navarran centers, that are only for Navarrans and their descendants, and these are favored by the current political party in power in Nafarroa, Unión del Pueblo Navarro. This party is not necessarily interested in relations with the other Basque centers because they define themselves separately as Navarrese, and not as generically Basque. The Foral Community of Nafarroa has not reached out to non-Navarrese Basques abroad, although President Miguel Sanz did visit various Centro Navarro organizations in Argentina in 2002 with success. Relations between Nafarroa and diaspora communities remain mainly personal contacts and networks, rather than institutionalized relationships, although this may change in the near future.

The three provinces in Iparralde have no official local-government relations with diaspora institutions.

However, several nongovernmental organizations, cultural associations, and privately funded activities maintain networks, especially with the Basques of Paris and with those of California. Regardless of the lack of institutional relations, personal networks are recent and strong. Basque dance troupes, choirs, athletes, and musicians from Iparralde have toured the diaspora communities through personal invitations of center leaders with personal and center funding. The government of Euskadi also incorporates various institutions and artists from Nafarroa and Iparralde into its diaspora projects.

THE LAW OF RELATIONS WITH THE BASQUE COMMUNITIES IN THE EXTERIOR: LEY 8/1994

THE LAW of Relations with Basque Communities Outside the Autonomous Community of the Basque Country, Ley 8/1994, was passed by the Basque parliament of Euskadi in May 1994. The Basque government had decided to make a qualitative change in the relations between the institutions of the homeland and those of the Basque communities abroad. Institutional development and increasing self-government provided a substantial foundation for a new start. The passage of the law signaled a new stage in the history of relations between the Autonomous Basque Government and Basque institutions in the diaspora and was described by parliamentarians as being a means of repaying "our historic debt to Basques overseas" (Sainz de la Maza 1994, 14). President José Antonio Ardanza also described the law as a starting point that would mark a new direction in relations between the Basque Country and Basques and their centers around the world.

Article 1 of the law stipulates a desire to preserve and reinforce links and to support and intensify relations between the Basque government, as well as other homeland institutions, with the Basque populations in the diaspora. It specifically mentions promoting diaspora projects which will spread, stimulate, and develop Basque culture and the homeland economy. It also establishes as permanent budgetary requests for diaspora grants. It strengthens networks linking Basques abroad, the Basque government, and various academic, cultural, economic, and religious institutions in the homeland.

LEY 8/1994 PROVIDES for a registry of Basque centers that are officially recognized by the Basque Autonomous Government, and it establishes the requirements for members of those centers also to register individually and be recognized for possible benefits. Each center is required to collect the names, birthplaces, ancestral town names, languages spoken, and citizenships held by its members. It endows registered members of Basque institutions that are registered with the Basque government with material benefits as well as psychological empowerment. The material benefits include, among other things, the ability to attend universities in the Basque Country, to receive senior citizens' pensions, to qualify for public housing in Euskadi (only the three provinces), and to apply for grants for the diaspora community's projects. The law sets the requirements for eligibility for benefits and distinguishes between benefits for members of Basque centers and for the institutions themselves. It also distinguishes between categories of benefits for the Basques who remain overseas and for those who return to the Basque Country.

Because Article 1 of Ley 8/1994 specifically mentions promoting activities to disseminate, stimulate, and develop Basque culture and Euskadi's economy (Article 1 section 3), some diaspora and Euskadi opposition party members have questioned the Basque government's instrumental motives for using the diaspora for economic gain for the homeland economy, then subsequently exploiting this economic gain to further the election objectives of the PNV.

These comments surface only occasionally and are usually swept aside, although they raise provocative issues. In other transnational populations, homeland politicians campaign to their diaspora communities. In Spain, in the Autonomous Community of Galicia, for example, the diaspora vote actually makes a significant electoral difference, as it did recently by giving approximately half a million votes from Galicians abroad to elect Manuel Fraga Iribarne as the autonomous community's president. In Euskadi and in Nafarroa, however, political parties do not actively campaign for the parliament outside their respective autonomous communities because the Basque diaspora vote does not make an electoral difference. Although approximately thirteen thousand foreign Basques are registered in Nafarroa, the government has not separated the statistics and given data on their voting patterns in the Autonomous Foral Community. The total number of qualified diaspora voters for the 2001 election in Euskadi was 32,858—of whom only 10,552 actually voted. This represents not even one percentage point (only .7 percent) of the total 1,414,269 votes cast in that election.

THE MAJORITY of Basques I have interviewed admit they do not know enough about politics to distinguish between the political parties and they do not maintain their Spanish citizenship, which is required to vote. Politics remains a secondary factor to cultural preservation.

The Basque Parliament is a unicameral legislative body, with twenty-five representatives from each of the three provinces of Euskadi elected to four-year terms. Various political parties are represented proportionally, according to the popular vote. In addition to making the laws of the Basque Autonomous Community, the parliament also is responsible for designating Euskadi's senators serving in the Spanish state legislative body, the Cortes. *Photograph by the author.*

BENEFITS FOR BASQUE ORGANIZATIONS, CENTERS, AND
INDIVIDUAL MEMBERS

FOR DIASPORA organizations to participate in the
Basque government's benefits programs, they
must be "recognized" by proving they comply with the
requirements of Ley 8/1994. The law requires democratic
organizational structures for recognition, and the associations must request recognition and follow the procedures to obtain it. They must have a valid constitution
filed with the judicial system of the country in which
they reside, and their fundamental objectives must
include the maintenance of Basque culture and ties with
the Basque Country, its people, history, language, and
culture. The Basque government also has recognized fed-
erations of Basque centers in Argentina, the Federación
de Entidades Vasco Argentinos, FEVA; in the United
States, the North American Basque Organizations,
NABO, and in Uruguay, the Federación de Instituciones
Vascas del Uruguay, FIVU.

The statutory benefits specifically given to registered
organizations in Ley 8/1994 include:

A) Access to information of a public nature, with a
social, cultural, or economic content; B) The right to
participation in different forms of expression of Basque
homeland social, cultural, and economic life that contribute to the external diaspora projection of such; C)
Treatment identical to that of homeland associations;
D) The right to ask the Basque Autonomous Community to participate in activities organized by a diaspora
center to promote Basque culture; E) Center participation in programs, missions, and delegations organized
by Basque homeland institutions in the center's territorial area; F) The right to request and receive advice
on social, economic, or labor matters in the Basque
Country; G) The right to a supply of material designed

to facilitate the transmission of knowledge of Basque history, culture, language, and social reality; H) Collaboration in activities of communication centered on the Autonomous Community, such as EITB, and *Euskal Etxeak*, the journal; I) The right to be heard via the advisory council and to attend the World Congresses of Basque Collectivities; J) The organization of courses to learn the Basque language. (Article 8, section 1 of Ley 8/1994)

BASQUE CENTERS also qualify to receive financial and other types of assistance. The law specifically mentions support for temporarily covering the operating costs of centers, maintenance of the infrastructure of their buildings, the promotion of activities and programs related to the homeland, and economic assistance for especially needy members (Article 8, section 3).

The members of Basque communities to whom the benefits and rights apply are defined as those resident abroad and their dependents. Included are those who fall under Article 7, section 2 of the Statutes of Autonomy: persons "who specifically request it shall enjoy the same political rights as those living in the Basque Country, if their last legal residence in Spain was in Euskadi, and provided they retain their Spanish nationality [citizenship]." The law specifically lists those evacuated during the Spanish Civil War and those exiled after the war for aid.

The principle of territoriality has been raised when determining to whom these rights belong. Should they belong to those Basques born in any of the seven provinces of Euskal Herria, or just those

Professor William A. Douglass addressed the Second World Congress of Basque Collectivities in Vitoria-Gasteiz in 1999. The opening address at the seat of the Basque presidency, the *lehendakaritza*, encouraged Basque delegates to debate the future of Basque identity in the diaspora and to prepare for changes and evolution in its relations with the Basque government.
Photograph by Basque Government Press Agency.

born in the three provinces of contemporary political boundaries of Euskadi? It is the government of Euskadi that is funding the benefits, and they have determined that anyone born in one of the seven provinces who returns to one of the three provinces in the jurisdiction of Euskadi will qualify for these services.

THE LAW also lists specific rights for individual members of diaspora organizations. These include access to the Basque cultural heritage via libraries, archives, museums, and other cultural property and institutions.

It specifies that language curricula are to be provided to students free of charge, and educational, cultural, and economic exchanges for individuals are to be promoted by the Basque government. The University of the Basque Country accepts qualified diaspora students on an equal footing with resident Basques, which is extremely beneficial for South American Basque students who are looking to future careers in Europe. After receiving an education, those Basques who are interested in creating a business in Euskadi can receive free technical and legal advice in regard to the creation of their enterprise. Benefits also include access to health and social services and public housing. Those who qualify financially "may have access to means of financial support to be used to facilitate their return voyage" (Article 11, section 3).

SOME DIASPORA Basques are demanding "rights" and benefits from the homeland while they stay in the diaspora. Several Basques in South America have argued that they "have a right" to Basque government benefits whether or not they are registered members of Basque centers. They also believe that anyone born in the Basque Country should have full access to all benefits, even if they cannot go to the homeland to receive them. For example, if there is health-care coverage for returning diaspora Basques who will move their residences to the homeland, there should be the same benefits for those who, for whatever reasons, cannot leave their host country. This is an example of extraterritoriality in identity and in political administration.

THE WORLD CONGRESS OF BASQUE COLLECTIVITIES
Importantly, Ley 8/1994 also directs a World Congress of Basque Collectivities be held every four years as a forum for intradiasporic relations among the Basque communities themselves and between the diaspora

Table 22-1

Diaspora Voting, 1990, 1994, 1998, and 2001 Parliamentary Elections in Euskadi

	1990 Diaspora	1994 Diaspora	1998 Diaspora	2001 Diaspora
Registered Voters	7,005	14,373	26,396	32,858
Actual Voters	2,152	3,119	6,888	10,552
	30.7%	21.7%	26.1%	32%
Parties	**Diaspora votes**			
PNV	647	978	2,011	EAJ-PNV/EA
	30.1%	31.4%	32%	4165 39.5%
PSOE	523	858	1,500	PSE-EE/PSOE
	24.3%	27.5%	24.3%	2161 20.5%
PP	205	431	1,343	PP
	9.5%	13.8%	21.7%	2898 27.5%
HB/EH	204	312	522	EH 625
	9.5%	10%	8.5%	5.9%
IU	0	31	256	EB-IU
	0%	1%	4.2%	384 3.6%
EA	105	251	378	Others
	4.9%	8.1%	6.1%	159 1.5%
Others	468	258	166	Not valid
	21.8%	8.3%	2.7%	160 1.5%
Not valid	0	0	712	
TOTAL	2,152	3,119	6,176	
	100%	100%	100%	

communities and the government of the Basque Autonomous Community. They create a Four-Year Plan of Institutional Action for proposed projects with the homeland. The First Congress of Basque Communities (Vitoria-Gasteiz, 1995) opened the floodgates for horizontal exchange between the Basques of different countries, in addition to strengthening vertical ties between diaspora communities and their homeland government. It facilitated the establishment of intercommunications between the diaspora organizations, and the delegates themselves established personal friendships that have evolved into institutional ties. For example, they organized exchanges of Basque dance groups between the United States and

Election data compiled from Basque Government Department of Interior published results.

PNV: Partido Nacionalista Vasco; PSOE: Partido Socialista Obrero Español; PP: Partido Popular; HB/EH: Herri Batasuna/Euskal Herritarrok. IU: Izquierda Unida; EA: Eusko Alkartasuna. (Totoricagüena 2004, 189).

We see a significant increase with each election in the number of diaspora registered voters as shown in the top row. This is a result of increased communication and information about registration and voter qualifications in addition to more information regarding homeland political parties. Diaspora Basques have access to information via the Internet and feel more knowledgeable about casting a vote. There is consistent support for the conservative Basque nationalist coalition PNV-EA, significantly increasing support for the conservative Spanish state-wide PP, and slightly decreasing support for the illegalized HB or EH. Diaspora voting patterns are quite similar to homeland results.

Argentina, and Basque delegations from Peru, Uruguay, Mexico, Canada, and Australia traveled to the Jaialdi International Basque Festival in Boise, Idaho, in 2000. Diaspora communities exchange newsletters, and Internet users check each others' Basque Web pages.

DURING THE first three congresses, delegates convened to discuss each congress's draft Four-Year Plan of Institutional Action and additional topics, such as allowing non-Basque participation at the centers, Basque language maintenance, attracting new members, especially youths, and keeping current members active. The first congress began with four general objectives: to preserve the structure and infrastructure of the Basque centers; to promote and maintain Basque identity, culture, and language; to establish effective channels of communication and information with Euskadi, and to associate the younger generations with the life and activities of the Basque centers and through the centers to Euskadi.

Because of the success of the congresses, the Basque diaspora communities have promoted a qualitative change in relations between themselves and the institutions of the homeland. The Law of Relations with the Basque Communities Outside the Autonomous Community of the Basque Country proved to be a helpful legal and political tool that enabled both the homeland government and the Basque communities and centers to reinforce their joint activities and networks. Ley 8/1994 institutionalizes relations and networks of Basque transnationalism and formulates mechanisms that facilitate cooperation, collaboration, and communication.

POLICY FORMULATION FOR THE DIASPORA

Ley 8/1994 created an Advisory Council for Relations with Basque Communities that usually meets once a year

Delegates attending the Second World Congress of
Basque Collectivities represented Basque communities
in sixteen countries and, together, they created and
debated the Four Year Plan of Institutional Action for
diaspora programs and homeland relations.
Photograph by Basque Government Press Agency.

for discussion and analysis of diaspora programs and
communications. It consists of the *lehendakari*, the general secretary for exterior action, the director of relations
with Basque collectivities, fourteen other representatives
of Basque government departments and institutions,
such as Euskaltzaindia, the Basque Language Academy,
and three assessors who have lived in and/or have
researched the diaspora communities. This advisory
council also communicates with Basque institutions in
Nafarroa and Iparralde. The council's role is still mainly
symbolic, and there is no political or administrative
power attached to this group. Initially appointed by the
lehendakari in 1995, the three assessors were elected at

Table 22-2
Basque Diaspora Policy Creation and Implementation

Basque Diaspora elects	Basque Autonomous Government appoints
Congress of Basque Collectivities	Advisory Council for Relations with Basque Communities
Creates suggestions for the four-year plan	Responds to suggestions for the four-year plan

Implementation of four-year plan of institutional action by diaspora centers and the Basque government (Totoricagüena 2004, 167).

the congresses of 1999 and 2003, by the World Congress delegates themselves.

INCLUDED IN the 1999 four-year plan were the responsibilities of reciprocated aid that the homeland might expect from the diaspora communities. While the diaspora needs tangible materials for educating others about Basque issues, the homeland needs an international voice. According to Iñaki Aguirre, secretary for foreign action for the Basque government, the centers' thousands of members could act as goodwill ambassadors for the Basque Country.

Initial 1987 appropriations for the entire combined diaspora communities in nineteen countries applying for aid totaled five million pesetas (40,650 U.S. dollars). The total diaspora grants for 2001 equaled 213,870,301 pesetas (1,108,131 U.S. dollars), but by 2003, they were decreased to 770,766.30 Euros (886,381 U.S. dollars). These grants support specific projects such as Basque center building maintenance, cultural celebrations and promotions, language courses, expenses for choirs, dance troupes, and athletes, conferences and academic research on Basque themes, and Urazandi: Basques Across the Seas, the book series that compiles the histories of the most important Basque diaspora communities.

IN ADDITION to grants, in 1998 the Basque government negotiated with the Banco Bilbao Vizcaya to allow special lower interest rates for loans to diaspora Basque centers. The Basque government acted as the guarantor. The 4.75 percent interest rate was advantageous for centers in countries with floating rates and where borrowers were paying more than triple that rate. Sixteen centers in Argentina, Uruguay, and Mexico took loans to carry out investment in infrastructure and to renovate their facilities. The total loans equaled approximately 1.6 million dollars (*Euskal Etxeak* no. 41 [1999]: 10), but unfortunately, several of the Argentine loans became problematic when their economic crisis hit at the new millennium. Funds expected to be used for grant projects in 2002 had to be used to cover delinquent loan payments, and the next year's total diaspora grant budget was decreased.

Benefiting from the positive reputation and status of the Basque populations, the Basque government also established political and economic policies to promote commercial networks. In 1992, the Basque government

The Ajuria Enea Palace was built in 1918 for Serafín Ajuria as his family mansion. Between 1966 and 1974, it was the home of a religious college until it was purchased by the Diputation of Araba for an art museum. In 1980, the palace was inaugurated as the official personal residence of the Basque president, also serving as the president's office.
Photograph by the author.

----

created Basque foundations and institutes in Chile, Mexico, Argentina, Venezuela, and later in the United States and Uruguay. Prominent Basque business leaders, engineers, and lawyers from the host societies combined with expert economists and specialists from Euskal Herria to create the business and economic *institutos* and *fundaciones*. These entities were charged with producing and designing international trade between the homeland and diaspora host countries.

THE DIASPORA itself actually established the concept of economic networks. Now the idea was to create industrial and business relationships between the Basque provinces and the host country enterprises using Basque connections and economic clout. Basque Country businesses would use the diaspora Basques' contacts and personal networks to make inroads into the South American Mercosur trading block (Argentina, Brazil, Paraguay, and Uruguay) with investment, production, and distribution for the reconversion of industrial societies. These institutes and foundations mediated the investment of thirty-five Basque firms in Latin American countries during 1997 and 1998 alone (Legarreta interview, 1999). Although the American Basque Foundation of the United States has since dissolved, the others continue to expand and in 2003 were elevated to the level of Basque delegations by the Basque government.

CONCLUSION

The Basque communities are proving to be effective and significant nonstate actors, working on behalf of their homeland government, institutions, and businesses. There is a marked difference between the passive policy of the 1980s and the decidedly more active one of the 1990s and the new millennium. The Basque government has only begun to harness the potential of the diaspora communities. It has been nudged into the spotlight by a diaspora waiting since the days of the government-in-exile. However, the honeymoon period is now ending, and the euphoria of having an autonomous government and enjoying economic prosperity, with gifts of grants and subsidies for the Basque centers and their members, may not last forever. Control of the Basque government by nationalist coalitions may not last, either, and the nonpartisan, nonpolitical, and heretofore almost nonpoliticized and unmobilized diaspora may flirt with a change of status.

There is a need for an institution in the homeland to receive these diaspora requests and visits. Just as Basques established cultural centers in the host societies to receive new immigrants and to help them settle into their new societies, the homeland now needs institutions to receive Basques from the diaspora returning to settle, study, or visit and research their own families, their Basque history, and their homeland.

FOR BASQUES, the scope and speed of information flows influence cultural patterns and diaspora consciousness, as do the effects of the availability and accessibility of Internet and satellite Euskaltelebista, as we saw in Lesson 18. However, these active ethnics have linked themselves simultaneously to networks of relationships and meaning from both host and home country since times of marine trade to Spanish colonialism, through the Basque government-in-exile period to contemporary Basque centers. As we can recall, Benedict Anderson has said that "communities are to be distinguished, not by their falsity/genuineness, but by the style in which they are imagined" (Anderson 1991, 6). The dispersed Basque diaspora communities have been imagined as ethnic diaspora communities promoting cultural preservation and sustained ethnic identity, over centuries in some cases; as groups maintaining homeland trade, labor, immigration, and cultural ties; as transnational networks of solidarity with co-ethnics; and as a community with a shared collective history and myths of its idealized homeland. These diaspora ethnics range from Basque ethnic fundamentalists to annual festival attendees similar to "Christmas Catholics." However, regardless of the frequency or intensity of their ethnicity maintenance, many define themselves as tied to other Basques around the world.

REGARDLESS OF which parties control politics, future Basque governments could use the effects of globalization and transnationalism to the advantage of all, with diaspora business and economic development, cultural enhancement, language revitalization, spiritual and psychological augmentation, and intensification in regard to ethnic identity. Or, to the detriment of all Basques, they could underestimate the power of ethnic identity and patronize with condescension or ignore the new model of deterritorialized loyalties and the opportunities that await (Totoricagüena 2004, 208). The lack of a leadership role in the collaboration between the government and the Basque diaspora could be occupied to the advantage of homeland and diaspora community Basques alike. The question is, who will lead?

Lesson twenty-two

BIBLIOGRAPHY

Anderson, Benedict. 1991. *Imagined Communities: Reflections on the Origin and Spread of Nationalism.* London: Verso.

Basch, Linda, Nina Glick Schiller, and Cristina Szanton Blanc. 1994. *Nations Unbound: Transnational Projects, Postcolonial Predicaments, and Deterritorialized Nation-States.* Amsterdam: Gordon and Breach Science Publishers.

Brunn, Stanley D. 1996. "The Internationalization of Diasporas in a Shrinking World." In *The Network of Diasporas,* ed. Georges Prévélakis. Paris: Cyprus Research Center KYKEM.

Castells, Manuel. 1997. *The Power of Identity. The Information Age: Economy, Society and Culture.* Vol. 2. Oxford: Blackwell.

Clifford, James. 1997. "Diasporas." In *The Ethnicity Reader: Nationalism, Multiculturalism, and Migration,* ed. Montserrat Guibernau and John Rex. Cambridge: Polity Press.

Cohen, Robin. 1997. *Global Diasporas: An Introduction.* London: University College London Press.

Dahan, Michael, and Gabriel Sheffer. 2001. "Ethnic Groups and Distance Shrinking Technologies." *Nationalism and Ethnic Politics* 7, no. 1 (Spring): 85–107

Elkins, David J. 1997. "Globalization, Telecommunication, and Virtual Ethnic Communities." *International Political Science Review* 18, no 2: 139–52.

Escobedo Mansilla, Ronald, Ana de Zabala Beascoechea, and Oscar Alvarez Gila. 1996. *Emigración y redes sociales de los vascos en América.* Gasteiz-Vitoria: Servicio Editorial Universidad del Pais Vasco.

Esman, Milton J. 1984. "Diasporas and International Relations." In *Modern Diasporas in International Politics,* ed. Gabriel Sheffer. London: Croom Helm.

Featherstone, Mike. 1995. *Undoing Culture: Globalization, Postmodernism, and Identity.* London: Sage.

Gellner, Ernest. 1983. *Nations and Nationalism.* Ithaca: Cornell University Press.

Hall, Stuart. 1991. "Old and New Identities, Old and New Ethnicities." In *Culture, Globalization, and the World System: Contemporary Conditions for the Representation of Identity,* ed. Anthony D. King. Basingstoke, UK: Macmillian Education.

———. 1997. "Diaspora and Detours in Identity." In *Identity and Difference,* ed. Kathryn Woodward. London: Sage.

Held, David, et al. 1999. *Global Transformations: Politics, Economics, and Culture.* Stanford: Stanford University Press.

Lavie, Smadar, and Ted Swedenburg, eds. 1996. *Displacement, Diaspora, and Geographies of Identity.* Durham, N.C.: Duke University Press.

Pérez-Agote, Alfonoso. 1999. *La identidad colectiva y su dimensión política.* Leioa, Euskadi: Facultad de Ciéncias Sociales, Universidad del País Vasco.

Portés, Alejandro, Luís E. Guarniza, and Patricia Landolt. 1999. "The Study of Transnationalism: Pitfalls and Promise of an Emergent Research Field." *Ethnic and Racial Studies* 22, no. 2 (March): 217–37.

Prévélakis, Georges, ed. 1996. *The Network of Diasporas.* Paris: Cyprus Research Center KYKEM.

Safran, William. 1991. "Diasporas in Modern Societies: Myths of Homeland and Return." *Diasporas: A Journal of Transnational Studies* 1 no. 1 : 83–98.

Sainz de la Maza, Karmelo. 1994. Speech given to the Basque Parliament of Euskadi. Quoted in *Law of Relations with Basque Communities Outside the Autonomous Community of the Basque Country.* Vitoria-Gasteiz: Servicio Central de Publicaciones del Gobierno Vasco.

Shain, Yossi. 1989. *The Frontiers of Loyalty: Political Exiles in the Age of the Nation-State.* Middletown, Conn.: Wesleyan University Press.

Sheffer, Gabriel, edi. 1984. *Modern Diasporas in International Politics.* London: Croom Helm.

———. 1996. "Wither the Study of Ethnic Diasporas? Some Theoretical, Definitional, Analytical, and Comparative Considerations." In *The Network of Diasporas,* ed. Georges Prévélakis. Paris: Cyprus Research Center KYKEM.

Tölölyan, Khachig. 1996. "Rethinking Diaspora(s): State-less Power in the Transnational Moment." *Diaspora* 5, no. 1: 3–36.

Totoricagüena, Gloria. 2004. *Identity, Culture, and Politics in the Basque Diaspora.* Reno: University of Nevada Press.

————. 2002. "El País Vasco visto desde la diáspora: Análisis de las relaciones institucionales entre el País Vasco y la diáspora vasca." *Eusko Ikaskuntza XV Congreso Internacional Select Papers.* Donostia–San Sebastián: Eusko Ikaskuntza.

————. 2000. "Celebrating Basque Diasporic Identity in Ethnic Festivals: Anatomy of a Basque Community." *Revista Internacional de los Estudios Vascos* 45, no. 2 (July–December): 569-98.

————. 2000. "Downloading Identity in the Basque Diaspora: Utilizing the Internet to Create and Maintain Ethnic Identity." *Nevada Historical Society Quarterly* 43, no. 2 (Summer): 140–54.

————. 1999. "Shrinking World, Expanding Diaspora: Globalization and Basque Diasporic Identity." In *The Basque Diaspora/La diaspora vasca,* ed. William A. Douglass, Carmelo Urza, Linda White, and Joseba Zulaika. Reno: Basque Studies Program, University of Nevada Press.

————. 1998. "'Rethinking Ethnicity: Arguments and Explorations' A Critique of Richard Jenkins." *Nations and Nationalism: Journal of the Association for the Study of Ethnicity and Nationalism* 4, part 4 (October): 237–41.

————, and William A. Douglass. 1999. "Los vascos en la Argentina." In *La inmigración Española en la Argentina,* ed. Alejandro Fernandez and Jose C. Moya. Buenos Aires: Editorial Biblos.

Van Hear, Nicolas 1998. *New Diasporas: The Mass Exodus, Dispersal, and Regrouping of Migrant Communities*. London: UCL Press.

Vertovec, Steven. 1999. "Conceiving and Researching Transnationalism." *Ethnic and Racial Studies* 22, no. 2 (March): 447–62.

REQUIRED READING

Eusko Jaurlaritza–Basque Government of Euskadi. *Law of Relations with Basque Communities Outside the Autonomous Community of the Basque Country. Ley 8/1994.*

Eusko Jaurlaritza–Basque Government of Euskadi. *Euskaldunak Munduan, Building the Future. Congress of Basque Communities*, 1995, pp 17–29, 33–41.

Eusko Jaurlaritza–Basque Government of Euskadi. *World Congress on Basque Communities*, 1999, pp 33–40.

Khachig Tölölyan, "Rethinking Diaspora(s): Stateless Power in the Transnational Moment," *Diaspora* 5, no. 1 (1996): 3–36.

Gloria Totoricagüena, *Identity, Culture, and Politics in the Basque Diaspora* (Reno: University of Nevada Press, 2004), chapter 6, pp 155–91.

WRITTEN LESSON FOR SUBMISSION

What are the overall general goals of the Public Law 8/1994 (Ley 8/1994)? Do you think that Ley 8/1994 and the World Congresses of Basque Collectivities of 1995, 1999, and 2003 have been substantial, or mainly symbolic? How would you measure this? What would you expect might be the issues of the 2007 World Congress? Please give examples from our readings for your opinion.

Bibliography

BOOKS AND ARTICLES

Abrams, Dominic, and Michael A. Hogg, eds. 1990. *Social Identity Theory: Constructive and Critical Advances*. New York: Harvester Wheatsheaf.

Adelman, Jeremy. 1995. "European Migration to Argentina, 1880–1930." In *The Cambridge Survey of World Migration*, ed. Robin Cohen. Cambridge: Cambridge University Press.

Aguirre, José Antonio. 1978. *Veinte años de gestión del Gobierno Vasco (1936–1956)*. Durango: Leopoldo Zugaza.

Ahedo, Igor. 2003. *Entre la frustración y la esperanza: Políticas de desarrollo e institucionalización en Iparralde*. Oñati: Instituto Vasco de la Comunidad Autónoma de Euskadi.

Aizpurua, Xabier. 1995. *Euskararen jarraipena: La continuidad del Euskera*. Vitoria-Gasteiz: Servicio Central de Publicaciones del Gobierno Vasco.

Alba, Richard D. 1990. *Ethnic Identity: The Transformation of White America*. New Haven: Yale University Press.

———. 1985. *Italian Americans: Into the Twilight of Ethnicity*. Englewood Cliffs, N.J.: Prentice Hall.

Alday, Alberto. 1999. "Vasco-navarros en el Nuevo Mundo: Una identidad dual." In *The Basque Diaspora/La diáspora vasca*, ed. William A. Douglass, Carmelo Urza, Linda White, and Joseba Zulaika. Reno: University of Nevada, Reno, Basque Studies Program and University of Nevada Press.

Alonso, Andoni, and Iñaki Arzoz. 1999. "Basque Identity on the Internet." In *Basque Cultural Studies*, ed.

William A. Douglass et al. Reno: Basque Studies Program, 1999.

Alonso Carballés, Jesús J. 1998. *1937 Los niños vascos evacuados a Francia y Bélgica: Historia y memoria de un éxodo infantil, 1936–1940*. Bilbao: Asociación de Niños Evacuados.

Altman, Ida. 1995. "Spanish Migration to the Americas." In *The Cambridge Survey of World Migration*, ed. Robin Cohen. Cambridge: Cambridge University Press.

Álvarez Gila, Óscar. 1996. "Vascos y Vascongados: Luchas ideológicas entre Carlistas y Nacionalistas en los centros vascos del Río de la Plata (1900–1930)." In *Emigración y redes sociales de los vascos en América*, ed. Ronald Escobedo Mansilla, Ana de Zabala Beascoechea, and Óscar Álvarez Gila. Vitoria-Gasteiz: Universidad del País Vasco.

———. 1995. "La formación de la colectividad inmigrante vasca en los países del Río de la Plata (siglo XIX)." *Estudios Migratorios Latinoamericanos* 10: 215–48.

Amezaga Clark, Miren. 1991. *Nere aita: El exilio vasco en América*. Donostia–San Sebastián: Editorial Txertoa.

Anasagasti, Iñaki, ed. 1988. *Homenaje al Comité Pro-Inmigración Vasca en Argentina (1940)*. San Sebastián–Donostia: Editorial Txertoa.

Anderson, Benedict. 1991. *Imagined Communities: Reflections on the Origin and Spread of Nationalism*. London: Verso.

Anthias, Floya. 1992. "Cultural Identity and the Politics of Ethnicity." In *Ethnicity, Class, Gender and Migration: Greek-Cypriots in Britain*. Aldershot, UK: Avebury.

Anthias, Floya, and Nira Yuval-Davis. 1993. *Racialized Boundaries: Race, Nation, Gender, Colour, and Class and the Anti-Racist Struggle*. London: Routledge.

Appadurai, Arjun. 1996. *Modernity at Large: Cultural Dimensions of Globalization*. Minneapolis: University of Minnesota Press.

Aramburu Zudaire, José Miguel, and Jesús María Usunáriz Garayoa. 1991. "La emigración de Navarros y Guipuzcoanos hacia el Nuevo Mundo durante la edad moderna: Fuentes y estado de la cuestión." In *La emigración española a ultramar, 1492–1914*, ed. Antonio Eiras Roel. Madrid: Ediciones Tabapress.

Arana y Goiri, Sabino de. 1965. *Obras completas de Arana y Goiri-tar Sabin*. Buenos Aires: Editorial Sabindiar Batza.

Aranaz Zuza, Ignacio, et al. 1992. *Navarros en América: Cinco crónicas*. Pamplona: Gobierno de Navarra.

Archdeacon, Thomas. J. 1985. "Problems and Possibilities in the Study of American Immigration and Ethnic History." *International Migration Review* 69, no. 19 (Spring): 112–34.

Arrien, Gregorio. 1991. *Niños vascos evacuados a Gran Bretaña 1937–1940*. Bilbao: Asociación de Niños Evacuados.

———. 1983. *La Generación del exilio: Génesis de las escuelas vascas y las colonias escolares, 1932–1940*. Bilbao: ONURA

Artís-Gener, Avelí. 1976. *La diáspora republicana*. Barcelona: Editorial Euros.

Astigarraga de, Andoni. 1986. *Abertzales en la Argentina*. Bilbao: Ediciones Alderdi Argitaldaria.

Azcona Pastor, José Manuel. 1992. *Los paraísos posibles: Historia de la inmigración vasca a Argentina y Uruguay en el siglo XIX*. Bilbao: Universidad de Duesto.

Azcona Pastor, José Manuel, Fernando Muru Ronda, and Inés García-Albi de Biedma. 1996. *Historia de la emigración vasca al Uruguay en el siglo XX*. Montevideo: Ministerio de Educación y Cultura, Archivo General de la Nación.

Baines, Dudley. 1991. *Emigration from Europe, 1815–1930*. London: Macmillan Education.

Bakalian, Anny P. 1993. *Armenian Americans: From Being to Feeling Armenian*. New Brunswick, N.J.: Transaction.

Balfour, Sebastian. 1995. "The Loss of Empire, Regenerationism, and the Forging of a Myth of National Identity." In *Spanish Cultural Studies: An Introduction, The Struggle for Modernity*, ed. Helen Graham and Jo Labanyi. Oxford: Oxford University Press.

Bard, Rachel. 1982. *Navarra: The Durable Kingdom*. Reno: University of Nevada Press.

Barkham, Selma Huxley. 1989. *The Basque Coast of Newfoundland*. Plum Point, Newf.: Great Northern Peninsula Development Corporation.

Barth, Fredrik, ed. 1969. *Ethnic Groups and Boundaries: The Social Organization of Culture Difference*. London: George Allen and Unwin.

Basch, Linda, Nina Glick Schiller, and Cristina Szanton Blanc. 1994. *Nations Unbound: Transnational Projects, Postcolonial Predicaments, and Deterritorialized Nation-States*. Amsterdam: Gordon and Breach Science Publishers.

Beltza [pseud.]. 1977. *El nacionalismo vasco en el exilio, 1937–1960*. Donostia–San Sebastián: Editorial Txertoa.

Ben-Ami, Shlomo. 1991. "Basque Nationalism between Archaism and Modernity." *Journal of Contemporary History* 26, nos. 3–4: 493–521.

Bengoetxea, Joxerramon. 1991. "Nationalism and Self-Determination: The Basque Case." In *Issues of Self-Determination*, ed. William Twining. Aberdeen: Aberdeen University Press.

Ben-Rafael, Eliezer. 1994. *Language, Identity, and Social Division: The Case of Israel*. Oxford: Clarendon Press.

Bernard, William S. 1971. "New Directions in Integration and Ethnicity." *International Migration Review* 5, no. 4 (Winter): 464–73.

Berry, John. 1992. "Acculturation and Adaptation in a New Society." *International Migration* 30: 69–85.

Berry, John W., and R. C. Annis, eds. 1988. *Ethnic Psychology: Research and Practice with Immigrants, Refugees, Native Peoples, Ethnic Groups, and Sojourners*. Lisse, Netherlands: Swets and Zeitlinger.

Bilbao Azkarreta, Jon, ed. 1992. *América y los vascos*. Bilbao: Eusko Jaurlaritza.

———. 1958. *Vascos en Cuba, 1492–1511*. Buenos Aires: Editorial Vasca Ekin.

Billig, Michael. 1995. *Banal Nationalism*. Thousand Oaks, Calif.: Sage.

Boski, Pawel. 1988. "Retention and Acquisition of National Self-Identity in Polish Immigrants to Canada: Criterial and Correlated Attributes." In *Ethnic Psychology: Research and Practice with Immigrants, Refugees, Native Peoples, Ethnic Groups, and Sojourners*, ed. John W. Berry and R. C. Annis. Lisse, Netherlands: Swets and Zeitlinger.

Bottomley, Gillian. 1995. "Southern European Migration to Australia: Diasporic Networks and Cultural Transformations." In *The Cambridge Survey of World Migration*, ed. Robin Cohen. Cambridge: Cambridge University Press.

Boyd, Monica. 1989. "Family and Personal Networks in International Migration: Recent Developments and

New Agendas." *International Migration Review* 23, no. 3: 638–70.

Branaa, Jean-Eric. 1989. *Les Basques de l'Amérique/ Basques from America*. Bayonne: Jean-Eric Branaa.

Brass, Paul R. 1991. *Ethnicity and Nationalism: Theory and Comparison*. New Delhi: Sage.

Brettell, Caroline B., and Rita Simon. 1986. "Immigrant Women: An Introduction." In *International Migration: The Female Experience*, ed. Caroline Brettell and Rita Simon. Totowa, N.J.: Rowman and Allanheld.

Bullen, Margaret. 2003. *Basque Gender Studies*. Basque Textbook Series. Reno: Center for Basque Studies.

Brunn, Stanley D. 1996. "The Internationalization of Diasporas in a Shrinking World." In *The Networks of Diaspora*, ed. Georges Prévélakis. Nicosia: Cyprus Research Center KYKEM.

Button, James. 1992. "Australia: In Search of Itself." *Time Magazine*. May 4.

Campani, Giovanna. 1995. "Women Migrants: From Marginal Subjects to Social Actor." In *The Cambridge Survey of World Migration*, ed. Robin Cohen. Cambridge: Cambridge University Press.

Caro Baroja, Julio. 1998. *Ser o no ser vasco*. Trans. Antonio Carreira. Madrid: Editorial Espasa Calpe.

———. 1971. *Los vascos*. 4th ed. Madrid: Ediciones ISTMO.

Carr, Raymond. 1982. *Spain 1808–1975*. Oxford: Clarendon Press.

Castells, Manuel. 1997. *The Power of Identity*. Vol. 2 of *The Information Age: Economy, Society and Culture*. Oxford: Blackwell.

———. 1996. *The Rise of the Network Society*. Vol. 1 of *The Information Age: Economy, Society, Culture*. Oxford: Blackwell.

Castles, Stephen, and Mark J. Miller. 1993. *The Age of Migration: International Population Movements in the Modern World*. London: Macmillan.

Castles, Stephen, et al. 1996. "Australia: Multi-Ethnic Community Without Nationalism?" In *Ethnicity*, ed. John Hutchinson and Anthony D. Smith. Oxford: Oxford University Press.

Cavalli-Sforza, Luigi Luca, and Francesco Cavalli-Sforza. 1995. *The Great Human Diasporas: The History of Diversity and Evolution*, trans. Sarah Thorne. Reading, Penn.: Addison-Wesley.

Cava Mesa, Begona. 1996. "El asociacionismo vasco en Argentina: Política cultural." In *Emigración y redes sociales de los vascos en América*, ed. Ronald Escobedo Mansilla, Ana de Zabala Beascoechea, and Óscar Álvarez Gila. Vitoria-Gasteiz: Universidad del País Vasco.

Caviglia, Maria Jorgelina, and Daniel Villar. 1994. *Inmigración vasca en Argentina: Vete a América*. Vitoria-Gasteiz: Departamento de Cultura Gobierno Vasco.

Chant, Sylvia, ed. 1992. *Gender and Migration in Developing Countries*. London: Bellhaven Press.

Cieraad, Irene, ed. *At Home: An Anthropology of Domestic Space*. Syracuse: Syracuse University Press. 1999.

Clark, Robert P. 1992. "Territorial Devolution as a Strategy to Resolve Ethnic Conflict: Basque Self-Governance in Spain's Autonomous Community System." In *Ethnic and Racial Minorities in Advanced Industrial Democracies*, ed. Anthony M. Messina. Contributions in Ethnic Studies, no. 29. Westport, Conn.: Greenwood Press.

———. 1984. *The Basque Insurgents: ETA, 1952–1980*. Madison: University of Wisconsin Press.

Clark, Robert P. 1979. *The Basques: The Franco Years and Beyond*. Reno: University of Nevada Press.

———, and Michael H. Haltzel, eds. 1987. *Spain in the 1980s: The Democratic Transition and a New International Role*. Cambridge: Ballinger.

Claval, Paul. 1996. "Diasporas and Politics: An Overview." In *The Networks of Diaspora*, ed. Georges Prévélakis. Nicosia: Cyprus Research Center KYKEM.

Clifford, James. 1997. "Diasporas." In *The Ethnicity Reader: Nationalism, Multiculturalism, and Migration*, ed. Montserrat Guibernau and John Rex. Cambridge: Polity Press.

Climo, Jacob. 1990. "Transmitting Ethnicity Through Oral Narratives." *Ethnic Groups* 8: 163–80.

Cohen, Anthony P. 1993. "Culture as Identity: An Anthropologist's View." *New Literary History* 24, no. 1: 195–209.

Cohen, Robin. 1997. "Diasporas, the Nation-State, and Globalization." In *Global History and Migrations*, ed. Wang Gungwu. Boulder, Colo.: Westview Press.

———. 1997. *Global Diasporas: An Introduction*. London: University College London Press.

———.1996. "Diaspora and the Nation-State: From Victims to Challengers." *International Affairs* 72, no. 3: 507–20.

———. 1994. *Frontiers of Identity: The British and the Rest*. London: Longman.

———, ed. 1995. *The Cambridge Survey of World Migration*. Cambridge: Cambridge University Press.

———, and Zig Layton-Henry, eds. 1997. *The Politics of Migration*. Cheltenham,UK : Edward Elgar.

Coleman, David. 1993. "The World on the Move? International Migration in 1992." Paper presented at the European Population Conference, U.N.

Commission for Europe, U.N. Population Fund, Geneva, Switzerland. March.

Collins, Roger. 1986. *The Basques*. Oxford: Basil Blackwell.

———. 1983. *Early Medieval Spain: Unity in Diversity, 400–1000*. New York: St. Martin's Press.

Collinson, Sarah. 1994. *Europe and International Migration*. London: Royal Institute of International Affairs.

Comet I Codina, Robert. 1990. "Minority Languages in Spain." In *Minority Languages*, Monographic Series 71, *Western and Eastern European Papers. Fourth International Conference on Minority Languages*, vol. 2, ed. Durk Gorter et al. Clevedon, UK : Multilingual Matters.

Congleton, Roger D. 1995. "Ethnic Clubs, Ethnic Conflict, and Ethnic Nationalism." In *Nationalism and Rationality*, ed. Albert Breton et al. Cambridge: Cambridge University Press.

Connor, Walker. 1996. "Beyond Reason: The Nature of the Ethnonational Bond." In *Ethnicity*, ed. John Hutchinson and Anthony D. Smith. Oxford: Oxford University Press.

———. 1994. *Ethnonationalism: The Quest for Understanding*. Princeton: Princeton University Press.

———. 1993. "Diasporas and the Formation of Foreign Policy: The U.S. in Comparative Perspective." In *Diasporas in World Politics: The Greeks in Comparative Perspective*, ed. Dimitri C. Constas and Athanassios G. Platias. London: Macmillan.

———. 1984. "The Impact of Homelands upon Diasporas." In *Modern Diasporas in International Politics*, ed. Gabriel Sheffer. London: Croom Helm.

Connor, Walker. 1978. "A Nation Is a Nation, Is a State, Is an Ethnic Group, Is a..." *Ethnic and Racial Studies* 1, no. 4 (October): 377–400.

———. 1972. "Nation-Building or Nation-Destroying?" *World Politics* 24, no. 3: 319–55.

Constantinou, Stavros T. 1996. "Greek American Networks." In *The Networks of Diaspora*, ed. George Prévélakis. Nicosia: Cyprus Research Center KYKEM.

Conversi, Daniele. 1997. *The Basques, the Catalans and Spain: Alternative Routes to Nationalist Mobilisation.* London: Hurst.

Corcuera Atienza, Javier. 1991. *Política y derecho: La construcción de la autonomía vasca.* Madrid: Centro de Estudios Constitucionales.

Dahan, Michael, and Gabriel Sheffer. 2001. "Ethnic Groups and Distance Shrinking Technologies." *Nationalism and Ethnic Politics* 7, no. 1 (Spring): 85–107.

da Silva, Milton M. 1975. "Modernization and Ethnic Conflict: The Case of the Basques." *Comparative Politics* 7, no. 2 (January): 227–51.

Decroos, Jean F. 1983. *The Long Journey Home: Social Integration and Ethnicity Maintenance Among Urban Basques in the San Francisco Bay Region.* Reno: University of Nevada, Reno, Basque Studies Program.

Del Valle, Teresa. 1997. "El género en la construcción de la identidad nacionalista." *Ankulegi: Revista de Antropología Social* 1 (November): 9–22.

———. 1993. *Gendered Anthropology.* London: Routledge

———. 1985. "Basque Ethnic Identity in a Time of Rapid Change." In *Iberian Identity: Essays on the Nature of Identity in Portugal and Spain*, ed. Richard Herr and John H. R. Polt. Berkeley: University of California Institute of International Studies.

Demetriou, Madeline. 1998. "Diasporic Identities, Loyalty, and the Political Process." Paper presented at Aalborg University, School of Postgraduate Interdisciplinary Research on Interculturalism and Transnationality (SPIRIT).

De Ugalde, Martín. 1979. *Conflicto lingüístico en Euskadi*. Euskaltzaindia, SIADECO: Ediciones Vascas.

De Vos, George, and Lola Romanucci-Ross, eds. 1975. *Ethnic Identity: Cultural Continuities and Change*. Palo Alto, Calif.: Mayfield.

Díez Medrano, Juan.1995. *Divided Nations: Class, Politics, and Nationalism in the Basque Country and Catalonia*. Ithaca: Cornell University Press.

Douglas, Mary. 1983. "How Identity Problems Disappear." In *Identity: Personal and Socio-Cultural, A Symposium*, ed. Anita Jacobson-Widding. Atlantic Highlands, N.J.: Humanities Press.

Douglass, William A. 2003. *La vasconia global: Ensayos sobre las diásporas vascas*. Serie Urazandi, no. 2.Vitoria-Gasteiz: Eusko Jaurlaritzaren Argitalpen Zerbitzu Nagusia, Servicio Central de Publicaciones del Gobierno Vasco.

———. 2001. "The Basques." In *The Australian People: An Encyclopedia of the Nation, Its People, and Their Origins*, ed. James Jupp. 2d ed. Cambridge: Cambridge University Press.

———. 2000. "Basques in Australia." http:// www.euskonews.com Issue #72. 2000/3/24–31.

———. 1999. "Creating the New Basque Diaspora." In *Basque Politics and Nationalism on the Eve of the Millennium*, ed. William A. Douglass et al. Basque Studies Program Occasional Papers Series, no. 6. Reno: University of Nevada, Reno, Basque Studies Program.

Douglass, William A. 1996. *Azúcar margo: Vida y fortuna de los ortadores de caña italianos y vascos en la Australia tropical.* Trans. Xabier Cillero Goiriastuena. Bilbao: Servicio Editorial Universidad del País Vasco.

————. 1992. "Basque Ethnic Resurgence: Consolidation or Crisis of Heritage." Paper presented to the American Association of Anthropology, San Francisco.

————. 1989. "Annotations Regarding Basque Traditional Political Thought in the Sixteenth Century." In *Essays in Basque Social Anthropology and History,* ed. William A. Douglass. Basque Studies Program Occasional Papers Series, no. 4. Reno: University of Nevada, Reno, Basque Studies Program.

————. 1989. "Factors in the Formation of the New-World Basque Emigrant Diaspora." In *Essays in Basque Social Anthropology and History,* ed. William A. Douglass. Basque Studies Program Occasional Papers Series, no. 4. Reno: University of Nevada, Reno, Basque Studies Program.

————. 1985. "Politics, Ideology, and the Fueros in Vizcaya during the Initial Phase of the Liberal Triennium (1820)." In *Basque Politics: A Case Study in Ethnic Nationalism,* ed. William A. Douglass. Reno: Associated Faculty Press, Basque Studies Program, University of Nevada, Reno.

————. 1984. "Sheep Ranchers and Sugar Growers: Property Transmission in the Basque Immigrant Family of the American West and Australia." In *Households: Comparative and Historical Studies of the Domestic Group,* ed. Robert McC. Notting, Richard R. Wilk, and Eric J. Arnould. Berkeley: University of California Press.

————. 1980. "Inventing an Ethnic Identity: The First Basque Festival." *Halcyon 1980: A Journal of the Humanities:* 115–30.

Douglass, William A. 1979. "Basque Immigrants: Contrasting Patterns of Adaptation in Argentina and the American West." In *Currents in Anthropology: Essays in Honor of Sol Tax*, ed. Robert Hinshaw. New York: Mouton.

———, ed. 1989. *Essays in Basque Social Anthropology and History*. Reno: Basque Studies Program, University of Nevada, Reno.

———, ed. 1985. *Basque Politics: A Case Study in Ethnic Nationalism*. Reno: University of Nevada, Reno, Basque Studies Program.

———, and Gloria Totoricagüena. 1999. "Los vascos en la Argentina," in *La Inmigración Española en la Argentina*, ed Alejandro Fernandez and Jose C. Moya. Buenos Aires: Editorial Biblos.

———, and Jon Bilbao. 1975. *Amerikanuak: Basques in the New World*. Reno: University of Nevada Press.

Dow, James R., ed. 1991. *Language and Ethnicity: Focusschrift in Honor of Joshua A. Fishman on the Occasion of His 65th Birthday*. Vol. 2. Amsterdam: John Benjamins.

Dupla, Antonio. 1992. *Presencia vasca en América 1492–1992: Una mirada crítica*. Donostia-San Sebastián: Tercera Prensa-Hirugarren Prentsa.

Durando, Dario. 1993. "The Rediscovery of Ethnic Identity." *Telos: A Quarterly Journal of Critical Thought* 97 (Fall): 21–31.

Echave, Baltasar de. 1971. *Discursos de la antigüedad de la lengua Cantabra Bascongada*. Bilbao: Edición Separada de la Gran Enciclopedia Vasca.

Echeverría, Jeronima. 2000. "Expansion and Eclipse of the Basque Boarding House in the American West." *Nevada Historical Society Quarterly*, no. 2 (Summer): 127–39.

Echeverría, Jeronima. 1999. "The Basque *Hotelera*: Implications for Broader Study." In *The Basque Diaspora/La diáspora vasca*, ed. William A. Douglass, Carmelo Urza, Linda White, and Joseba Zulaika. Reno: Basque Studies Program, pp.239–48.

———. 1999. *Home Away from Home: A History of the Basque Boardinghouses*. Reno: University of Nevada Press.

Edwards, John. 1985. *Language, Society, and Identity*. Oxford: Basil Blackwell.

Eiras Roel, Antonio, ed. 1991. *La emigración española a ultramar, 1492–1914*. Madrid: Ediciones Tabapress.

Ekstrand, Lars, ed. 1986. *Ethnic Minorities and Immigrants in a Cross-Cultural Perspective*. Berwyn, Pa.: Swets North America.

Elazar, Daniel J. 1984. "The Jewish People as the Classic Diaspora: A Political Analysis." In *Modern Diasporas in International Politics*, ed. Gabriel Sheffer. London: Croom Helm.

Elkins, David J. 1997. "Globalization, Telecommunication, and Virtual Ethnic Communities." *International Political Science Review* 18, no. 2: 139–52.

Eller, Jack David, and Reed M. Coughlan. 1993. "The Poverty of Primordialism: The Demystification of Ethnic Attachments." *Ethnic and Racial Studies* 16, no. 2 (April): 183–202.

Epstein, A.L. 1978. *Ethos and Identity: Three Studies in Ethnicity*. London: Tavistock.

Erdmans, Mary Patrice. 1995. "Immigrants and Ethnics: Conflict and Identity in Chicago Polonia." *Sociological Quarterly* 36, no. 1: 175–95.

Eriksen, Thomas Hylland. 1993. *Ethnicity and Nationalism: Anthropological Perspectives*. London: Pluto Press.

Escobedo Mansilla, Ronald, Ana de Zabala Beascoechea, and Óscar Álvarez Gila, eds. 1996. *Emigración y redes sociales de los vascos en América.* Vitoria-Gasteiz: Servicio Editorial Universidad del País Vasco.

Esman, Milton J. 1995. "Ethnic Actors in International Politics." *Nationalism and Ethnic Politics* 1, no. 1 (Spring): 111–25.

———. 1986. "Diasporas and International Relations." In *Modern Diasporas in International Politics*, ed. Gabriel Sheffer. London: Croom Helm.

Esman, Milton J., and Shibley Telhami, eds. 1995. *International Organizations and Ethnic Conflict.* Ithaca: Cornell University Press.

Falcoff, Mark, and Fredrick B. Pike. 1982. *The Spanish Civil War, 1936–39: American Hemisphere Perspectives.* Lincoln: University of Nebraska Press.

Fawcett, James T. 1989. "Networks, Linkages, and Migration Systems." *International Migration Review* 23, no. 3: 671–80.

Featherstone, Mike. 1995. *Undoing Culture: Globalization, Postmodernism, and Identity.* London: Sage.

Federación de Entidades Vasco Argentinas. 1984. Vitoria-Gasteiz: Servicio Central de Publicaciones del Gobierno Vasco.

Felipe y Lorenzo, Emilio de. 1991. "El Real Seminario Bascongado de Vergara y sus alumnos de ultramar." In *América y los vascos: Presencia vasca en América*, ed. Jon Bilbao. Vitoria-Gasteiz: Gobierno Vasco Departamento de Cultura.

Fernández, Alberto. 1972. *Emigración republicana española (1939–1945).* Madrid: Gráficas Color.

Fernández de Casadevante Romani, Carlos. 1985. *La frontera hispano-francesa y las relaciones de vecindad: Especial referencia al sector fronterizo del País Vasco.* Bilbao: Servicio Editorial de la Universidad del País Vasco.

Fernández de Pinedo, Emiliano. 1993. *La emigración vasca a América, siglos XIX y XX.* Gijón, Asturias: Ediciones Jucar.

Finch, Henry. 1995. "Uruguayan Migration." In *The Cambridge Survey of World Migration,* ed. Robin Cohen. Cambridge: Cambridge University Press.

Fishman, Joshua. 1997. *In Praise of the Beloved Language: A Comparative View of Positive Ethnolinguistic Consciousness.* New York: Mouton de Gruyter.

————. 1989. *Language and Ethnicity in Minority Sociolinguistic Perspective.* Clevedon, UK: Multilingual Matters.

————, et al., eds. 1985. *The Rise and Fall of Ethnic Revival: Perspectives on Language and Ethnicity.* New York: Mouton.

Foley, Larry. 1967. "The Basques—Strongmen of the Canefields." *People Magazine* (Australia). October 18.

Galindez, Jesús de. 1984. *Presencia vasca en América.* Vitoria-Gasteiz: Servicio Central de Publicaciones del Gobierno Vasco.

Gans, Herbert J. 1994. "Symbolic Ethnicity and Symbolic Religiosity: Towards a Comparison of Ethnic and Religious Acculturation." *Ethnic and Racial Studies* 17, no. 4 (October): 577–89.

————. 1992. "Second Generation Decline: Scenarios for the Economic and Ethnic Futures of the Post-1965 America Immigrants." *Ethnic and Racial Studies* 15, no. 2 (April): 173–92.

————. 1979. "Symbolic Ethnicity: The Future of Ethnic Groups and Cultures in America." *Ethnic and Racial Studies* 2, no. 1 (January): 1–20.

Garcia, Caterina. 1995. "The Autonomous Communities and External Relations." In *Democratic Spain: Reshaping External Relations in a Changing World*, ed. Richard Gillespie, Fernando Rodrigo, and Jonathon Story. London: Routledge.

García de Cortázar, Fernando, and Manuel Montero. 1980. *Historia contemporánea del País Vasco: De las Cortes de Cádiz al Estatuto de Guernica*. San Sebastián: Editorial Txertoa.

García de Cortázar, José Angel, et al., eds. 1979. *Introducción a la historia medieval de Alava, Guipuzcoa y Vizcaya en sus textos*. San Sebastián: Editorial Txertoa.

Garmendia, Mari Karmen, and Xabier Aizpurua. 1990. "A Demolinguistic Analysis of the Basque Autonomous Community Derived from the Census of 1986." In *Minority Languages*. Monographic Series 71, *Western and Eastern European Papers. Fourth International Conference on Minority Languages*, vol. 2, ed. Durk Gorter et al. Clevedon, UK: Multilingual Matters.

Garritz, Amaya, and Javier Sanchiz. 1999. "Estudios vascos en México." In *The Basque Diaspora/La diáspora vasca*, ed. William A. Douglass, Carmelo Urza, Linda White, and Joseba Zulaika. Reno: Basque Studies Program, University of Nevada, Reno.

Geertz, Clifford. 1973. "The Integrative Revolution: Primordial Sentiments and Civil Politics in the New States." In *The Interpretation of Cultures: Selected Essays*. New York: Basic Books.

Gellner, Ernest. 1983. *Nations and Nationalism*. Ithaca: Cornell University Press.

Giddens, Anthony. 1991. *Modernity and Self-Identity*. Cambridge: Polity Press.

Giles, Howard, and Patricia Johnson. 1987. "Ethnolinguistic Identity Theory: Social Psychological Approach to Language Maintenance." *International Journal of the Sociology of Language* 68: 69–99.

Gjerde, Jon. 1997. *The Minds of the West: Ethnocultural Evolution in the Rural Middle West, 1830–1917.* Chapel Hill: University of North Carolina Press.

Glazer, Nathan, and Daniel P. Moynihan, eds. 1975. *Ethnicity: Theory and Experience.* Cambridge: Harvard University Press.

———. 1970. *Beyond the Melting Pot: The Negroes, Puerto Ricans, Jews, Italians, and Irish of New York City.* 2d ed. Cambridge, Mass.: MIT Press.

Glick Schiller, Nina, Linda Basch, and Christina Szanton Blanc. 1994. "From Migrant to Transmigrant: Theorizing Transnational Migration." *Anthropological Quarterly* 68, no. 1 (January): 48–63.

Gómez Prieto, Julia. 1991. "La emigración vizcaína hacia América. Los Indianos de Balmaseda: Siglos XVI–XIX." In *La emigración española a ultramar, 1492–1914,* ed. Antonio Eiras Roel. Madrid: Ediciones Tabapress.

Goyhenetxe, Eukeni. 1985. *Historia de Iparralde: Desde los orígenes a nuestros días.* Donostia-San Sebastián: Editorial Txertoa.

Graham, Helen, and Jo Labanyi, eds. 1995. *Spanish Cultural Studies: An Introduction. The Struggle for Modernity.* Oxford: Oxford University Press.

Greeley, Andrew M. 1974. *Ethnicity in the United States: A Preliminary Reconnaissance.* New York: John Wiley and Sons.

Greenwood, Davydd J. 1977. "Continuity in Change: Spanish Basque Ethnicity as a Historical Process." In *Ethnic Conflict in the Western World: Conference on Ethnic Pluralism and Conflict in Contemporary*

Western Europe and Canada, , ed. Milton Esman. Ithaca: Cornell University Press.

Grinberg, Leon, and Rebeca Grinberg. 1989. *Psychoanalytic Perspectives on Migration and Exile.* Trans. Nancy Festinger. New Haven: Yale University Press.

Grosby, Steven. 1994. "The Verdict of History: The Inexpugnable Tie of Primordiality—A Response to Eller and Coughlan." *Ethnic and Racial Studies* 17, no. 2 (January): 164–71.

Guaresti, Juan José. 1950. "Notas para un Apunte sobre : La influencia vasca en la Argentina." *Boletín del Instituto Americano de Estudios Vascos* 1, no. 1 (April–June).

Guibernau, Montserrat, and John Rex, eds. 1997. *The Ethnicity Reader: Nationalism, Multiculturalism, and Migration.* Cambridge: Polity Press.

Gurr, Ted Robert. 1993. *Minorities at Risk: A Global View of Ethnopolitical Conflicts.* Washington, D.C.: United States Institute of Peace Press.

———. 1993. "Why Minorities Rebel: A Global Analysis of Communal Mobilization and Conflict since 1945." *International Political Science Review* 14, no. 2 (April): 161–201.

Haarmann, Harald. 1986. "Language in Ethnicity: A View of Basic Ecological Relations." In *Contributions to the Sociology of Language,* no. 44, ed. Joshua A. Fishman. Berlin: Mouton de Gruyter.

Hall, Stuart. 1997. "Diaspora and Detours in Identity." In *Identity and Difference,* ed. Kathryn Woodward. London: Sage.

———. 1991. "Old and New Identities, Old and New Ethnicities." In *Culture, Globalization, and the World System: Contemporary Conditions for the*

Representation of Identity, ed. Anthony D. King. Basingstoke, UK : Macmillian Education.

Hansen, Marcus Lee. 1937. "Who Shall Inherit America?" In *American Immigrants and Their Generations: Studies and Commentaries on the Hansen Thesis After Fifty Years*, ed. Peter Kivisto and Dag Blanck. Urbana: University of Illinois Press, 1990.

Hardin, Russell. 1995. "Self-Interest, Group Identity." In *Nationalism and Rationality*, ed. Albert Breton et al. Cambridge: Cambridge University Press.

Harik, Iliya. 1984. "Modern Diasporas in International Politics." In *Diasporas and Communal Conflicts*, ed. Gabriel Sheffer. London: Croom Helm.

Hechter, Michael. 1996. "Ethnicity and Rational Choice Theory." In *Ethnicity*, ed. John Hutchinson and Anthony D. Smith. Oxford: Oxford University Press.

———. 1978. "Group Formation and the Cultural Division of Labor." *American Journal of Sociology* 84, no. 2: 293–319.

Held, David, et al. 1999. *Global Transformations: Politics, Economics, and Culture*. Stanford: Stanford University Press.

Helmreich, Stefan. 1992. "Kinship, Nation, and Paul Gilroy's Concept of Diaspora." *Diaspora* 2, no. 2 (Fall): 243–49.

Henry, Frances, ed. 1976. *Ethnicity in the Americas*. The Hague: Mouton.

Hertzberg, Arthur. 1996. "Israel and the Diaspora: A Relationship Reexamined." *Israel Affairs* 2, nos. 3-4 (Spring–Summer): 169–83.

Hobsbawm, Eric J. 1992. *Nations and Nationalism since 1780: Programme, Myth, Reality*. 2d ed. Cambridge: Cambridge University Press.

———, and Terence Ranger, eds. 1983. *The Invention of Tradition*. Cambridge: Cambridge University Press.

Hooson, David. 1994. *Geography and National Identity.* Oxford: Blackwell.

Horowitz, Donald L. 1985. *Ethnic Groups in Conflict.* Berkeley: University of California Press.

Huntington, Samuel. 1997. "The Erosion of American National Interest." *Foreign Affairs* 76, no. 5 (September–October): 28–49.

Hutchinson, John, and Anthony D. Smith, eds. 1996. *Ethnicity.* Oxford: Oxford University Press.

———, eds. 1994. *Nationalism.* Oxford: Oxford University Press.

Iberlin, Dollie, and David Romtvedt, eds. 1995. *Buffalotarrak: An Anthology of the Basque People of Buffalo, Wyoming.* Buffalo, Wyo.: Red Hills Publications.

Ignatieff, Michael. 1993. *Blood and Belonging: Journeys into the New Nationalism.* Toronto: Penguin Books.

Iriani Zalakain, Marcelino. 2000. *Hacer América: Los vascos en la pampa húmeda, Argentina (1840–1920).* Leioa: Universidad del País Vasco.

Jacob, James E. 1994. *Hills of Conflict: Basque Nationalism in France.* Reno: University of Nevada Press.

———. 1985. "Politics, Ideology, and the Fueros in Vizcaya during the Initial Phase of the Liberal Triennium (1820)." In *Basque Politics: A Case Study in Ethnic Nationalism,* ed. William A. Douglass. Reno: University of Nevada, Reno, Basque Studies Program.

Jacobson-Widding, Anita, ed. 1983. *Identity: Personal and Social-Cultural, A Symposium.* Atlantic Heights, N.J.: Humanities Press.

Jakobovits, Immanuel. 1991. "Israel-Diaspora Relations and Anglo-Jewish Perspective." In *Israel and Diaspora Jewry: Ideological and Political Perspectives,* ed. Eliezer Don-Yehiya. Vol. 3 of *Comparative Jewish Politics*. Jerusalem: Bar-Ilan University Press.

Jáuregui, Gurutz, José Manuel Castells, and Xabier Iriondo. 1997. *La institucionalización jurídica y política de Vasconia*. Donostia–San Sebastián: Eusko Ikaskuntza.

Jáuregui Bereciartu, Gurutz. 1986. *Contra el estado-nación: En torno al hecho y la cuestión nacional*. Madrid: Siglo XXI de España Editores.

———. 1981. *Ideología y estrategia política de ETA: Análisis de su evolución entre 1959 y 1968*. Madrid: Siglo XXI de España Editores.

Jenkins, Richard. 1997. *Rethinking Ethnicity: Arguments and Explorations*. London: Sage.

Jiménez de Aberasturi, Juan Carlos, coordinator. 1982. *Estudios de Historia Contemporánea del País Vasco*. San Sebastián: Haranburu Editor.

Jupp, James, and Marie Kabala, 1993. "The Ethnic Lobby and Immigration Policy." In *The Politics of Australian Immigration*, ed. James Jupp and Marie Kabala. Canberra: Australian Government Publishing Service.

Kamen, Henry. 1983. *Spain 1469–1714: A Society of Conflict*. London: Longman Group.

Kecmanovic, Dusan. 1996. *Mass Psychology of Ethnonationalism*. New York: Plenum Press.

Kedourie, Elie. 1993. *Nationalism*. 4th ed. Oxford: Blackwell.

Kenny, Michael. 1976. "Twentieth Century Spanish Expatriate Ties with the Homeland: Remigration and Its Consequences." In *The Changing Faces of Rural Spain*, ed. Joseph B. Aceves and William A. Douglass. New York: John Wiley and Sons.

King, Anthony. 1991. "Introduction: Spaces of Culture, Spaces of Knowledge." In *Culture, Globalization and the World-System: Contemporary Conditions* for the Representation of Identity, ed. Anthony King. Basingstock, UK: Macmillan Education.

King, Charles, and Neil J. Melvin, eds. 1998. *Nations Abroad: Diaspora Politics and International Relations in the Former Soviet Union*. Boulder, Colo.: Westview Press.

King, Russell, ed. 1993. *Mass Migrations in Europe: The Legacy and the Future*. London: Belhaven Press.

Kivisto, Peter. 1989. *The Ethnic Enigma: The Salience of Ethnicity for European Origin Groups*. Philadelphia: Balch Institute Press.

Kolor-Panov, Dona. 1996. "Video and the Diasporic Imagination of Selfhood: A Case Study of the Croatians in Australia." *Cultural Studies* 10, no. 2 (May): 288–314.

Lacarra, José Maria. 1972. *Historia política del Reino de Navarra: Desde sus orígenes hasta su incorporación a Castilla*. Vol. 1. Pamplona: Editorial Aranzadi.

Lafourcade, Maite. 1999. "Sistemas de herencia y transmisión de la propiedad en Iparralde bajo el Antiguo Régimen." In *Vasconia: Cuadernos de Historia-Geografía*. Donostia-San Sebastián: Eusko Ikaskuntza.

Landau, Jacob M. 1986. "Diaspora and Language." In *Modern Diasporas in International Politics*, ed. Gabriel Sheffer. London: Croom Helm.

Las Casas, Bartolomé de. 1575–1625?. *Apologética historia sumaria. Cuanto a las cualidades, dispusición, descripción, cielo y suelo destas tierras, y condiciones naturales, policias, repúblicas, manera de vivir, e costumbres de las gentes destas Indias occidentales y meridionales cuyo imperio soberano pertenece a los reyes de Castilla*, ed. Edmundo O'Gorman. Vols. 1 and 2. 3rd ed. Mexico City: Universidad Nacional Autónoma de México.

Lavie, Smadar, and Ted Swedenburg, eds. 1996. *Displacement, Diaspora, and Geographies of Identity.* Durham, N.C.: Duke University Press.

Legarreta, Dorothy. 1985. "Basque Refugee Children as Expatriates: Political Catalysts in Europe and America." In *Basque Politics: A Case Study in Ethnic Nationalism,* ed. William A. Douglass. Reno: Basque Studies Program Occasional Papers Series, no.2 Associated Faculty Press Inc. and Basque Studies Program.

———. 1984. *The Guernica Generation: Basque Refugee Children of the Spanish Civil War.* Reno: University of Nevada Press.

Leonardo, Micaela di. 1984. *The Varieties of Ethnic Experience: Kinship, Class, and Gender Among California Italian-Americans.* Ithaca: Cornell University Press.

Letamendia, Francisco. 1997. "Basque Nationalism and Cross-Border Co-operation Between the Southern and Northern Basque Countries." *Regional and Federal Studies* 7, no. 2 (Summer): 25–41.

Lettler, Willy, and M.A. Leguineche. 1967. "Cortadores de caña en Australia." *La Actualidad Española,* no. 804 (June).

Levitt, Peggy. 2001. *The Transnational Villagers.* Berkeley: University of California Press.

Levitt, Peggy, and Mary C. Waters, eds. 2002.*The Changing Face of Home: The Transnational Lives of the Second Generation.* New York: Russell Sage Foundation.

Lieberson, Stanley. 1985. "Unhyphenated Whites in the United States." *Ethnic and Racial Studies* 8, no. 1 (January): 159–80.

Lieberson, Stanley, and Mary Waters. 1988. *From Many Strands: Ethnic and Racial Groups in Contemporary America*. New York: Russell Sage Foundation.

Liebkind, Karmela. 1983. "Dimensions of Identity in Multiple Group Allegiance." In *Identity: Personal and Social-Cultural, A Symposium*, ed. Anita Jacobson-Widding. Atlantic Heights, N.J.: Humanities Press.

Liebman, Charles S. 1991. "Israel in the Mind of American Jewry." In *Israel and Diaspora Jewry: Ideological and Political Perspectives*, ed. Eliezer Don-Yehiya. Vol. 3 of *Comparative Jewish Politics*. Jerusalem: Bar-Ilan University Press.

Linz, Juan J. 1986. *Conflicto en Euskadi*. Madrid: Espasa Calpe.

———. 1985. *New Nationalisms and the Developed West: Toward Explanation*. Boston: Allen and Unwin.

Livermore, Harold. 1958. *A History of Spain*. London: George Allen & Unwin.

Llera Ramo, Francisco José. 1994. *Los vascos y la política. El proceso político vasco: Elecciones, partidos, opinión pública y legitimación en el País Vasco, 1977–1992*. Bilbo: Argitarapen Zerbitzua Euskal Herriko Uniberstitatea.

———. 1985. *Postfranquismo y fuerzas políticas en Euskadi: Sociología electoral del País Vasco*. Bilbao: Servicio Editorial Universidad del País Vasco.

Lyman, Stanford M., and William A. Douglass. 1973. "Ethnicity: Strategies of Collective and Individual Impression Management." *Social Research* 40, no. 4 (Summer): 344–65.

Lynch, John. 1964. *Empire and Absolutism, 1516–1598*. Vol. 1 of *Spain Under the Habsburgs*. Oxford: Basil Blackwell.

MacDonald, John S., and Leatrice D. MacDonald. 1974. "Chain Migration, Ethnic Neighbourhood Formation, and Social Networks." In *An Urban World*, ed. Charles Tilly. Boston: Little, Brown.

Macdonald, Nancy. 1987. *Homage to the Spanish Exiles: Voices from the Spanish Civil War*. New York: Human Sciences Press.

Madariaga, Salvador de. 1950. *Cuadro histórico de las Indias: Introducción a Bolívar*. Buenos Aires: Editorial Sudamericana.

Malkki, Liisa H. 1995. "Refugees and Exile: From 'Refugee Studies' to the National Order of Things." *Annual Review of Anthropology*.: 495–523.

Marenales Rossi, Marta. 1991. *La aventura vasca: Destino—Montevideo*. Montevideo: Centro Vasco Euskal Erria y Gobierno Vasco.

Marenales Rossi, Martha, and Juan Carlos Luzuriaga. 1990. *Vascos en el Uruguay*. Nuestras Raíces, no. 4. Montevideo: Editorial Nuestra Tierra.

Mar-Molinero, Clare, and Angel Smith, eds. 1996. *Nationalism and the Nation in the Iberian Peninsula: Competing and Conflicting Identities*. Oxford: Berg.

Márques Ortiz, Reyes. 1996. "Colectividad vasca y asociacionismo en Argentina." In *Emigración y redes sociales de los vascos en América*, ed. Ronald Escobedo Mansilla, Ana de Zabala Beascoechea, and Óscar Álvarez Gila. Vitoria-Gasteiz: Universidad del País Vasco.

Martín Rubio, Carmen. 1996. "Vascos en Potosí: Minas y mineros según una fuente inédita de Arzans y Vela." In *Emigración y redes sociales de los vascos en América*, ed. Ronald Escobedo Mansilla, Ana de Zabala Beascoechea, and Óscar Álvarez Gila. Vitoria-Gasteiz: Universidad del País Vasco.

Matsuo, Hisako. 1992. "Identificational Assimilation of Japanese Americans: A Reassessment of Primordial and Circumstantialism." *Sociological Perspectives* 35, no. 3: 505–52.

McAllister, Ian. 1995. "Occupational Mobility Among Immigrants: The Impact of Migration on Economic Success in Australia." *International Migration Review* 29, no. 2 (Summer): 441–67.

McKay, James. 1982. "An Explanatory Synthesis of Primordial and Mobilizationist Approaches to Ethnic Phenomena." *Ethnic and Racial Studies* 5, no. 4 (October): 395–420.

McKay, James, and Frank Lewins. 1978. "Ethnicity and the Ethnic Group: A Conceptual Analysis and Reformulation." *Ethnic and Racial Studies* 1, no. 4 (October): 412–27.

Medina, Xabier. 1997. *Los otros vascos: Las emigraciones vascas en el siglo XX*. Madrid: Editorial Fundamentos, Colección Ciencia.

Mettler, Willy, and M. A. Leguineche. 1967. "Cortadores de caña en Australia." *La Actualidad Española* 804 (June 1): 20–24.

Michelena, Luís. 1985. *Lengua e historia*. Madrid: Paraninfo.

Moch, Leslie Page. 1992. *Moving Europeans: Migration in Western Europe Since 1650*. Bloomington: Indiana University Press.

Monreal Zia, Gregorio. 1999. "El estatuto en su perspectiva histórica." *Euskonews & Media* 51 (22–29 October). www.euskonews.com.

———. 1996. "La institucionalización pública y la especificidad de las juntas generales." *Revista Internacional de los Estudios Vascos* 41, no. 2: 455–58.

———. 1992. "Larramendi: Madurez y crisis del régimen foral." In *Manuel de Larramendi: Hirugarren mendeurrena, 1690–1990*, ed. Joseba Andoni Lakarra. Andoain: Andoain Udala.

Monreal Zia, Gregorio. 1989. "Annotations Regarding Basque Traditional Political Thought in the Sixteenth Century." In *Essays in Basque Social Anthropology and History*, ed. William A. Douglass. Basque Studies Program Occasional Papers Series, no. 4. Reno: University of Nevada, Reno, Basque Studies Program.

Moreno, Luís. 1995. "Multiple Ethnoterritorial Concurrence in Spain." *Nationalism and Ethnic Politics* 1, no. 1 (Spring): 11–32.

Moya, Jose C. 1998. *Cousins and Strangers: Spanish Immigrants in Buenos Aires, 1850–1930*. Berkeley: University of California Press.

Moynihan, Daniel Patrick. 1993. *Pandemonium: Ethnicity in International Politics*. Oxford: Oxford University Press.

Murphy, Alexander, and Nancy Leeper. 1996. "Southeast Europeans in the Cities of the West: Changing Networks in a Changing World." In *The Network of Diasporas*, ed. Georges Prévélakis. Nicosia: Cyprus Research Center KYKEM.

Nadal, Jorge. 1966. La población española

Nagel, Joanne. 1995. "American Indian Ethnic Renewal: Politics and the Resurgence of Identity." *American Sociological Review* 60 (December): 947–65.

———. 1994. "Constructing Ethnicity: Creating and Recreating Ethnic Identity and Culture." *Social Problems* 41, no. 1 (February): 152–76.

Neto, Felix. 1995. "Predictors of Satisfaction with Life Among Second Generation Migrants." *Social Indicators Research: An Interdisciplinary Journal for Quality-of-Life Measurement* 35, no. 1 (May): 93–116.

Newman, Saul. 1996. *Ethnoregional Conflict in Democracies: Mostly Ballots, Rarely Bullets.*

Contributions in Political Science, no. 373. Westport, Conn.: Greenwood Press.

Nuñez Astrain, Luis C. 1997. *The Basques: Their Struggle for Independence*. Trans. Meic Stephens. Falmouth, Wales: Welsh Academic Press.

———. 1977. *La sociedad vasca actual*. San Sebastián: Editorial Txertoa.

Okamura, Jonathan Y. 1998. *Imagining the Filipino American Diaspora: Transnational Relations, Identities, and Communities*. London: Garland.

O'Leary, Brendan. 1998. "Ernest Gellner's Diagnoses of Nationalism: A Critical Overview, or, What Is Living and What Is Dead in Ernest Gellner's Philosophy of Nationalism?" In *The State of the Nation: Ernest Gellner and the Theory of Nationalism*, ed. John Hall. Cambridge: Cambridge University Press.

Olzak, Susan. 1983. "Contemporary Ethnic Mobilization." *Annual Review of Sociology* 9: 355–74.

———, and Joane Nagel, eds. 1986. *Competitive Ethnic Relations*. Orlando: Academic Press.

Ordaz Romay, Mari Ángeles. 1996. "El FBI y los vascos del exilio de 1939 en Estados Unidos." In *Emigración y redes sociales de los vascos en América*, ed. Ronald Escobedo Mansilla, Ana de Zabala Beascoechea, and Óscar Álvarez Gila. Vitoria-Gasteiz: Universidad del País Vasco.

Ormond, P. S. 1926. *The Basques and Their Country: Dealing Chiefly with the French Provinces*. London: Simpkin, Marshall, Hamilton, Kent and Company.

Orúe, Carlos. 1996. *Sydneyko Gure Txoko: 30 Urteurrena*. Newtown, New South Wales: El Faro Printing.

Ossa Echaburu, Rafael. 1963. *Pastores y pelotaris vascos en U.S.A.* Bilbao: Ediciones de la Caja de Ahorros Vizcaína.

Paquette, Mary Grace. 1982. *Basques to Bakersfield.* Bakersfield, Calif.: Kern County Historical Society.

Palacios Fernández, Emilio, ed. *Memoria del exilio vasco: Cultura, pensamiento y literatura de loa escritores transterrados en 1939.* Madrid: Editorial Biblioteca Nueva.

Panossian, Razmik. 1998. "The Armenians: Conflicting Identities and the Politics of Division." In *Nations Abroad: Diaspora Politics and International Relations in the Former Soviet Union,* ed. Charles King and Neil J. Melvin. Boulder, Colo.: Westview Press.

Payne, Stanley G. 1985. "Navarra and Basque Nationalism." In *Basque Politics: A Case Study in Ethnic Nationalism,* ed. William A. Douglass. Reno: University of Nevada, Reno, Basque Studies Program.

————. 1975. *Basque Nationalism.* Reno: University of Nevada Press.

Peltz, Rakhmiel. 1991. "Ethnic Identity and Aging: Children of Jewish Immigrants Return to Their First Language." In *Language and Ethnicity: Focusshrift in Honor of Joshua A. Fishman,* ed. James R. Dow. Vol. 2. Amsterdam: John Benjamins.

Pérez-Agote, Alfonso. 1999. *La identidad colectiva y su dimensión política.* Leioa: Facultad de Ciencias Sociales, Universidad del País Vasco.

————. 1987. *El nacionalismo vasco a la salida del Franquismo.* Madrid: Centro de Investigaciones Sociológicas.

————. 1986. "The Role of Religion in the Definition of a Symbolic Conflict: Religion and the Basque Problem." *Social Compass (International Review of Sociology of Religion)* 33, no. 4: 419–35.

Pérez-Agote, Alfonso. 1984. *La reproducción del nacionalismo: El caso vasco.* Madrid: Centro de Investigaciones Sociológicas.

———, ed.1989. *Sociología del nacionalismo.* Vitoria-Gasteiz: Servicio Editorial Universidad del País Vasco Gobierno Vasco.

———, Jesús Azcona, and Ander Gurrutxaga. 1997. *Mantener la identidad: Los vascos del Río Carabelas.* Bilbao: Servicio Editorial de la Universidad del País Vasco.

Pérez de Arenaza Múgica, José Maria, and Javier Lasagabaster Olazábal, eds. 1991. *América y los vascos: Presencia vasca en América.* Gasteiz: Departamento de Cultura, Gobierno Vasco.

Petersen, William, Michael Novak, and Phillip Gleason, eds. 1982. *Concepts of Ethnicity.* Cambridge: Belknap Press of Harvard University Press.

Phinney, Jean S., and Mary Jane Rotheram. 1987. *Children's Ethnic Socialization: Pluralism and Development.* London: Sage.

Pieterse, Jan Nederveen. 1996. "Varieties of Ethnic Politics and Ethnicity Discourse." In *The Politics of Difference: Ethnic Premises in a World of Power,* ed. Edwin N. Wilmsen and Patrick McAllisten. Chicago: University of Chicago Press.

Pildain Salazar, María Pilar. 1984. *Ir a América: La emigración vasca a América.* Donostia–San Sebastián: Sociedad Guipuzcoana de Ediciones y Publicaciones.

Portes, Alejandro. 1999. "Conclusion: Towards a New World. The Origins and Effects of Transnational Activities." *Ethnic and Racial Studies* 22, no. 2 (March): 463–77.

———, Luis E. Guarniza, and Patricia Landolt. 1999. "The Study of Transnationalism: Pitfalls and Promise of an Emergent Research Field." *Ethnic and Racial Studies* 22, no. 2 (March): 217–37.

Portes, Alejandro. , and Rubén G. Rumbaut. 1990. *Immigrant America: A Portrait.* Berkeley: University of California Press.

Preston, Paul. 1994. *Franco: A Biography.* New York: Basic Books.

————. 1990. *The Politics of Revenge: Fascism and the Military in Twentieth-Century Spain.* London: Unwin Hyman.

Prévélakis, Georges, ed. 1996. *The Network of Diasporas.* Nicosia: Cyprus Research Center KYKEM.

Querol, Javier. 1959. "Al Margen de un Congreso." *Sábado Gráfico,* no. 166 (December 5).

Quijada, Mónica. 1991. *Aires de república, Aires de cruzada: La Guerra Civil Española en Argentina.* Barcelona: Sendai Ediciones.

Quiroz Paz-Soldán, Eusebio. 1996. "Los vascos en la ciudad de Arequipa." In *Emigración y redes sociales de los vascos en América,* ed. Ronald Escobedo Mansilla, Ana de Zabala Beascoechea, and Óscar Álvarez Gila. Vitoria-Gasteiz: Universidad del País Vasco.

Ramirez Goicoechea, Eugenia. 1991. *De jóvenes y sus identidades: Socioantropología de la etnicidad de Euskadi.* Madrid: Siglo XX de España Editores, Centro de Investigaciones Sociológicas.

Roldán, José Manuel. 1989. *Historia de España.* Madrid: Ediciones Eurolatinas.

Roosens, Eugene E. 1989. *Creating Ethnicity: The Process of Ethnogenesis.* Frontiers of Anthropology Series, no. 5. London: Sage.

Rowles, Graham, and Shularrit Reinharz. 1988. *Qualitative Gerontology.* New York: Springer.

Rubinstein, William. David. 1995. "Melbourne Jewry: A Diaspora Community with a Vigorous Jewish Identity." *Jewish Journal of Sociology* 37, no. 2 (December): 81–99.

Ruiz de Azua, Estibaliz. 1992. *Vascongadas y América*. Madrid: Editorial MAPFRE.

Ruiz Olabuénaga, José Ignacio, et al. 1983. *La lucha del euskera en la Comunidad Autónoma Vasca: Una encuesta básica—conocimiento, uso actitudes*. Gasteiz: Servicio Central de Publicaciones del Gobierno Vasco.

Rumbaut, Ruben G. 1994. "The Crucible Within: Ethnic Identity, Self-Esteem, and Segmented Assimilation Among Children of Immigrants." *International Migration Review* 28, no. 4 (Winter): 748–94.

Sachdev, Itesh, and Richard Bourhis. 1990. "Language and Social Identification." In *Social Identity Theory: Constructive and Critical Advances*, ed. Dominic Abrams and Michael A. Hogg. London: Harvester Wheatsheaf.

Safran, William. 1995. "Ethnicity and Citizenship: The Canadian Case." *Nationalism and Ethnic Politics* 1, no. 3 (Autumn): 107–11.

———. 1995. "Nations, Ethnic Groups, States, and Politics: A Preface and an Agenda." *Nationalism and Ethnic Politics* 1, no. 1 (Spring): 1–10.

———. 1991. "Diasporas in Modern Societies: Myths of Homeland and Return." *Diasporas: A Journal of Transnational Studies* 1, no. 1: 83–98.

Sainz de la Maza, Karmelo. 1994. Speech given to the Basque Parliament of Euskadi, quoted in *Law of Relations with Basque Communities outside the Autonomous Community of the Basque Country*, Vitoria-Gasteiz: Servicio Central de Publicaciones del Gobierno Vasco.

Sanchez, Maria-José. 1992. "Les Espagnols en Belgique au XXe Siècle." In *Histoire des étrangers et de l'Immigration en Belgique: De la préhistoire à nos jours.* Brussels: Editions Vie Ouvrière, Centre Bruxellois d'Action Interculturelle.

Sánchez-Albornoz, Claudio. 1978. *El régimen de la tierra en el reino asturleonés hace mil años.* Buenos Aires: Instituto de Historia de España, Universidad de Buenos Aires.

Sandberg, Neil C. 1974. *Ethnic Identity and Assimilation: The Polish-American Community.* New York: Praeger.

San Sebastián, Koldo. 1998. *El exilio vasco en América: 1936–1946. Acción del gobierno.* Donostia–San Sebastián: Editorial Txertoa.

————. 1991. *The Basque Archives: Vascos en Estados Unidos (1939–1943).* Donostia–San Sebastián: Editorial Txertoa.

San Sebastián, Koldo, and Peru Ajuria. 1989. *El exilio vasco en Venezuela.* Vitoria-Gasteiz: Servicio Central de Publicaciones Gobierno Vasco.

Santiso González, Maria Concepción. 1991. "La segunda guerra Carlista y su repercusión en la emigración Guipuzcoana a América." In *La emigración española a ultramar, 1492–1914,* ed. Antonio Eiras Roel. Madrid: Ediciones Tabapress.

Sarrailh de Ihartza, Fernando. 1964. *Vasconia.* Buenos Aires: Ediciones Norbait.

Sarramone, Alberto. Sayas Abengoechea, Juan José. 1999. *Los abuelos vascos que vinieron de Francia.* Buenos Aires: Editorial Biblos Azul.

————.1999. "De Vascones a Romanos para volver a ser Vascones." *Revista Internacional de los Estudios Vascos* 44: 147–84.

————. 1995. *Los abuelos vascos en el Río de la Plata.* Buenos Aires: Editorial Biblos Azul.

Sarramone, Alberto.1994. *Los vascos en la antigüedad*.
Madrid: Ediciones Cátedra.

Scott, George M., Jr. 1990. "A Resynthesis of the
Primordial and Circumstantial Approaches to Ethnic
Group Solidarity: Towards an Explanatory Model."
Ethnic and Racial Studies 13, no. 2 (April): 147–71.

Scott, William A., Ruth Scott, and John Stumpf. 1989.
*Adaptation of Immigrants: Individual Differences
and Determinants*. Oxford: Pergamon Press.

Shafir, Gershon. 1995. *Immigrants and Nationalists:
Ethnic Conflict and Accommodation in Catalonia, the
Basque Country, Latvia, and Estonia*. Albany: State
University of New York Press.

Shain, Yossi. 1994. "Ethnic Diasporas and U.S. Foreign
Policy." *Political Science Quarterly* 109, no. 5
(Winter): 811–41.

———. 1994. "Marketing the Democratic Creed
Abroad: U.S. Diasporic Politics in the Era of
Multiculturalism." *Diaspora: A Journal of
Transnational Studies* 3, no. 1 (Spring): 85–111.

———. 1989. *The Frontiers of Loyalty: Political Exiles
in the Age of the Nation-State*. Middleton, Conn.:
Wesleyan University Press.

———. ed. 1991. *Governments-in-Exile in the
Contemporary World of Politics*. London: Routledge,
Chapman and Hall.

———, and Juan J. Linz. 1995. *Between States: Interim
Governments and Democratic Transitions*. New York:
Cambridge University Press.

Sheffer, Gabriel, 2003. *Diaspora Politics: At Home
Abroad*. Cambridge: Cambridge University Press.

———. 1996. "Whither the Study of Ethnic Diasporas?
Some Theoretical, Definitional, Analytical, and
Comparative Considerations." In *The Network of*

Diasporas, ed. Georges Prévélakis. Nicosia: Cyprus Research Center KYKEM.

Shain, Yossi. 1994. "Ethno-National Diasporas and Security." *Survival* 36, no. 1 (Spring): 60–79.

———, ed. 1986. *Modern Diasporas in International Politics*. London: Croom Helm.

Shils, Edward. 1981. *Tradition*. London: Faber and Faber.

Siegrist de Gentile, Nora, and Óscar Álvarez Gila. 1998. *De la Ría del Nervión al Río de la Plata: Estudio histórico de un proceso migratorio, 1750–1850*. Pamplona: Newbook Ediciones.

Simic, Andrei. 1985. "Ethnicity as a Resource for the Aged: An Anthropological Perspective." *Journal of Applied Gerontology* 4: 6–17.

Simon, Rita James, and Caroline B. Brettle, eds. 1986. *International Migration: The Female Experience* Totowa, N.J.: Rowan and Allanheld.

Slobin, Mark. 1994. "Music in Diaspora: The View from Euro-America." *Diaspora* 3, no. 3 (Winter): 243–51.

Smith, Anthony D. 1995. *Nations and Nationalism in a Global Era*. Cambridge: Polity Press.

———. 1995. "Zionism and Diaspora Nationalism." *Israel Affairs* 2, no. 2 (Winter): 1–19.

———. 1994. "The Problem of National Identity: Ancient, Medieval and Modern?" *Ethnic and Racial Studies* 17, no. 3 (July): 375–99.

———. 1991. *National Identity*. London: Penguin Books.

———. 1986. *The Ethnic Origins of Nations*. Oxford: Blackwell.

———. 1984. "Negotiating Ethnicity in an Uncertain Environment." *Ethnic and Racial Studies* 7, no. 3: 360–72.

———. 1983. *Theories of Nationalism*. 2d ed. New York: Holmes and Meier.

Smith, Anthony D. 1981. *The Ethnic Revival*. Cambridge: Cambridge University Press.

Smolicz, J. J. 1977. "Australia: From Migrant Country to Multicultural Nation." *International Migration Review* 31, no. 1 (Spring): 171–86.

Sørensen, Ninna Nyberg. 1995. "Roots, Routes, and Transnational Attractions: Dominican Migration, Gender, and Cultural Change." In *Ethnicity, Gender, and the Subversion of Nationalism*, ed. Fiona Wilson and Bodil Folke Frederiksen. London: Frank Cass.

Sowell, Thomas. 1996. *Migrations and Cultures: A World View*. New York: Basic Books.

———. 1981. *Ethnic America: A History*. New York: Basic Books.

Spicer, Edward. 1971. "Persistent Identity Systems." *Science* 174, no. 4011: 795–800.

Stack, John F., Jr., ed. 1981. *Ethnic Identities in a Transnational World*. Westport, Conn.: Greenwood Press.

Stevens, Christine A. 1995. "The Illusion of Social Inclusion: Cambodian Youth in South Australia." *Diaspora* 4, no. 1: 59–75.

Stoller, Eleanor Palo. 1996. "Sauna, Sisu, and Sibelius: Ethnic Identity Among Finnish Americans." *Sociological Quarterly* 37, no. 1: 146–75.

Suárez Fernández, Luís. 1959. *Navegación y comercio en el Golfo de Vizcaya: Un estudio sobre la política marinera de la casa de Trastamara*. Madrid: Consejo Superior de Investigaciones Científicas, Escuela de Estudios Medievales.

Subtelny, Orest. 1991. *Ukrainians in North America: An Illustrated History*. Toronto: University of Toronto Press.

Tajfel, Henri. 1982. *Social Identity and Intergroup Relations*. Cambridge: Cambridge University Press.

Tajfel, Henri. 1981. *Human Groups and Social Categories*. Cambridge: Cambridge University Press.

———, ed. 1984. *The Social Dimension: European Development in Social Psychology*. Vol. 2. Cambridge: Cambridge University Press.

———, ed. 1978. *Differentiation Between Social Groups: Studies in the Social Psychology of Intergroup Relations*. London: Academic Press.

Tajfel, Henri, and Turner, J. C. 1979. "An Integrative Theory of Intergroup Conflict." In *The Social Psychology of Intergroup Relations*, ed. S. Worchel and W. G. Austin. Monterey, Calif.: Brooks-Cole.

Tamayo Salaberri, Virginia. 1994. *La autonomía vasca contemporánea: Foralidad y estatutismo (1975–1979)*. San Sebastián: Instituto Vasco de Administración Pública.

Tejerina Montana, Benjamín. 1992. *Nacionalismo y lengua: Los procesos de cambio lingüístico en el País Vasco*. Madrid: Centro de Investigaciones Sociológicas, Siglo Veintiuno de España.

Temple, Bogusia. 1996. "Time Travels: Time, Oral Histories, and British-Polish Identities." *Time and Society* 5 (February): 85–96.

Thomas, Hugh. 2001. *The Spanish Civil War*. New York: The Modern Library.

Tilly, Charles. 1990. "Transplanted Networks." In *Immigration Reconsidered: History, Sociology, and Politics*, ed. Virginia Yans-McLaughlin. New York: Oxford University Press.

———, ed. 1974. *An Urban World*. Boston: Little, Brown.

Tölölyan, Khachig. 1996. "Rethinking Diaspora(s): Stateless Power in the Transnation Moment." *Diaspora* 5, no. 1: 3–36.

Totoricagüena, Gloria. 2004. *The Basques of New York: A Cosmopolitan Experience*. 2d ed. Basque Migration

and Diaspora Studies Series, no. 2. Reno: Center for
Basque Studies, University of Nevada, Reno.

Totoricagüena, Gloria. 2004. *Identity, Culture, and
Politics: Comparing the Basque Diaspora.* Reno:
University of Nevada Press.

———. 2003. *The Basques of Boise: Dreamers and
Doers.* Urazandi: Basques Across the Seas Series, no.
3. Vitoria-Gasteiz: Central Publication Service of the
Basque Government.

———. 2003. *Diáspora vasca comparada: Etnicidad,
cultura, y política en las colectividades.* Serie
Urazandi, no. 1. Vitoria-Gasteiz: Eusko Jaurlaritza.

———. 2003. "Euskal Herria visto desde la diáspora:
Análisis de las relaciones institucionales entre Euskal
Herria y la diáspora vasca." *Eusko Ikaskuntza XV
Congreso Internacional.* Donostia–San Sebastián:
Eusko Ikaskuntza.

———. 2003. "Identities Across Borders." Conference of
the Armenian Institute. London, England. February
2003.

———. 2003. "Interconnected Disconnectedness: How
Diaspora Basque Women Maintain Ethnic Identity."
In *Amatxi, Amuma, Amona: Writings in Honor
of Basque Women,* ed. Linda White and Cameron
Watson. Reno: Center for Basque Studies, University
of Nevada, Reno.

———. 2003. "NOKA: Euskal emakume artean."
Emakunde, no. 51 (June).

———. 2002. "Vascos en el Oeste Americano." In
Enciclopedia General Ilustrada del País Vasco.
www.eusko-ikaskuntza.org. Donostia–SanSebastián:
Editorial Auñamendi.

———. 2001. "Una aproximación al desarrollo de la
diáspora vasca." In *Kanpoko Etxe berria: Emigración*

vasca a América siglos XIX–XX. Bilbao: Museo Arqueológico, Etnográfico e Histórico Vasco.

Totoricagüena, Gloria. 2001. "La identidad contemporánea de los vascos en la diáspora." *Eusko Ikaskuntza Euskonews and Media Electronic Journal*, no. 121 (May). www.euskonews.com.

———. 2001. "The North American Basque Organizations." *Eusko Ikaskuntza Euskonews and Media Electronic Journal*, no. 119 (April). www.euskonews.com.

———. 2000. "Celebrating Basque Diasporic Identity in Ethnic Festivals: Anatomy of a Basque Community." *Revista Internacional de Estudios Vascos* 45, no. 2 (Fall): 569–98.

———. 2000. "Downloading Identity in the Basque Diaspora: Utilizing the Internet to Create and Maintain Ethnic Identity." *Nevada Historical Society Quarterly* 43, no. 2 (Summer): 140–54.

———. 2000. "Izan zirelako gara, izan garelako izango gara. Because of Them We Are. Because of Us They Will Be." *Eusko Etxea*, no. 47, pp 16–23.

———. 1999. "Shrinking World, Expanding Diaspora: Globalization and Basque Diasporic Identity." In *The Basque Diaspora/La diaspora Vasca*, ed. William A. Douglass, Carmelo Urza, Linda White, and Joseba Zulaika. Reno: University of Nevada, Reno, Basque Studies Program and University of Nevada Press.

———, with William A. Douglass. 1999. "Los vascos en la Argentina." In *La inmigración española en la Argentina*, ed. Alejandro Fernández and José. Moya. Buenos Aires: Editorial Biblos.

Tovar, Antonio. 1957. *The Basque Language*. Trans. Herbert Pierrepont Houghton. Philadelphia: University of Pennsylvania Press.

Tuñón de Lara, Manuel, et al. 1987. *La Guerra Civil en el País Vasco: 50 años después*. Bilbao: Servicio Editorial Universidad del País Vasco.

Turuzeta, Josu. 1995. *Cien años de nacionalismo vasco, 1895–1995*. Bilbao: Editorial Iparraguirre.

Tusell, Javier, and Alicia Alted. 1991. "The Government of the Spanish Republic in Exile: (1939–1977)." In *Governments-in-Exile in Contemporary World Politics*, ed. Yossi Shain. London: Routledge, Chapman and Hall.

Tusell, Javier, et al., eds. 1995. *Historia de la transición y consolidación democrática en España (1975–1986)*. Vol. 1 of *International Congress: History of the Transition and the Democratic Consolidation in Spain (1975–1986)*. Department of Contemporary History, UNED and UNAM. Madrid: Pardo.

Twining, William. 1991. *Issues of Self-Determination*. Aberdeen: Aberdeen University Press.

Ugalde Solano, Mercedes. 1993. *Mujeres y nacionalismo vasco: Genesis y desarollo de Emakume Abertzale Batza, 1906–1936*. Bilbao: Servicio Editorial Universidad del País Vasco.

Ugalde Zubiri, Alexander. 1996. *La acción exterior del nacionalismo vasco, (1890–1939): Historia, pensamiento y relaciones internacionales*. Bilbao: Gobierno Vasco Colección Tesis Doctorales, Instituto Vasco de Administración Pública.

Untracht, Oppi. 1997. *Traditional Jewelry of India*. London: Thames and Hudson.

Urla, Jacqueline. 1988. 1993. "Cultural Politics in an Age of Statistics: Numbers, Nations, and the Making of Basque Identity." *American Ethnologist* 20, no. 4: 818–43.

Urla, Jacqueline. "Ethnic Protest and Social Planning: A Look at Basque Language Revival." *Cultural Anthropology* 3, no. 4 (November): 379–94.

Urquijo, Iñaki Bernardo. 1993. *Galindez: La tumba abierta. Los vascos y los Estados Unidos.* Vitoria-Gasteiz: Servicio Central de Publicaciones del Gobierno Vasco.

Urza, Carmelo. 1993. *Solitude: Art and Symbolism in the National Basque Monument.* Reno: University of Nevada Press.

Van den Berghe, Pierre L. 1996. "Does Race Matter?" In *Ethnicity*, ed. John Hutchinson and Anthony D. Smith. Oxford: Oxford University Press.

———. 1981. *The Ethnic Phenomenon.* New York: Elsevier.

———. 1978. "Race and Ethnicity: A Sociobiological Perspective." *Ethnic and Racial Studies* 1, no. 4 (October): 401–11.

Van Hear, Nicolas. 1998. *New Diasporas: The Mass Exodus, Dispersal and Regrouping of Migrant Communities.* London: UCL Press.

Van Houdenhoven, Jan Pieter, and Tineke M. Willemsen, eds. 1989. *Ethnic Minorities: Social Psychological Perspectives.* Amsterdam: Swets and Zeitlinger.

Van Knippenburg, Ad F. M. 1984. "Intergroup Differences in Group Perceptions." In *The Social Dimension: European Development in Social Psychology*, ed. Henri Tajfel. Vol. 2. Cambridge: Cambridge University Press.

Vázquez de Prada Vallejo, Valentín, and Jesus Mari Usunariz Garayoa. 1991. "La emigración navarra hacia América en el siglo XVII." In *América y los vascos: Presencia vasca en América*, ed. Jon Bilbao. Gasteiz: Departamento de Cultura, Gobierno Vasco.

Vertovec, Steven. 1999. "Conceiving and Researching Transnationalism." *Ethnic and Racial Studies* 22, no. 2 (March): 447–62.

Waters, Mary C. 1990. *Ethnic Options: Choosing Identities in America*. Berkeley: University of California Press.

Waters, Tony. 1995. "Towards a Theory of Ethnic Identity and Migration: The Formation of Ethnic Enclaves by Migrant Germans in Russia and North America." *International Migration Review* 29, no. 2 (Summer): 515–44.

Watson, Cameron. 2003. *Modern Basque History: Eighteenth Century to the Present*. Basque Textbook Series. Reno: Center for Basque Studies.

Weber-Newth, Inge. 1995. "Ethnic Germans Come Home to the Fatherland." *Debatte* 1: 126–42.

Weinrich, Peter. 1986. "Identity Development in Migrant Offspring: Theory and Practice." In *Ethnic Minorities and Immigrants in a Cross-Cultural Perspective*, ed. Lars Ekstrand. Berwyn, Penn.: Swets North America.

Wicklund, Robert A., and Peter M. Gollwitzer. *Symbolic Self-Completion*. Hillsdale, N.J.: Lawrence Erlbaum Associates. 1982.

Wilson, Andrew. 1998. "The Ukrainians: Engaging the Eastern Diaspora." In *Nations Abroad: Diaspora Politics and International Relations in the Former Soviet Union*, ed. Charles King and Neil J. Melvin. Boulder, Colo.: Westview Press.

Wilson, Fiona, and Bodil Folke Frederiksen, eds. 1995. *Ethnicity, Gender, and the Subversion of Nationalism*. London: Frank Cass.

Winland, Daphne N. 1995. "We Are Now an Actual Nation: The Impact of National Independence on the Croatian Diaspora in Canada." *Diaspora* 4, no. 1 (Spring): 3–29.

Yancey, William, Eugene Ericksen, and Richard Juliani. 1976. "Emergent Ethnicity: A Review and a Reformulation." *American Sociological Review* 41 (June): 391–403.

Yinger, Milton J. 1985. "Ethnicity." *Annual Review of Sociology* 11: 151–80.

———. 1981. "Toward a Theory of Assimilation and Dissimilation." *Ethnic and Racial Studies* 4, no. 3 (July): 249–64.

Zabaleta, Iñaki. 1999. "The Basques in the International Press: Coverage by the *New York Times* (1950–1996)." In *Basque Politics and Nationalism on the Eve of the Millenium*, ed. William A. Douglass et al. Basque Studies Program Occasional Papers Series, no. 6. Reno: University of Nevada, Reno, Basque Studies Program.

Zirakzadeh, Cyrus Ernesto. 1991. *A Rebellious People: Basques, Protests, and Politics.* Reno: University of Nevada Press.

Zubiri, Nancy. 1998. *A Travel Guide to Basque America: Families, Feasts, and Festivals.* Reno: University of Nevada Press.

Zulaika, Joseba. 1998. "Tropics of Terror: From Guernica's 'Natives' to Global 'Terrorists." *Social Identities* 4, no. 1: 93–108.

BASQUE GOVERNMENT OFFICIAL PUBLICATIONS

1999. Eusko Jaurlaritza–Basque Government of Euskadi. *World Congress on Basque Communities, 1999.* Vitoria-Gasteiz: Eusko Jaurlaritza.

1995. Eusko Jaurlaritza–Basque Government of Euskadi. *Euskaldunak Munduan, Building the Future. Congress of Basque Communities, 1995.* Vitoria-Gasteiz: Eusko Jaurlaritza.

1994. Law of Relations with Basque Communities Outside the Autonomous Community of the Basque Country. Vitoria-Gasteiz: Eusko Jaurlaritza Argitalpen Zerbitzu Nagusia.

1992. General Secretary for Linguistic Policy. *Comparencia, a petición propia, de la Secretaría General de Política Lingüística ante la Comisión de Instituciones e Interior del Parlamento Vasco.* Vitoria-Gasteiz: Gobierno Vasco.

1992. *Descripción general da la situación sociolinguística da la Comunidad Autónoma del País Vasco.* Vitoria-Gasteiz: Gobierno Vasco.

1991. General Secretary for Linguistic Policy. *Comparencia, a petición propia, de la Secretaría General de Política Lingüística ante la Comisión de Instituciones e Interior del Parlamento Vasco.* Vitoria-Gasteiz: Gobierno Vasco.

1986. *Basic Law of the Standardization of the Use of Basque.* Vitoria-Gasteiz: Evagraf, S. Coop.

1989. *Análisis demolingüístico de la Comunidad Autónoma Vasca derivado del padrón de 1986.* Vitoria-Gasteiz: Gráficas Santamaría.

UNPUBLISHED PAPERS AND PAMPHLETS

Arrizabalaga, Marie-Pierre. 1986. "A Statistical Study of Basque Immigration into California, Nevada, Idaho, and Wyoming Between 1900 and 1910." MA thesis, University of Nevada, Reno, Center for Basque Studies.

Castelli, Joseph Roy. 1980. "Basques in the Western United States: A Functional Approach to Determination of Cultural Presence in the Geographic Landscape." PhD diss., East Stroudsburg State College.

Coleman, D. 1993. "The World on the Move? International Migration in 1992." Paper presented at the European Population Conference, U.N. Commission for Europe, U.N. Population Fund, March, in Geneva, Switzerland.

Douglass, William A. 1995. "Studying the Basque Presence in North America." Unpublished paper, Basques in Mexico Conference, 1995.

———. " Basques in the Antipodes."

Edlefsen, John B. "En nombre de la verdad y la justicia lea este folleto: La verdad siempre prevalece." 1970. Melbourne, Australia: Basque Community of Melbourne.

———. 1948. "A Sociological Study of the Basques of Southwest Idaho." PhD diss., Washington State University.

Gaarder, Lorin R. 1976. "The Basques of Mexico: An Historical and Contemporary Portrait." PhD diss., University of Utah.

Hendry, Barbara Ann. 1992. "Ethnicity and Identity in a Basque Borderland: Rioja Alavesa, Spain." PhD diss., University of Florida.

Herri Batasuna, Herri Enbaxada. 1997. "Manifesto to the Public Opinion and the International Community." Pamphlet distributed to Belgian media, labor unions, and politicians. Brussels.

"Informe sobre la colectividad vasca en Uruguay 1995." Report to the Basque Congress of Basque Collectivities from Basque Centers in Uruguay. Gasteiz.

Iztueta, Paulo. 1993. "Revisión de los conceptos: Comunidad, nación, estado, identidad en relación con la lengua." Paper presented to the Conference on Language and Collective Identity, July, Euskal Herriko Unibertsitatea, Donostia–San Sebastián.

Larrañaga, Iñaki. 1993. "Comunidad lingüística y percepción de la identidad nacional." Paper presented at Conference on Language and Collective Identity, July, Euskal Herriko Unibertsitatea, Donostia–San Sebastián.

Larumbe, Josefina, and María Fernanda Astigarraga. 1998. "Bibliotecas existentes en entidades vascas de la República Argentina: Informe de situación." Report to the Euzko Etxea of La Plata, Argentina, for the American Congress of Basque Centers.

Laurak Bat Basque Center, 1997. "El futuro de los centros vascos y su relación con el País Vasco." Paper presented to the American Congress of Basque Centers, November, Buenos Aires, Argentina.

Thursby, Jacqueline S. 1994. "Basque Women of the American West." PhD diss., Bowling Green State University.

Totoricagüena, Gloria. 2003. Inaugural keynote address to the Third World Congress of Basque Collectivities. "Aurrera Goaz." July 14. Vitoria-Gasteiz.

———. 2000. "Comparing the Basque Diaspora: Ethnonationalism, Transnationalism and Identity Maintenance in Argentina, Australia, Belgium, Peru, the United States of America, and Uruguay." PhD diss., London School of Economics and Political Science.

Ybarrola, Steven. 1983. "Intermarriage, Assimilation, and Ethnicity Maintenance: A Basque-American Case Study." MA thesis, Brown University, Department of Anthropology.

NEWSLETTERS, NEWSPAPERS, AND JOURNALS

Basque Studies Program Newsletter. 1981–2004. University of Nevada, Reno, Basque Studies Center, Center for Basque Studies.

Journal of Basque Studies. 1983–1998. Indiana University of Pennsylvania, Indiana, Pa.

La Revista de los Vascos. Magazine of Haize Hegoa. June 1994–February 1995. Montevideo, Uruguay.

Society of Basque Studies in America. 1988–2004. Brooklyn, N.Y. and Naperville, Ill.

TRACES. An electronic bulletin established by the Transnational Communities Project. Oxford University. Oxford, England. www.transcomm.ox.ac.uk.

Voice of the Basques. 1974–1978. Boise, Idaho.

Pictures

Anna M. Aguirre, 221
Esteban Aspiazu Family Collection, New York, 225
Alberto Azua family collection, 324
Jon Balanzategi and Eugenia Oleaga family collection, 379, 394, 489
Basque Government Press Agency, 407, 530, 535
Basque Government Urazandi Collection, 189, 428
The Basque Library, University of Nevada, Reno. 158, 197, 204, 209, 217, 228, 245, 248, 253, 256, 261, 268, 363, 366, 451
Bryan Day, 499
DEIA, 163, 294, 297, 350
Euskal Etxea, Basque Government publication, 155
Euskal Etxeak, 399, 402, 433, 436, 441, 507, 510
Eulalia Abaitua Allende Salazar, courtesy of the Basque Archaeological, Ethnographic, and Historical Museum, Bilbao, 48, 57, 78, 85, 88, 308, 418, 473, 476, 481, 484
Francisco de Mendieta, 65
Totoricagüena Family Collection, cover photo
New York Euzko Etxea, 105
Alberto Urberuaga Ortuzar, 382
Carlos Orue and the Sydney'ko Gure Txoko, 358
San Francisco Basque Cultural Center, 468
La Tarde, Bilbao newspaper, 116
Peter Toja Jr. Family Collection, 273, 276, 300
Mary Lou Urrutia, 212
Voice of the Basques, 303
Javier Amorebieta Zuñega, 347, 371, 374

Index

A

C

E

I

L

Lakebed, Alejandro, correspondent of official government-in-exile bulletin who attempted to disseminate information about homeland, 376

Landa, Claudia, 254
owner of Hogar Hotel in Salt Lake City Utah, a boarding house, 228

Larralde Aguirre, José, 260, 290

Larrañaga, Cipriano, 320

Lasagabaster, Javier, 171

Lasarte Arana, José María
Basque government-in-exile delegate in South America, 290

La Tarde, Bilbao newspaper, picture page reference, 594

Lauburu, the Basque four-headed cross, 456

Laurac Bat, 177–78

Laurak Bat and Laurac Bat, 164, 196, 432.
See also Revista Laurak Bat
protest against Abolitionary Foral Law caused formation of the Basque centers, 168

Law of Relations with Basque Communities in Exterior, provides for registry of centers and endows registered members with material benefits, 525

Law on Political Responsibilities, made crime for anyone over age of fourteen to have "helped to undermine public order" since October 1,1934, 283

leaders in late nineteenth and twentieth centuries became concerned with integration based on national or ethnic identity, 49–50

Legarreta Bilbao, Josu, led Office of Relations with Basque Communities to its enormously successful worldwide diaspora programs, 399

Legarreta, Dorothy, 341

Legarreta, Saturnino, 260

Leizaola, Jesús María, under his leadership Basque government-in-exile continued Christian Democratic, pro-European and international policies, 336

Leiçarraga, Ioannes, 75

U

V

Valdivia, Lieutenant Governor Pedro de, 159
Van den Berghe, Pierre 106, 118
Vasconia, La (later La Baskonia)
  Basque periodical published in Argentina, 21, 164, 178, 287
  publication began in 1893, 287
Venezuela, colonization of, 133–34
Basques from Venezuela sent radio broadcasts into Iparralde
  during Franco dictatorship when Euskara was outlawed and
  political dissent was crushed, 402
Victoria, ship that Elcano used to circumnavigate the Earth,
  192
Viña, Angel, 260
violence as necessary, contagious destructive violence that
  supports struggle, 289
virtual communities: potentially as fundamental in identity
  building and in process of socialization as physical,
  geographical communities, 440
Vizcaíno hotel of Ogden Utah, 254
Vizcaíno, Juan, 96, 130. See also Juan de la Cosa
Voice of the Basques, picture page reference, 594

W

Waters, Mary, 117
Western Range Association
  began to recruit sheepherders in Peru (1971) and Mexico
    (1973), 219
  enticed Basques to come to American West and work three-
    year contracts as sheepherders, 212
  pushed goal of recruiting Basques to come to the American
    West to work as sheepherders, 218
Western Union or MoneyGram, money sent home via, 419
White Australia Policy, Basques unaffected by racist policies
  because of European origins, 356
Winnemucca area, Nevada, boardinghouses in, 249–50
women in centers, Basque cultural centers served as social
  spaces for reconstitution of homeland gender roles with
  women assuming places of power and prestige, 469

Colophon

This book was edited by Bud Bynack and indexed by Lawrence Feldman. It was laid out and produced by Gunnlaugur SE Briem, who also designed the typeface, BriemAnvil.

It was printed and bound by Fidlar Doubleday of Kalamazoo, Michigan.

The Basque Studies textbook series

87319698R00392

Made in the USA
San Bernardino, CA
03 September 2018